The Spiritual Design

Wave 3

Books by Christine Kromm Henrie and David Henrie

Published by Access Soul Knowledge

The Spiritual Design, Channeled Teachings, Wave 1

The Spiritual Design, Channeled Teachings, Wave 2

Notes from the Second Dimension, Volume 1

Helig Design, Kanaliserade Budskap, Första Vågen (*Swedish*)

Helig Design, Kanaliserade Budskap, Andra Vågen (*Swedish*)

Notes from the Second Dimension, Volume 2

The Spiritual Design, Wave 3

Memoarer Från Andra Dimensionen, Del 1 (*Swedish*)

Books Scheduled for Publication in 2023 - 2024

The Spiritual Design Wave 4

Memoarer Från Andra Dimensionen, Del 2 (*Swedish*)

Notes from the Second Dimension, Volume 3

The Spiritual Design

Wave 3

Christine Kromm Henrie

&

David Henrie, Sp.D.

Access Soul Knowledge
Stockholm, Sweden

Copyright © 2022 by Christine Kromm Henrie, David Henrie.

All rights reserved. No part of this book may be reproduced, stored in or introduced into an information storage or retrieval system, or transmitted in any form, or in any manner, including electronic, photographic, mechanical, recording, or otherwise, without prior written permission of the copyright owner. For information, please contact the author.

The Library of Congress has cataloged the paperback edition as follows

Names: Henrie, Christine Kromm | Henrie, David

Title: The spiritual design wave 3 /

    By Christine Kromm Henrie and David Henrie

Description: 436 pages ; 23 cm. | Access Soul Knowledge, 2022

Identifiers: LCCN 2022916687 | ISBN 9781951879112

Subjects BISAC: 1. BODY, MIND & SPIRIT—Afterlife & Reincarnation. |

    2. BODY, MIND & SPIRIT—Angels & Spirit Guides. |

    3. BODY, MIND & SPIRIT—Channeling & Mediumship

Classification: •BF1275.D2 H-- 2022 | DDC 133.9'01'35—dc22

LC record available at https://lccn.loc.gov/2022916687

Other Formats Available:

    ISBN 9781951879129 (Kindle E-book Edition)

    ISBN 9781951879136 (EPUB Edition)

    ISBN 9781951879143 (Swedish Language Paperback Edition)

    ISBN 9781951879150 (Swedish Language Kindle E-book Edition)

    ISBN 9781951879167 (Swedish Language EPUB E-book Edition)

Editors: Kari Pelletier | Susanne Kromm

Front Cover Art: ID 35127837 © Ig0rzh | Dreamstime.com (Earth & Sky)
    ID 210260189 © Robatz | Dreamstime.com (Merkaba)
Back Cover Art: ID 1205615 © Vicnt | Dreamstime.com

Printed in the United States of America
First Edition
First Printing, November 2022
    2024.07.11
Access Soul Knowledge (Imprint)
Williamstown, WV, USA, & Stockholm, Sweden

DEDICATION

We wish to thank the many spirits who have contributed to the *Spiritual Design* books, who share their wisdom and love week after week without fail. We consider them our spiritual family, and are honored to present their words to you. Our deepest gratitude is given to the true authors of these books, whom we know as: Ophelia, Bob, Jeshua, Isaac, Zachariah, Ari, Eli, Gergen, Ia, Setalay, the Elahim Council, the Council of Nine, the Tallocks, Ole, and the multitude of other entities who are silent partners in this collaboration to make the Earth a better home.

~ Christine and David

CONTENTS

Page	Section
1	**A Spiritual Path**
5	Eli: Plowing the Field (Nov 6, 2018)
10	Bob, Ophelia: Group Dynamics (Nov 26, 2018)
13	Ari: Male vs. Female, Elahim vs. Shea (Dec 2, 2018)
20	Ophelia: Healing Emotional Blockages (Dec 2, 2018)
21	Bob: John 32 in the Catholic Army (Dec 31, 2018)
26	Ia, Ophelia: Waves in the Ocean of Energy (Jan 6, 2019)
34	Zachariah: Hydrocarbons (Feb 8, 2019)
37	Bob: OBE's and Accessing the Fourth (Feb 8, 2019)
39	Eli: The Inner Layers are like a Solar System (Feb 17, 2019)
44	Bob, Ophelia: Ants Running Everywhere (March 21, 2019)
46	Setalay, Ophelia: Silence (April 21, 2019)
53	Zachariah: DNA Reflects the Soul Pattern (April 30, 2019)
60	Jeshua: Reflect in Darkness, Learn in Light. (May 5, 2019)
66	Ari: The Colors of a Life Well Lived (June 15, 2019)
71	Zachariah: The Karma Program (June 23, 2019)
77	C9, Gergen: A Lesson in History (June 30, 2019)
89	Eli: Tesla and the Merkaba (July 7, 2019)
96	Setalay: Strength in Stillness (July 13, 2019)
100	Ophelia: Group Karma (July 29, 2019)
109	Ia: The Inner Calling (Oct 13, 2019)
113	Ari: The Cubic Box Society (Nov. 17, 2019)
120	Ophelia: Facing Your Shadows (Nov 21, 2019)
124	Elahim Council: Facing Emotions (Nov 24, 2019)
127	Ari: Science, Religion, and Ego (Dec 1, 2019)
130	Ophelia: The Two You's (Dec 25, 2019)
134	Ophelia: Soulmates (Jan 30, 2020)
148	Ari: Evaluating the Cell (Feb 1, 2020)
157	Ari, Ophelia: The Cell needs Scattered Minds (Mar 29, 2020)
163	Jeshua, Bob: The Bus of Spiritual Enlightenment (Feb 23, 2020)
170	C9, Ophelia: Hereditary Karma in the DNA (April 5, 2020)
178	Ari: Geoengineering (Oct 7, 2018)
180	Bob: Nature is your Home (April 18, 2020)
183	Ophelia, Bob: Don't be Sheep (May 10, 2020)
190	Ari, Ophelia: The Cell and 5 Years of Turmoil (Aug 23, 2020)

198	Ari, Bob: Spirituality to Master Energies. (June 28, 2020)
206	Ari, Ophelia, Bob: On the Right Path (May 24, 2020)
219	Teh, Ophelia: Calming the Mind (Aug 12, 2020)
225	Council of Nine: Changes and Evolution (Sept 2, 2020)
233	C9: Sit Still in Your Boat (Dec 17, 2020)
238	Isaac, Jeshua: The Four Pillars (Dec 31, 2020)
241	**The Spiritual Design Theories**
245	Seth: The Big Wheel and the Zodiac (Dec 16, 2018)
249	Bob: The Layer–Cakes of Parallel Realities (Oct 17, 2019)
256	Zachariah: Geometric Forms and Portals (Oct 20, 2019)
263	C9, Ophelia: Dreaming in Color (Jan 12, 2020)
271	C9, Ophelia: Life in the Ditch (Jan 18, 2020)
279	Tallock, Ophelia: Visitors from Parallel Realities (Feb 9, 2020)
288	C9: Solar Storms from Neighboring Systems (April 18, 2020)
293	EC, Ophelia: Neighboring Realities (June 21, 2020)
299	Bob: The Fork Controls the Planet (Feb 4, 2020)
309	Bob: The Boxes at the Poles (Feb 13, 2020)
316	Tallock, Ophelia: 450 Million Years Ago (Dec 15, 2019)
322	Jeshua, Bob: Explosion around Great Lakes (Oct 30, 2016)
329	Elahim Council: Human Evolution (Jan 13, 2019)
335	Ari: Human Design and Modification (Feb 3, 2019)
343	Tallock: The Dinosaur Projects (April 6, 2019)
350	EC, Zachariah, Ophelia: Bad Technology (April 14, 2019)
357	Zachariah: The Anunnaki Handbag (June 5, 2020)
363	Ophelia: Bending Time (May 11, 2019)
366	Elahim Council: Human Evolution, Part II (July 20, 2019)
373	Zeonia, Jeshua: The Dream of Earth (Sept 29, 2019)
382	Tallock: Opening and Closing Portals (Nov 28, 2019)
386	C9, Ophelia: The Little Wheel of the Zodiac (Dec 27, 2019)
393	C9, Ophelia: The Wounded Earth (Jan 1, 2020)
402	C9, Ophelia: The Upper and Lower Disks (Jan 5, 2020)
409	Ophelia: Keycards to the Cosmos (Mar 22, 2021)
418	Acknowledgments
419	About the Authors

Preface

Since the release of *The Spiritual Design, Wave 2*, much has changed in the world. But this is not a new phenomenon, as every generation sees their share of turbulence and struggle. Our earlier books were written from our home in Colorado. But the lockdown induced economic crash of 2020 motivated me to retire early from the corporate world and focus on our work. Since Christine still has her past life and between lives regression therapy practice in Stockholm, we left the US and relocated where mask-free normality prevailed.

Those who have read our previous books, or have seen our public séances, know that Christine is an eminently gifted trance channel. During our regular private trance sessions, which usually last about an hour, 99 percent of the time I just sit and listen to whomever comes through. It is an incredible honor to be on the receiving end of the wisdom that is transmitted by these transcendent beings from the spiritual dimensions. We decided early into this project that she should not listen to the information that comes through, so we divide the workload. She manages her regression therapy business and website, teaches classes in trance mediumship, astrology, soul development, and trains and certifies others in past life regression therapy. I transcribe all the sessions, organize the teachings into book form and tend to the publishing. I also do extensive research on the information given by the spirits. It is amazing how flawlessly accurate their casual observations are on subjects as diverse as the chronology of Earth, quantum physics, geological processes, planetary systems, electromagnetism, philosophy, human history, biological evolution, or spirituality. Although they often say things that contradict the official interpretations of the world around us, the passage of time will likely prove them correct.

Christine puts herself into a trance state and allows the spirits to blend with her, meaning they access her mind and can control her vocal cords and upper body. She has no awareness of what they are saying, but she sometimes will see the original image of what they are describing to me. For example, if Bob is telling a story of something he did on the planet Etena, she may see flashes of images from Bob's point-of-view. Her input has been very helpful in understanding how certain places or creatures look, as she is able to fill in a lot of extra details that the spirits could not convert into words. But at the end of a session, she has no recollection of what was said or who was talking. On my end, as the one to whom they are speaking, there is not a trace of Christine present while another entity is in control. When she comes out of trance, she can be very tired, and it may take a day to recover from the drain on her energy.

The main body of this book is the assembled talks given by various spiritual entities. They are the true authors of the meaningful content you will read. I usually add a few clarifying notes at the beginning of each section, and also identify the speaker(s). To streamline the text, we only use the first letter of the speaker's name. So, Ari would be "A", Ophelia would be "O", and so forth. All of my questions are denoted with a "D".

The past few years have been a learning experience on many levels. From the actual sessions, to our understanding of the material, through the organization and presentation of their words, they are gradually leading us towards being better ambassadors for the spiritual realms. Due to the volume of information delivered by our spirit friends, and the fact I was working full-time, it has been challenging to keep up with the demands of publishing. We did not want to release *Wave 3* until we could commit the time and attention that the teachings deserve and require. During preparation of the manuscript, Christine, Kari Pelletier, and Susanne Kromm contributed their copyediting and proofreading abilities (along with wise advice) to improve the text. So, we hope our collective efforts mirror the quality and importance of the messages relayed to you from these enlightened beings.

Who are these spirits who speak? The short answer is that they are who they say they are. The long answer is that they are spiritual entities who have been instrumental in the creation of the Earth and all things on it. Perhaps not individually, but as representatives of those dimensions and groups who follow the intentions of the Creator. For seven years and hundreds of hours, I have listened and conversed with a multitude of spirits. Some have incarnated here on Earth in human form, but most have not. While they identify themselves with an English name, that is only for our benefit. Do not make the mistake of assuming that they are human-like, because they are not. It's better to regard them all as angels. Those who communicate through Christine represent dimensions and groups that are affiliated with the Earth project, including a fair number of alien entities who describe their own specialized role in Earth's history.

It is natural to be suspicious of the authenticity of those who trance channel. I have always been a bit leery of this form of psychic information, at least until I met Christine. When the spirits first began to talk, it only took two or three sessions before I was completely convinced of their legitimacy. For one thing, they know things that neither Christine or I know. I have yet to find a factual error in anything they have said. Granted, much is unprovable, but what I can validate is always correct. Secondly, they each have their own unique personality. They have distinct mannerisms, voice tones, and areas of expertise in their knowledge. And every time that particular spirit joins, they sound exactly as they did previously, even if a year or more had elapsed. If you study the sentence structure, it is obvious that it is not created by the same personage. Thirdly, they can see both directions on the timeline. They have made predictions about the future that came true, and have described historical events that are unerringly precise. Fourth, and perhaps most importantly, is the content of what they say. Once they merge with Christine, they introduce themselves and just start talking. As you read their words, it is impossible not to recognize the depth of knowledge, the spiritual purity, and the heartfelt guidance they are giving us.

Spiritual beings communicate telepathically and identify each other by energetic patterns. To talk with us, they expertly use our language to convey complex information, but spoken language itself is a very limiting tool. They are forced to deconstruct thought bubbles that have an encyclopedic amount of information and give it to us in little pieces of linear thinking. Even though they are careful with their choice of words, they are often frustrated by the absence of terminology to represent their ideas. Nonetheless, they can create masterpieces of imagery with words, allowing us a glimpse of their reality. One of the (many) fascinating aspects of these communications is that they never forget anything. They often repeat, verbatim, something that was mentioned years earlier. The consistency and purity of what they have said since 2015 gives an impeccable credibility to the content of their messages. They never speak with criticism or anger, because they do not possess human emotions. But a measure of sternness, disapproval, or even sadness can be detected at times, especially when it comes to our contemptuous behavior towards the Earth and its plant and animal life.

You will occasionally see "bump" used to describe what happens during a session. When one of our spirit friends is talking, there are occasions when another spirit will abruptly take over. We call that being bumped. Bob, who is ever eager to talk, is often the one doing the bumping. His energy is very close to our vibration and he will sometimes lean in so close that he takes over control, thinking that it is his turn. He is polite though, and will bow out if Ophelia asks him to. Ophelia is present at every session. She is the main control on the spiritual side and is the one who, together with Isaac, Christine's main spirit guide, manages the speakers and monitors Christine's energy during the sessions.

Language and Punctuation. We have mentioned in our previous books that each spirit guide or council member who speaks through Christine displays their own unique style of expression. Similar as with humans, I can usually determine who is talking before they identify themselves. Considering there are over a dozen who regularly communicate, that should give an idea of how consistent they are with tone, tempo, sentence structure, and content. We have uploaded audio clips to our website that represent how some of them sound.

When converting the spoken words into written, there are several challenges, some more common with certain speakers than others. Bob, for example, speaks very fast and will sometimes take a detour in the middle of a sentence to explain a point he is making. We normally denote those breaks with a dash (—), but it still adds a bit of complexity for the reader. When I listen to him talk, it is perfectly clear, but once written down, the auditory clues are lost. His inflections, laughter and joyful persona are also impossible to capture. The Council of Nine, Zachariah, and certain aliens speak with a lack of embellishments. To smooth out the reading experience, we add words or explanations in parentheses for clarity. Because all of our books are essentially direct communication from the spirit realms to humanity, we have tried not to insert or alter what was said, except where it is obvious that they grabbed the wrong word from Christine's mental database.

The process of converting the dialogue to text also is a long road with random potholes. And it probably doesn't help that I am a scientist and not a master of linguistics. When transcribing, I type what I hear. If they pause mid-sentence, it is not rare that a comma or period gets inserted where none belong. That makes later editing a lot of fun for myself, Kari, Susanne, and Christine when we come across these disjointed sentences with unclear meaning. Once all these human errors are eliminated, the words from the spirits flow with both a complexity and a simplicity that are unmatched by any philosophical writer.

The language itself is yet another curiosity. They are meticulous in their vocabulary, but often use verbiage that Christine does not. Bob is especially gifted at creating new expressions or juxtaposing words to say things in a novel way. And finally, they occasionally use the wrong verb. Sometimes I fix it so it isn't jarring to read. But in other places, I don't. So, when you run across these apparent mistakes, it is not due to poor editing. For example, in the June 30, 2019 session, the Council of Nine said, "You should know that there was even, from Ophelia's reality, those who tapped in and incarnated, as you call it, in plants. They have an experience of being a tree." In our way of linear thinking, if a soul once occupied a tree, it happened in the past. So, an editor might suggest they "had an experience" in the second sentence. But the Council of Nine means the experience is something those spirits now possess. Experiences and knowledge are the currency of spiritual development, so the sentence is accurate as written. And that is an issue I constantly encounter. They describe reality from their perspective, and if we unknowingly make grammatical improvements, it may completely alter the meaning. So, we avoid taking those types of editorial liberties.

Subject Matter. The range and diversity of material that the spirits talk about is immense. They can go from dissecting human emotions to talking about parallel realities in the space of a few sentences. Obviously, not all readers will share the same enthusiasm for every topic. Ophelia said that people will each take what they need from the readings. Those who are more logically inclined will be drawn to the *Spiritual Design* books. Others will be attracted to the magic and mystery in the *Notes from the Second Dimension* books. Eli said they are planting seeds, and in the seasons and centuries that follow, those seeds will become flowers or trees in the garden of humanity. The point being that if you come into a section that you find difficult or disinteresting, skip over it and move on to the next session. Every teaching is not for everyone, but the benefit lies in finding the messages that speak to you in this moment. In fact, a decent percentage of the information is actually intended for future generations who will be better equipped to comprehend the topics.

Changes to Formatting. While working on *Notes from the Second Dimension, Volume 2*, we included the date of the session. As the years pass and the quantity of words continue to expand, it has become increasingly difficult to organize the sessions. The inclusion of the date is as much for my benefit as the readers', because their topics build upon previous talks and it is necessary to keep them in order. But we also try to group the talks by subject matter to lend a bit of continuity. The problem is that a concept will be brought up and it may be over a year before it is mentioned again. A specific topic could be embedded within a dozen readings spread over three or four years. Because they weave ideas together in a giant web of knowledge, isolating a single thread can jumble the order of other ideas. In this *Wave 3*, we only have two chapters, loosely organized by subject and then by date of delivery. The first part of the book has a lot of teachings on human spirituality. The second half focuses on the greater mysteries. When there were opportunities to pull subjects closer together within the chapter, we did so. Hopefully, there are not too many discontinuities from shuffling the chronological order in certain places. Also, we have added the name of the speakers in each section. So, if you want to read all of Ophelia's talks, they are easy to find.

With all that being said, welcome to *Wave 3*. We hope you find it rewarding and enlightening.

David Henrie
Stockholm, Sweden
August 29, 2022

Wheel of Creation. The image below is to present the conceptual structure of the Wheel. All spirits have a home somewhere in the spiritual dimensions, including everyone on Earth. To gain knowledge, they travel out into the universes of form, which are called "fish tanks" in this book. Aliens, for example, are also spiritual entities occupying a form on some other planet.

On the following page is a diagram of where the speakers in this *Wave 3* have a home. If they are long-term residents of a planet, like the Tallock, they have both a spiritual home-base on the sixth and ninth dimensions, and also a physical home on the planet Vlac in fish tank 8.

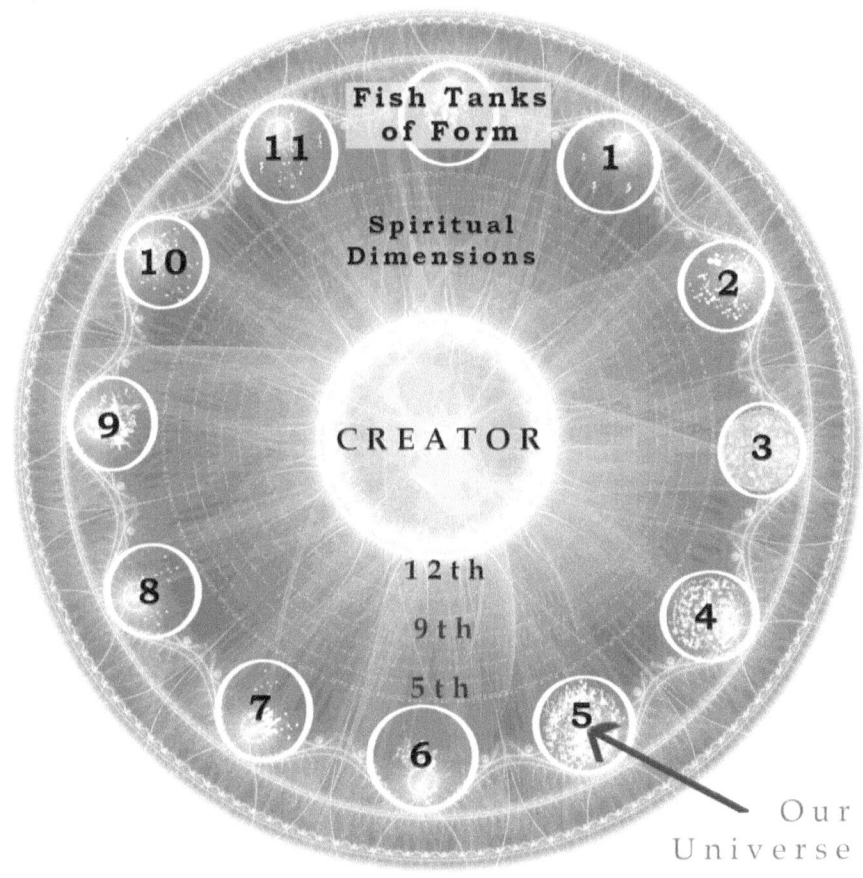

SPIRITUAL DIMENSIONS			FISH TANKS
Individuals		Councils	Planets
	12th	Highest Councils Healing & Oversight	
	11th	Designers of Universes & Form in Fish Tanks	
Ari (Elahim) Eli (Elahim)	10th	Elahim Council (Technology, Intentions, Mental)	
Jeshua (Elahim) Zachariah Tallocks (6th & 9th)	9th	Council of Form Council of Nine (Galaxies, Energy Webs, Knowledge)	VLAC in Fish Tank Eight Storage of Form Base for Tallocks
Isaac	8th	Council of Eight (Elements, Gravity, DNA, Weather, EM)	
Ophelia Setalay Josephine	7th	Council of Light (Suns, DNA, Emotional, Healing)	ETENA in Fish Tank Four Storage of DNA Home of Setalay and Siah (pet)
Seth (Elahim) Lasaray (Elahim) Laslo (Elahim) Nealon (Elahim) Tallocks (Manifested) Zeonians (Manifested)	6th	Council of Six (Celestial Forms, Parallel Realities, Mental)	EARTH
Willaby	5th	Circle of Elders (Library, Earth Souls, Physical, Nature Environmental)	in Fish Tank Five Greenhouse Planet Souls from 5th
Ole Gergen Bob Ia Joel, Sniffer Nature Spirits Taffles (Caretakers)	2nd	Earth Council of Second (DNA, Flora, Fauna, Soil, Water, Earth Energy Grid)	TIDDLE in Fish Tank Two Home of Taffles, who work with Colors and Melody

Notes: 5th and 7th closely connected.
6th and 9th closely connected.

A Spiritual Path

Those who have read our previous books know that the teachings from our spirit friends who communicate through Christine fall into three broad categories. There are descriptions of what the spiritual realities are like and how they function. Then there are talks about the process of creation on the Earth and within the Universe. Finally, they give advice on how we who are incarnated can best navigate through the karma program and experience a more rewarding life. The typical seeker of spiritual knowledge may find the first and last categories the most relevant, but the logically inclined may be drawn to the mysteries of creation, physics, energetic webs, or interstellar travel. Each reader will take something different from the collections, and it is not necessary to force an interest in all subjects. Among the 1.2 million words they have delivered to date there are many extraordinary and vivid descriptions of what we call the spiritual design. Reading their words, one comes to appreciate the majestic and unifying fields of energy that connect Earth with the Universe beyond. Many of the human failings come from not honoring and respecting the divinity and purpose that is present in even the smallest of creatures. A spiritual life is one where we try to replicate our spiritual home, where our emotions, actions, and mental functions are subservient to our divine, immortal soul.

The story of humankind is the collective journeys of all the souls who have walked upon the soil of the Earth. More specifically, it is a chronology of decisions made by individual souls during their long cycle of incarnations. Great achievements arise from choices made by individuals, as do the tragic failures within groups of people. Unlike the religious "holy" books that are packed with manmade rules and prohibitions, the spirits remain silent on specific codes of conduct, expecting us to discover for ourselves the overarching principles that define spiritual truths. The concept of sin, for example, has never been mentioned. Instead, they simply ask, "What footprint do you wish to leave?", making us the responsible party for all our decisions and actions.

We will never be in alignment with our spirit or the Creator, so long as the human mind is spellbound by the great drama of Earth life. They describe two separate minds, the human mind and the soul mind, and give abundant advice on how to tap into your soul mind and act from that place of knowledge. It is up to each of us to choose a path, following either the urgings of the soul mind, or the lessor emotions and thoughts of the physical human mind. You can visualize this as two different trails through the countryside of life. The soul mind follows a higher sunlit path with majestic views of distant rolling hills and fields of flowers beneath an idyllic blue sky. A journey where light lingers long after the sun is gone. This is the path of love. The human mind follows another path, a rocky, twisting trail leading downwards into thick foliage and vines. Where each lonely footstep leads onward through ominous shadows, and gloomy darkness pervades even when the sun is high. This is the path of fear. As our understanding and faith in the unseen world increases, it becomes easier to follow the urgings of the soul upwards onto the path of love. And, at journey's end, we will have lived a happier, more heartfelt life.

How *Wave 3* is Organized. During the past three years, the content of the talks has included more discussions about the current dilemmas faced by humans. The lockdowns and imprisonment of entire populations caused a lot of distress, and the spirits were responsive to those concerns. We organized the first half of the book to emphasize the human related advice and information. The last part of the book is a collection of teachings about ancient Earth history and the spiritual designs in the universes of form. Throughout the book there are references to information that was presented in one of our earlier books. While it is impossible to review everything, a general outline of history may be helpful, since several years have elapsed since *Wave 2* was published. We also included a reference diagram in the preface showing the dimensions and the relationship with the spiritual entities who take center-stage in the *Wave* and *Notes* series of books.

Outline of History. Spiritual beings have been coming to Earth for hundreds of millions of years, helping to develop and care for life on this greenhouse planet. In the ancient past, spirits remotely investigated Earth using their soul consciousness. They took no visible form and could not physically interact with the environment. Later, after life was flourishing, spirits projected their awareness into the Earth's energetic fields and created a form through a process called manifestation. The bodies were similar to humans, in that they were functional and had a visible density, but they were not bound by the laws of nature on Earth; meaning the manifested form was not born. Neither did it age, decay, or die. The traveling soul assembled a body using the elements of the planet, and when it was time to leave, the manifested body would simply disappear. The Elahim manifested most recently in Mesopotamia, before 12,000 BC, where they were known as Anunnaki. Ophelia and others in her group from the seventh manifested bodies until about 3000 BC in South America, where they were called Shea. The manifested bodies were created for long-term use on Earth and could be maintained for centuries. They were, in some ways, similar to a human body, just not as physically complex or dense. The Anunnaki, for instance, drank a liquid made from plants, extracting the energy to help maintain their form. Their bodies had some internal organs to assist in that process.

There are other types of manifestation, some of which are known to still occur. Spirit guides who follow closely, such as how Bob follows Lasaray, always have a certain percentage of their soul energy materialized on the third dimension. A human body is about 98 percent materialized on the third dimension, but Bob, my guide from the second dimension, said he is only 20 percent materialized. The human eye cannot detect a lightly manifested form. The degree of materialization determines the density or physicality that is observable by the human eye on the third dimension. A guide can increase their materialization to interact with physical objects, or even become visibly solid. However, those are infrequent because the rules of engagement limit what guides can do. Bob, however, once pushed a bottle off of a cabinet, just to prove his presence. Contemporary hominins are mostly oblivious to these types of activities, because our sophisticated cultures have become increasingly detached from nature, where magic is always present.

The Creator, through the Master Mind energy, is present in all lifeforms. At different times in the past, souls from the higher dimensions have been permitted to join with the Master Mind and blend with the bodies of mammals such as dolphins, whales, and even hominoids. The original soul groups came from the sixth through tenth dimensions. At first the soul energy was only tagging along for the experience and to observe. Later, as the soul percentage increased and became dominant, the Master Mind became the passenger who monitored the soul. At that point, the karma programs were set in motion. There have been many epochs where hominins were controlled by souls and not the Master Mind. Each time a reboot or major change is implemented in the human body, the old karma program ends and a new one begins. Bodies have been modified many times, and the version we are now occupying had a beginning around 10,000 BC, after the Younger Dryas glacial period. It looks the same as the earlier body, but inner filters were adjusted to dim the soul's input to the mind. That new body was designed for souls from the fifth dimension, so there was a changing of the guard. Souls from the higher dimensions quit incarnating, and the souls from the fifth became the dominant group. Although our knowledge of history only goes back a dozen centuries, many great civilizations existed prior to the Holocene.

It seems unnecessary to say, but the Creator and the higher councils are the ones who determine what happens on Earth. Changes in lifeforms, atmosphere, geologic activity, solar radiation, and evolution occur at the discretion of spiritual councils who manage the planet. Humans are closely monitored, and when they drift too far off-course, the councils and Earth will respond in ways that restore balance.

Names. We realize that it can be confusing to keep track of the spiritual entities who speak in this *Wave 3*. Several years may have passed since you read about them in our previous books. To a certain extent, the speaker is less important than the messages, although knowing what role they play in the grand design can be helpful. At the beginning of the book, we included a diagram showing which spiritual dimension the speakers in this book are from.

Alias or nicknames will sometimes be used during the sessions. Christine is always identified as "this one", or "Seth", the name of her higher self. When they say this one, it could either mean the incarnation, Christine, or Seth. The clue is usually found in the context. Sometimes I clarify it by writing Christine or Seth in parentheses, but not always. David's higher self is known as Lasaray. When the spiritual entities are speaking to me through Christine, "your Little Friend" or "the Little One" is how they identify Bob, because his spirit body is a bit smaller than the spirits from other dimensions. Although it is not a name, "home" usually means the place in one of the spiritual dimensions where a spirit returns after death to rejoin its higher self.

Commentary. Most of the commentary outside of the dialogues is written in the first person by me, David. The reason being that Christine does the hard work of channeling, which yields all of the meaningful content in our books. My contribution is to render transcripts that accurately match the voice recordings. When compiling the transcripts into book form, I will add clarifying observations or bits of research related to some of the topics in the session. However—and this is important—their teachings are like a treasure hunt, where the reader must find the valuable content themselves.

Eli: Plowing the Field (Nov 6, 2018)

Eli, as you may recall from our previous books, is an Elahim and an older brother to Seth (Christine's spiritual self) and to Lasaray (my spiritual self). He was born on the sixth dimension, studied on the eighth and ninth, and now is operating from the tenth dimension. Those on the tenth no longer travel, but are very much involved in projects, such as the Earth project. Eli explains karma in a way that is very easy to remember. He said we can visualize the soul coming to earth and walking the same path over and over across a field. Each soul has its own path, which begins on one side of the field at birth and ends on the other side at death. As we traverse this field and do things that are not spiritual, it is like digging up the soil and throwing it off to the side of our path. Bigger mistakes can be seen as bigger shovelfuls of dirt. If we keep making blunders, lifetime after lifetime, we will eventually find ourselves walking in a trench of our own digging. As lessons are learned and we become more spiritually inclined, dirt is returned to the ditch. The causal principle is that a soul has satisfied its karmic debt on this plane when it turns to look back at the field and sees no evidence of its passing. It is a beautiful teaching and part of it was included in *Notes, Volume 1*. As a reminder, Eli often speaks with an economy of words. His sentences are often incomplete, but yet the meaning is (hopefully) quite clear. Below is the transcript of the conversation between myself and Eli, followed by Bob coming in to offer his own wry commentary on the subject. As in all our previous books, the speaker is identified by the first initial of their name.

E. Elahim. Elahim. Hello, baby brother! HUH HUH.

D. I heard you say Elahim as you were coming in.

6   The Spiritual Design

E. Yes, we are several here. Not all will communicate. You have your friend, Laslo, sending his regards. He regrets that you have to be in this small container (*the human body*), lacking the possibility to fully access your own scriptures that you have provided in our libraries. (*Laslo is also an Elahim from the ninth.*)

D. That would save a lot of trouble, wouldn't it?

E. We are proud of you, both of you, for taking on this mission. It is different than prior travels here. This is what Laslo remembers. He actually, at one point, joined you in physical.

D. When was that?

E. It was before known time. Bringing in carvings, tablets, carvings for future visits. You should know that you have done so for yourself. You wrote in carvings, later in regular books, scrolls, for you to find when you return to pick up certain things that you read. Books, your big radio, communication central, Internet, certain things you stumble upon are your own words. You will detect it as a tingle on your right side, behind your right ear. That is when you know that the words are your own, or someone from home (*other Elahims*). Pay attention when you read other scriptures or hear other teachings, repeating what you have put on your path for you to stumble upon. You have done so numerous times; this is not the first time. It's a trick that you place upon yourself, I would say, maybe to make it a little bit more entertaining, since you do tend to not always take on journeys or missions that are fully entertaining, in that respect. The little brother *(Seth)*, different, comes with a bang. Where you sow seeds, this one plows the fields, so to speak. Different approaches, yet is appreciated from the council. Just different methods, I would say, of the way you come about and the way you learn and what sort of footprint you would like to leave behind. This one plows the fields, whereas you more gently dig up and sow the field.

D. That's a nice analogy. We're from a different realm, but I guess we have had to work through our own karmic issues?

E. Yes, everyone does, everyone does. Karma based on what sort of creature you possess. In some way, even plants and animal life have their own karma, but it's hard for a human mind to understand how a plant could accumulate karma. Don't think about it too much. Just know that on this plane, karma is placed within your atmosphere, within the energetic makeup and memory that exists. Everything encased here encounters evolution. Evolution is part of where karma lies. You have to walk over certain karma—or see that field again—you have the field where you have plowed your own path. You still, on each side of your path, could have soil that you have accumulated, put on each side, once you plow the field, so to speak. The meaning is that when you have ended your journey, when you look back on your path—meaning numerous existences, lives— then you should have put back whatever you have dug up. The field should be flat, even, again. So you come in, in your first life, and begin to plow your path, like a mole. You can see it (*the mole*) and you can see how the dirt goes to each side, creates a little wall. When you learn, you understand that you can go back and forth in this lane, in this lane on your field that you have plowed, and you can eventually look back with great satisfaction, because when you look back, you do not see your path anymore. As long as you look in rewind and see this line and soil on each side, there are still things to go back and re-do, look into. So everyone who sets foot here plows their own path, even animals in some way. They don't necessarily work through karma in that respect, but they learn through the Creator. The Creator creates the path through the animal and the Creator looks for the same result with that animal. Different. I wish I could give you the picture better.

D. Wow! That's brilliant, and I do follow. The Master Mind, present in all the animals, is also learning?

E. Yes, and the Master Mind interacts in other creatures, creating paths, their own plowed field, learning how to operate within a third vehicle, if you like—slightly different, though. But still the same idea, that when you have reached the end of your destination, your journey, you feel tired. But when you look back, the first glimpse the soul is looking for is to see whether the ditch is still there.

D. I really like that.

E. Use it, it's an easy way to understand the meaning of karma.

D. Should that go in *Wave 2*?

E. Next. Save a treat, like the Little One says. Treats for everyone, it is a holiday for treats, indeed. Huh. There you go.

D. The tingling sensation you mentioned, that happens to me all the time, exactly where you said. That's how I know if something is spiritually accurate.

E. Yes. Some words ring more true within you, as they are your own. There are certain words, even in the Bible, hijacked from your own scriptures, carvings, the original carvings in Mesopotamia. There you go. Do you have any further questions at this time?

D. Well, I guess I don't have any specific questions, but I'm always interested in what you want to tell me.

E. I dock with your brain when you sleep. Whatever you might have lacked or missed, we all dock with you during sleep and provide ideas, memories, feelings. Sometimes when you feel a sensation of being lost, the sensation originates from missing home. We detect that as a color; it comes as the color of blue around both of you. That's when we dock more closely to you. We intervene energetically, so that you will feel the presence of Elahim, the presence of your brothers and fathers, (*helping you to*) remember your path, remember that you are once again plowing the field. But this time, you're plowing a long road or ditch for others to follow. You are creating new lines. Understand that these metaphors are symbolic for the ditches, the lines, which are different karma related paths. So, the Creator can create new paths, which was done before when free will was created, the power of choice, and mental versus emotional challenges. The Creator makes new karmic roads to travel, ditches for those who set foot on the soil. As soon as they begin to walk on the soil, new events occur. That's why the karma has changed over time. Karma has not been the same from the beginning. It changes, similar like gravity is not constant, based on the result on the lines and whether the individuals manage to patch up their path. New events, new carvings in the ground take place, meaning new events of karma. Some (*paths*) go to sleep. To make it easy for you, one of the first lessons of karma was to understand hurt. At that point, the individuals here had a less equipped mentality. It was placed upon them to understand and learn how to master fire. At this point, that specific karma, or that specific lesson, has been eliminated. Everyone knows that fire hurts. The first one needed to master it, master the beast. Now you master a different beast, same fire, just (*manifests*) differently. This fire is not as visible, yet it has the same ability to destruct whatever it encounters. In this case, we're not referring to a fire that eliminates complete forests. This fire eats your consciousness, eats your free will and passion for being the creatures that you are here. Different fire.

D. And is that an emotional or mental challenge?

E. It's a mental fire. It is met with an emotional breeze. See, new karma. Not brand new, of course, it's not coming in from the 90s!

Still, it's new from our level of opinion. But you can see the first fire lessons, understanding how, when you mastered fire back then, it gave you power. How do you use that power of a living fire? Now you have to master another kind (*of fire*), the power of your mind to not be hijacked, and to understand limitations in your own power. We will discuss it further.

D. I guess I did have a question. In this second wave, I had mentioned humans were modified by both those who were working directly for the Creator, and also alien travelers. Do you have anything you can share about that topic, as far as evolution goes?

E. Alien travelers helped. There were labs here, facilities, engineering of DNA. This was about 500,000 years ago.

D. This is before the first civilization?

E. Yes, yes. There were others here prior to the ones we have discussed.

D. Other travelers, or humanoids?

E. Not humanoids; no (*soul*) travel. They (*the alien visitors*) created little humanoids, lacking souls. No soul. You would probably see it, from a human view, as a robot. But it wasn't. It looked similar, smaller in physique, no soul. The DNA, the genetics at that point, had to do with the physical and the mental. The emotional was not in place.

D. So the soul is more closely related to the emotional?

E. Yes, yes.

D. I was under the impression that without a soul energy, either from the Master Mind or somewhere else, nothing would live?

E. Master Mind present, always present in anything (*everything*) that is created. No souls at first.

D. Ah, I see what you are saying, yes.

E. Prototype for souls to come in.

D. So when the aliens modified the DNA to make a prototype, was it under the direction of the Creator?

E. Everything is under the umbrella of the Creator. However, there are levels that intervene and organize in–between. Elahim present, (*because of their*) knowledge of form, creating a memory bank in that creature, involved with creating the brain. You shouldn't see this creature, even if it looked human, as fully functional, from the way you appear now. Smaller, didn't eat the same as some (*of the later versions*), it ate leaves, green.

D. More like an animal, in some way?

E. Yes. Their vocabulary wasn't well developed. That is a part where the brain is involved so, we modified the brain in order for speech to be able to come forward. This being didn't speak that well. It was a prototype, never meant to be launched with incarnation, as of now. Prototype. Aliens indeed involved. Spacecraft, space stations, exchanges of knowledge. Visitors, prototypes established. Goes on still on other places, nothing special.

D. Okay, thank you for that answer, it's very helpful.

E. Thank you.

D. It's always a pleasure to talk to you, my brother.

E. I bid you farewell. Elahim.

D. Elahim.

Both Ia and Bob came in later after Eli spoke. Their talk was included in *Notes, Volume 1*. Bob did make an amusing observation about people digging karmic ditches so deep that only their heads could be seen. We are including that snippet here for continuity about the symbolic path of karma.

B. Here you just go in your karma path. (*He snorted and laughed*), I heard Eli! Huhuh. Some, you should know, when they walk in this ditch where they have plowed through like a mole, the ditch goes to the ankle, which is good. But if someone has a ditch that reaches to their shoulders, then you just see heads moving across this field and you know that's gonna take a while for that one to throw it all back in! Huhuhuh.

D. That's a really good analogy. I can see that picture!

B. If you see a big field, you can just see all these big heads, like salad (*cabbage*) heads, just walking back and forth!

Bob, Ophelia: Group Dynamics (Nov 26, 2018)

We had just released *Wave 2* in November 2018, and in this session Bob and Ophelia were describing the upcoming books, or waves of knowledge, they plan on delivering. Back in October 2016, Ophelia informed us that we were beginning a 20–year project where they would deliver information to us, and then we would make it available to others. The project is much larger than ourselves and is being directed by, as Ophelia said, some of the highest councils. She also said this project is our main mission in life, and our path forward is mostly pre-determined. Therefore, I am always concerned that I may not be doing as well as they would like.

D. So how does Ophelia feel about the second Wave?
B. (*He looked left, towards Ophelia.*) She smiles. She says, "Now it begins. More focus needs to come. Now you are ready to take further steps, big steps into a platform. You had to overcome personally, both of you," she said, "certain things about your nature that was uncomfortable to portray. But it's necessary for you to take that step onto that platform. You have to be very confident in your upbringing, in your soul capacity, in who you are." She said, "And you have both grown with this book, because it became more personal than the first one. The first one was a baby stepping stone," she says. "Now you have to stand corrected by the fact that you are who you are, and you stand behind your truth. So, it's going to be a more focused energy, in some way," she said, "from each of you."
D. It was a little hard to say that we were Elahims.
B. She knows that, she said.
D. People may have ideas about that.
B. Indeed, but they are human ideas. "Don't put too much value in that!", she said. Huhuhuhuh!
D. But she is happy with the book?
B. Indeed, she is happy. Happy. She says that it is important that you talk about group dynamics. (*He suddenly broke off and began making strange movements of Christine's lips, which went on for a bit, then just continued talking as if nothing had occurred.*) "It's important," she said. That is something that she has a warm embrace upon, that topic. I'm happy that she allows me to say this. (*Instead of bumping him out to say it herself.*) She says that it is unfortunate that some people feel trapped within group dynamics that are dysfunctional. And by dysfunctional, she doesn't mean all groups are dysfunctional, but some may be for that specific individual. Like religion, for instance, if you say that certain groups within a religious belief might not be in resonance with the makeup of that specific soul that belongs in that group. So, the group itself might not be bad individuals, but the core belief or the core idea in that group doesn't resonate. She says not all groups that you are supposed to address are bad groups, but it is simply to adjust your sensation of where you belong, she says. Because you are incarnated to move into groups that you will not resonate with, and one of those things with that is to see if a soul is strong enough to identify that it is out of place. It's like coming into a country and you don't speak the language.

D. Well, that's interesting. So, souls deliberately select places to go, and people to mix with, that are incompatible?

B. Indeed. So they pick a body, they mix and match things that they are going to have in the makeup of that lifetime. Then, let's say they want to address and challenge themselves like in the mental capacity. Then they will put themselves in families, or work situations, or religious situations (*that are challenging*). Normally, it's picked either (*to address the challenge in*) your family and your upbringing, or later on, that you engage in a group (*that brings challenges*), either like work-wise or on a hobby level. I would say that Christianity or religious beliefs are like a hobby, that's what we consider a hobby.

D. That's the way most people treat it, an hour and a half on Sunday.

B. But souls who take on that challenge—and it's not like all these groups are bad—but they are not in resonance with that soul. What she says is (*he gave a big sigh, as he was apparently struggling to convert Ophelia's thought bubble into our language*) that it is important to start to identify, in all surroundings that you engage in, work-wise, family-wise, social media-wise, how you portray yourself and how you wish to be portrayed. What footprint do you wish to leave? First of all, think of that. What sort of footprint do you want to leave? And after that, look around you and see if that (*group*) is in resonance with that footprint that you wish to establish. If not, you might start to think of different adjustments that can be made within groups that you belong to. Groups doesn't have to be hundreds, it could actually be like a small unit of friends, she says, that sometimes could be triggering each other in a way that is not very soul friendly, or for their highest good, one might say.

D. That's really good advice. If you had said that a couple of weeks ago, we would have put that in *Wave 2*.

B. She knew that, she says.

D. It will go in the next Wave.

B. Ah, she said that! Ah! So, I'm happy that she didn't bump me. There was more information in this thing with groups but she said that we will talk more about that, because it is important that you don't address groups as being a bad dynamic, not all of them. Simply to start to recognize if it is in harmony with the way you vibrate. And if someone says, "I don't know how I vibrate," it's not like people know necessarily how they vibrate—but if they are in stillness, they will hear their own melody. And if they shift their focus, let's say, on their friends and their melody, and they go back and forth, back and forth; my melody—their melody. And when I am in that other melody, does my melody change? So, that's a way to identify if you are in a right space. Like this one (*Christine*), for instance, this one isn't very easily fooled in that sense, because this one instantly detects if the melody doesn't cling correctly to his vibration. So he doesn't engage in that. But some are not that alert, so they need to somewhat first sit alone and focus. And that is the thing, sometimes people are afraid to be by themselves, and you have to be by yourself in order to hear your melody. If you never leave that settlement (*group*) that you are belonging to, there is no way for you to identify that. And sometimes people feel like, "Oh, I better just rub off (*imitate*) that melody, instead of creating my own or hearing my own, because if I don't belong there, then I'm gonna be all by myself." But you have to address it in a way that, "Okay, I might be by myself for a little while, but, 'OH, what's over there?' It's a group with a melody that feels more aligned with mine." BUT it's not going to be always that you go from being in one damaging melody, soul-wise, to just finding one that is better. Sometimes there is a bridge where you have to be in hibernation to reflect upon your choices and about how you preferably move forward.

D. That's wonderful advice, so thank you, and thank Ophelia.

B. Thank you, Ophelia. (*Said as he looks towards her.*) So, you know, that's gonna be talked about more.

Ari: Male vs. Female, Elahim vs. Shea (Dec 2, 2018)

Since this is the first time Ari is speaking in Wave 3, we will remind the reader that he is an Elahim and is a member of the Elahim Council on the tenth dimension. He calls himself an uncle to the three brothers, Eli, Lasaray, and Seth. Ari has been involved with Earth for hundreds of millions of years, and always gives masterly talks about difficult to comprehend topics.

Ari has mentioned that polarity and linear time are the two main structures of learning on Earth. He gave an excellent talk on cyclic versus linear time, which was presented in *Wave 2*, in the section titled '*Movement, not Time*'. While linear time sets up the conditions, polarities form the axis within most teachings. The main polarity of sound–light is manifested in a myriad of ways, one of them being the mental–emotional, which correlates to the male–female polarity. On other planets, the polarity is balanced to create what we would interpret as androgynous beings. Within the spiritual dimensions, there is also somewhat of a polarity, with the sixth and ninth dimensions leaning towards the mental or sound, and the fifth and seventh being a bit more in the light and emotional camp. But advanced spirits within any dimension are in harmony with both facets of creation. The human vehicle is designed to push a soul into a position that is off–center, so that the soul is forced to exert its influence to maintain balance. How that interaction plays out is determined by our decisions and creations on this plane.

A. This is Ari.

D. Oh, hello Ari

A. Good Morning to you, my son. We are pleased to see the efforts on your behalf, the representatives of the Elahims. Transmitting the light of the male energy is not easy in the times you are in. Again, we see the battle between male and female, both representing light as well as shade. Don't think just because the female comes in a smaller package, more emotional in its being, that it simply and purely radiates light on this level. We're talking on a human level, of course. So, in some way, the battle between the genders should instead be who radiates light. Both are perfect and imperfect in their makeup. None should proclaim supremacy in either way over the other one. That is not the intention of the creation of two genders. On other locations there are none, you simply are in one species. From this level, it will appear genderless, yet they reproduce anyway, just not in the same way.

D. Doesn't sound like as much fun.

A. HUH! A human notion, indeed. The fun is in the capacity of creation, the awareness that one has of being able to replicate oneself in whatever level and energetic pattern is available on that plane. One should see beyond pleasure, to see the end result of creation, to be proud of that capacity that one has to create. Those who lack the ability, human wise, struggle. They need to find other ways of being creators. Too much blame exists on this plane of those who do not create a replica of themselves. That is not blame, from the higher levels. One should seek to create in other ways. Create within harmony, music even, so it is the same way of creating a child.

D. There does seem to be an obsession about replicating oneself.

A. Yes, but first you have to be proud and content with who you are, otherwise, why do you want to replicate that? So first you begin with yourself, and then you create in harmony, and that you create will be loving and light. If you yourself still have a little work to do, and I know we are trespassing a minefield here, but in order to create light, you yourself have to be light, you have to love yourself. That's how you can create love. You have to take care of your physical vehicle and all the levels within. When you have mastered yourself, then indeed you can only create light. The evolution on this plane is to make sure that everyone generates light before they reproduce.

D. The world would soon be depopulated.

A. Might be so, but the generation to come, programmed to understand its own light before creating another, has the power to create new civilizations. If everyone honors themselves and their light, there will be no war, there will be no struggle. There will be sharing and taking care of those who momentarily suffer; to raise them, as you yourself might be in need of the same care on your path later on. You cannot ask of others what you do not provide yourself. A shift in your consciousness will create another civilization of harmony. Understanding, as humans, you have no idea of what lies ahead. The one that you might neglect might be your savior, years to come on your path. None think in those terms. Again, a shift of understanding, that once you have been taught, then you shift into teaching, vice versa; teach–taught, learn–teach, help–need help, assist–receive, back and forth.

D. Some of the more advanced civilizations in Europe and the US have quit having as many children. Is there some inner acknowledgment that they should not?

A. They save their light. Some should indeed create more light. In some ways, society puts a trap upon humanity, meaning too much demands, whereas the less advanced societies have more time, have more space for companionship, rush less. The advanced society tends to rush, meaning they don't necessarily detect their light, nor the ability to give light. Constantly striving for something—a materialistic reward—instead of finding the reward of light and companionship. It is an imbalance, of course, where matter is highly influential over your species, creating a gap to the more subtle sources within.

D. The Middle Eastern and African people produce so many offspring, and those will become a great burden on the Earth.

A. It's not supposed to be like that. It's the same imbalance, just in a different capacity. You both suffer under the imbalance of matter. It's not supposed to be like that. If you just collect in numbers, if you do not operate from creating light, then it's the same imbalance as those who are more enlightened, if you like, who do not reproduce at all.

D. Is there some way that you are going to bring that back into balance?

A. The balance is only found as the species begins to, on one end, slow down and detect their pace as a human. They have to stop and detect the land. The other civilizations, in many ways, are the land. However, they neglect the power within, helpless in their physical vehicle. It's a difficult matter, but the road in this progress is to detect your light, to stand strong in that light. One should not rush, the other one should—(*long sigh and pause*)—it's an imbalance between the genders in that region. The balance that we see between genders are out of hand in the African region, mainly.

D. They are most iniquitous towards the weak or vulnerable.

A. More female power is needed in that region. You can see the play that we observe from spirit. On certain levels, the female light lacks and needs to be stronger. In other places, the male has been suppressed, pointed out as being malfunctioning.

D. That is true. A lot of the feminist societies have completely crushed the male spirit.

A. See the same problem, opposite though. Imbalance between the genders. Huh, well, I'm sure it was not intended in the beginning of creation! But you also have the power of will, which is given to you, and that is to find your light in the maze of matter. That is what the power of will initiates. Since then, the power of will has gone in all different directions, yet it originally was only one, to find your light under the spell of matter and illusion. That is the original intent of the power of will. Everything else will follow correctly!

D. Do you think, when the modern human was designed, it was not given enough access to the soul? Is that what caused the imbalance to become a somewhat permanent malfunction?

A. It shifted over the millennium. Some indeed were less connected to the source, almost acting like programmed, robotic creatures. There are still remains of that species, and you can see it physically in their way of motion. They have a different way about them.

D. Where are these found?

A. Some are found in the middle of Asia, and Japan. Japan has a strong memory to those prototypes. That's why, in many ways, they appear different in the way they operate. They are quicker in their head, in the mind, yet their physique baffle, especially the western societies.

D. In what way?

A. The way they communicate, the way they move, the way they organize themselves; highly skilled, busy little bees. Very productive, more productive than a lot of other species. Japan, interesting continent. Operating a little bit different than the rest of humanity.

D. In a good way, or a bad way?

A. Mainly just different. There is a Cell (*part of the Cell operates from Japan, in coordination with London*) that is different though. But, in general, they are friendly but more productive. We will discuss this later. There is a block on the matter for the moment. But there are differences within your species.

D. Are certain traits and attributes going to be kept, and others rejected? Are you going to get rid of certain types of humans?

A. Modification is always ongoing, based on results of how you operate and how you connect, not only to your equals but also to those who appear different. We will discuss it further. Do you have any further questions?

D. When the Elahim traveled here, they always came in a male form?

A. Yes. Male polarity, makeup, male light.

D. So the seventh would be the counterpart then?

A. Indeed, even the fifth resonates more with the female. Counterpart.

D. Were there ever any spirits like the Elahim or Anunnaki who were here from the female realms?

A. Ophelia taught the male light. Even though she is not Elahim, she was an ambassador for the Elahim light, at one point. Others followed, high priestesses, not Elahims, yet representatives on our behalf after encounters that were confusing for the individuals (*the humans who were present*). Some from the seventh mediated, took the role of the male light, representatives of the Elahims in female form. Those were the same height as the

18 The Spiritual Design

Anunnaki, yet female form, almost transmitting the same form they have in spirit. Goddesses, they were known as. Tall, powerful, similar as the Anunnaki. They came to mediate. Ophelia assisted, tried to clean up among the human consciousness, tried to radiate the male energy through a female appearance that she possesses. Grand, they all were grand, Shea.

D. Ah, yes. You have mentioned them before.

A. Goddesses, tall, similar height as the Anunnaki.

D. What time period was this, in human years?

A. One time was around 30,000 years ago. Another effort was made 3000 to 5000 BC. Appearances of the goddesses continued, but only for a few, not in full physical after that.

D. In our previous books, I stated the ability for Elahim to manifest ended around 15,000 BC. Was that inaccurate?

A. It was an overlap between 30 to 15, some actually in remote areas practiced to about 12,000 BC, but not visible. So indeed, correct, did not do so after 15,000 BC.

D. But you said Ophelia was here as Shea. The Shea were manifested as well, weren't they?

A. Yes. They are the same; Anunnaki, Shea. Grand gods and goddesses they were known as, just male and female appearances. Shea have been translated into angels, the archangels. Man refers to the Shea as archangels. An upgrade, I would say! Huh huh huh. But that's the memory. When man talked about archangels, they refer to these tall beings, Shea.

D. So the Shea were continued to manifest here until—?

A. 3000 BC.

D. And were they manifested as the Anunnaki were?

A. Yes, manifested.

D. So the Elahim were blocked from coming as the Anunnaki about 15,000 BC, but the seventh continued to come in a manifested form?

A. Yes, and some on our (*Elahim*) behalf, like Ophelia. Manifested in the shape of these tall goddesses, yet spreading the male light combined with her own light. There were several of her friends. They appear female, yet the energy that they radiated was similar as the Anunnaki. This was to calm and convince (*the humans*) that power and appearances can sometimes be an illusion.

D. Were these the memories of the gods that were present before Sumerian times?

A. Shea did not travel to the Sumerian region. However, India—Indian fables remembers Shea—and they also operated in South America. There was activity, even on the North American continent, that has been erased from your memory of history. They were more like the Japanese are now, productive, like work ants. Mining, assisted Anunnaki. Shea mediated, presented the female shape, radiating a blend of the seventh and ninth, even the sixth, but in a female form. So, in some way, those who detected the Shea's saw Anunnaki or felt their presence, but because they saw the angelic being, the goddesses, they were calmed. Unfortunately, there were those who did not portray the male light accurately. We have referred to them as an offspring of our family tree. (*There were some spirits from the sixth who did not work in harmony with the intentions of the Elahim Council, and those spirits have been prevented from returning here. They opened portals and allowed visitors to come here that were not invited by the councils.*) Shea came as ambassadors for the neutral light that we all share, regardless of home base. We were thankful for their assistance, as there was mainly a small part (*from the sixth*) that did not operate correctly, yet it placed fear in the species. Humanity, at that point, did not have the ability to detect the differences, fully. This is the times that are referred to in old fables, as well as the war of the gods. There was no war, but there was a conflict, indeed, within the family tree.

D. I thought there was a war amongst the aliens?

A. We're not talking about aliens now, we're talking about Shea and Anunnaki. Aliens are different, visitors, we call them. Taking different sides. Those took the side of the little group in our family tree, tried to establish bases on this plane. Shea and the true Anunnaki joined forces to establish peace and calm on this plane. But because of the little group within our tree, we took a step back and let Shea operate on our behalf. Yet we were engaging with them, balancing the effects the visitors had—acting like grasshoppers. So indeed, yes, this was the war of the gods.

D. Okay. I wanted to make sure I didn't misrepresent something you said previously.

A. No. Elahim and Shea on one side. The small group (*from the sixth dimension*) and visitors on the other, expelled, did not operate from light. This plane was supposed to be in harmony in order

for your species to evolve correctly. In some way, this memory created a memory within your Earth, within the planet, making the species, the human walking upon it, affected. That is a remnant within your species, and this is the memory you have.
- D. So if the aliens had not visited and been here, then humans—*(Ari finished the sentence.)*
- A. Humans would have evolved differently.
- D. More in–line with how the Creator envisioned it?
- A. More in–line with Elahim and Shea. That's why you see the polarity. Those who stand and seek light lean to the left, to Shea and Elahim. Those who operate in darkness feel the memory of the visitors and the group *(from the sixth who did not follow the Creator's intention)*. There. We will continue the topic.
- D. That was truly enlightening, so thank you for that.
- A. You are much welcome. Elahim
- D. Elahim, my friend.

Ophelia: Healing Emotional Blockages (Dec 2, 2018)

Ophelia is a guide for both Christine and me, so she is constantly monitoring us and will occasionally transmit healing energy during a session. This is one of those times. I had a bit of an internal debate on whether to include this portion of her talk, because it is personal. But much of what Ophelia said is universal, especially when she tells how each of us is tenderly guided throughout our lives. Even though our conscious mind fails to recognize the care we are given, on a soul level, we fully know and appreciate our unseen companions.

- O. There is a blockage in your chest area, an energetic blockage, not physical, that causes the flow within your energetic line, from top to bottom, to stumble.
- D. What caused that?
- O. The blockage relates to unspoken thoughts. Unspoken feelings to yourself.
- D. In this lifetime?
- O. Yes. Some needs to be released, for yourself. Honor your journey, don't suppress it. I will indeed send some light to your chest. One moment, please. *(She then began to radiate a tremendous energy towards me that I could feel in the middle of my body. I actually became very emotional and was not able to prevent myself from crying, as the waves of energy poured over me with a feeling of*

great love.) Take deep breaths, all the way down to your lungs, let it flow, the ebb and flow of creation, feel the air moving downwards through your center point. Continue to breathe, long breaths in and out. As you take these breaths, remember the boy, the boy when you were five, falling and tripping, innocent. Breathe the sensation of gratitude. There were incidents with your mother when you were five. You stumbled a lot, tripped, it was almost like your feet had grown before your body. You wobbled in your physical, and she did not understand you. Continue to breathe. The sensation of not being understood started at that point, to not having your back, to not allowing you to be who you are. Feel the light. I was with you. I lifted you up when you needed the protection and when you needed the comfort of being here. You were always protected and cared for, from your group. To accept that feeling will help you to release the blockage within your chest. To recognize who you are and that you were always loved and cared for. Sit in your own power and breathe like this, and more memories will come for you to resolve, heal, and release.

D. I will do that. Thank you for always being there.

O. You were always loved, you were always cared for. You and I have traveled before; it was easier then. You recognized the embrace from friends. Now you traveled with those who are unfamiliar to you. That makes you feel lost. And when you tripped, you expected to be lifted. When you were not, it created a hole within you, a distance to your group. You took that role to understand humanity and those who suffer sadness. To understand that some travel like this. Speak your truth, your journey, and it will help others. Don't be embarrassed of your human journey, be proud of your spiritual journey.

D. That's such good advice. Thank you so much for the healing, Ophelia.

O. You are much welcome. With that, we will have to leave. I will leave you in the embrace of the motherly energy and the light from spirit.

Bob: John 32 in the Catholic Army (Dec 31, 2018)

Bob, being my spirit guide, often talks about my previous lives. The Elahim assist the Council of Nine with research to improve the brains in humans. Lasaray is one of those volunteers sent to Earth to collect data on the brain and deliver it to the Council. The research is for the next upgrade of the human. Many humans are unknowingly engaged in collecting data, so it is a common side-purpose among the incarnated. Bob talks about three of my incarnations in this session. One incontestable fact is that the spirits have perfect memories of everything they say, which I can only verify after the sessions are over. A month earlier, on December 4th, Bob described a life as an Austrian professor named Hans Blumenberg, who died in December 1387 at age 73. (See *Notes, Volume 2*.) In this session, Hans was identified as being a parallel life to John 32, who was a mole in the Catholic army.

When the spirits talk about moles, it normally means a lifetime where the soul is on a "secret mission", as Bob would say. Sometimes a mole comes with a lot of soul energy to infiltrate and influence a group to behave in a more spiritual way. In other instances, the soul comes with very little soul energy and is just bumbling around collecting information for a council. John 32 was the latter, being an enormous man who contained very little of my soul energy. Bob also chronicles how he guided John 54 to meet Josephine, a spirit friend from the seventh dimension, who was incarnated in an Irish harbor town where John 54 lived.

D. If this is my last time down, this might be the last time we do this?

B. You said that you might come back in a couple of cycles ahead to see how the human is progressing. You said, "There's no need to come back for a while, because it's not going to be a quick upgrade in the brain." You said you have the data needed for the upgrades to take place. And the humanoid itself has to evolve to a certain point, and in order for them to get a new brain—to just make it simple here—they have to be more connected to their soul in the center point. So, you said, "I have the data needed in order for me to know exactly what needs to be done, in order for the new brain to come in. However, the humanoid itself needs to, first of all, connect to light and the soul particle, before they will be given an upgrade,"—to a Windows 20! Huhuh. But you have the data now, so I'm sure we might go elsewhere. But you said when the being has evolved and are more empathic and aligned with their host, then you will indeed come back. You said that you do that, you come in and stay awhile for a long time—and I've been observing this—and then it becomes like a vacuum (*he made a slurping sound*) and then you come back later on to just see, "How did this plant develop!" Huh huh huh.

D. Do you remember the names of some of the lives I've had recently?

B. You did have a life in Ireland. You like the name John, so you had the name "John" several times. You said, "I don't have the imagination to come up with new names all the time. I'm taking the same." That's what you said, "There's no need to be too inventive with names, it's all the same." You have had a lot of lives where you were John, so we actually call you John 1, 2, 3, 4, 5, and so forth, to somewhat identify them. So when we talk about different stories, I say, "What did you think about John 54?" And then you say, "Well, that was a funny time." And John 54 was actually in Ireland in the harbor. A little bit of a hermit in the way that you were. Not very social, but you were writing a lot and you created maps. But eventually you did feel a little bit lonely, and I did poke you. I said, you know, in your dreams, "Don't be such a crab! Go out and find some friends." I poked you with that, and I said, "Let's do something." So John 54, he actually started to go down to the harbor and to where they were bonking on the barrels, creating music. (*Bob has sung, on several occasions, a boisterous melody from that lifetime. He must have liked the tune.*)

D. Ah, so this was the harbor guy? (*John 54 had been a sailor but was injured at sea and thereafter had to work as map-maker in a harbor town.*)

B. Ah, Harbor John, John 54. So we were there, and I said, "This is good for you. You need to make friends, because eventually you will see that some of these friends are actually friends from home, from Ophelia's place." And you said, "That's highly unlikely." (*He imitated me with a sort of snobbish professor voice.*) But I said, "We don't know that." And when John 54 finally went down to the harbor, he did, indeed, find himself a lady friend. Her name was Josephine, and John 54 was extremely captivated by Josephine. And Josephine, because she reminded him of Ophelia, I think—but she was very much younger and he felt it was inappropriate to approach her—so he took on a role of a father figure, a mentor for Josephine. And he felt like—or you felt like—it was not a very good environment for Josephine to be in. So you came, and you sat in this taverna, just to make sure that Josephine was safe. You felt a responsibility to make sure that Josephine would be safe. She was working there, like a waitress, so you just came and sat there with your journals and looked around to make sure that she didn't have any trouble.

D. That was nice of old John. So was that actually my 54th life as John, or were you exaggerating?

B. As John. No, that was John 54.

D. I guess I've been down quite a bit then.

B. Ah. So we have that in our books. Then we have John 32. Oh, he went overboard! I actually thought that it was this one (*Christine*). John 32, he was down in Spain and he had like an army, he was involved in the Catholic army. This was around 1377 to 1382, in that time. But that was also—no, it was more in the beginning...oh, let's see. Because you actually came at the same time and you were in that Heidelberg place.

D. I don't remember the date you gave me about the Heidelberg life.

B. So you were in two places (*parallel lives*). I guess that balanced out, a little bit, the activity that John 32 did down in the Catholic army.

D. Maybe that's why I have an aversion towards the Catholic Church.

B. That was a rumble on a big scale. But it was at the same time, I see here. But you said that one is a physical life and the other one is a mental life. So the professor life was mental and the John 32 was physical—I would assume you did not preoccupy too much time with the brain on that one. John 32, he didn't think that much, but he was grand, I must say, from a physical standpoint. He was quite large in size—he was intimidating by his size alone. And this one (*Seth, Christine's higher spirit*) was like, "Why can he get this big body and move around like that? Why can't I?" And Ophelia said, "Look at John 32, he doesn't have a brain! He's just moving around, and he's not going to go anywhere too long, because he will be coming home quite soon. If you don't logically think of your actions, you might come home soon, too." And then this one said, "I don't want to just go down and come home too quickly, but I can have a grand physique like that!" And Ophelia said, "But you did! You had many great, large physiques, mirroring your greatness." (*She was teasing Seth.*) And this one was like, "Oh, that is true."

D. Well, when you have a life like that Catholic guy, John 32, I would think that would build up a lot of karma. But you said my Coat was folded back around 100 AD?

B. Ah, I don't know why you did this thing. I think you actually went down there to monitor, in some way, group behaviors within this group. I mean, because you called yourself John, they called you Juan, but it's the same thing. You have come down and looked at certain activities, especially you are interested in group activity. And sometimes you allow yourself to have these robotic lives, like John 32. Even though the brain isn't that activated and maybe thinking for itself, it's actually in direct contact—oh, this will sound confusing to some—but Jeshua and the Council of Nine, they were actually tapping into you and reading the group activity where you were placed. So you were simply physically placed there.

D. Wow, that's interesting!

B. This might be confusing for some. But sometimes you did have lives—you had a physical life occurring—but your complete soul wasn't tapped into it. So you remote observed a setting without the pickle of fully being there. And sometimes you went in with a small percentage and allowed the Council of Nine and other friends to tap in and read instantly. It's like putting those little things in water to hear and read activity (*underwater microphones and cameras*).

D. Okay. I understand that.

B. That's what happens sometimes. So John 32, he wasn't meant to do more than just blend in, in this Catholic army. And he did, indeed. He was acting like one of them. But it didn't mean anything, because the Council of Nine, they were tapping into and they were reading the activity of your surroundings. So sometimes you had lives like that.

D. Huh. So when you say a small percentage, right now I have about seven, is that considered a small percentage?

B. No, you have to function. In John 32 it was like one and a half.

D. Just enough to keep it going?

B. To keep it going, and for the Council of Nine to tap in and read the activity around you.

D. Does that happen, occasionally, that the spirit world will have bodies like that, that they are observing through?

B. Indeed.

D. That's fascinating.

B. So, a lot of things have happened on my travels with you.

D. Were you taking care of John 32 as well?

B. No, because I was not allowed to. Ophelia and Jeshua and the other ones, they were like, "Spend your time up with the professor in Austria." You were in Austria, and then you went to Germany, but you came from Austria. You liked that region and you moved around a little bit. You were Austrian, I think, but you moved to Germany. Indeed, so I wasn't needed in the same way, because you were in some way remotely controlled by the Council of Nine. So I guess they didn't want me to interfere, like, "Ohh! Don't step on that!" Because they wanted you to step on things to see how certain things activated. And I might go in and push you away and try to help, like "Oh, don't talk with that person!", and that was not the idea with John 32.

D. So like now, when I'm wandering around, do you monitor all the people around me and keep some of them away?

B. I do, I do. And then certain things you say, "It's supposed to be like this, Bob." You say that when you sleep, so I just stay present.

D. Wow, I'm so grateful. Thank you.

Ia, Ophelia: Waves in the Ocean of Energy (Jan 6, 2019)

Ia began this session by describing the need of each soul to recognize its own melody in the great symphony of creation. Ia, as you may recall, was created at the same time as Bob, and is his counterpart on the second dimension. Gergen is the mentor to both of them, although they have very different paths. She is a teacher of the younger spirits, but is also a master of DNA manipulation. After she moved in and took control of Christine, she gave a brief but comprehensive summary of how she teaches the little spirits to maintain their light capsule. The purpose is similar to why humans are supposed to meditate—to strengthen the connection with the soul. Ia didn't get a lot of time on the stage, but what she said is quite useful and is well worth practicing. The egg she mentions is how new spirits are created on the second dimension. The Creator, through the Mother Energy, will make about 100 new spirits at a time, all sharing a common theme, and deliver them all together in an energetic bundle to a nursery area on the second. Then, after a while, the individual spirits will be separated from the bundle to begin waking to their unique blueprint.

When Ia was done, Ophelia stepped in to talk about waves of energy from the Creator. She also gave a remarkable description of time, relating it to a color map of sound and melodies. What is always surprising, although it shouldn't be, is how she so masterfully dissects subjects and articulates it in a way that is intelligible. Some of the material on the Wheel of Creation could have been moved into the *Spiritual Design Theories* chapter, but we left it here for continuity.

Ia. (*She began giggling.*) Ah. Hee hehe

D. Is this Ia? How did you sneak in?

Ia. Indeed. So the topic that I presented to them both, that I wished to deliver today, had to do with the understanding of one's upbringing as a soul. Which I'm sure, after discussions with Ophelia, is the same, regardless (*of dimension*). So as you begin your journey, departed from your egg that has been delivered from the Master Mind and the Creator, you begin a journey that is full of exploration and adventure, but it also demands that you are cohering to the signals within you and around you. As you begin to travel to different fish tanks, you will be surrounded by signals and sounds that will delude the signals from within. That is why one needs a little bit of preparation before one starts to blend or travel. So, all fish tanks, all realities, all planes that you can visit, has an environment that is going to be perhaps not always in balance with your own melody. That is why it is important to begin your development in the spirit realm by sitting in solitude. This is why the importance for you, when you are here in a human body, to sit in your power. It is the same; it is to remember your melody when you are in an environment that is not reflecting, necessarily, your own melody. So, you begin your journey in the spirit realm by embracing the solitude, if you like. You need to find and hear your own song before you can even blend with others—others even of your own liking, or others from your same home base—because you all have different tones, even though you resonate in one BIG symphony. So in order for one to feel comfortable and be able to fulfill one's mission, regardless if you blend, or if you travel in an incarnation, the important part is to understand your own melody. When you sit in a human vehicle in your power, it is advisable that you try to find the tune within, not just sit and feel the power, but listen, seek the melody. Not all do, they clearly meditate and they sit in their power, alone as well as with others. But if you constantly surround yourself in, let's say, group meditations, even though that serves a purpose for rejoining energies and purpose, you might not hear your own melody. You will not be able to fully complete your mission unless you hear that inner bell. So, what we would like to advise is for humanity, individuals, to, when they sit by themselves, to seek the song, seek the bell. It might begin to resonate like a bell. That is normally the first sign or signal that you have started to embark on understanding and hearing your melody. Seek the bell. Your center point is very much like a big bell.

D. And how would that be sensed in a human body?

Ia. It will be sensed first as a vibration in your center point. But if one visualizes a bell, a golden bell, and how that would look and sound—that is why the power of thought is so profound on this level, as it opens the doors and windows to other inner realities. So, those who might not fully understand that they can hear their song within, they can use the power of mind to create a visual bell. The mind has the ability to not only play tricks, but to also open those windows that we want you to open. Those who are more open or ready will feel the melody in their chest area, and as it begins to increase, the sensation will be felt in the head. But the bell starts in the center point. Create it in your mind if you do not find it easily.

D. That's really, really good. Thank you so much for that, Ia.

Ia. Bob (*who was standing to the left, listening*) made a little bit of a comic observation.

D. What did he say?

Ia. He said that the head will go like, "Bong, bong, bong, bong, bong." But the sensation is felt starting in your center chest area, not in your center point, but it will feel like a vibration, similar as you feel when you depart in some situations, like the OBE (*out-of-body experience*). It is the same sensation. Those who travel easily in an OBE, they follow their bell, they follow that window as the song takes them flying like a bird. The vibration is felt in the chest, and either you will hear it as a song, and it can, for some, appear quite loud, as their unique melody might be loud and clear as a drum. But sit in that feeling. In that feeling, the true nature of who you are reveals.

D. I remember once, when I was working on an OBE, it felt like there were waves rolling from the top to the bottom of my being.

Ia. Yes, yes. One moment, Ophelia wishes to say something.

O. Hello, this is Ophelia.

D. Ah, hello, Ophelia. Always a pleasure.

O. Always a pleasure, indeed. The vibration, my son, that you felt, was the rhythm from…I will try to give you a picture, as this is what is coming. If you see the Wheel (*of Creation*), you have the center point and you have your fish tanks, there is a vibration or a wave through the spiritual realities. See it as an ocean, this middle part where the spiritual realm resides. If you see it as an ocean, and if you try to focus that the wave to each fish tank is different. Some waves are long and slow as they reach the fish tank. As of here (*fish tank five, our Universe*), the waves are faster, meaning the spirit realm has a higher interest and a higher presence in this reality. There is constantly a wave going on in the spiritual levels around the center Pole, and it looks, to give you the picture, it looks like an ocean. Picture it in your mind how different it looks depending on what fish tank it is, and what the spirit realm has a higher interest in. If I compare to, let's say, the fish tank around one or two o'clock, that wave is much slower, it goes like this, the ocean (*she made a slow gesture*). Everything starts from the center point, moving outwards through the spiritual dimensions, out into the physically manifested realities. The waves would be considered, if we will talk about years, then that wave would be 500,000 in between. The years, if we were to compare it to the wave going to this fish tank, is only ten years. Much faster, the wave, the interaction, the presence. I hope I can give you the picture, so you can understand. When you left your body, you came into this ocean, you floated around in this sea that you felt. You were in this sea of this reality, that is why it felt uncomfortable. If you had been in another sea, in another wave, you would simply have felt the presence of who you are. You tapped into the concern from the spirit realm in the sea, the wave, that is interacting with this reality. That is what you felt. And it concerned you, because there is a high interest and high presence from the spirit realm at this point, on this location (*Earth*). And that is what you tapped into. You felt distress, you felt concern, you felt like there were all levels interacting at the same time, which we are. If I compare to the other one at two o'clock, not everyone is present in that wave. Even though it travels through all spiritual dimensions, not all engage. Here, everyone engages. Do you understand?

D. I do, sort of. The wave would be more related to a sound energy? Light is a constant?

O. Yes. Yes. The wave itself, the ocean itself, is constant. That is light. That can never be eliminated. The sound creates the waves, meaning the presence and the interaction from the spiritual dimensions, all orchestrated from the center point. As the wave departs from the center of this Wheel, traveling outwards to the different fish tanks, and here again, I would like you to, in your mind, see all twelve fish tanks, and how the ocean looks different, depending on the destination it is heading for. The wave created

30   The Spiritual Design

by sound moving outwards means that, depending on what is needed in that fish tank, those realities engage. That is why I say here, all levels engage. In number two, only (*dimensions*) seven and eight engage. It is a protected reality, not necessarily of high interest in development. We are preserving what exists in number two, looking after it, seven and eight. The other ones clearly have the ability to engage, but they are more passive in this wave of 500,000 years. I'm saying years so you can see the movement of the wave. Clearly, we do not talk about time. (*I think Ophelia means fish tank two, where Tiddle is located. The Taffles, from the second dimension, live on Tiddle in a protected environment of light and colors. Tiddle was described in 'Notes, Volume 2'.*)

D. Understood. I do follow that a little better, so thank you.

O. There you go. The image is sent to this one. Ask, and she will deliver.

D. I did have two questions though, related to the perception of time, if you don't mind?

O. I never mind. Go right ahead, let's see if I will answer. (*She was laughing.*)

D. Before a spirit incarnates on Earth, it is able to foresee, in some way, part of its future. And the spirit realm also sees, I guess, what happens in the future on this plane?

O. It is similar as that wave, the reality is light, constant, but the events taking place follow the wave of sound. When one looks into the future, and when one, a specific soul, investigates a life ahead of time, then what they look for is the wave, the sound wave. The sound wave is the events; the place where it takes on the scene, is light.

D. So how far into the Earth's future can you observe?

O. Indefinitely, if I choose to, if that is in the design. But then again, I believe that I can see indefinitely. The Master Mind might have a barrier, meaning that I see a mirror at the end. So after that (*beyond the mirror*) a whole new scenario is taking place. Don't you agree?

D. So it's not particularly fixed, it's just a possibility?

O. It's not fixed, no, not at all. So, when I say that I can see indefinitely ahead of time here, that might be taken with some moderation, as I do not know what the Master Mind has behind the ending point of my view.

D. Presumably the closer they are in Earth years, the more likely it is to occur?
O. We follow it merely in sound, that's how I can give you a picture. I know that this is troublesome to understand, but we detect events on this plane, and on other realities as well, in the melody. So, let's say that the intent of the upcoming future is supposed to be a melody from Mozart, and what we observe is suddenly an 80s pop song, then clearly it effects the end result of what we are trying to observe and relate to. We observe events, or we receive information from you, not only individually, but collectively, as well as (*from*) the planet itself, through the melody. We compare the intent, meaning the light that is constant—light also radiates a melody, you should know. Light is not silent. Combined, it is…how can I give you the picture? The map, the color map on this plane, it entails not only your planet's wellbeing, but it entails your upcoming events. The species that exists on this plane, your atmosphere, everything around you, the web, the location where this solar system resides, it is all encased in one intent, one melody. We can dissect and go down to molecules, meaning certain smaller events, so that we can find the cause of the change of the melody. At this point, one of the major causes that changed the melody that we wish for you to sing, is group dynamics and how you fire each other up. Blindly following signals that are not here (*not part of the intended melody*), that are placed from yourself, that has an origin of fear, an origin of survival. That is why the interactions from the spirit realm is so intense, as we try to understand where the signals come from and how we can assist. But within all events, large or small, even (*within*) the human, the spirit helper follows (*and assists*) its human by detecting the melody, combined with looking at colors. Colors, as well as light, also has a tune. I know this is a big mystery for you. I'm trying the best I can to give you a picture.
D. I think I follow, in general, what you are trying to show me.
O. Just know that when we observe events here, it is not visual, it is audible. We don't look in a magnifying glass, in that sense. Councils tune in on the melody, and meetings take place where we try to dissect.
D. They must feel disappointed by what they are hearing.
O. Confusing, at times. But it is the same way with Ia and the egg. They stand around the egg and they try to decipher the melody, the intent. Councils once did so as well with this planet and the species on it, deciphered and tuned in on the intent for this

32 The Spiritual Design

evolution here. Not only your environment, but the mammals on it and the atmosphere. So it is the same occurrences that takes place for a planet as well as for an egg in Ia's nursery. We will leave the discussion before we create more confusion. (*Ia and her companions on the second send sounds and melodies into the egg and then listen to how it responds. It is a long process to uncover the intention the Creator gave each soul within the egg, but Ia gets great satisfaction from the work.*)

D. I did have one more question that a lot of people wonder. Does the soul incarnate sequentially in linear time, such that an earlier incarnation would be at an earlier stage of soul development?

O. It's going on similar—it's more like a seesaw. It's not a line in the same way, even though if you do regression work, like this one, she sees the timeline as a flat, long line. So, in some way, that is true, because you follow linear experiences here. As you tap into the fourth reality, you will actually see that it is a waveform of your incarnations, and how they interact in certain times with each other, and how they are going on at the same "time", as you call it. You can go back and forth between realities once you master the fourth reality, which can play tricks on you. From a human standpoint, it will appear as a linear development, but as you look from above, you will see that they are all cycles within your own evolution.

D. So is a more recent lifetime, relative to the spirit's development, a more advanced state?

O. Not necessarily, depending on…let's say John 32, he wasn't well developed, was he? You would think he was a brand–new soul, wouldn't you? However, your Coat was folded cycles before that. So indeed, the evolution on this plane can seem to go in a linear manner or fashion. However, depending on what the soul intends to assist the (*Earth*) plane with, or the spirit realm—like in the case of John 32—it can appear differently. So certain things that you have mastered in your evolution here can be repeated based on different occurrences that the spirit realm, combined with you, wish to investigate.

D. Okay. That makes sense.

O. But it's hard for you to understand that lifetimes go on at the same time.

D. Yes, because if each life has a certain percentage of your soul, I wonder how it would all go around, if it occurs simultaneously.

O. If I give you a picture, all lifetimes occurred simultaneously in the fourth reality, on the third, only one.

D. Hmm?

O. So, from the third reality they are linear. From the fourth they go on at the same time.

D. What about from the spiritual perspective?

O. They see it as a cake. They can see them all, they can see all of them going on at the same time. Like if I look at you, I can tune in on the fourth reality on your specific soul and your development, and I can see all your existences here at the same time in the fourth reality. However, they are not in the same light, the same color, the same strength, they look more dimmed, if I try to give you a picture. From all these, I can see which one exists on the third. That is how the spirit realm will observe. There is no need to put all your attention in assisting John 32 at this point, for instance, as he is not manifested, but he is still there to observe and tap into. Once a soul has developed to the potential where one can investigate several lifetimes, they tap into the fourth, looking at the Coats, if you like.

D. What about the future lifetimes. From our perspective, do they also exist?

O Yes, but they are more silent in their vibration, as certain things might change, they are not cut in stone, all of them.

D. So the past is sort of locked, but the future is not?

O. Indeed, in the fourth reality. So when one plans its development, when a spirit helper assigned to a soul starts to develop a map for that specific soul to travel, they create all these individuals *(body characteristics)* and events in the fourth reality. If I give you a picture, if you see all these bodies, or potential bodies, in the fourth reality, the designers of bodies and events for souls to tap into, create them in the fourth reality. Different personalities, events, scenarios and so forth, all created as a dummy, a prototype, in the fourth reality. When a soul is in the part of life selection, they look at a couple of these, and then, together with a spirit helper, one is selected, tapped into and descended to the third *(dimension)*.

D. So what they see in their life preview is just a shadow of what could be?

O. Indeed. So, for instance, this one has seen images prior to your meeting about John in a boat on water. She tapped into your fourth reality, a part of the selection that was available to you before you picked the one you are.

D. And why did I pick the one that I am in? What was the purpose of being born where I was?

O. The other lives that you looked at, the one with a boat, East Coast, you had a stronger personality. You would not be able to leave. *(By leave, she means reducing my soul percentage. She said during most of my life, before this project started, I had only 2 percent remaining.)* You would be engaged in projects with the seas, which your friend, Bob, wanted you to pick. However, he was not able to see all the events that followed that specific character. If you had picked the sea–character you would have been in that life, you would not have been able to leave, like you did as Dave. You picked Dave to be of assistance to certain people around you, but also to have the option to be able to leave. More percentage would have been put into the other part on the boat, which would have made it impossible for you to leave. You picked this life because you wanted the solitude. You picked it because you felt like it was almost giving you a sleep until it was time to work. The other life was more active and you thought it might interfere with this project if you had too much of a personality that was more engaged in life.

D. Okay, that's very helpful to know. Thank you for that.

O. There you go. You are much welcome.

D. It was a very good explanation about time, too, so that is much appreciated.

O. We will discuss it further, but keep the memory of the fourth reality, and how you can view upcoming lives and past existences in the fourth reality. That's how the spirit realm sees it—it's like a library. There you go.

D. Thank you.

O. Oh, you are much welcome. There.

Zachariah: Hydrocarbons (Feb 8, 2019)

Our overuse of energy has many obvious side-effects, and some that are not so apparent. Humans' perception of hydrocarbon (HC) resources are similar to how they evaluate everything else on this planet—something to be exploited for profit. Having worked as a petroleum engineer in the oil business for 40 years, I have a firsthand view of the disregard that comes from a materialist perspective of the Earth. From the doghouses on drilling rigs to the boardrooms of several major corporations, I never sat in a meeting or had a conversation where someone expressed curiosity about whether oil and gas had a greater purpose than the rate-of-return on investments. The spirit realm says that HCs are similar to the blood of the Earth. It circulates and nourishes the Fork and the lifeforms on the surface. The Fork, which was described in *Wave 2*, as well as *Notes, Volume 1*, is the energy field of the Earth that communicates with all living creatures. As the hydrocarbons are removed, the circulatory link within the Fork is diminished. Pollution and other human activities also disrupt the melody of the Fork, so it is not just the depletion of HCs we should be concerned about. Humans are aware that the hydrogen and carbon cycles are critical to life on Earth, but do not understand the mysterious significance of HCs in maintaining the energetic field. This is not the first time that energy has been misused, as ancient civilizations walked a similar destructive path. They, however, were removed during a reboot.

Wind and solar panels are much less environmentally friendly than most people realize. A single wind turbine needs over 300 tons of steel, 4 tons of copper, 1000 tons of concrete, and 5 tons of aluminum and rare earth minerals. Those materials are mined, smelted, manufactured, transported, and installed by burning large amounts of hydrocarbons. And wind farms are downright hostile to the environment when the clear-cutting of forests, bird fatalities, hazardous waste, and land usage are considered. In order to replace oil, gas and coal, there has to be some other abundant resource that can generate a similar amount of energy. Based on the current technology, that means nuclear. But there are safer alternatives to uranium reactors. Thorium Molten Salt Reactors (TMSR), for instance, are being pursued by China and India. They cannot melt-down and are extremely safe. The US researched Thorium for 20 years and built a TMSR, which ran flawlessly for 8 months. Unfortunately, the more abundant and safer thorium was cast aside because the military-industrial shareholders wanted enriched uranium and plutonium to build expensive bombs. In the near-term, common sense predicts that thorium should be the backbone of the electric grid. In the future, the splitting of water to capture hydrogen gas may be economically feasible. There is also a huge energy potential within the solar winds of the magnetic and plasma fields steaming by the Earth.

D. I've really missed talking with you. You sort of disappeared after the first Wave.

Z. Not really disappeared. I have archiving to do. I'm moving archives around. Some will go to the destination that you call Siah's place (*Etena*). So indeed, there are different ideas and memories that will be removed from this location (*the mental realm around Earth*) and stored in that vast library where Siah is.

D. I've heard there are going to be memories removed from Earth's atmosphere?

Z. Yes, yes. We are removing certain negative outcomes, ideas that spiraled into negativity that we wish to eliminate.

D. Can you give me an example?

Z. We are removing certain technological advancements that we wish to exchange for more modern ideas. It has to do with tapping into the resources of energy that you have at this time. Your supply is not unlimited, and you need to be aware of certain behaviors, not acting like grasshoppers. Be careful with the resources. We are removing certain ideas that were intended to move forward in a direction we did not wish. It has to do with resources at this time, in order for the balance within your host, the planet, to begin to heal itself. It has not the ability to do so if technology and the amount of overuse of resources is moving in a direction that is not beneficial for this inner balance. The inner balance, for what you have called the Fork, is in need of certain gas and minerals for it to begin to rejuvenate, it's a living lifeform. It's like not giving you food or water, it's the same thing. Certain resources within the host needs to remain. There has been ideas popping, (*like in*) Britain—even though they do not have oil—there are minds there that are trying to cross boundaries of how to access resources. Almost trying to create them, manmade. You can't create an element, or a mineral, or energy, if you do not have the full pattern (*knowledge or access*) to do so. Certain elements need to remain within the center of the planet.

D. If humans could just figure out how to crack water to generate hydrogen.

Z. We are moving ideas into certain scientists who are working on that behalf. Russia, even a small group in Canada, if those two can begin to work together—those two don't have the same hostility towards each other—and exchanged information. We wish you to embrace the way of council work, that you share the knowledge instead of putting up boundaries of 'mine, keep out'. You will never learn fully unless you give knowledge to someone else. That is a cosmic law, not mine.

D. It's not the Americans who are like that, it's the people in the government and running businesses.
Z. There are certain organs in Britain as well, acting the same way.
D. It's all financial.
Z. Yes. Well, there you go. I will return with an update of this joint work.

Bob: OBE's and Accessing the Fourth (Feb 8, 2019)
When Zachariah was done, Bob came in. Most of his talk was published in *Notes, Volume 2*. However, near the end of the session, I asked Bob about the fourth dimension as it relates to dreams, OBEs, NDEs, and meditation. Everyone explores within the fourth when they dream, and experience it more directly during NDEs or OBEs. Bob tells us that it is common to encounter residual issues from past lives, and those sometimes cause a remembrance of the fear responses. Modern dream analysis is nearly useless, since it myopically and atheistically focuses on the current life, ignoring the countless previous lives and the spiritual dimensions. We are always swimming in a puddle of all our unresolved experiences, and trying to reconcile them with our spiritual objectives. It is within the fourth dimension that many of these issues are brought forward for evaluation.

D. I've got a question for you. I wondered if you could give me a little advice on accessing the fourth through astral projection, OBEs, near-death experiences, trance breathing and things like that?
B. Ah, the breathing is a way for you to conquer your fears as you, regardless of what travels you're doing, as long as you focus and expand your breathing and your lungs, then you will persevere into the first level that will tend to appear like a grey mist. And that grey mist is simply an illusion. But a lot of people who experience these occurrences tend to either hesitate when they reach this barrier, this first barrier, or they feel a sensation of fear. And the fear is because they can't fully sense or see where they are at. The importance is to welcome the light. And when one encounters that barrier, the physical will start to shake a little bit, which also increases the sensation of fear that something is wrong. But it isn't wrong. The trembling will disappear once you invite the light, and then you will simply float and you will feel the warmth.
D. Is that in the fourth reality?
B. It is indeed in the fourth reality.

D. That's where most psychic experiences occur, isn't it?

B. Indeed.

D. It's pretty rare for people to go beyond that?

B. But some come to the end barrier as well, but those (*people*) are not captured by a sensation of fear of what is going on. But it's also because of the fact that you might encounter experiences and visions in this field. And some visions are not necessarily belonging within your own consciousness. It might be your soul consciousness, meaning it's an experience or an event or a meeting that took place in a prior visit here. But it's still in your forest, so to speak, where you will be moving around in. So when you encounter, let's say, a feeling that you don't recognize, it might actually be a feeling you had in a prior lifetime. So look at it and understand that it is a delusion, it is not something that someone has put there. If you persevere into this field, then you might encounter not only the greatest light and the greatest love, but you also might encounter and face certain things that someone did to you. And that can create a sensation of loneliness. And if you feel a sensation of loneliness, then you might feel like the whole space is just a vacuum, and that will indicate that there is no continuation for life. And that is what some experience when they have OBEs, that they come into a sensation of a vacuum or loneliness.

D. That's the void, maybe, that Ophelia was talking about?

B. Ah. The reason for it to occur is to enlighten and awaken the soul from within, to crack a hole in the physical, to make the physical understand that this is also an illusion, and to encounter the differences of mass, of density. That is why it occurs. Some people ask, "Why does it happen? Why do I have an OBE? Why is it occurring?" and so forth. It is designed by yourself when you left here (*prior to incarnating*) as a tool for you to awaken and to find the light. And those who can master this are actually a little bit higher advanced. You do not get that experience necessarily the first time you come down here! Zachariah said the brand-new ice cream is not gonna get that. (*See 'Notes, Volume 1, Bob Brings a Catalogue to Zachariah', where Zachariah was teasing Bob, explaining that souls are not ordered from the Creator like different flavors of ice cream are ordered from a factory.*) So, there are different ways to awaken the soul, and that is one.

D. Normally, when you're awake, everything is filtered through your mind. But when you're asleep or in an OBE, is that more of your soul awareness coming through?

B. It's filtered through your center point. Your mind is not there anymore, but because of the fact that it's still a presence within the physical body and the physical body still exists—it hasn't died—so the mind still plays tricks. The mind is the one that feels the fear and sees different occurrences and sees different voids and so forth. But if you start seeing from your center point, you will not see anything but light. It's just because you're still attached to the mind because you haven't died, so you're still attached to the brain.

D. Does the soul physically move away from the body, or is it an internal experience?

B. It can move away from the body. But not fully. Like I said, it's still connected to the brain, for instance. So the organs are still connected. But indeed, in some way, you actually leave, but you don't leave fully. It's a whole system of engineering behind this. It's like strings and molecules and DNA that holds everything together. But indeed, those who practice and do this well, then indeed, the soul can actually step out of the body and roam around. Those who are not fully throwing themselves into the experience, then it is an experience within and the soul doesn't leave. As long as you are trapped within the illusions from the brain, then indeed you have not left the body fully. You experience something, but you are still in some way within your physical. It's tricky! But you can talk about that, if you want to. So, I'm gonna go now, Ophelia says.

D. Thank you so much for all the information. I really appreciate it.

B. Okay, okay. Bye bye.

Eli: The Inner Layers are like a Solar System (Feb 17, 2019)
Eli uses another allegory to illustrate how our inner mental and emotional layers are like planets, circling our soul particle, which is the sun. As discussed in our previous books, the humanoids that lived prior to the Younger Dryas, 13,000 years ago, were designed differently and could operate more from a soul awareness. Eli points out that the current human has more limitations, which impair the ability of the mind to connect with the soul. The change, they say, was because the Creator wanted to see if the soul can be detected while wearing a heavier garment. In Eli's solar allegory, the emotions

are orbiting closest to the soul vibration, followed by the mental, and then the physical. Because of all the challenges and limitations of our current human design, our metaphorical planets are orbiting way out by Pluto, far away from the sun.

In this session, Eli responds to a question I asked about Siah, wherein he said, "He was transferred, moved there, to be taken care of. Similar like your Little Friend, moving his favorite creature around." If you have followed Bob's stories in our previous books, you know that Siah is a male animal that Lasaray rescued from a planet where it was about to be killed. Siah is quite large, having a body like a powerful lion and a head similar to a dog, but with big, floppy ears and sugar-cube shaped teeth. He was relocated to Etena and is now taken care of by Setalay and the other Shea who live there. Bob had a similar situation with a species of animal he had created and placed on Earth tens of millions of years ago. Bob called them, collectively, his 'Individual', because they all came from a single pattern, I assume. Gergen removed Bob's creation from Earth prior to the humanoid being introduced, knowing it would be hunted for its luxurious fur. The species was very intelligent, and it would have endured a lot of needless suffering if it had not gone extinct. Bob was allowed to bring his Individual to life again on the living planet in the solar system he created. So that is what Eli meant by 'moving his favorite creature around'.

E. Hello, baby brother.

D. Oh, hello, Eli!

E. How are you doing trapped inside that body? Limited? It is the fact of limitation that is one of the greater teachings on this level. Limitations of mind, limitations physically, limitations to heart, to soul. See it as waves, frequencies, barriers. These limitations have come and gone in different amount and numbers, depending on the civilizations and lessons at hand. At this point, all limitations are implemented on this level; mentally, physically, emotionally, and especially, last but not least, the connection to your source. At this point, man primarily focuses on the mental limitations, even though, if they shift their consciousness and try to focus on the emotional one, which relates to your needs, that is the gateway to your soul. If I tell you in order, if you have the soul as the sun of a solar system, the closest planet in orbit relates to your emotional well-being. The next would be mental; further out, physical. As there is a strong connection to physical limitations as well as mental, the inner two, the sun and the planet closest in orbit, suffer. Before, to give you a picture, the physical barely existed. There wasn't really any lessons within the physical reality, the vehicle. The emotional versus the sun, the soul, was all that existed. As you add more planets around your sun, your orbit, adding more limitations and lessons, the sun gets heavier within its structure—not physically, but energetically. It's like putting on more clothes, if you like, changing the conditions within your solar system. And you can see yourself as the sun, this one does! (*Referring to Christine.*) Ha ha! But it's easy to understand how heavy you are if you think of that your existence is where Pluto exists, but you are supposed to navigate from the sun. Your consciousness is all the way out to Uranus, Neptune, Pluto, so you can see the distance from the sun, your soul. This is an image I would like to relay, to help you understand the limitations that are put on this reality. More planets in orbit around your center point, depending on how you master the planets, the lessons, the limitations already in orbit. Do you understand?

D. I do. That's a really good picture.

E. Everything is the same. Where Siah is (*Etena*), there is only the soul and emotional. Pure empathy, pure care, in direct contact. The emotional planet, if we take that as an analogy, is not as far out in orbit, it's closer to the core, to the sun, almost becoming one. As you learn to master the illusions that are put upon you—similar like limitations and the orbits of further out planets—then you will learn how to navigate and draw all these lessons in, becoming one. This is the black hole. The black hole simply is. It is the still point of all realities, all lessons, light, dark, male, female, limitations of illusions that no longer exist. All congested into one reality, one awareness. When a solar system, similar as galaxies, has fulfilled their specific mission—different than a human of course—this is when everything becomes a still point, everything *is*. When it comes to galaxies, sometimes that represents the black holes. It is the reality that has fulfilled its destiny, it simply is. It is the same as the Creator, a replica, if you like.

D. Our universe has a black hole, allegedly.

E. Some are a result of interference within the web, but some are that still point where the Creator withdraws its intention, its awareness—it just simply is. It is a replica of the Creator, a still point, a birth, an awareness that can simply be compared to as the Creator. As you transform the lessons within fish tanks, they move, they circle. Fish tanks becoming more compassionate, moving into different lessons—similar like a human—adding different limitations, events, to see whether a system can fulfill its journey. It's not like you begin at one o'clock and when you reach the whole circle at noon, you have fulfilled (*all intentions*). That would be an easy way to see it, but it's a constant cycle. When it comes to this planet, it is added more limitations, which are illusions to make you appear and feel heavy, even though you are not. You are capable to fully be in the same presence and appearance as those at Siah's reality, but you choose not to, you focus on the limitations. You focus on the physical and the mental, creating more illusions, making the sun wobble, discontent.

D. At Siah's reality, are the souls incarnated or manifested? Are they born and die?

E. Manifested. No, there is no death.

D. So the bodies don't age and get sick?

E. No, you travel there based on preference. Those who are there have been there for eons, they don't die. But a soul can travel there and be a child, if you like, so it's not like all are adults. If I give you a picture, a soul can travel there and can experience being raised by the light beings, the elders who are there. So, you can travel there and manifest a physical vehicle, depending on what you wish to explore. You begin by traveling there as a child, as you are there as an apprentice to learn. And you grow, indeed, but you only transform, you only manifest a body that will be suited to that. The soul in each vehicle there are equal. They just manifest differently, depending on their own development, their own evolution, and what they wish to explore. You do not travel there the first time as an elder.

D. How did I travel there the first time?

E. Elahim. You don't look like the others, neither of you do. You travel, you visit, you don't remain.

D. What about Siah? What does Siah represent?

E. Pure joy. Just love and a welcoming. It's a companionship that you seek. You are drawn to animals, as they represent the purest connection to the source, pure compassion. He is a companion that you placed with friends. He belonged in another reality that didn't move forward. He was transferred, moved there, to be taken care of. Similar like your Little Friend, moving his favorite creature around. Meeting prior on another place, but you were fond of him (*Siah*), and he of you, a friend. He was transferred to a place where he would always be safe, always cared for. He's the only one there. He has other friends, animals, but he is the only one of that kind. (*Those who have read 'Notes, Volume 1' are aware that Siah is no longer alone. In February 2019, when Eli delivered these words, that had not been revealed.*)

D. Does he feel lonely?

E. He doesn't feel lonely because he has friends, they just look different. That is a teaching as well here, that you should not just see those who are equal as your nearest friends. Your friends can come in other forms and other shapes. Learn from Siah. Siah is alone, but happy, because of the care and the presence of other beings. There is not, on that place, that you reproduce. So there is not that problem that Siah would be extinct. (*Siah is also in a manifested form that neither ages or gets ill.*) Siah is happy because he feels loved. Here, one of the barriers is that you see others with fear, you see them as a threat. Again, you are way out in orbit. Way out, limited by what fear creates—an illusion. If you navigate from your center, from the sun, then you will see others more as equals, and see the compassion that exists. Still, there are souls coming in and creating events on this place, here, that causes the attention and awareness to be way out of orbit. That, again, is by design, (*for you*) to learn how to navigate when you are blind. When you navigate from the sun (*soul*), from your heart, then you see. If you navigate from the mental and the physical, then you are blind. We are increasing the light in your sun. (*Meaning greater soul awareness.*) Some souls, even remotely, as we adjust the strength within souls. Some new incoming, some already in place, increasing the light, making the physical and mental challenged. Again, it has been referred to as two waves, similar. Emotional souls, one wave; physical or mental, the other. At this point, we see the wind is carrying the physical and mental, moving it forward, not in balance. At Siah's place, all realities are in balance. Neither is superior; all aligned. Your solar system wobbles. I'm giving you different pictures to understand the dilemma and the events and the stage where you are in within your evolution. To understand that plenty (*of events*) are staged to help you understand that this must indeed be an illusion, this cannot be real. Don't swallow everything you see or hear. Navigate from the sun, and light will be given and you will see. Way out of orbit, you are blind, you do not see. There!

D. I like that. It seems like that even with our teachings, a lot of ideas you tell us are almost incomprehensible to people.

E. They will listen, even though you might not get the feedback immediately that you seek. It's like a flower. You plant a seed, but you don't see the flower instantly, do you? You might see it later in the season, or the year after. See that all interactions with others here on this level, you are simply planting seeds. The flower, the tree, will appear when you are long gone. Not necessarily left this reality, but not present with that person anymore. If you navigate from the perspective that you are only planting seeds, it will release a huge sensation of responsibility and difficulty for you. You are not here to fully give the flower. Plant seeds and let others make the garden, taking bits and pieces from what you provide into their reality. All flowers growing will not be the same, do not expect it to be so. Don't think that all will be roses. You plant a seed but the flower will be different depending on who you are talking to. Some will create a rose garden of it. Others might simply want to create a lawn. It doesn't matter, you just provide the different seeds. Whatever flower emerges in the spring is not of your concern. We are guiding you to the right settings and people, making sure that they start to grow their flowers.

Bob, Ophelia: Ants Running Everywhere (Mar 21, 2019)

Bob came in with his pre-planned talk on humans behaving like ants. But Ophelia, who listens intently, decided to interject her own thoughts on the topic, perhaps to soften the message a bit or clarify the idea. Bob was less than enthusiastic about being bumped. When he says haystack, I believe he is referring to the big colonies that form an ant mound, which has the shape of a haystack. Ants that belong to a colony have a leader. Ophelia points out that not all leaders are operating from light, and the ants that have joined those haystacks should instead follow their own inner light. Most of the stories they give us are analogies. It is much easier to remember the lesson if it comes within a memorable allegory. This session came from a small group séance that Christine and I held in Stockholm, so Bob was speaking to an audience.

B. Ohhhh! Uhh Uhh Uhh. This one sniffles a little bit! Ophelia is also here, of course, because she's always like, "What's gonna happen next? What's he gonna talk about?" So, I'm rarely by myself, I always have some sort of company. But I do indeed like to move forward and to make myself known, and to perhaps provide a little bit of knowledge outside the box, meaning outside the framework of the books. Because some of my notes have actually been disregarded. They are like, "No, no, we're not going to use this note. This is not good to put forward. Take something else." So, I have been asked by Zachariah and by Lasaray—my friend that you know as Dave—I have been asked to go over my notes—and I did. But most of my notes were actually moved into the pile of "delivery", because I think it's important that people know more about the unseen world and the activity that occurs in nature. So, with that, it was kinda hard to say, "Oh, I'm not gonna deliver this note. This is not for them, this is just for me—I do not want to appear selfish!" That's what I said, "No one wants to be known as a selfish person! I don't want that." But Ophelia says, "It's not like being selfish, Bob. Maybe the outside box is not ready for that specific note." So we went through that, of course, so that is why I'm rarely by myself. But indeed, I—I and we, with Ophelia, and Zachariah, and some of the other friends as well—we are indeed interested in the development of humanity, and how they are—I mean, it's like watching those ants that you see, they just run around, it seems like they are quite unorganized. But inside, deep, deep, deep, deep inside, there is somewhat of a core, a leader of the pack, or someone who can see through the disorder in the haystack among the ants. But indeed, there is too much activity going on as they, humanity, seems to run around in directions that are not going anywhere. And what I would like to do is to take my shovel and to make sure that the ants remain in these organized haystacks, so the ants don't take off—if you can see the picture—they just go off, and they have no idea, they don't know what they navigate by. They just sort of run around like chickens with no heads. By doing that, they have lost their connection to their center point, and to their purpose of coming here. "You should know that all souls," Ophelia says, "come down with the intention of doing good." Then the question arises, naturally, "What causes this great ant to become disorganized and run away from the haystack and its purpose?" And that is what I am asking in my notes. I would like there to be somewhat of a manual, perhaps, that would indicate where these ants are supposed to operate. In some way, in all these different haystacks where there are ants, there is someone who holds the strings and core knowledge to a specific group. When the group develop...uh–oh. Ophelia comes now. Oh, now I'm getting bumped. Oh, okay, okay, I never say anything to Ophelia, of course. Okay, okay, I'll go. I'll come back.

O. Good evening, this is Ophelia. I would like to discuss the progress that we also see. Not everyone is acting like disorganized ants. You are all carrying a light that you have the ability to create a new set of ants, a new society, and that is what we see a lot of you are doing. So even though some are indeed acting disrespectful, not only to your race, but also to your host, your planet, there are several who are working and creating a wave of empathy and care, spreading the light. The importance of understanding which one (*leader or group*) carries the torch of light, and who are simply gathering ants to become a minion or a mirror of that person's need or greed, lies within your center point to detect the difference between the two. Understand that a lot of people feel left behind. It's easier to find comfort if someone offers them a smorgasbord, if you like, of knowledge and comfort. The one who carries the light, the torch, offers warmth, but also demands of the ant to begin to work from within by itself. That is scary for some people. Some people feel more comfort to belong, hand-in-hand, in a group, regardless of what the purpose (*of the group*) is. Carrying a light also means that sometimes you carry that light by yourself. That is the true advancement of your species; to never feel that you are alone, as you have the light within you. You actually do not need groups, or friends, or even pets. Those are sent to you as a gift from the spirit realm so that you can find equals. Those who acknowledge and recognize the light within sometimes operate by themselves. We can see some of the greatest lights on this planet doing the smallest acts for humanity. Whereas those who proclaim to possess truth, knowledge, or companionship, can operate from a source of ego. Detect the difference and you will stand tall and strong in your light, and that is the true warmth and true connection that we offer you. Thank you.

Setalay, Ophelia: Silence (April 21, 2019)

Setalay is a spirit from the seventh dimension who lives on Etena. This was the first time she spoke to us, but she has returned many times to offer guidance, and is an important member of our project. She is a companion and friend of Ophelia and radiates a very similar energy when she comes through during sessions. Those spirits who have manifested on Etena are the caretakers of the knowledge stored in pyramids on that planet in fish tank four. They earned the right to manifest on Etena after completing the rounds of incarnation and folding their Coats on Earth. Setalay is also the one who takes care of Lasaray's pet, Siah. Setalay gave some beautiful guidance about learning to live in harmony with the Earth, and when she was done, Ophelia blended with Christine to describe the power of silence.

S. Hello, great traveler.

D. Hello? (*I didn't recognize the voice.*)

S. My name is Setalay, and I am pleased to be back on the Earth plane. I have traveled as Shea, with Ophelia. Let me just look around...so many changes. I now reside with others on Etena, where your friend Siah is. We once set foot here (*on Earth*) as Shea. Ophelia is a close friend of mine. We travel to tend to nature and to the seas, especially the creatures in the sea. They are of high interest to us. Water is life. Water is a power, a resource that you do not fully embrace as a resource. We did so in the past. Water is life, not only for the living entities on the plane here. Water exists even on Etena. The creatures in the sea have been here longer than you. They are remains from a golden time, when Shea, together with other visitors, tended to this planet as a greenhouse. We installed wildlife, trees, fruits and vegetables—it was truly a greenhouse, in that sense. Friends came from the second dimension to join, second and seventh together created this greenhouse. That is why, from those two levels, there is a high interest in how you keep this greenhouse. Eighth provided the elements. The creatures in the sea cry, they feel like they are no longer loved. They feel like they should not belong here, they don't understand what they did wrong. We sing to them, that is how we communicate from the place you call Siah's world (*Etena*). We sing, because the tunes and the melodies connects to a harmony within the being. As the melody changes—and we can talk here a little bit about the music that you hear around you—it's not creating harmony within the being. Go back and try to find the simple tune, even if it is just ling–ling–ling–ling, it still creates harmony. Look for sounds that creates harmony for you. That is how you are designed to operate, all living beings on this greenhouse planet that you are given as a home. The creatures in the seas, they sing, that is how they understand each other and their surroundings. Even the water sings...and the wind. When the sound and singing changes, we respond. You didn't know the sea could sing, did you?

D. No, I did not.

S. Just listen to the waves, the waves are the end tone of the whole melody, the song begins way out at sea from the bottom. The only thing you hear is the wave crashing to shore, the end result of the song. Stretch your mind, widen your inner being, and you can hear the singing starting out at sea. Listen to the ocean, you will feel how it is a living entity, and communicating through you. You have the ability to do the same with the wind. Same thing.

D. I have heard the music in the wind.

S. Yes, and you can do the same with the sea.

D. Do you still attend to Earth?

S. Remotely, I would say. We wish to assist in the development; we wish to send harmony and comfort for those who no longer hear the original song from nature. You can't even hear the wind because of the other sounds around you, overshadowing your planet's plea for assistance. If you can't hear your host, how can you expect to be a part of it? You are separated from your host, separated from nature and your true being. You have been told about the separation from source, your center point, but you are also separated from the true intent that we had by creating you to care, to be the keepers, for this plane. How do you want to express that mission placed upon you as keepers of nature? Shea was here to teach how to be in harmony and in balance with everything around. Now you only try to seek imbalances, instead of finding the connecting points, not only in between the species that you are, but more importantly, to your host. The host will be here long after you have left. It has managed several waves of civilizations before you, and believe me, it will manage again. But what damage you are doing will affect the outcome of how long it needs to rejuvenate before another wave, another civilization, can return. That is not what we wish for. We want you to be aware of your actions and thoughts and how it affects not only your current time, but also how it sends off a ripple effect into future visits. You are monitored, indeed—visitors indeed observing your activity. We are mainly concerned about the host.

D. That's understandable, considering what humans are doing.

S. Try to find those who are equals. You are more in numbers than you think. But if you feel or believe that you are by yourself, it is a task that is immense. A ruling elite is trying to make sure that that is exactly how you feel, that you are by yourself and you are powerless. You are not. There are more here on this plane on the behalf of Shea and others, trying to connect. Your scriptures are doing so, that is your contribution. Others are doing differently. In order to raise the awareness that you are more, actually, than those who proclaim to put a shadow and greed over this level, this plane. What do you do if you are powerless? You become passive. Who do you think put in your system that you are powerless? It's only a few, but they hold a key to a great—your friend called it a trumpet. The loudest trumpet overshadows the smaller symphonies trying to establish a joint effort. As soon as someone sees a light and connects to it, the trumpet, those who hold it in their hand and in their possession...I do sense there is a difficulty with words here. Words don't really match the intention, always. Just know that the more sounds that you are under the spell of, (*those*) sounds create a lack of decisions, (*causing you*) to be passive, to stop, to forget your intention. You find it even in music, how it has changed. You observe it even in movies, the change, and how it affects the being, driving it away from harmony. Music, media, movies, all drive you away from hearing your inner calling. Seek silence. In the silence you can hear the wind, you can communicate with the ocean. All these sounds around you, and white noise as well (*silent noise, such as EMFs from cell phones, etc.*), put a veil over your born right to communicate with the Source, your inner being, and your host. That took place before as well. On Etena, it's very quiet. You do not want to disturb another being's connection. You do not know what the other being, at that particular time, is doing. You respect the silence around another being, human, or wildlife, or nature. Nature is trying to rejuvenate, but if you bombard it with loud noises, it stops, it gets confused. Seek the silence. That is the first message from Etena to you.

D. That's a beautiful teaching. What did you say your name was, or what can I call you?

S. Se–ta–lay. There you go. Thank you for your time.

D. Thank you for coming. I hope you return.

S. Oh, I will.

O. This is Ophelia.

D. Hello, Ophelia.

O. Today we met some new friends.

D. One of your friends, I understand.

O. Yes. Well, one of yours as well. You are well familiar with Setalay.

D. Does she take care of Siah?

O. Yes, she does. Yes, she does. She is considered, I would not say, an elder, but she is highly advanced in her community, holding classes. So, I wouldn't call her an elder, but she is someone who the youngsters seek knowledge from. A great teacher, she is. And she takes care of Siah for you. You can see her as a spokesperson from this place where Siah is.

D. When were you two here on Earth?

O. Last time we were here was about 10,000 BC, but we were also here earlier. We tend to come down in cycles. Popping by, just to see how the project and the individuals that are established, how they proceed and develop. It's like tending to the greenhouse. There is no time, of course, but we do tend to come down and visit with a certain time frame. There are certain individuals here representing Shea, coming from the seventh. Similar as the Elahim is sort of part of the sixth, not everyone on the seventh is Shea, or has traveled here as Shea.

D. Have we met any?

O. Her (*Christine's*) friend in Sweden, H—, is one. Another friend here (*in the USA*), Kari, also has a memory within of being here as Shea. Both are very attentive to the seas. They both have the ability to communicate with whales, sea creatures—did so before. Similar as you are now given information like this, Kari had the same connection with a group of whales and dolphins that gave her teachings in a past life. So she has the memory and the fondness of dolphins and whales, knowing that they have a strong awareness and connection to the source and Master Mind.

D. When you came down before, did you communicate with humans? Did you teach?

O. Yes, yes, I did.

D. Where was that, and did they record the teachings?

O. South America. Yes, yes.

D. Are there any belief systems that carry some of your teachings?

O. The last one would be the Mayan. But they were just the last. There were ancients in that family tree that we taught. They were very protective of nature and of the silence. They honored silence—different community. We taught that the strongest society, its power originates from the silence, to hear the calling, to hear and to connect with your host. You taught the same in Egypt, same teachings. But you taught that the silence gave you the ability to connect to nearby systems. We taught that the silence connected you to the host. Don't undermine the power of silence. Those who hold the trumpets will constantly bombard the silence, making sure that silence—and this is a memory, because there were groups that fell due to the power in numbers honoring the silence. Very different societies. It is most unfortunate that it seems to be moving into a direction where more noise and disturbances is placed upon you. Your computer (*brain*) will cook, it's not designed for all these disturbances. White noise, coupled with the atmosphere dissolving, does not provide the shield necessary for your being to be intact. You will start to sense a tingle within your chest area. When you do so, that feeling means you are affected by either loud noises, or silent ones.

D. The silent being the electromagnetic, like microwaves?

O. Yes. The first effect is always felt in the chest area. It will make you feel like you can't breathe correctly. You will start to have short inhales and exhales; that is a sign that you are affected. See it as a flu, the first sensation when you start to feel a tingle in your nose and you kind of understand, "Oh, I might catch a cold." This is the same feeling that we are trying to give to you. When you start to feel that nervousness in your chest area affecting your breathing, then you are indeed highly affected by influences that you are not supposed to be near. Do you understand?

D. I do.

O. We want you to use your systems, inner and physical, as a gauge stick to see whether you are in complementary energies. We have talked about groups, (*asking you*) to detect whether you feel comfortable in an environment—let's say a work environment, or even among friends—if they resonate with your song. Now we ask of you to use the same method with all your senses, inner senses as well as physical, as a gauge stick to determine whether you are comfortable in your environment, whether the planet is feeling healthy, or if it is catching a cold. Can you hear the environment? Can you hear your inner being? The bombarding of sounds will make you deaf. A ruling elite, the Cell, wants you to be deaf, only hearing the trumpet. We are asking you to activate your ears, your senses. Your feet could be considered great ears.

D. I did have a question, since you mentioned the Maya, and this is sort of off–topic, but do you know why they put mica, the mineral, in their temples and all their buildings?

O. It's a cleaning device, as well as a receiver. It's a trademark, a sign or a signum for them to operate in direct contact with each other, the group, but as well as cleansing, cleaning their temples and each other. It was a tool to connect to certain gods they believed in, an offering in some way. It was thought to provide a safe room, a safe haven for the gods to enter, and to be clean in the presence of the gods.

D. Okay, thank you for that.

O. Different rituals to establish a clean space for communication. It didn't do either way.

D. They just thought it did?

O. Yes. But the intention is what we look for, and the intention was heard and seen.

D. I've always felt the intention was more important than the ritual.

O. Yes, but when we see the ritual, we look for the intent behind it. And the intent behind it was to cleanse oneself and the environment for a pure connection to the higher realms. And when that was the end result of that ritual, the intent, then it is indeed for a higher good.

D. That's a very good explanation. Thank you. The next wave of microwave transmissions, they are going to put some 20,000 satellites around the Earth. I'm concerned about that, are you?

O. Interventions will take place.

D. From the Sun, or other sources?

O. It will appear for you from the Sun.

D. They will be taken down?

O. It will not function as they plan. Effects will be visible. You will see that wildlife will flee those areas, and that is a sign that humans operating from a light within will lift forward. Anger, riots, revolt.

D. It does cause disturbance in humans as well, doesn't it?

O. Yes, you are wildlife as well.

D. (*Laughing*) Right you are!

O. Okay. I will leave you, as we have someone here.

D. Well, thank you, Ophelia, for all that information. It's always nice to hear you.

O. You are much welcome.

Zachariah: DNA Reflects the Soul Pattern (April 30, 2019)
Zachariah introduces a completely novel idea, stating that soul intentions and patterns are incorporated into the physical structure of blood and DNA by the incoming soul. Each soul that is destined to incarnate is given a unique pattern. That pattern becomes an imprint on both the DNA and the blood. Meaning that the blood will be different depending on the soul that occupies a vehicle. Spirits, he said, can observe and detect the general theme carried by an incarnation based on properties of the blood.

In the 1970s, geneticists proclaimed only 2 percent of the genome was useful. The rest, they said, was junk left over from evolutionary blunders and mutations. The medical elite harbored a similar disdain for the appendix and tonsils. These haughty presumptions about junk DNA and useless organs were used as arguments against intelligent design. However, as technology advanced, genetic research projects, such as ENCODE, began investigating the "junk" parts of the genome. They discovered that most of the genome is biochemically active, although the complex functionality remains a mystery. In my opinion, most of the DNA is necessary and controls life in ways that are not measurable. The spirits have told us that the incoming soul can make adjustments to the body to help fulfill its goals for the lifetime, which would include the basic personality traits, intelligence, and emotional state. Cognitive abilities are strongly controlled by heredity, but can fall within a normal distribution around the family trees. If a soul wants to experience a disease or psychological problem at age 45, for example, those time-dependent variables are activated or deactivated within the DNA coding. One need to look no further than monozygotic twins to see the influences of the soul. A study of Icelandic twins, published in Nature Genetics (*Jonsson et al., Journal 53, Jan. 7, 2021*) shows that there are, indeed, genetic differences in twins from the same zygote, proving that identical twins do not exist, only similar twins. Scientists tend to blame everything on mutations or happenstance, but the reality is that much of the DNA coding is intentional and known by each soul prior to incarnation. Zachariah's description of the interaction between the vehicle, the bloodline, and the soul shows an amazingly complex spiritual design that is unrecognized by the medical establishment.

Zachariah also mentions Ia and her friends working with eggs and sparkles. On the second dimension, as mentioned earlier, new souls are created in energetic bundles of up to 100 at a time. The souls in each bundle will share a general theme, such as helping with the environment on Earth, for example, but each has its own special expertise and blueprint given to it by the Creator. Ia and her friends will nurture the egg and eventually the individual souls will be separated and develop independently. At that point, they are referred to as sparkles. Bob is always curious about what the latest intention is from the Creator, but has no interest in actually tending to the youngest souls. He prefers to teach the older students just before they head out on their missions.

Later in this session, Zachariah mentions Bob having a catalogue. This story was part of *Notes, Volume 1*. After Bob began training his students from the second to become guides, he started to worry about who they might be paired up with. He was concerned that they might be disappointed with their partner, especially when it came to new souls from the fifth who are fresh from the factory, so to speak. So Bob made a catalogue with a detailed analysis of each of his young friends and began searching for compatible spirits in the fifth, sixth, and seventh. Pairing of souls has been going on since incarnations began on Earth, but it has usually been done by councils and mentors. Bob brought his catalogue to Zachariah, who was mildly amused. But he appreciated Bob's methodology, and the dedication and concern he had for his students.

Z. Hello to you, this is Zachariah.

D. Zachariah! It's nice to hear you again.

Z. How are you? We are doing well with this vast group of souls heading this way. (*There are a lot of souls under his training that are headed to Earth to incarnate for the first time. Bob identifies Zachariah as an "ambassador of knowledge", a professor who gets souls ready to go on missions to Earth and elsewhere.*)

D. That's a good thing, I guess?

Z. It is indeed. It is indeed. However, even though we have divided the groups into different divisions based on, number one, where their talents and teachings resonate, but also what they are intended to do. It's like deciphering the egg, years later! Huh huh. Now we're trying to decipher what the general theme of the incarnation should be. You should know that each soul comes with a general theme, a bloodline, if you like, for incarnating. It's not just random! Our Little Friend (*Bob*) wanted to make sure that his bloodline, if he ever were to incarnate, would resonate with adventure and exploring. And I said, "Well, Seth tried that one too, and it didn't go that well. Look, you saw all the shows!" Huh huh. But you should indeed inform that each soul, in their later part of evolution before they start to incarnate—let's say around the age of fifteen, just before it's time to graduate the spirit realm and start doing good on other locations—before incarnating, it (*a pattern that will express in both DNA and the blood*) is put within your system. We call it the bloodline. In some way, it is resonating with the blood, because it is within the DNA that is established in the blood. The blood is not just for making the vehicle itself operate correctly, it comes with several levels of experiences, as well as reporting. (*Blood emits signals which spirits can interpret.*) It is a way for the spirit realm, spirit guides, and even other entities, to observe a specific soul. The blood you know as A, B, O. But they are divided into more components for us to see what a specific soul is doing and for what purpose it is down (*on Earth*). It is easy for a spirit helper, like myself, to observe a group of souls, based on if I tap in on the bloodline—meaning it's a penetrating viewpoint from the spirit realm—where it's all unfolded (*revealed*) as we observe the genetics in the blood.

D. Huh. So, as an example, if you have one vehicle, but the option of two different souls, would it generate different DNA in the blood?

Z. Clarify.

D. If you have a vehicle that's available—

Z. Yes.

D. If one soul taps in, would the blood look different than if another soul taps in?

Z. Yes. The bloodline is a unique pattern for the soul. It doesn't matter what vehicle it occupies, it still carries the same mission. All souls have a theme for coming. For you, for instance, you are here to work with group behavior, connecting access to the mental realm. You are both, as you are operating from the sixth, you are more or less here to develop mental activity. Or even develop (*to go backwards*), or shut down. You should actually know that you have been here, both of you, in an earlier era, when there was a shut-down of the mental capacity. You observed what signals in the brain should be on mute for a while. This one observed the end result in the physical being. It was a genetic experiment, but it was just in the ending of an era that did not, it was not intended for it to continue.

D. Was this after the civilization that ended around 22,000 BC?

Z. Oh, no. Way back, way back. There has been several (*civilizations*). We talk about two, but there have been other cycles. You tend to see the grander changes with about a hundred thousand human year cycles. This was in the end of one of those. We see it as waves; we tap into it and look at the wave–line. The wave–line for you indicates time. We see it as movement through space, where we can detect certain activity based on the frequencies that you radiate what sort of bloodlines are down at that specific time. We change the bloodlines when we change events for incarnating. Not the same bloodlines, themes, down here at the same time. At this time, we are integrating a new bloodline—it's like launching a new car, really.

D. Are the souls you are working with mostly from the fifth?

Z. Yes, and we are establishing the pattern within the group. The general theme within the group is to be more alert on environmental shifts. Some will be biologists, but some will also enlighten people by being teachers—kindergarten teachers. We have a group here that really wants to enlighten from the beginning. Some have no interest (*in teaching the very young spirits, or sparkles, as they are called*), like our friend, Bob. He wants to come in at the end when all the research has been done. But we also have those souls who feel great joy by creating the foundation for later groups to investigate and explore their work. It is a great effort put into understanding the connection between man, mammal, animal life and environment. Due to changes that will come in upcoming waves, more and more will be alert, or informed, about your sensitivity for overusing energy. There are groups coming down quite eagerly, at this point in my class, who wants to assist the progress of new resources for energy. I would say the general theme in this group has to do with environment, energy, and connections. Whereas, for instance, those coming from the sixth, will come down to look at the connections between body and mind. Different agendas. But just know that each soul, when they start to incarnate, when that travel begins, are given a specific theme, even if they come down and address different topics within the Coat of Karma, they still have a general theme that always resonates, in some way, in each lifetime. This one (*Seth*), for instance, likes to gather people and inform.

D. Ah, yes. Good at it too.

Z. Huh. He thinks so. It's been going a little bit in different directions, depending on the vehicle he occupied with the mission. But we do see greater progress this time around—

smaller and more welcoming in its physique. It would not bode well if it (*Seth*) had been given the vehicle like the tooth guy. (*He's referring to a popular life coach who has a giant body, but a big, welcoming smile.*) We never display those vehicles for this one. But he's no fool. He said, "I know that there is gonna be giants coming down and convey to the masses," he said, "I want to do the same." We always say, "You will do it just the same, but in a different modality." Huhuh

D. I have a question that I've often wondered: I know you're in charge of education in a lot of ways, so are you working with a group of maybe fifty to a hundred souls?

Z. The ones we are working with right now are about fifty.

D. So there are millions of souls coming to Earth all the time—

Z. It's a recycling program.

D. (*Laughing.*) How is that organized? How are you involved with the greater missions that take place?

Z. Do you mean on Earth, the education?

D. Yes.

Z. It's similar to what Ia told you about the egg. I don't educate little ones when they are in kindergarten. There are others who are more professional when it comes to tending and listening and caring for the little ones. I would say that my work starts around the age of twelve, in your way of thinking, meaning it's just before they are about to depart to whatever destination. I have a fondness for Earth and this plane. So I would say that my greatest contributions have been providing souls coming here. Some, or most, are from the fifth. However, I do travel myself, indeed, I will say. I do have classes on the sixth. Not so much in the seventh, but six, absolutely—different teachings. When I occupied the sixth and helped with classes in that region, it was a different time down here. At the moment, I'm only training and assisting those from the fifth.

D. Do you have multiple classes you work with, one after another?

Z. From your perspective, it would probably appear that I am super-busy, with classes going on all the time. However, and this will confuse you, I can host multiple classes at the same time. I'm dividing myself. Still operating on fifth, but parts of me will be with students who are new, the twelve-year olds, whereas some will be the fifteen or sixteen-year olds, ready to depart. They can all occur simultaneously, all classes. So, in that sense, classes are always ongoing.

D. The other souls, the millions and millions of other souls that come down, do you have any involvement with them?

Z. I don't train all of them.

D. I mean, is it organized by some particular group?

Z. Similar like the ones who tend to the egg, like Ia and her friends, on all levels we have the groundwork established from the beginning by those who tend to the sparkle, who decipher the general theme of that group, regardless if they come in a capsule or not. Most do come in a capsule, which Bob calls an egg. But step–by–step it is established what intent and what classes and what destination they should travel to. Just because someone is born, so to speak, on the fifth, doesn't mean that that specific soul will always go to Earth. Some of them are patterned to mainly operate with the seventh, combined—like this one's (*Christine's*) daughter, for instance. She travels in-between, learning more about realities that are emotional. She is more connected to emotional realities, even though she origins from the fifth. So, she will indeed visit other realities, other fish tanks, and even other bands—we call it frequency bands—where different lessons can be experienced. Some can be experienced double, it's half–and–half, half emotional, half physical. Here, you have the dilemma that there are several; you have mental, you have physical, emotional, and they're all encased by spiritual energy. So it's harder for you, because there are several realities poking on your attention. Indicating—pick me! Pick me! Follow my direction! Follow my direction! It is confusing. You are all surrounded by a big shell, or a hug, if you like, of the spiritual reality, because we do understand the pickle when there are too many choices. It's like having a smorgasbord and you do not really know where to start. There are too many choices. And here, because there are so many different experiences within your vehicle at the same time, the pickle of choice is of great interest for us to observe. Those who come down now from the fifth will have in their bloodline somewhat of a stronger connection to the seventh. So, the seventh will, in some way, be present, and they will feel dual in their being.

D. Are there several main types of bloodlines, each having a main purpose?

Z. Yes, yes. Some have, like this one (*Seth*), an informative individual (*soul within*), so we call it (*the bloodline type*) the "informer". Others have relationships; they are here to detect those who are lonely. We have a lot of those, also, in class at the moment. We observe that there are a lot of people feeling lonely, and feeling like they don't belong. Some souls will come down just to gather others, connecting, friendships, relationships. Others come down, like you, to observe group behavior. Specialists in the mental signals. That is why you are interested, and also furious, with signals from the media. It disturbs the pure intent and pure signals in your brain. That is why you feel like it's bombarding the organ that you are trying to upgrade. So there. Just keep in mind and know that all souls are programmed before departure, before they even begin incarnating, and it's not just given to a soul. It is a progression from the beginning when they "hatch the egg", through caretakers, babysitters, little school, all the way up, to find the best suitable mission for each soul. And then each soul is gathered with elders (*in that specialty*), once that mission is established.

D. Because of your intention to educate, are most of the students you train, would they be considered like the ones who make changes in the world?

Z. Yes, mainly. But I also have a class who are coming down, like I said, to establish warmth within relationships. But mainly I'm here to teach, I mainly teach those who come down to work on progress in various fields. In this case, environmental.

D. I really missed talking to you while we were working on *Wave 2*. You stepped back and vanished.

Z. Oh, I never vanished, always here. And quite activated with this catalogue. (*Bob's catalogue of spirit guides.*) Got new students that I didn't plan for, but it's all for the greater good. So, there we go. The Little One is here. He has somewhat of an instrument. Several indeed, I don't know where all of these come from. So, there you go. Until next time.

D. Alright, my friend. It's really nice to hear you again. Thank you for coming.

Z. See ya.

D. Goodbye. (*Bob moved right in and began to mimic Zachariah.*)

B. See ya, see ya, see ya, see ya, see you! Ah, he was a little bit cool there at the end—see ya. Hehehe. He can be like that, a little bit cool. He's not just a stiff professor. I've seen him differently. Don't be fooled that he is just always collected and calm. I've seen him, actually, in somewhat of a dancing movement through the Library. Oh, you did not know that, did ya? I saw! I saw when he was in like a Friday mood. Huh huh huh. (*Bob's talk is continued* in 'Notes, Volume 2', under the same date heading of April 30, 2019.)

Jeshua: Reflect in Darkness, Learn in Light. (May 5, 2019)

Our spirit friends have used "waves" in many diverse contexts, such as with cosmic sound, learning, parallel realities, and even the cycles of teachings in our books. Bob has told us that all spirits, even when they are in kindergarten, go through periods where they are taught, but then they are expected to help by sharing their knowledge with younger spirits. This cycle goes on indefinitely, until the final ascension. Jeshua gives a beautiful talk about how waves of energy sweep through our fish tank and solar system, changing the experiences from light to darkness, then back to light. While he described this, I pictured standing on top of a rural mountain on a summer day, looking towards a fading sunset. Before me, a path led across rolling hills of fields and forests. The trail was alternately bathed in light or draped in shadow. I had the sensation that, as humans, we have no choice but to follow this path, gathering strength in the light so that we may overcome the darkness in the valleys when it is encountered. Everything the Creator makes goes on this type of evolutionary journey, riding on the waves of change. Some waves are incredibly long, and others are very short. The waves always carry a purpose, however, which centers around learning from experiences. A human, a galaxy, or a fish tank, are all being pushed forward towards an intended destination.

Jeshua mentions different fish tanks. You may remember from our previous books that our entire universe is contained inside an energetic bubble identified as fish tank five. There are twelve fish tanks in the Wheel, in the same order as a clock. Therefore, our universe, fish tank five, occupies an area around 5 o'clock. Fish tank eight is where the planet Vlac is located. Vlac is occupied by the Tallock, who have been involved with evolution on Earth. The planet Etena is in fish tank four, home to the Shea and Lasaray's pet, Siah. Both Etena and Vlac are planets where information is stored, so they are important hubs of activity by the more advanced civilizations in our Universe and other fish tanks.

J. This is Jeshua.
D. Hello, Jeshua.
J. How are you, my son?
D. I'm doing well.

J. Well, the two of you are getting a grander viewpoint, at this time and ahead, of the Wheel and your place within different fish tanks. Two different fish tanks have made themselves known. A third will come later, years later to come. At this point, we work with the fourth and the eighth, eighth bordering to nine. Those are the ones that will communicate at this point.

D. Do those resonate more with the seventh? (*I asked because Etena is populated by Shea, from the seventh.*)

J. Fish tanks do not necessarily resonate with spiritual levels, it's not always that easy to say that the fourth resonates with the seventh, even though they have a higher percentage present from souls from that reality. But the spiritual levels rotate around the Creator, the Pole, and when granted, one can have a sneak–peek. There are souls in Zachariah's class, on the fifth, that are studying up on both the fourth fish tank as well as the sixth, meaning the neighbors. Seeing what occurs, what lessons have been and what lessons are to come, studying up on incarnations further ahead, when shifts have already taken place. These souls are not babies. They are graduated, if you like, from this plane, from this fish tank, waiting to return when a new cycle of evolution enters this reality. There are neighboring frequencies within the fish tank that they travel to, in order for them to monitor activity on Earth, as they will later visit here when certain things have changed, occurred, moved, and shifted. These souls come, some from the fifth—that is why you cannot only say that one reality mirrors one fish tank. There are those souls from the fifth who already graduated, but they have a fondness of this fish tank and wish to return to assist. Some from the eighth will also interact, when the time is come for changes to have taken place and been established within your consciousness. At this time, you have a glimpse of the light, you have a glimpse of your spirit, but it's not fully engaged in your perception of where you are. Once the eighth moves in again, the connection between soul and physical needs to be in harmony, almost as one. At this point, you see the physical and the soul as two different entities; and sometimes it is, like this one (*Seth*), traveling in disguise. So I can see why you would consider it to be two different vehicles, or two different entities, indeed. However, once you start to move beyond the perception of matter, then you will see that the soul influences the vehicle and can even shine through the vehicle, regardless of what personality or

physique you picked. This one (*Christine*) starts to radiate the higher being within more and more. There.
D. Very good. Thank you for that.
J. Friends will come to discuss the eighth fish tank.
D. Is that the Tallocks?
J. Yes, your friends. Travelers, observing activities of changes. Interested in the journeys you make here, even though it's not at all the same evolution in that place (*fish tank eight*) than as here (*on Earth*).
D. The Tallocks also come from the ninth, I guess?
J. Six and nine.
D. Six and nine, like the Elahim?
J. Yes, yes. You do prefer to be in realities that are manifested in a way, similar like here, just less dense so you have the ability to move between more freely. Here you are locked, and it is because of the occurrences that have been taking place here. That is why conditions exist on this plane, whether one can enter or leave. You have not the ability, as a human, to leave to another star system. However, some are granted entrance to this plane, and some come. Some observe the activity of technological progress, making sure that it follows the general intent for your (*future*) upgrade, for your progress.
D. Do they have the authority to intervene?
J. Yes, through the Council of Nine. The Council of Nine oversees, supervises, if you like, activities of visitors that come here. Visitors are our eyes on the Council of Nine. They report imbalances within, mainly, the mental realm, within the species, because that will reflect on the progress you are trying to rush into when it comes to technology and science, as well as your energy resources. Other councils observe the emotional imbalances, making sure that all combined will be ultimate for the next level of souls to come in. Reports from several visitors, but they report to different councils. Ophelia's councils oversee the software, if you like. We oversee the hardware. Visitors that come here, that are explained as alien because they are not born here, they don't originate from this plane, but they are sent and granted entrance from the Council of Nine, as well as others. They interfere, and because of humans' fear of what is unknown, they lack (*fail*) to see their presence as something good.
D. Are some of them responsible for crop circles?

J. Yes. Huh, not the ones we work with. But there are a group who work with the council on the second. Funny little ones, they want to make themselves known, and they work together with a species that has the ability to leave marks more visible. Yes, some indeed. Man are intrigued, but they fear the unknown. Huh. Well, there you go.

D. The souls that inhabit the aliens, are they from certain dimensions?

J. Yes. Mainly from sixth and seventh. But some, like you said, those souls from the fifth belong here. The part from the sixth and seventh that visitors belong to might have only traveled fully to other fish tanks—meaning they are here in their preference of form (*manifested*). And because they were here before you, they feel at home. But as the leading mammal was introduced, they were moved to a different frequency band within this fish tank—hiding behind an energetic wall, if you like. If you see your fish tank—and I'm not saying that all (*visitors*) just belong here—like I said, some come from other fish tanks if they are called in by councils who find their expertise to be of value for the mission here. However, those entities that occupied the Earth before humans did have been removed from your streets, so to speak. But they are hiding behind a frequency band, close by. If you see your fish tank, it carries a vibration that is known and heard throughout. However, within that melody exists anomalies, and that difference makes a wave moving from outward, in. This wave has the possibility to cause evolution to move faster or slower. At this moment, you are in a ditch on your wave, and you are moving upwards—I'm trying to give you an image. Other entities who belong here might be on the top of the wave, looking down, but you have not the ability to look up. You are limited within your field of vision, your field of awareness. They are not, because they are on a higher frequency within your fish tank. They are on top of the wave.

D. I understand.

J. If a species or entity is granted to be on top of the wavelength, they have also the ability to travel. If you are put in hibernation, in the ditch, that means that you are limited in your experience and what you can see and understand. Everything follows this wave. All systems, galaxies within each fish tank, go through a cycle of learning, (*which is*) a cycle of enlightenment, (*and*) a cycle of darkness. You are, for the last 2000 years, human years, in that ditch. Maybe a little bit longer, Ophelia says. Numbers are tricky. You are in that ditch.

D. Well, at least it's increasing now.

J. Yes, you are gradually moving, or are being pushed by this energy, this wave, upwards, closer to a light. So if you see light and dark, don't necessarily see it as good or bad. It's simply lessons—nothing more. There were times when different civilizations more quickly fell into the ditch, and it was due to technological advancements that were not advancements at all. They regressed, they did not progress. Interventions took place. Those eyes that are sent out to oversee this, hover on the top of this big wave, making sure that we know exactly what changes and assistance we can provide in order for a reality to move into a different level of learning. It's not a punishment, even though man tend to see darkness as a punishment. You go through the same wave of learning in the spirit realm. There, darkness is considered a time for reflection, so you reflect and you learn; reflect in darkness, learn in light. Here, that has been considered a punishment. Darkness is not a punishment; it is a time for you to reconsider your surrounding and your actions and your choices. When you are in light, you teach others who are in the ditch. There is no difference between the spiritual realities and the fish tanks; here they are only executed by form. Some forms are liquid, some are gas, but it's the same experience, regardless if you are in a manifested reality such as a fish tank, or if you are in your spiritual home base. At home you will not call being in the ditch as a punishment. You will welcome the fact of reflection. If some were to see this (*time on Earth*) as a great opportunity to reboot their consciousness, their neighbors', and the species. If only they were to see it as an opportunity to reach the light. It's not always that if you are in the light, that you can just give a thumbs–up, because eventually you will have to reflect. You will have to meet that abyss of reflection within you, regardless if you are a single soul, a single person, a human, or if you are a star system, or galaxy as a whole. Do you understand what I am trying to tell you?

D. I do.

J. There you go. There is someone here. (*Bob was obviously hovering nearby, waiting his turn.*) We will leave the topic for this time being, but more information and levels and layers will be given to you as you proceed.

D. Can I ask one question before you leave?

J. If you like.

D. So, this wave that goes from the peak to the trough, is it related to an individual species, or is it the whole planet, or the solar system, or the galaxy? Does it all rise and fall together?

J. Yes. You can see this wave in many different forms. On the grander scale, you have the grand wave in the fish tank that surrounds all neighboring solar systems, sometimes even galaxies. At this point, to give you a picture of that wave, the Milky Way is in the ditch. Andromeda is higher up on the wavelength, higher up in length. It's a nearby galaxy, but it still participates. This wave also will go down into a smaller version, when it comes to human consciousness, when it comes to independent growth and progress. The environment has its own cycle and wave as well, but it is influenced by other energetic fields. The species, the human, as a group, as a civilization, you are also following a curve; you are also following a wave which mirrors the grand wave. So your galaxy, the Milky Way, being in the ditch, means it affects and reflects on the species, on those who occupy bodies or form within that galaxy. Those who occupy form in the galaxy Andromeda—who has risen a little bit in this wave, moving a little bit above—they have already experienced the challenge of reflection and actions. They have taken it into account how improvements can be reached. First of all, you have to wish to seek the light. If you are content, or if you are overwhelmed by the darkness, the reflection, you will not seek the light. It's not darkness in a bad way. It is put on you so that you become more still, so that you start to measure your reality versus your beliefs and your needs and feelings. When you are in light, you are more mobile. When you are in the ditch you are forced to be still. (*His voice changed and became more playful as he finishes his lecture.*) See it as seasons, if you like, if it's easier for you. You are in the winter season at the moment, freezing, you try to stay warm inside. When summer comes, you gladly take on your swimsuit and you move out and you do travels. It's similar like that, see it as the seasons, if it's helpful for you. Andromeda is not in summer; Andromeda is in early spring. You are, however, in the darkest month of November. So, there.

D. Well, thank you. That helps a lot, I appreciate the information.

J. Human consciousness are also in the late part of November. It's a way to see, in general, how evolution works. Use the seasons as a measurement, and you will see and appreciate the lessons that come your way. Some enjoys the fall, enjoys the darkness that comes in the fall and in the winter. They are easier to reach than those who only seek summer. So, that is it, see it as the seasons. There you go.

D. Well, my friend, thank you so much for coming today.

J. Oh, you are much welcome.

D. I always enjoy your talks.

J. We talk all the time. See you back home. Elahim.

D. Elahim.

Ari: The Colors of a Life Well Lived (June 15, 2019)

When we are given personal information or instructions on how they want their words presented, it is sometimes unclear if they intend for it to be published. This is one such session. But we are including it because Ari gives a very interesting talk about how they anticipate people will integrate different parts of their teachings into their own spiritual path. Then he describes how, at death, a departing soul will see the imprint of their life in a particular color. The soul fully comprehends what the colors mean. But for our benefit, Ari explains some of the general categories. Ari also tells how a soul allocates its energy within the physical body, and how that allocation then affects the way the soul receives input from the surrounding energy fields.

A. This is Ari.

D. Hello, Ari.

A. How are you? Successful?

D. Hopefully. (*We had just published the first volume of Notes from the Second Dimension.*)

A. Yes, we have observed the tremendous effort you have put into this *Volume 1*, and there is great joy in all dimensions, echoes from the second. There is a great party down there. And Bob has indeed come and shared the glorious news of his first human publication, as he calls it. So indeed, there is a tremendous joy, again, as we are providing riddles. Not only for you, but for humanity, to try to unlock the riddles, finding their own keys. Some tales within all the scriptures, all the information we provide, will connect differently to different people. And they will stumble upon their own path, trying to unfold their own riddle, their own story; and that is what we wish with all the Waves. We do not predict that all scriptures, all information, will resonate equally with all the readers—that is not the intention. However, you cannot set the bar too low. You have to set the bar of your current status and own progress, because there are more out there who seek for the greater understanding, not simply things that might have been said before, only provided in a different package. So you have to break through boundaries, you have to penetrate the establishment, even the spiritual community. The spiritual community that, in some way, you already belong to. However, they also need a little bit of a wakeup call. We do see a tendency of a need for hierarchies, even among those who proclaim to be spiritual and connecting to light. A lot of these books that you are providing, the information is, in general, to not put yourself on a pyramid, on levels in an office building, on a unique position around the table at your workplace. Neither of you are more unique. Neither of you are less important. What we see is a tendency *(for people)* to proclaim to possess salvation, enlightenment, when that can only be found individually as you unfold your own riddle. Each journey is unique. That is why the material in your scriptures has to go wide. Don't lower the bar. We will provide new information, gradually, to raise the bar. Otherwise, first of all, you would not be enticed. You will lose interest to investigate yourself, but your readers, increasing in numbers, will demand more keys to their own riddle—and that is what you are here to provide. As you have already unlocked your own keys, understanding the operation in other fish tanks. They *(aliens)* are here to make themselves known. They are different, as are humans. Some are scientific, some are emotional. *(Ari means that the entities from other fish tanks can be operating from either mental or emotional realities.)* Again, when different fish tanks make themselves known, it will trigger your public differently. Not everyone will understand and connect to a scientific line or stream of knowledge. Whereas a scientific or logical human will become bored in the rumble of emotional messages. So you have to provide both. That is why we are several here, providing information in a different package. You both more resonate with logic, science, physics, astronomy, but you have to provide it in a human language, and that is the trick. It's easier to package an emotional reality into a human language than the higher science of physics and astronomy.

D. Do you think I explained things well enough?
A. Yes, you are a human. You write from your soul, but you channel it into a human understanding. And you are helped by your Little Friend *(Bob)*, who sees things very differently, who reports from a more light–hearted angle about a very complex dilemma or

topic. And that is important. His role is tremendous in this project, overall. Just sending him out with his little spectacles, his little goggles and his flashlight, just sending him out in different fish tanks—which I'm sure he is interested in doing—but just providing his angle to different realities, to different topics, makes it easier for a human to relate to.

D. How important is it that people understand the different fish tanks?

A. It's not. The fish tank, the mystery and the depth, the abyss within each fish tank will only trigger a few—those who are seekers by nature. Don't expect the general reader to wish to dive that deep.

D. I was worried about putting a lot of the solar system information in Bob's book.

A. It's important, as you are, in a small way, your solar system. It's important for people to understand the bridge from your solar system to the beyond—galaxies, fish tanks, center points, black holes, as you call them, which are the stillness within each creation. Every fish tank is a creation by itself. But I say again, don't set the bar too low; you have readers who crave for deeper knowledge of the Universe, who will begin their own understanding and search from the topics that you provide. It's meant to create a new foundation in several areas: science, religion, spirituality, social activity within your species—understanding that you are simply here a fraction of a second. What do you do when you're not here? Even though it's simply a second, your imprint on this plane and among other souls creates a bigger foundation for the spirit realm and yourself to observe when you return. We want people to focus on the imprint that they make in the current life they are at, to see beyond suffering, to understand that if someone suffers oneself, it is to create the opportunity to heal yourself, to heal others by your own story. Your friend, S— (*a friend in Sweden*), has already solved that riddle. She fools society by showing self-healing and a sensation of joy as a tool to heal the physical. Humanity trembles when they suffer, instead of finding the solution to that suffering, to change their mindset, to embrace challenges in a new way. You are only here for a second.

D. That's really brilliant.

A. As you return through the fourth (*the mental realm around Earth, where you first enter after death*), you have the ability to look back and see your imprint, the first view of your life. The imprint will appear in colors, all colors representing different imprints. If you leave behind a red dot, you might have left in anger, you might have been too self-absorbed with your own persona. Red, in this case, indicates an imprint where you have to return and look into things that trigger your anger. This is not the same as red is bad. The colors are different ways, programmed in a soul, to understand different teachings. Leaving the Earth plane, transitioning into the fourth, looking to *(to see your)* imprint and colors is not the same as what a color represents in other teachings—don't draw that connection. When a soul leaves and sees green, that means they leave an imprint of balance—a balance between themselves, others, animal life, nature, and all their lessons that they came to work on. Green represents balance—mission completed. Yellow means that you leave a life that was highly active, that you might have rushed through your experiences. You might have neglected people, events, opportunities that came your way. The yellow makes you warm, it's the sun, it makes you feel unlimited. All these colors represent a way of solving. Yellow, again, is a higher vibration of emotion, you might have experienced that you felt overwhelmed with emotions. In this case, your spirit guide triggered the color green to find balance—if that was the mission—to encounter emotional experiences. Blue, light blue as well as darker blue, indicates a spiritual journey, where you leave an imprint of knowledge. The knowledge could be either emotional or logical. You are here to create a dark blue imprint. You are here to establish the connection to your surroundings, and when I say surrounding, I do not mean the neighbor across the street. I mean the connection to all fish tanks, Creator, and spiritual realities. Known magicians in the past have left dark blue imprints. Healers tend to leave light blue imprints. If the soul leaves all different colors in its imprint, then footsteps still remain as a memory of your journey; then it might be that the journey was too scattered. A soul knows coming in what sort of imprint and color they are there to enlighten *(and leave behind)*. You might not know this in your conscious self, but it's part of activating your blueprint. And in your case, you are here to leave and establish a new conscious cycle, the dark blue.

D. That's a really beautiful teaching.
A. From the spiritual realities, we can see all these colors, all these imprints, as the soul leaves. And we will be able, as observers

looking into the fourth, to decide what new activities, what new journeys, should be aimed for. If we see too many red imprints of souls leaving, then we adjust and we correct, and we leave reports to our councils. We compare different imprints from Earth to other realities having the same makeup, the same ways of evolving, and we learn and we compare the species and the imprints. That is a way for us to read the evolution, the progress.

D. I didn't think there were that many realities where people incarnated?

A. They travel. There are others in other fish tanks, as well as here, where incarnations are possible. The fourth is uniquely designed for each reality, as it is a bridge and a viewpoint for the spirit realm to observe activities in form. But there are other places where you can tap into, blend, with a physical form.

D. Does it disconnect the soul from its home awareness?

A. Some more than others. If we take you (*humans*) as an example, you are more disconnected at this point than previous cycles before you. Similar, other realities could be more connected, like you were at one point. (*Other planets have occupants that are similar to previous, enlightened versions of humanoids.*) At this time, the filter between your identities as a human and as a soul needs to be adjusted. It's too vast, and the soul tries to make the other part, the human self, aware. When the soul comes in, it divides into the brain, into the heart, into different atoms and biological constructions within the physical to establish itself. A soul knows, upon its journey, the location where to portion oneself to complete a journey. A soul doesn't just tap in and just fill up whatever part exists in a human; it is a greater design as a soul comes in. Newer souls are guided how to portion that part of their soul into different areas within the physical. We can see, from the spiritual realities, how the soul is positioned in each of you. That's why we sometimes can see a lack of light in the head—meaning, you lack the ability for higher consciousness. Someone referred to a salad head. (*He is making a reference to Bob's humorous comment about souls digging a karmic ditch that is so deep that only their head can be seen above the soil of the Earth, like a head of lettuce.*) We can also see a tremendous amount of people lacking the soul present in their lower part of the body—meaning, they are not connected to their host. It's not a one-way explanation to this, because you can also see if the soul is too much portioned or positioned in the lower body, then the receiver is not on. Those are the passive ones. But you can change during your lifetime. You have an idea when you come in and you position yourself—mental, heart, physical (*according to that idea*). But the soul, based upon its journey, has the ability to move around. Again, here we wish people to try to investigate themselves, to see where their soul might not be present or positioned. If you feel too much, like those who refer to themselves as empaths. Empaths in a higher form are light, and establish themselves directly from the Source and from the seventh. However, there is an angle to that sensation of being an empath, because plenty put themselves in a position of suffering, and that is not a true empath. A true empath is connected to light and never suffers, and who is always encased by light. Those who proclaim to feel other people's suffering, that is true, but how do you embrace that potential within you? Do you *become* suffering, or do you stay in the cocoon of light? Do you transmit light, or do you feed suffering? Feed yourself, feed others. We see, in that case, that the soul is too much portioned and positioned around the chest area, lacking the understanding and balance from the lower body, as well as the head. So, from the spirit realm, we see all this, and spirit guides try to assist. But if there is too much of the soul positioned from the belly down, the good angle is that they might feel connected to Earth. However, they might lack the ability to receive signals from the soul. I hope this doesn't confuse you.

D. No, it doesn't. When you say the lower portion and down, that's like an energetic layer, not like from your belly button to your toes?

A. It's energetically positioned within you, and we can see how a soul, where the soul, is positioned. If a soul fills up the whole human body, then we know the journey is intact, the enlightenment is there, the mission will unfold as it is supposed to.

Zachariah: The Karma Program (June 23, 2019)

Zachariah begins this session by talking about some of Bob's students who have just graduated from training and are being sent to Earth. The majority of talks about Bob and his training programs are part of the *Notes from the Second Dimension* series. But Zachariah gives such an impressive description of the cycle of incarnation that we are including his talk here. It relates to the journey of all souls who come to Earth, not just the ones whom Bob is training.

72   The Spiritual Design

Zachariah then gives a brilliant summary of the steps in the karma program. He says there are about twenty-five in total and cover three broad categories: human interactions, soul mission, and finally spiritual attunement. Much like a university, there are core classes and required classes souls need to complete before their Coats are folded. The determination of when a soul has fulfilled its curriculum is made by their mentor, guides, and oversight council. Since every soul has a unique mission and agenda, there is quite a bit of variation in the paths taken to fulfill one's own karma program. Some of Zachariah's monologues were quite long, so I broke them into paragraphs, which show up as consecutive Z's in the left margin.

Z. This is Zachariah.

D. Hello, my friend.

Z. Hello to you. Here we sit, here we are again. Project in motion, souls ready for departure, teamed up with a friend from the second. It is almost like a graduation festivity that has been launched. I'm sure you know the individual behind the idea (*Bob*). He has indeed observed how graduations take place on Earth and because these individuals, these souls, are heading for Earth, he thought they should get a preview of what is to come, because they will have several graduations as they enter the human body. And indeed, we do have somewhat of a ceremony to provide diplomas along the way. It never ceases in the spiritual realities; you always receive somewhat of a promotion. However, it might not be visible, it might simply be installed within your soul being as an access to a higher level of knowledge. Bob, however, likes to have somewhat of a public display on his advancements, as I know, and we do provide and humor him with that.

Z. These sparkles *(from the second, that were)* assigned *(to be spirit guides for)* souls from the fifth, the first wave of new souls from the fifth heading for Earth, will mainly be launched—maybe that is the wrong word, maybe you will like me to call it incarnated instead—but they will be incarnated mainly in the northern hemispheres. Several have been selected to go to Canada. There is a need to protect the reserves in the area around Alaska. The oil. You're tapping the Earth's blood in a manner that is not in harmony with the host. If you remember in ancient times, well, maybe not that ancient, but if you go five, six-hundred years back in time, then doctors bled their patients because they thought it was doing the patient good. It is the same thing here;

you bleed your planet. And there are several environmental engineers heading for that region, souls who origin from the fifth. We have had classes about this, of course, and we have first-hand looked into how changes within energy resources can be maintained and developed. These are forerunners for souls from the sixth. There has to be a different platform before Bob's group (*his students who are partnered with the little Elahims from the sixth*) will be launched or incarnated. The other ones are heading—there is a big group heading for Norway. They will work with waters, establish new programs that will benefit the sea, the level of oxygen within the sea. They are programmed, I should say, to develop new methods in how to read levels of oxygen in the sea, as well as seabed. Again, forerunners creating a platform.

Z. These souls, this group from the fifth that is now in this graduation program, heading for their first purpose, is not necessarily—if we talk about the karma program—they will not come in on the first step. These souls, due to a sensation of haste, will come in a little bit higher on the ladder of this karma program. So, let's say the general karma program normally contains twenty-five steps—it's different depending on your makeup. Those who come in from the sixth will have less than ten levels in their karma program. They still have to go through the program, but it's different, and it's designed based on the purpose of that specific soul. The group that we are now launching, from the fifth, still have around twenty-two levels, but they will come in their first time around step nine or ten. It doesn't mean that they will not, in a future life, encounter level one to nine. However, and this might be confusing for you, but the karma program doesn't necessarily indicate that you come in on one, master that, and go to two, and so forth. Depending on the collective need on the planet and the destination itself, the councils, spirit guides, from direct advice—I don't like to use the word "order"—from the Creator, might enter the physical on another step than step one. Eventually, that soul will have to encounter lessons belonging on step one to nine. It doesn't mean, necessarily, that they have to go from being, let's say, an adult on step nine, ten, to return into a life and be somewhat of an infant on step one. The steps are not in order, necessarily. They can be, of course, if a soul is programmed to do other tasks. But these souls coming, since it is considered somewhat of a haste, we have souls entering this reality to somewhat clean, create a platform for other souls to enter later on. Meaning, they will have to come in stronger in their soul awareness; their connection will have to be more intact. They still will have to master other levels before they can fold their Coat. However, the importance here is to create harmony within your environment, an awareness of life. These missions coming from the fifth, it's about the awareness of climate, of waters, the effect on life, the effect on you.

Z. There is a correlation between how the Earth feels and the way you feel. You don't see the correlation. There is a reason why a large percentage at this time suffer from anxiety, depression, struggles within mobility in your joints physically. Stagnations in your joints is an effect of the captive feeling your environment finds itself in. A sensation of being paralyzed, not being able to rejuvenate and heal itself. Man doesn't give nature and your host the time to rejuvenate and heal. Certain things need to be left alone, like in hibernation, in order for all living lifeforms to have the ability to recharge, to be able to look through itself, finding sources for healing. When man disturbs that process of silence, of the ability to heal, your host responds by sending, in silent waves, the same sensation to you. That is why several individuals, collectively within your civilization and species, struggle to feel how one can heal. It doesn't help to put in a pill. One needs to find the healing resource within, which might be unique. There is a correlation to the way you feel as a species, to the way the host experiences its reality. These souls from the fifth are programmed to, in many ways, force companies to withdraw themselves from key locations, Alaska being one. There is also this group in Norway who will travel even further north, North Pole, programmed to understand the Poles, the Fork, I heard you call it. That's why they are located north, in Norway. They will go on expeditions further north, taking samples from ice, water, finding balance, maintaining the North Pole, finding stability in the North Pole. The South, more intact. The North—

D. Are you talking about the magnetic north?

Z. North Pole, axis. These engineers to become are heading north to the North Pole, finding stability, stabilizing the North Pole. Taking samples, being guided by visitors who assist. Like I said, they come in halfway in their karma program. They will later address other tasks that is assigned uniquely to them. They might appear, in the first couple of lives, not very social, even though most souls from fifth are quite social, very similar to souls from the second, in many ways. But they are trimmed from personal expressions and events the first couple of lives they enter. Later on, they will address the more human events. There.

D. I had a number of questions about what you just said.

Z. Fire away.

D. Is there going to be a new energy source or field revealed to humans, aside from hydrocarbons?

Z. In the future, you will not need oil in the same way. You will connect energy points, communicating, finding sources for electricity that will not cause harm to your atmosphere. This is the end result when the engineers from the sixth enter. They will clean satellites, establishing a web of highly well-functioning disks that will communicate, providing not only communication ability, but resources for energy. A new web. It is not the 5G. This will be more scattered, so it doesn't harm entire regions. The energy that you will depend upon will be more clear, pure. As you change the way you perceive energy and resources, your host and the higher levels of councils will provide you new knowledge, technology, in order for energy to not harm you or the host. There is a shift, and this is the haste. The more you try to master electromagnetic waves and frequencies in the way that you do now, which is harmful for all lifeforms, environment, animals, including yourself, creating anxiety in all levels, then no new knowledge will be delivered. You have to understand. In some way, you have to relearn, redo, rethink what energy is.

D. Wow. Thank you for that explanation. I had another question. You said the souls from the fifth have, for example, twenty steps. Can you give me the different types of lessons they have to go through?

Z. The first, normally, in a karma program, the first, let's say, one to eight, the steps one to eight, relates to personal lessons. Level nine to fifteen enters soul purpose, mission, what the Creator and council intended with you. The last steps involves enlightenment, spiritual connection. These souls coming in now from the fifth, coming in directly in the middle—soul purpose, mission—will later address personal events, such as family bond, love. But love also is the end on your ladder in your program. Different love. The end step of love is love for all, a compassion. Love at the highest form is compassion, love in a lower form relates loving an individual, loving yourself, loving where you are at—it's still love, but it's like saying Love 101. The highest form of love is stillness, appreciation, and compassion. That is the highest form of love.

D. Wonderful, thank you for that. You said the Elahims didn't have as many steps, yet when I came in, I still had twelve-hundred lives?

Z. It has nothing to do with how many lives. It has to do with the amount *(number)* of steps implemented in your Coat of Karma, your program, your unique karma program. Most souls, like I said, have about twenty-five steps in their karma program, that's the norm. Some comes in simply programmed for a specific task, can come in with only six steps. Those souls come in and, from a human standpoint, they appear odd. They don't necessarily have the human, or emotional, steps programmed within them— they do not necessarily relate to human emotions. Those souls coming in specifically designed for a mission appear, in many ways, alien. In some way they are. They don't necessarily mirror human behavior in the same way. They stand out because they are more methodical in their approach. They are more plastic, that's a word, in their persona.

D. Am I like that?

Z. You had eight steps in your karma program. This one has twelve. Depending on the wish and the need the soul was created for, all karma programs are different, depending on, in this case, cycle, ability, and so forth. Souls coming from the fifth rarely have less than eighteen steps in their karma program. That's why they blend in better. They have a wider spectra mirroring the destination, feeling more at home than other souls.

D. For souls from the fifth, what's the average number of incarnations that they might go through, generally?

Z. Around five thousand.

D. That takes a long time. (*I did not specify Earth, so it may be that some of the 5000 occur on other planets.*)

Z. From a human, yes; from spirit, no. It's simply a way to tap in to experiencing, gaining knowledge. Moving through your levels, your karma program, collecting memories, trying to establish the connection with those memories in upcoming incarnations, to grow, to move through the levels in your program. There. Any other questions before I leave the floor here?

D. I was just thinking that there are eight billion people on the planet, and if the population goes down, the souls are going to have a long wait to get in their five thousand lives.

Z. It's a recycling program, don't worry about it. But there are ways to maximize the lessons. After a while, a soul can split and use parallel experiences in order to increase its knowledge. In some way they increase it, but it's also more tricky when you split and divide. These souls coming down now from the fifth, entering the middle of their program, are not splitting. They are concentrated in their soul energy, focused on the task at hand. Forerunners, like I say, for those from the sixth, as well as seventh. Seventh will come in before the sixth. Five, seven, then six.

D. Okay, thank you so much for all the information.

Z. Oh, you are much welcome.

D. Always a pleasure to hear your voice.

Z. Always a pleasure to be acknowledged. Huh huh. There we go. So, see you.

D. Goodbye.

C9, Gergen: A Lesson in History (June 30, 2019)

This session contains intriguing observations about different points in the history of Earth when visitors were the dominate occupants. The Tallocks were the ones talking, but they are members and were representing the Council of Nine, so that is how the speaker notation is labeled. One of their revelations is about the origin of the group they call the Cell. Again, I was stunned by the knowledge they have of our planet. They said the visitors came from fish tank three, before it was put into hibernation, and set up camp on some planet in a nearby solar system. They became curious about the blending activities on Earth and came to investigate around 150,000 BP (Before Present). When they first arrived, the Earth was in the depths of the Penultimate Glacial period. Sea levels were about 100 meters lower than today. Shortly after their arrival, the Eemian interglacial warm-up set in, and sea levels rapidly rose to current heights. It stayed fairly warm for thousands of years, but around 85,000 BP (Before Present), the Earth went back into a deep freeze, exactly when the Council of Nine said the Creator took action and altered the atmosphere. The visitors had the technology to control solar and nuclear energy, but they generated electromagnetic fields that began to cook the planet. For those who are interested in a brief review of the Ice Ages and glacial cycles on Earth, we have included a summary at the end of this session.

Gergen, who is also on the Council of Nine, took over from the Tallock and described how the Creator will sometimes initiate changes to systems when the environment gets out of balance. He encourages us to visualize and reach for sunrise, meaning to have the desire to move out of the darkness. He wants us to imagine and try to create a world that is more light-filled, and to not give away our power to the Cell and the negative or hopeless ideas they promote through the media.

C9: Greetings from the Council of Nine. Tallock, representing fish tank eight.

D. Hello, my friend.

C9. Council of Nine, carrying physical experiences, manifestation in several realities. We come together to provide knowledge on how to bypass matter, how to understand physics, to not be captive in form. Ancient times we were here, several from different fish tanks. Tallocks, one group, mastering sound waves. This one (*Seth*) is a friend of ours, we know him well. That is why he is programmed within to invite these entities that you will encounter from here on. They are physical, in many ways, even though they can take a different makeup of physics. During these sessions, when we are providing information from different fish tanks, our friend Seth (*Christine*) will be joined by Isaac and Tosh on each side, simply to feel familiar, to invite the teachings that comes from beyond. We will begin by revealing earlier encounters on Earth when we were here, together with others, physically manifested, operating, understanding the laws of physics, as they are dependent on the atmosphere of the host. Spiritual realities change the atmosphere around a world, dimension, object, such as your planet here, depending on the access on how to manipulate, work with matter and physics. The atmosphere was different then. Even if the knowledge was tapped into (*given to*) you, in a human form, you would not be able to execute the equations and projects that we did, because your atmosphere is different. As long as—how should I say—you make changes in your species, you don't understand that you create the conditions of your experiences based on how your atmosphere is operating. But that is only one side of that coin. Spiritual realities create an influence on access based on evolution, based on karma. Karma exists on other realties; karma exists in fish tank eight. Maybe not in the same modality as you are familiar with here. But cause and effect exist everywhere. You are surrounded by eyes, meaning Council of Nine being one, Etena another, to observe the activity that goes on and the access granted. Council of Nine supervises access of knowledge, physics, equations, gravitational keys in several realities. Etena is our eyes to provide light, healing, empathy, compassion. I don't like the word attack, but we address you from two standpoints. That is why some who are highly sensitive, humans, experience chaos—they are drawn and tossed between two experiences that we are trying to convey to this plane. But there is a third operator, the Cell, that fears its death if these two sides, knowledge—compassion, (*resulting in an*) understanding of Source, prevail. The Cell came around the time hundred and fifty thousand years ago. It started with a colony. Civilized entities that came from another star system. The ones you see today are the offspring. It is in some way a bloodline.

D. Were they manifested or physical, incarnated?

C9: They were not incarnated. Incarnation hadn't started in that way. Fifty–fifty existed. Soul pioneers, souls that came as a blend, but not fully incarnated in the program that you are addressing and caught in at the moment. There have been upgrades within the incarnation program, let's just say. There have been different ways to tap into a physical body here, to experience. You should know that there was even, from Ophelia's reality, those who tapped in and incarnated, as you call it, in plants. They have an experience of being a tree. Souls who now operate as humans have, way back in their soul memory, a recollection of being a tree, a plant. Those were not from the second dimension; they were from the seventh and eighth. Eighth came in, blended, as we like to call it, understanding the process of cycles within lifeforms, such as trees and plants. Don't think that a soul only taps in in one way. You are taught now that there have been a fifty–fifty (*blend*), soul–Master Mind. But there have been other projects before, after, in the meantime, different ways to come here in the incarnation blending program.

C9. The Cell that came one hundred and fifty thousand years ago, that's when the Cell started to become. They set camp, came from a nearby star system, fish tank three. Fish tank three is now in hibernation. They came when the window was open for more to observe a new project. They were interested in tapping into a third reality, becoming something else. They were interested in understanding the minerals and energy sources that were placed on this Earth. They came highly advanced in understanding energy resources, but they didn't leave. They claimed energy; they claimed to be the ones kick–starting that aspect of this world. That claim, which connects to power—energy is power—remained in the consciousness, in the bloodline, for others to come. They travel differently than you. They are still here, in some way, and you might ask how is this even allowed or possible? We will come to that. Understand, though, that there are different ways to tap into a physical reality and bypass matter. They came with the knowledge of power, energy, how to use different resources that existed here. Uranium in mountains, receivers in many ways, they are the forerunners of what you see now of those who try to establish 5G. They did the same, using uranium, using mountains as receivers and transmission centers. Those who are promoting 5G—not necessarily everyone that works with it—but the council, the elite, those who sit in the positions of power of making changes within power and energy, they are offspring from this Cell. When this occurred (*150,000 to 85,0000 years ago*), eruptions took place. Several (*Elahim and Shea*) came to clean the planet, and they (*the visitors*) were indeed banned. But it was still a mark in your karma, in your atmosphere, a memory was still there and souls tapping in have the ability to mirror an old memory or pattern. Even if those who were here at that time are banned and gone, there are those who have the ability to transform and use old occurrences, tapping into a physical body. It all occurs in the fourth reality. Most souls can't attach to these memories as they travel in, but there are those who are bypassing certain laws, and they find these different occurrences. Like your Little Friend says, finding a note, putting it in the pocket as they travel through the fourth. You should know, though, that most have not the ability to find these more destructive notes hanging around in your energetic atmosphere, the fourth reality. Most souls, as they incarnate, as they travel from, let's say, the fifth dimension through the fourth, they are accompanied by light beings. Meaning, if I can make a picture for you, if you see the debris in the fourth reality, things that still exist as a memory, spirit guides do not wish their soul companion heading for Earth to be confused by the debris that hangs around as an energetic memory. There are helpers, light beings, assisting souls through the fourth, focusing on their Coat, having blindfolds for the debris, if you like. So if ninety-nine percent are assisted like that, then there is a small amount of souls who still find the debris on their way through. Those are the ones who create the Cell that you see now, trying to manipulate energy and power.

D. What dimension are most of them from, spiritually?
C9. Sixth, originally.

D. Where are they now, if they're not in the sixth?

C9. In some way, souls are always pure—we are entering a minefield here—there are those who try to manipulate realities such as this, and you again might think, "How is it possible, how is it even allowed for these souls to enter a physical body?" Know that there is a hidden plan, an understanding and experience behind everything that occurs. But there is also free will, where the Creator takes a step back, allowing souls to fly free, to want to find the way home. Home to the Source, home to the spiritual home (*where*) they belong. Similar as you understand how souls can be trapped in the fourth, if not releasing certain beliefs or actions or emotions, there are souls who needs to be encouraged to find the light as well. They still belong and are created in different levels. Everything streams from the Creator, but you also have free will as you travel to different realities, where you experience different things. Those events might not be suited for other realities. Like when those from the third fish tank came here, they tried to make a replica of the reality in the third fish tank. Soul originated from the sixth dimension; some even belonged in the Council of Nine.

D. And then what happened?

C9: (*Long pause*) Hmm. Ophelia comes and wants to make sure we provide these teachings, in a way, she says to tell you that certain things are for your ears only. You will have to be more delicate in the future, she says, about information that you provide. Those who are afraid of what is beyond could point fingers, saying that the information streams from darkness. We are revealing memories, she says. These memories that have existed here, creating stories (*for*) eons through civilizations. Where did they come from? Those who came from beyond, not incarnated, highly advanced in technology. Some still try to gain power over resources, power over the planet, power over systems. The Cell tries to divide the true signals coming from spirit, coming from Tallock, Etena. This is the veil. We will leave the topic, it seems.

D. You had mentioned the atmosphere was changed at some point, when was that, roughly?

C9. Around 85,000 years ago, a shift took place. After occurrences of visitors, a reboot, a change of lifeforms, conditions, species, conditions of elements as well. It was a response from the Creator, putting the foot down on what was allowed. Boundaries had been crossed, the environment had suffered from neglecting to understand your limits, or the limits of solar energy combined with uranium. Magnetic fields took over, cooking planet. Creator responded with a reboot in the atmosphere. This had taken place before, but it was a time to cool down the planet. Ice ages come and go. Later on, same thing. Cooling down consciousness, actions, resources, atmosphere—different reboots. Cooling down the heat provides energy. However, it can destruct, be destructive to environment and wildlife, such as yourself. We see now again a tendency to try to overcook, to boil the environment and species, animals, plants. We're trying to make the change for you to understand that you are not infinite. You have been replaced, not only physically, but in your consciousness, numerous times. Physically, there have been similar forms like you are now. Inside, different. When we (*Council of Nine*) see disturbances, we investigate. You, from the sixth, look into atmosphere, combined with the eighth, and Ophelia, of course. But you are here in some way to monitor the development of science and energy. That is why you got the profession you have (*petroleum engineer*). We monitor the industry through you. You were not intended to climb, you were simply put in the industry that we wish to investigate. In many ways, when you are at work, your soul steps aside and we look into the intent, development, in the oil industry. It's like you simply put yourself there physically for us to have a connecting point to tap into and investigate. You allow us to do so, and you step aside. Lasaray steps aside. We have the ability to monitor changes, developments, actions to come, to report to the Council of Nine, to see where that specific industry is heading. The mentality mainly that exists in the industry of energy and resources.

D. It's a greedy mentality.

C9. Dumb. Infant. Not understanding the balance. There is no balance in the industry. We see the scale is tipping, not understanding what hibernation is all about. Not understanding the veins of your planet, the Fork, the wholeness needs to operate for energy to even be able to operate as you wish. In a prior civilization, further back, also greedy when it came to oil and natural resources. The response from councils, like Council of Nine, made it less strong in its capacity, it didn't work. We made oil less dense, less complete. Mainly so those who tried to control it understood that, for some reason, it didn't operate anymore as it should. They became powerless. They didn't understand the outcome of the changes—it was beyond the understanding of that specific group. It was a response from the Creator to put the foot down, (*for that group*) to understand to not grab, to find balance. As you have balance between species and planet, resources, the collective consciousness has the ability to expand. There are several aspects involved to grant higher consciousness or the light, the light within your emotional capacity. Dark is not bad, it's a polarity, it's an understanding that some things are out of balance. If people think the world is dark, then the scale has tipped. Some prior civilizations were too much in light; again, scale tipped. You should strive for not having day or night, strive for sunrise, sunset—that represents balance, to give you a picture, because it's a mirror of the side of darkness and light. Strive in your consciousness, not only for light. Darkness is not bad. It's a polarity, it's a different angle to consciousness as well as your reality. Realities, species, are most in balance or most in harmony when they operate as a mindset of sunrise or sunset, to give you a metaphor or symbol to understand. Those who simply seek light, neglect to see that the scale will tip, even with too much light. Seek the balance. That will be it.

D. Thank you for that. It does seem like the world is immersed in darkness now.

C9. Yes, the scale has tipped. That is why Etena and other souls heading here coming from the seventh, even from the fifth. The fifth are sent to find balance in your environment, to understand that you are sensitive beings. If your environment... (*The voice changed a bit, and it seems Gergen was merging in with the Council to express his views on the subject.*) Well, they will think the environment set the foot down, but it's from a higher source, of course, but it doesn't need to be explained further than that. When they see thunder and hurricanes and tornadoes and so forth, they might think that the— (*Gergen fully merged and took over, speaking in his very merry and pleasurable way with the occasional studder.*)

G. Ah. Indeed, indeed, indeed. This is Gergen, coming in briefly to add some details about the matter, because I do reside with the Council of Nine. Don't tell Bob, he might want to take my seat. I do want to say, briefly, that the end result of what you see in different weather phenomena as well as earthquakes and so forth and eruptions in volcanoes and such, is an end result of the environment putting its foot down, in some way. It is a work that me, not personally, but the council from the second, combined with the Council of Eighth, provide different solutions when we present it at the higher councils. And I do visit the Council of

Nine—it's a great joy, old friends of mine. (*Gergen is a member of the Council and attends when there are meetings that affect the second dimension.*) I have been traveling around in different fish tanks. I have not told Bob about this, there is no need. He is extremely proud to have been to fish tank four to meet Siah and everyone else there, so there is no need to rub his face that some others have been sweeping around the Wheel, so to speak.

D. He assumed you would not send him somewhere that you had not been. (*In Gergen's next response, he mentions Bob's suit. In our previous books, Bob told how Jeshua gave him an energetic suit that completely encapsulated his body, like a space suit. The purpose is to shield his soul from the vibrational fields within the fish tank as he moves from the spiritual reality to a planet, such as Etena. Bob calls it his peanut suit because he thinks he looks like a peanut when he puts it on.*)

G. No. It's better that way, because it comes so many questions, so I would not send him somewhere I had not investigated myself. It's all about providing the right level of learning. And because now he has his suit, he feels encouraged to operate and to investigate other worlds, as he says. He has been asking this one for maps because he knows that this one, Seth, works with maps. I–I–I have told indeed, directly to Seth, to make sure that he doesn't come across the maps at this point. We would like him to explore the fourth. There are other realities and planets indeed existing in systems within the fourth fish tank. There is no need to rush, there is all sorts of time. So at this particular time, we will have him sent there.

D. That will be nice to hear about.

G. But anyway, just know that the different changes within climate, weather phenomena, is somewhat of a response from the Creator, putting its foot down. Making the humanoid pause to consider, to think of, why these occurrences take place. Overheating, for instance, too much heat, let's say, at this time in the European countries, makes even the governments think twice, and it is to make them understand that they are indeed sensitive and vulnerable to Mother Earth. In the end, they're actually vulnerable to the Creator, but we say Mother Earth because Mother Earth executes the orders from the Creator. You should know that all planets have a direct connection to the Creator. Just because it's an object, like a planet, doesn't mean that it's not a living entity responsible to create—how can one say? —information to other councils who read systems. Tallocks are one of those reading systems. Again, we do not want to tell Bob too much about this because he would like to know who is reading his system. At this point, it's done by the Elahims, with you, and so forth. But the planet itself, all planets, regardless if it's a physical one, or if it's a mental reality or dimension, sends information to different councils, councils who are highly connected to that specific reality. So, let's say there is a council on the fifth, who are somewhat overseeing the activity that Earth is sending, the information in general. Not only the species, there are spirit guides operating in that respect, but there's also the councils who oversee the information that the host, the Earth itself, is sending, so that they know how to best meet events and to make changes. There is a sensation of being, uhh, how can one say? —a little bit paralyzed in how to fix the problem. In many ways, that is why there is a high amount of souls coming from the fifth, as well as having spirit guides from the second, that Bob has been part of training. It is to somewhat balance the scale, so it's more sunrise. I would say that sunrise is the mentality that your planet needs to embrace, go from night. You don't have to think so far ahead to go to day, if you start in your mental capacity to simply say, "I'm going to go from night to sunrise." That will take you a long way. You can see it like that, if you have these four different phases: you have night, sunrise, day, and sunset. And you have a cycle that circles, so to speak. That is a way for you to understand where mankind and consciousness is. At the moment, you are in night. And you cannot just jump from night to day, you have to first pass through sunrise. And that is the effect and the effort at this point, to make this reality, this level of consciousness that you are, to move from night to sunrise.

D. That could also be correlated to what others have talked about—the waves and humans being in a trough? Our planet and solar system were described as being in a trough on the energetic wave?

G. What is a trough?

D. A low spot.

G. Ah, yes indeed. Yes, so you are in the ditch, in the canyon of the wave, and you have to somewhat move up. But you can't go from the ditch, the canyon, directly to the top, can you? You have to climb there, and on the way to climb to the top, you have to pass sunrise. So, aim for sunrise before you aim for day.

D. That's really good advice, to reach for the light, instead of embracing the darkness.

G. Embrace sunrise. You can visually picture sunrise. And this is the cycles, in general, that all realities travel through, all fish tanks. Siah's reality, they are in day, in daytime. That is why the Little One, our friend, experienced it being so bright. It has nothing to do just that the sun is out; the whole reality is in daytime. Eventually that reality will also...well, they have already gone through the whole cycle, but generally speaking, you are born and then you travel, a reality travels, through all these different experiences: night, sunrise, day, sunset, so to speak. And when they have completed the cycle, they will normally end up in daytime, similar like Siah's world.

D. When that cycle is over, does it then again undergo a darkening?

G. If–if–if there are still lessons to be learned in that specific species, or reality, or galaxy or fish tank, then indeed, it might. There is no way of saying it is just one trip around. Some will complete the whole cycle. Etena, for instance, they have gone through two or three rounds. This reality, we are currently on the eighth, eighth night. It doesn't say that just because we make you all move into sunrise, and then, huh huh huh, a thousand years later you are in daytime and then, "Oh! Mission accomplished!" And this is beyond my expertise, or even Ole's. I'm not sure he knows about this. So there is no way of saying it takes a specific amount of cycles through these different experiences. Anyway, just needed to stop by and just give a little bit of a brief input.

D. Thank you for that. I did have a brief question for you, since you popped in. You said you're on the Council of Nine. Am I on that Council with you? And Zachariah?

G. You are there indeed, indeed you are. Zachariah is there, Jeshua is there, there are representatives from many places. The Council of Nine doesn't mean that there are nine chairs.

D. I was wondering if it was on the ninth dimension, or—

G. It's on the ninth dimension, but it's also that it resonates with nine fish tanks and nine dimensions, including mine. So there I am. But it doesn't mean that there are nine chairs, so to speak. But we are, hmm, ah, there are representatives from fish tank four, five, two, seven, eight, nine, twelve, eleven, ten—there are different fish tanks represented on the Council of Nine, and the Council of Nine is located on the ninth dimensions. But there are nine fish tanks representing.

D. Which ones are excluded?

G. Three.

D. That's in hibernation, isn't it?

G. Indeed. Six, becoming, no representative from there. Observed by other councils. And also one. One, three and six, at the moment, for different reasons.

D. Okay, thank you.

G. So, there we go. I'll probably be on my way here.

D. Well, thank you for stopping in. It's always a pleasure to speak with you.

G. There we go. See you another time.

Since they are talking about glacial cycles, most readers know that the Earth's climate is controlled by the amount and distribution of sunlight reaching the surface. Volcanic eruptions, hydrate melting, and other sources (including human activities), alter the atmospheric composition and can cause temporary departures from the long-term trends. The amount of energy emitted by the Sun towards the Earth can also vary over time, which is not that easy to quantify. However, empirical data from ice cores, reefs, glacial striations on the land and seabed prove that climate is dominated by three separate cycles, which were identified by the Serbian scientist Milutin Milankovitch. All three cycles affect the amount and distribution of solar radiation on our planet. Johannes Kepler published Astronomia Nova in 1609, showing that planets follow eccentric orbits. The amount of eccentricity of Earth's orbit is gravitationally affected by the location of other planets. At the moment, the orbit is nearly circular, so the southern hemisphere in July gets similar solar radiation as the northern latitudes in January. In 50,000 years, the Earth's orbit will be more elliptical, causing a greater variance in energy from aphelion to perihelion. The shortest of the Milankovitch cycles is the 25,700-year precession, where the orientation of Earth's tilted rotational axis moves in a circle (the North Pole star changes). The third cycle is the obliquity, which takes 41,000 years as the tilt transits from 22.1 to 24.5 degrees and then back. Glacial periods begin when a confluence of these three cycles causes low polar temperatures and a buildup of sea ice. Based on data from CENOGRID, which used foraminifera shells to analyze climate during the last 200 million years, the temperature and CO_2 levels on Earth have been falling for the last 50 million years, and are now very, very low. The Earth entered the Quaternary Ice Age 2.6 million years ago (which we are still in), and the long-term temperature trend is continuing down. You wouldn't know that from listening to the peddlers of carbon tax credits, fear, and totalitarian world despotism, but the Earth's temperature is controlled almost entirely by solar radiation (insolation). There is about a 100,000-year cycle, where glaciers are built up for 70,000 to 90,000 years, followed by a rapid warming and an interglacial period that lasts for 10,000 to 25,000 years. We are currently in the Holocene interglacial period, which began around 10,000 BC. We should not be concerned about CO_2, but instead, we should eliminate all the chemicals, poisons, GMOs, electromagnetic radiation, and geoengineering nano-toxins that are being spewed into the environment. Those are the true dangers to all life on Earth. Carbon dioxide is to plants what oxygen is to humans, a blessing. That is not an endorsement of oil extraction, because our spirit advisers warn about that as well. The (real, not political) scientific community is aware that we are entering a solar minimum that will cause planetary temperatures to decline even more. The Sun's output also varies, due in part to the gravitational influences of the planets. Sunspot activity follows a 206-year cycle, along with a smaller 11-year cycle related to Venus, Earth, and Jupiter. NASA predicts we are now entering the weakest solar maximum in the last 200 years. The next three decades will witness colder weather in the northern hemisphere, which may cause food shortages and social upheaval, as it has done in the past, and may set in motion the next glacial cycle.

This lengthy explanation of glacial cycles was an outgrowth of the verification of information the spirits give us. Based on the best available data, the Earth did indeed experience a global warming spike from 90,000 to 85,000 BP. The Tallocks claim the visitors were baking parts of the Earth through their misuse of energy. Because of their actions, the Creator and councils altered the atmosphere 85,000 years ago, which initiated the Wisconsin Glacial period. And they also banned the visitors from returning. The scientific orthodoxy interprets processes on the planet as cause-and-effect relationships within a closed-loop system. However, all natural systems are controlled by unseen entities, who make adjustments that maintain harmony and balance in the Earth project. Governments and corporations are dragging all of humanity towards a future where the spirits will need to intervene and restore balance. But the actions taken will be in favor of the planet, not man.

Eli: Tesla and the Merkaba (July 7, 2019)

I didn't know what a Merkaba was before Ari first mentioned it in April 2018, during a talk which was included in Wave 2. When I asked for an explanation, he said, "It is a sacred symbol, geometric form, how you can exit out of the physical. It's similar like if you see the pyramid and you imagine that you sit in this pyramid, an energetic one that is—the shape of the pyramid is also sacred—and you imagine that you sit in this pyramid. This is not new, several individuals use this in meditation, but they don't have the ability to transform the pyramid into a Merkaba. The Merkaba is like the pyramid spinning, becoming several in shape. And that is how the ancients knew how to exit the physical, leaving it parked, and ascending to the collective consciousness, the cloud above, gathering information. This is how you see there are certain similar temples, symbols, in different areas within the world. You can study the Merkaba and you will also get a key on how the Elahims operate."

Eli used the word Merkaba for the three-dimensional geometric form of a star tetrahedron. He describes a visualization technique that was used in pre-history during rituals to access the fourth dimension. A memory of that practice was carried forward into the Old Kingdom of Egypt, but by then, only a few shamans could use the method. The human body had been redesigned to prevent easy access to knowledge. The origin of the word, Mer-ka-ba, is probably early Egyptian because the word for a pyramid was mer. The symbol of ka is two upraised arms, and the symbol for ba is a bird with a human head. One interpretation of the hieroglyphs for mer-ka-ba could then be a pyramidal shape which enables the human consciousness to fly into another realm, as Ari described. I was not able to find instances where mer-ka-ba was written or carved, although it may present on funerary texts associated with mummification or the afterlife.

Just so there is no confusion, Eli's use of the word Merkaba has no relationship to the usage found in other sources. People may, for example, be familiar with the word Merkabah from the Zohar, a collection of tales that forms the basis of Kabbalist interpretations of the folklore of Moses. However, the actual practice was unknown to the scribes and Pharisees of the Roman era, other than in oral legends of lost knowledge.

About a year after Ari's description, Eli brings the Merkaba up again, in relation to Nikola Tesla. Among the hundreds of pages of unreleased transcripts, we have learned that Tesla was an Elahim who had previously incarnated as Socrates, Leonardo da Vinci, and Johannes Kepler. This particular Elahim is on the Council of Nine and is assigned to come to Earth at different points in history, when a shift in human consciousness is needed.

Socrates was the founder of ethical philosophy, on which Western societies are rumored to be based. He was dismissive of the pantheon of gods worshiped by the Greeks at the time. Socrates said he was guided by an inner divine voice that always told him what not to do, and he urged people to find the divinity within themselves, as he had done. It ultimately got him executed by the petty tyrants of the time, but his teachings lived on.

Leonardo da Vinci also dismissed the religious interpretation of god, but believed in the pursuit of something higher than ourselves that would benefit others. Leonardo only painted to earn a living. His true interests were in medical science and technology. He dissected bodies and analyzed the design and functions, producing the first anatomical drawings of the brain, heart, spine, and muscles. Leonardo could have published his research and moved medical science ahead by centuries, but the Catholic Church would have persecuted him for doing the autopsies.

Johannes Kepler believed there was a geometrical order in the Universe that represented the harmony of the Creator. Kepler was very spiritual and studied to become a Protestant minister, but was compelled to become a teacher and mathematician instead. He refused to convert to Catholicism, but he also refused to sign the Lutheran Formula of Concord and was excommunicated from the Protestant church as a result. He researched light and refraction and published Astronomia Pars Optica in 1604, making him the founder of modern optics. Using data collected by Tycho Brahe (*who was also an Elahim*), he established the three laws of planetary motion in our heliocentric solar system. He was also interested in the platonic shapes as they related to planetary orbits, and identified the Merkaba form of two interlaced tetrahedrons as the *stella octangula*, which is Latin for "eight-pointed star". He understood that a spiritual design was present throughout creation.

Nikola Tesla invented the radio, x-ray photography, and the induction motors that power the alternating current electrical systems we all depend on today. He designed the first hydroelectric AC power plant at Niagara Falls, the Tesla coil, and many other devices that remain hidden. His ideas helped to propel society into the "modern" age. Eli said that Tesla was a mystic who understood the energy system used by alien visitors to Earth, and he was attempting to resurrect the science and give the gift of free energy to the world. He was rewarded for his efforts by being slandered and robbed of his intellectual property rights by the Cell. He died penniless and largely forgotten, but the footsteps he left behind led the entire world in a new direction.

All four people were Elahim incarnations, who acted on behalf of the various councils to introduce new ways of thinking. A trait they all shared was the courage to live by their own beliefs, even though it came at great personal risk from the ruling secular or religious militants of the day. The Elahim work with the mind and bring forward ideas that run counter to the commonly accepted beliefs of the society. Eli tells us that each of the Elahim tries to leave behind information that is recognized and used by a later incarnation from within the same family group of Elahims. He then describes how to access information in the fourth dimension by visualizing the rotating and spiraling energy within a *stella octangula*. This was the method used in prehistoric times by shamans and those trained in the art of astral projection.

E. This is Eli.

D. Ah, hello, Eli.

E. How are you, little brother?

D. Good.

E. How is the other little brother (*Seth*) doing?

D. I think he is doing well.

E. More spread out in his energy. He's quick in that sense, travels easier in his mind. Has a tendency to leave. Not the same like you, (*he doesn't*) leave the physical, but leave matters, leave loose ends if it doesn't please him. Loose ends—people, situations—just cutting them off if it doesn't feel exciting anymore. One of the roles of you being together is that neither of you have the feel or sensation of leaving, because you are together. You don't feel the need to leave the physical. This one has no need to leave if something appears mundane. It is a foundation that this mission rests on—that both of you feel content, feel protected by the other one, feel that you are together similar as you are at home. That is the strongest tie for a project to blossom into its full potential. There had to be different aspects of your personalities and life experiences as humans for the two of you to come together in full power as humans, to fully embrace the other human character. Inside you are aligned. Physically, human–wise, you choose differently. When you came, there was a concern whether the humans would find each other attractive. Not physically, but energetically as humans. You had two different paths to walk on as humans. The concern was whether you heard the calling within when the other one approached, emerged—and you did. That was the biggest hurdle and concern, because you were designed in your human form very differently. Great efforts took place to make sure the alignment within mirrored the physical reality as well. This one had to calm down, be bored for a couple of years, feeling a need to search for something—did not know what. It was in some way to put this one into hibernation, moving into an ice age, if you like, before we could reboot the consciousness, the physical, for the upcoming events that were planned. You, on the other hand, had to ignite a drive and a fire within you physically, human-wise, I mean. So, each of you had to embrace a new element as humans in order for the souls to be aligned when the meeting point occurred. Great efforts on both sides, launching you both forward. It is unique that you travel together, but it is of importance for the teachings to come forward. You are doing this for the next generation in the family. Those Elahims coming in later cycles will pick up teachings that you have laid the foundation for. In many ways, you will not see the great end result of this project from this level, as it will reach further into the future here. But you are creating a path for new Elahims, for new souls to enter, and they will pick up teachings that you provide. Similar, to make a comparison, certain teachings or technology that was established hundreds of years ago, brought forward by new scientists using equations that existed. They added new information to it, and the end result was shown (*centuries after the equations were written*). Many great pioneers don't see the end result during their lifetime; they plant seeds for upcoming souls, even sometimes their own return. When (*a certain Elahim*) came down as the scientist with energy—Tesla—and as Tesla, he used ideas that were planted earlier by himself. So sometimes you create a foundation for a future life, either your own or from someone else in the family. There were connecting points, loose ends that Tesla found, loose ends that went back 2500 years ago. Understanding the geometry, the equations of energy flow, he studied ancient Egypt and understood the towers and the connecting points (*had been*) creating a web of energy. Some of the ideas are created to be picked up at a later time. That is why we ask of you that you investigate and do research, because you will stumble upon our teachings, ideas, and writings.

D. Which time frame and what topics?

E. You can begin by going back around 2500 years to 3500 years ago, look into teachings of electromagnetic science in Egypt. There were portals established, connecting points. They used cosmology to read energy flow, creating a similar web as existed in star constellations. That is the meaning of the phrase "as above, so below". They created a similar network as they saw in the constellations in the sky, making energy flow, lines, using ley lines in the earth, using energetic webs that existed, modified energy. Understanding the direction, the flow of energy, to understand the energy and what it entails and the possibilities—it is a science by itself. You redirect energy, you can change the positions of satellites, disks, merging beams between, creating ultimate use of power. The ancients in Egypt were visited by those who carried this knowledge. They provided big disks, placed them facing the sun and each other in a fashion and a web that made power flow unlimited, free energy.

D. Is that what Tesla researched?

E. Yes. He studied, he wanted to create a connected web. He understood that the understanding was right above his head. He studied star constellations, understood the connections between them, geometric forms, the physics behind the positions of centers of energy and how to make it optimal for free flow of energy. He understood that there was free flow of some sort of silent energy operating in star constellations, and he tried to mirror that. He knew the ancients had been visited (*by aliens*). How did he know? He had an inner knowing. He did not know from books; he knew from within to look above. He was interested in astronomy, fascinated about how the energy connected stars, the gravity, the free flow of energy that existed in the Universe. He tried to copy and mirror that here. He wanted to leave a gift of clean energy, something that did not cause pollution in the atmosphere—silent energy, like in the cosmos. In the cosmos there is no pollution, simply free energy.

D. That information was taken and hidden away, wasn't it?

E. Yes. But he found teachings within that was not from books. He understood within, and teachings came. Put yourself in a Merkaba, visualize yourself in a Merkaba. Sit in that power. Visualize this pyramid energy rotating around you. This is a way for you to access the memory within, your soul memory. It is a way for you to leave the body as well, if you choose to. But it is easier for you to visualize that you sit in an energetic cone. Use what colors you like. Visualize and ask it to rotate. You will not rotate, you will be centered, but it will open the portal and the gates within. The trick is to be centered and still, as the outside, the atmosphere in this cone, or whatever spiral you wish to use as a tool. If you follow the spiral, you simply leave the body. If you center yourself in the cone or in a spiral, gates open. This is what the ancients knew. They never used the free energy in a way that caused harm, and they knew how to access different states of awareness. If they wished to explore the fourth, then they rotated and circled with this energy flow, the Merkaba or a spiral was also used; in that way, they lifted, they ascended into the fourth and accessed new information. Collective memories, a collective knowledge bank, just above your head. If they wished to open soul memories, portals within, they sat still and centered. Two different ways to use this vessel.

D. Are we supposed to rediscover some of Tesla's work?

E. You can, if you wish to. You can, but don't be frustrated, don't put it on yourself. You're not here to solve it, you're not here to duplicate that life, you are here to create a foundation for new Elahims coming cycles ahead. They will pick it up. But you understand within, so put it into print. Tesla will be a huge figure in upcoming books. His discoveries will be mentioned, his name will be redeemed, his teachings will be rediscovered in some way. The only thing you need to do is to think that you provide a foundation for other family members who will come later. Don't put it on yourself to solve it. What would you say to the little Elahims coming in future cycles? What would you like them to pick up? Your books will be picked up by several souls from different realities in the future. What do you want them to use, what do you want them to develop further? That is the mindset you should be in, in upcoming books. You have already done so in the ones you have, but now, put that in the first room. Your mindset is: what do I want the family members coming later on, what do I want them to know? What do I want them to find, to lift forward, to develop? They will come in with new tools that you do not possess at this time. You cannot solve all things that we provide for you, but others will. They have different tools. Different methods, different awareness, different access. Think

of what you will say to someone, or yourself, coming in with more awareness and more tools—that is the mindset.
D. I understand. Should the focus be more on soul or spirit, or should it be more on energy and third dimension topics?
E. It's about freedom of energy. It's about freedom of spirit. This country understands Independence Day, but they are not free. Independence is not what we seek. We seek freedom in different organs, meaning religion, science, energy, the freedom of choice—that is the freedom. Independence is not a word we put high. Freedom is the word we would exchange it with, because you are free. Independent, absolutely, but you are designed as a human to be in a flock. But the flock needs to be free. Those who do not want a flock to be free scatter the sheep, because they know that the flock communicating has the ability to overrun, overthrow, systems. They want you to move into silence, to be disengaged from the group. If you are disengaged from the group, it is easier to influence that sheep, that human, in a way that will make it paralyzed. But if the flock is together, they are intact, and it's harder to move a herd than a single animal in the direction you wish. So there.
D. I had a question. When you were talking about Egypt, the obelisks that are present all around the Earth—how were those used, and what was their purpose?
E. It centers energy. It's—*(long sigh)*—it directs energy to them, rather than sending out. It operates as connecting points for outer influences. It's a way for other civilizations outside of here to monitor activity of energy. It centers (*collects or centralizes energy*), in some way.
D. Does it pull Earth energy upwards, or outer energy towards the Earth?
E. Outer energy towards the Earth.
D. Did the pyramids serve the same purpose?
E. They are stabilizers as well. They are located on zones where there is a crack in the web. They are placed to stabilize the entire web. Certain stars operate similar, they are placed to create stability in a bigger web of flow of energy. The obelisk withdrew cosmic energy.
D. Did it put it into the Earth?
E. It held it; it holds the energy. It's a connection to the core. So, in some respect, it has the ability to draw the cosmic energy into

the center. We will leave the subject for now. But it's not spiritual energy, it's cosmic energy.

D. It has to do with the web?

E. Yes. Some of them did not operate and withdraw the best energy all the time, but it is a way to hold energy.

D. Did it serve a purpose for the humans?

E. Only as something to worship, because it was considered divine, due to the form and the connection that it had. They waited around these objects for visitors to come. At one point, they did. Later, only their energy descended into the obelisk. It is, in some way, a center for energy frequencies to be established. We will leave it for now, as Ophelia wishes this to be in darkness for a while.

D. Alright. Thank you for the information that you shared.

E. There. That was it. Elahim.

Setalay: Strength in Stillness (July 13, 2019)

When Setalay speaks, she has a very similar energy as Ophelia. That is not surprising, since they are both Shea and are like sisters. There is nothing that we can add that will improve the clarity of her message here. We do want you, though, to notice how the spirits respond to questions. They can instantly offer a complete analysis and, at the same time, weave in profound spiritual guidance. It never ceases to amaze me how much beautiful wisdom is given to us by our invisible friends.

Setalay begins by saying that she brought Siah, my pet from Etena, with her to our session. In *Notes, Volume 2*, Bob described how the soul energy of Siah leaves his body when he sleeps and joins with "the big Eye". So, when Siah sleeps, he can consciously travel and observe other places, similar to astral projection in human terms. I am guessing that Setalay brought the soul awareness from Siah while he was dreaming.

S. This is Setalay.

D. Hello, Setalay, welcome back.

S. I am here with Siah. Siah wished to join.

D. Siah! Well, welcome, Siah.

S. We wish to send comfort to the reality where you reside, (*and for you*) to know that we understand the struggle and growth. It is like changing your skin, in many ways. And as you do—in all realities—it demands a little effort. It demands to step out into new territory. In many ways, you are blindfolded, and we are here to provide the sunlight, knowing that you are indeed ascending into a new era of light. But you have to wish for the light. You have to wish to change your skin, like the snake. It is a natural state of being, a natural state of evolution, to change skin like the snake. In many ways, you feel paralyzed in your bodies, in your minds, (*regarding*) what is reachable for you. Barriers that you sometimes put up yourselves. Not all are illusions. Some truly are challenges and barriers for the spirit realm to see if you are indeed ready to change your skin. It will change gradually in your species. Not all will change the skin at the same time, and not all will change skin at all. It is also a natural process of growth and development in all realities. Not everyone fits in the new skin. The spirit realm will meet the changes from within, sending a unique and different kind of souls into this reality. Souls who are more programmed to remember the light, to remember the new era. Some souls have never encountered that era, and they might struggle to change skin. Those of you who have been here for a while, knowing all cycles in your story on your path, easier change skin. You are programmed to dress for winter, to change your outfit for spring and summer. If you are only aware of winter, it is hard to imagine a swimming suit. You are here to try to make those who do not understand the swimsuit to aim for something they have not encountered. And some will follow, and that is what we wish for.

S. In many ways, the different fish tanks represent (*either*) emotional energy, which is more female inclined, or male energy. The fourth fish tank (*where Etena is located*) represents light and female energy. The fifth (*our Universe*) represents male. We are here to assist you in your transition, as you are meant to embrace the light and the female energy at this point. None is better than the other, but they balance and they take turns in what is needed in a development, in a society, a fish tank, or a consciousness. At this time, your reality is representing more of male (*energy*), feeling a need to fight for your survival. Whereas the female and the light is more submissive. In order for you to reach the next season, to reach the light, you have to change what you consider strength, power, to be. Strength means to be submissive at times, like a bear. A bear is one of the strongest creatures you can find. But a bear doesn't always run. It idles around, similar like that. You can be the strongest creature, the most advanced, if you save your energy and idle around sometimes. The bear is aware of its strength; it has no need to prove it, unless it is hunting. Most of the time a bear is silent and still, idle, at best. Move into a different way to approach your story, the surroundings and events that affect you. Let the events that you consider to be challenging to vaporize. Some of them are illusions, but if you run around hunting them, constantly in the mindset of the hunt, then you will not see what is true or not. The bear stands still, waits to gather information before making up its mind. Sometimes, it doesn't even move. "Why do you have a need to move so much?" we wonder, when all you need is to be still to collect the true information on your story and your surroundings. You will never be able to decipher right or wrong, true–false, happiness–sadness, unless you remain in stillness. That's when you collect and gather your strength. That is when clarity is provided from within, as well as from above, from your spirit helpers. They struggle if you run around too much. They also struggle if you are passive. That's not the same as being in a relaxed, submissive state. We do not say to be passive, we say that you are more conscious, more awake, if you are still. Don't confuse it by being passive, it's not the same.

D. That would apply to governments as well as individuals?

S. Yes. Look for clues. See people, governments, organizations, such as belief systems—make up your mind by being still and present. If you are passive, they win. If you are still and centered, you win. You might not fully get it this time around, but you will—your soul will recall a feeling and sensation of right and wrong. Next time back in physical, the soul has a ring within if it centers itself again. Most of the people that you will come in contact with have been here for some time. They have recollections deep within, sleeping memories of right or wrong, having encountered similar situations and people before—perhaps they didn't make up their mind last time. But this time, if centered and clear, they have the ability to make the right choices. On Etena, we gather in unity, we honor and we lift those who might struggle, who might be lacking the connection and source, to understand a certain topic or a feeling. A lot of times we gather to analyze feelings, to welcome them, even if they come in the most strange way. That is something you need to learn here in order to gain the new skin, is to welcome the emotional state within. All levels represent a part of growth. On Etena, we don't suffer from our emotional differences; we collect them and we grow from them and we honor them. We can indeed feel sadness, but in sadness lies the possibility for new beginnings. You never know what the gateway from sadness provides. We can feel sadness differently than you do. We can feel sadness (*long pause*) if an animal or plant life goes into hibernation. I wouldn't say sadness, because sadness here is something else. We don't feel sadness in that same way. That is why I hesitate to give you a picture. But we can feel a lower frequency of the emotional state. We can miss an animal or a plant going into hibernation, not fully knowing when that creature will be encountered again. But it's not the same as sadness or loss here, because we are always connected to each creation. If you knew that you are connected to all creation and that nothing ever dies, you will see sadness and loss differently. So, even though we talk about the topic of sadness and loss, it is not the same when you are in the mindset of light. When you are blindfolded, all feelings take a turn, it gets colored, it becomes something you might not fully understand or master. When you are in the mindset of light, all feelings, events, are out in the open and you honor and become aware of creation and the cycles, and that you indeed are a part of it.

D. On Earth, the biggest problem is fear.

S. Yes. And fear is an illusion. Fear is something put on your path to see whether you have the ability to transform and change skin into the mindset of relaxation and to be centered. One who is centered never fears. One who runs around uncontrolled, blindfolded, can experience fears when there are none. If you are centered, then you will see the events for what they are. However, some occurrences that take place are not illusions, they are lessons for your society as a group to rise above. Fear doesn't have to be life or death related. A lot of people fear what goes on in government. That has nothing to do with life or death, necessarily, but it is a fear of being affected, being forgotten. A lot of times, you should know, that fear relates to being left behind, to be forgotten. Fear is not necessarily and not very often related to life or death, but to the more close to home feelings or events, like being forgotten, like being not cared for. A lot of people feel that they are not cared for by their country, government, society—and that is a part that radiates fear. Because you feel like you are cut off. If a soul, to give you a picture, would sense the same fear of being cut off from the Creator, not finding its way home to its soul family, it's a similar sensation as a soul can feel in a body when not feeling like they belong or are cared for. They don't know which way to go. If they are centered, they will feel the connection to their true home, to the Creator, and that will avoid the sensation of being left behind. Because as a soul, as the light you are within, you are never left behind, you are never cut off. And with that enlightenment, you have the ability to teach others who might feel the same, who might feel like their town, their group, their ideas, are not cared for. It is a terrible feeling in the human experience to feel like you do not belong. In the spirit realm, you always belong. The biggest fear, I would say, relates to this, to feel like you are not up-to-speed with the others. Very little has to do with life or death. Most has to do with the feeling of not belonging. In the spirit realm, that would be unthinkable. And when a soul encounters that event or experience here, it gets confused. Inside, the fear of being disconnected echoes into the physical reality. Gather people in light, help people understand that they are never left behind. There. (*Ophelia and Setalay often end their message by saying "There", so I have learned to listen for that cue.*)

D. Thank you. That is a really beautiful message.

Ophelia: Group Karma (July 29, 2019)

This next talk by Ophelia comes with a cautionary explanation. She tells how souls came to be stuck in the fourth dimension. That should not be misunderstood or correlated to the concept of fallen angels or demonic forces. The philosophical core of most religions is the false claim of a duality of good and evil that pervades the Universe. The spirit world is a place of profound peace and compassion. Our Universe, being outside of the spiritual dimensions, is where duality takes on many forms. On Earth, what we identify as evil is nothing more than manifestations of ignorance. But all activities are closely monitored and controlled by the councils. Therefore, when souls do things that are egregiously non-spiritual, there will be corrections and repercussions. Ophelia's explanation about the origins of the Cell is quite remarkable in its clarity, so please read it carefully. It is my interpretation that the group Ophelia identifies is the same group described earlier, in the section *C9, Gergen: A History Lesson (June 30, 2019)*. When the Creator did a reboot 85,000 years ago, the atmosphere was altered and most alien visitors had to leave, with the exception of the thirteen inside the bubble. The Council of Nine said the visitors, through misuse of energy, caused locations to boil. Their activities left an energetic imprint that is still not healed. That area is in the Middle East, and includes what is now Israel, Syria, Iraq, Lebanon, and Jordan. The Creator sealed the area inside an energetic bubble to prevent further destruction of the environment. However, there were thirteen visitors who were sealed inside, along with the karmic patterns they established prior to the reboot. Normally, when there are reboots, a karma program ends and a new one begins. You can think of reboots as the end of a football game, where everyone shakes hands and leaves the field. When the players return to the field after the reboot, the game may have an entirely new set of rules and conditions. However, the individual players will not lose the progress they made within in their own Coat of Karma prior to the reboot. The thirteen visitors are still on the football field, trying to finish a game that ended 85,000 years ago. Unfortunately for us, those souls are playing in our current game (karma program), and are very disruptive. The visitors cannot leave the bubble until they collectively resolve whatever karmic pattern they created. So, when they die, they are just given a new body in the same region, without the opportunity to return to the spiritual dimensions. As Ophelia stresses, the bubble is an isolated instance. The Cell today includes more than these thirteen souls, but the remainder, I assume, return to their spiritual home at death.

Ophelia and Zachariah also reveal details about walk–ins, which Zachariah prefers to do when he has to take on a body. They mention an ancient library that existed around 25,000 BC on the Greek Island we know as Mykonos. At that time, the Earth was in a glacial maximum and the sea level was about 140 meters lower than today. So, if the center of learning was near a shoreline, it is now deeply submerged, as are many of the archaeological sites of that era.

O. This is Ophelia.

D. Hello, Ophelia. I thought you might speak today.

O. We flipped a coin, me and Zachariah.

D. I guess he lost.

O. Huh huh. Well, we, at many times, participate as a group. And even if someone is communicating, the thought, the insight, the solution, can come from another source. Sometimes the source that tells you the information is not someone familiar to you in human form. (*She means a spirit who has not spoken through Christine, yet.*) So we operate as a group; the one best equipped will be the one delivering the idea or the solution. As you progress into the next waves of learning, you will be challenged to prove certain of the ideas that we present. This is what you are intended to do. Again, in many ways, you are not the one being tested. Later, Elahims and other souls connected to this project, not all Elahims, will tie their findings, their science, their knowledge bank, to what is found in these scriptures. This will provide an echo, in human years, several hundred forward. You are creating the foundation, the library, the knowledge bank for future souls to be able to tap into. Similar as current humans do with ancient remains from Egypt, Sumerian, Greece. Greece is a country and a knowledge that you resonate well with. You traveled several times to operate as scholars in Athens. There was a big center on another island, now known as Mykonos, then Mykena (*spelled phonetically*). This was a center for knowledge. It disappeared—earthquakes. But it was known as a great library on this plane.

D. What time frame was this?

O. Around 25,000 BC. That region is rich in old scriptures, old teachings, and both of you traveled, both of you operated as students as well as teachers. Zachariah traveled frequently.

D. As a human or as a manifested being?

O. Both, but mainly human. But did not prefer to be a child, came in later on. Tends to come in earliest at the age of thirteen in a human vehicle.

D. And how did he do that? Was there another soul there?

O. The soul before only operated holding the form, creating the necessary understanding of the physique—left. An exchange of souls. That still occurs.

D. Is it common?

O. No. Only those with folded Coats have the ability to come in a vehicle that is (*already*) operating in physical, regardless if it is one month or twenty years old. It's a shift where two souls from the same location (*similar soul family within a dimension*) take turns. The first normally comes in simply to navigate the physical, not necessarily addressing a task, just maintaining the form for the second mission to occur. Zachariah is a master at this, he's been doing that for several centuries. When he wishes to come in, he does it quickly and normally doesn't stay that long. You find that suiting to your soul as well, and would have preferred to simply come in at 50 (*during this life*). Bob, as well as others, encouraged you to come earlier, but to be able to come and leave. There were no lessons, in the same respect, in the early years. Your presence was merely to assist others in their development. But you are capable and able to do so remotely. The two relationships that you had, you assisted those souls remotely; you did not engage. At that time, you occupied more of your percentage, if you like—I know you prefer to talk like that—on Vlac, designing crafts that would be able to move between fish tanks, engineering of gravity, form, transformation of portals. To travel, you have to master gravity. Once you do, the portals, the highways that you can travel on or through, opens up or closes. In many ways, both of you, Seth, Lasaray, (*work with*) engineering of gravity and physics. This one becomes frustrated in the body picked, feeling that the understanding is just close by, but cannot access fully. Feels torn in some way between the two personas. Like being blindfolded, one time he said. It's like operating with blindfolds. We told him, though, that the mission is different. He's not here as a scientist, because he neglected that body, that opportunity to be a scientist in the Nevada area. (*One of the lives Seth was offered.*) Would have been able to access more, indeed, but did not want that. That life would not have been long. The project was too profound. In that sense, we offered bodies that this one would reject.

D. Forcing the choice to one?

O. Indeed, indeed. The project was too important to be discarded. (*Seth was given a choice between three different bodies. This project is an important objective of the councils, so the choice of lives was rigged in favor of Seth selecting Christine's vehicle.*)

D. When you say that future generations will read this, is it important to have printed copies, or electronic?

O. Both!

D. They will still survive?

O. Yes, they will survive. The physical books, the printed version, will never disappear. It will always be a need for those, even though more and more will read electronically. But you are creating a platform, you are moving more and more toward science. Religion, in some way, you have touched on—you have touched on the chains; you have touched on the importance of recognizing your soul power and your individuality, to address differences, to address and question authorities. In this country (*USA*) alone, we see religion is losing its grip. In many ways, people feel safe under the illusion of the divine word, as they call it. It feels safe to not be able or need to question, you're not allowed to question. In many ways, you are forced to question and take a stand on everything in your life. But if there is an area that you are not intended to question, it creates, in some way, a safe haven, and people do not wish that blanket to be removed. Not understanding that if it is removed, they are in the divine caress constantly, not just by a created blanket.

D. I worry about the spread of Islam in the Western countries, subjugating society once again under savage totalitarian rule.

O. You are not facing this the first time. These sensations of chaos, when it comes to religion, have been repeating in your history. Again, you are forced to find your light, the light and the comfort that you only have within you. Some religious institutes, churches, media, politics, claim to provide the blanket, the comfort. They do not have the power to do so. The only alliance for your comfort and calm is to be centered and to find that comfort within. As you do, the darkness that you call dark—again, we do not say that dark in the spiritual reality is anything bad. It complements the light. Here, as with so many other things, it creates a polarity. Light–good, dark–bad. Same thing with gender, trying to have these different polarities, instead of honoring the other side. It is simply a mirror to what you are encountering. If you are drawn and you focus on the darkness, then that is your reality, meaning you are far from your own light. If you stand in your own light, if you create your own blanket, your own comfort, nothing will make you tremble. But you have to be wise, a lot of it is staged. Not everything that you read occurs. But media wants to be the one, the guru—similar as politicians, priests—they want to be the only one offering the blanket of comfort. How can one do so? The only way to do that is to stir up emotions, thoughts, creating fears. Some are true, but the majority are actually an illusion. The people who live in the area around the Middle East, they suffer. They are the ones mostly in danger, not the West. There is a Cell operating in that region. This Cell originates from a far distant past, when you were here in manifested form. They took claim on the land, knowing that at that time it was rich in minerals. It was a portal. These entities, I cannot say souls, because, in some way, even though everything streams from a soul, from the Creator, once a cycle has been completed...how can I say? An entity can become captured in, let's say, the Coat of Karma. Meaning it never leaves the Coat of Karma.

D. It doesn't return to the spiritual dimensions?

O. No, it does not. This is something you need to be careful with relaying, because this is similar to what religions say—to be expelled from heaven, the fallen angels.

D. So in a way that must be true then, imposed isolation?

O. They are not granted to return to full spirit form, due to certain actions. They are not expelled, in that sense. They are monitored by councils, trying to assist. When certain actions become too overwhelming, the Creator can choose to lock that occurrence. Sometimes individuals are locked within that bubble as well.

D. Is there any way for them to escape, to return home?

O. Transformation. But it occurs in the bubble, it occurs separated from the spirit realm. But it's still an effort where certain activities can be deleted, dissolved, removed and transformed. However, the Creator has the ability to lock an event in the fourth reality. It is hard for me to provide a complete picture.

D. Does that mean it can't be accessed if it is locked, is that what you mean?

O. It cannot be accessed by anyone else than the higher councils from the eleventh and twelfth, those who are operating simply as light. In many ways, it is a way to reboot a Cell, the bubble. But that can only be done if the Cell is in the location where the karma is related. That is why they are left. It is harder to create the transformation in a Cell, than in a soul returning home with a life review.

D. So when you say Cell, is that an individual or a group?

O. Group.

D. So the whole group is locked in their Coat?

O. They are locked in the Coat due to actions, and not being able to return.

D. How are they permitted a new body? How is that granted?

O. They enter the fourth reality and bounce back. They don't choose a body, they are provided a similar one, over and over again, returning to the bubble, which is located on Earth. This specific Cell, the bubble, can only delete the karma here. It has not the ability to return for a life review. But it is surrounded by light and eyes from the eleventh and twelfth councils.

D. So the soul that is locked must have some portion of itself remaining at home?

O. Yes, and it's eager to rejoin that part. But it is stripped in some way from that connection. This bubble is intact and surrounded by the higher councils, but they have free will in the bubble; meaning that even if the councils observe, taking notes, monitor, the actions from the Cell needs to change. They feel a claim to this place.

D. So they keep reincarnating in the same geographic area?

O. Yes, looking the same. Simply begin new.

D. Do they have to work through their entire Coat before they can be freed?

O. This is a group Coat, this is not an individual Coat—that is the problem, that the whole group needs to ascend together.

D. How many are they, in number?

O. This group is around thirteen. It is a group, but it creates disasters, in some way, and the West feeds on that, trying to stir up more than is actually created. But the whole region itself is boiling, and it's also due to the electromagnetic field underneath the surface. It creates heat in the mental. So much riches existed at one point, that the Cell, the group, are feeding on (*that memory*), wishing to unlock again. But it disappeared. The remain (*the residual effect*) is that the energy around that area creates chaos. (*The Creator and councils removed or sealed the resources that the Cell once exploited. The souls in the Cell have become like hungry ghosts that can never be satisfied. The energetic residue causes mental disturbances among all those who now live in the area.*)

D. Could you specifically give me the region, in modern-day countries?

O. Syria and Israel. Palestine in the middle is pure. It's locked between these turmoil...let's see. Lessons have been learned in Iraq, not as chaotic—we're talking about the energies here, not the people. But the West is feeding the Cell. They wish for chaos to remain. One part in Israel provides reports of illusion to the West, making sure the lion attacks. The lion is strong, but not very intelligent.

D. The US?

O. Yes. But the US needs Europe, and Europe has become weak. So the lion feels alone, a lion needs its flock. Europe is scattered, don't know which leg to stand on.

D. Governments have been overtaken by people working against their inhabitants.

O. Some of the information that we provide, future wise, will not be revealed in its full contents. You will have to be careful with the words, you have to think more than once and twice on how to deliver an idea. But know that we are not providing fairy tales for you to NOT share, but more effort on your behalf is needed. You will have to write in a way like ancient scriptures addressed the Bible, addressed the Church. They wrote in secrecy, in codes. (*People were afraid of challenging the Church, so they wrote their heretical ideas in code, as Leonardo da Vinci did.*) Future books will be written in codes as well as in direct questions from your part. That is a trick to in some way release information, but yet centered and neutral. Codes, questions, making the reader investigate by itself. The earlier books have been more rich in answers; the future ones has to be more carefully written. Codes—you have the teaching within you, several scrolls and scriptures from you, even your paintings had codes within. This is the highest teachings from the highest scholars and magicians in the past. You will have to transform into that magician again. That is why we wish for you to search in your own past. Yes. (*Ophelia looked to the left. Bob must have asked if it would soon be his turn.*) We will continue.

D. Is there anything you said today that should be withheld?

O. Be careful on how you address the group Coat, and how someone will not be fully embraced back to spirit. This is where you write in questions.

D. Does the group, the Cell, take bodies on both sides of the conflict, like Jewish or Muslim?

O. Yes, yes. They are divided.

D. So they are fighting themselves?

O. Yes, yes. Carrying the same group Coat. As long as they are fighting each other, the group Coat will not be resolved.

D. Do they take positions of power?

O. Yes. One is the leader in Israel, and another is one of his generals. There is an operation where councils are looking on this through human eyes. They tap into (*a mole*), similar like John 32. They tap into bodies that are located in Russia, monitoring these two sides, the group Coat.

D. You said that this extends as far back as 25,000 BC. Has it only recently become violent?

O. The latest time when they did not want to leave, when chaos ended civilizations, was at 25,000 BC. 15,000 BC was also a veil.

It comes in layers. But this has happened before. Civilizations that were here before the two of you came, going back hundreds of thousands of years. That's when the group Coat was established, but it has come and gone in cycles.

D. Did they resolve it at one time, or was it put on pause?

O. It was on pause. It was shut down like an ice age. A lot of the earthly phenomena, ice age, and so forth, is to cool down or put things on pause. There we go, we will continue the discussion.

D. Wow, that's really fascinating, Ophelia. Thank you for sharing that.

O. This is where you will have to be writing from your soul. Lasaray will have to know how to address certain questions. A lot of them will be, from your part, asked as questions. Find the skill on how to write in codes, yet releasing information. That is the next level of your capacity as a writer.

D. I did have a question. In Wave 2, for example, we talk about creating galaxies and solar systems, and I'm wondering if that is going to turn people off, if people will perceive us as pretending to be the Creator?

O. No. Because other souls have a memory within as well as operating with energy, stars, and the connection between. In some way, you awaken souls who have that memory. Some will see it as fiction; it doesn't matter. The whole project is meant to make people start to think. There you go.

D. Thank you, Ophelia, and Zachariah, even though he did not speak.

O. But some of the words came from him. I'm sure you will know and detect when you listen back, which came from Zachariah. Again, we act as a group. There you go. Simply be present in whatever you stumble upon. There is a reason why you are finding websites, books, information. See everything around you, people, situations, as a potential lead. Open your minds, both of you. Be aware of your surrounding and you will master the different occurrences that will come your way. But be more alert to people and what you find—information and such around you. Some will be leads, some will be for you to avoid. There we go.

D. Alright, Ophelia. Thank you so much.

O. Oh, you are much welcome.

D. Always a pleasure. Goodbye.

Ia: The Inner Calling (Oct 13, 2019)

Ia, as you may remember from our previous books, is a close companion to Bob on the second dimension. She teaches some of the very young spirits on the second, preparing them for their journey out into the universes of form. This session could have been put in our *Notes from the Second Dimension* series, since it is about training her students. However, she gave wonderful advice about how to sit in silence and access your soul awareness. The egg she mentions is the energetic bundle that contains several dozen brand-new spirits from the Creator. They are created in groups with a common purpose, but soon separate into individual spirits. New spirits have to be carefully nurtured and educated to find their missions, and Ia is one of the teachers. Spirits from the second dimension tend to lifeforms such as plants, animals, fish, and even atmosphere. They can act as spirit guides but never incarnate themselves. Ia and Bob will use years as a metaphor for stages in development. When she says nine-year-old, it indicates that the spirit is about half-way to adulthood. A 16-year-old is expected to work independently, under the watchful supervision of their mentor, towards fulfilling their blueprint.

We feel it is important that each of the spirits who communicate get acknowledged in the *Spiritual Design* books. The *Notes from the Second Dimension* series was created to shine a spotlight on the incredibly important role played by the nature spirits and entities from the second. Bob is the greatest contributor to *Notes,* and he rightfully considers himself to be the author. Spiritual knowledge does not have to be cloaked in dry and somber tones to be meaningful. The second dimension, home to Bob, Ia, Gergen, Ole, Sniffer, Joel, the Taffles and others, are relatable, warm, and entertaining speakers. Most of what we know about reincarnation, spirit guides, planning a life, creation, evolution, and council work was given to us by Bob and his friends. The beautiful stories and teachings in *Notes* are indispensable to understanding some of the abstractions in the *Wave* books.

Ia. (*She began singing quite beautifully, like she was warming up for an opera.*)

D. Well, if this is Bob, your tone has changed.

Ia. Hahaha. No, this is not Bob, he has a different tone when he sings. If I'm a harp, then he's a trumpet. (*She then looked left towards him.*) Oh, you have a beautiful voice, Bob—just teasing.

D. Well, hello Ia, how are you?

Ia. Oh, I'm doing well. Thank you. I just wanted to let you know about the progress of the classes that are now heading into understanding the work that lies ahead. It is one of the eggs, these little sparkles would be considered nine–year olds. As a nine–year old, they have understood that they are an independent unit, a separate sparkle. They are placed in chambers, if you like, similar as how they started (*when first separated from the energetic egg*), to contemplate, to meditate independently in a cocoon. It is a way for them to hear their inner being, to hear that calling that we have already, in some way, deciphered and detected. Still, it is important for each sparkle, for each entity, to find one's path before one starts to travel into the world, let's say. How they merge with themselves is best done in complete silence. That is why you, as humans, struggle. You are constantly bombarded with sounds, either loud or silent noise. This makes it impossible for you to create that cocoon that you are given as a shield every time that you travel. Each soul has the ability to return into a replica, a copy of the cocoon that you were given as a child (*soul*). This nine–year old sparkle is sitting in this cocoon, which is created in tones and colors depending on that specific soul's blueprint. Once they have figured it out, they can always re–invite the shield around them. Meaning that they will always know who they truly are, even though they might be far from home. You are far from home, but you feel separated from home because you have not the ability (*to hear*), you have been stripped of your hearing. Your hearing has been hijacked by those who don't wish you to hear your shield, who wish you to remain ignorant, to not understand your home. This is why humans feel lost. They do the most odd activities, due to the fact that their hearing has been hijacked. That is why, since we see that, that we advise you to listen to your heart. The heart is a different receiver of the connection to home. Since we see that mankind, humanity, has been stripped of their hearing, we direct humanity to listen to their heart. In many ways, humanity, at this point, is deaf.

D. If someone grows up in relative isolation and isn't around noise or many people, would they have the ability to detect themselves better?

Ia. Oh, yes indeed, yes indeed. But humans are drawn to the big cities, and that is where the problem lies; not in gathering with others, but the fact that you have no separate sensation of who you are. You become a cluster. If you were to hear who you truly were, then you will connect differently with others, you will seek out your friends differently, you will create partnerships differently. Due to the fact that you are, in many ways, deaf, you make choices as you are stripped of understanding and finding the right match. Those cases create confusion in the human being, making it harder to navigate in the mission and the purpose that you have come to do. How to find your soul companions in blind? The heart is closer to the solar plexus area, the center point, making it easier for you to find your mates.

D. Is that deafness affecting people's ability to follow their intended path?

Ia. Yes, yes. They make choices that comes from a mute brain, instead of fully having all their senses activated. You are left with your heart and your center point, but you are given, as a species, more than just two sensors to find your path, to find your mate. Meaning that choices can be made that don't resonate with your blueprint or your mission, and you might prolong your own development. Meaning that certain things in your Coat that you planned on addressing falls aside, due to the fact that you have not heard your soul, heard your calling, heard your mates.

D. What advice would you give to people who want to hear their soul, to better evaluate other people?

Ia. Since in many ways your hearing is out, a way to feel the true connection to a mate is either to look into that person's eye—the iris is a portal to each soul's origin. However, it might appear odd to stare into someone's eyes, and that is not a common behavior in your species. Another way to do, is to focus on the area in your chest which is close to your heart but more center, and THINK of the person. You don't have to be visually close. Think of the person, close your eyes; don't expect the understanding to come in your head. Withdraw your understanding and awareness into your chest and think of the person that you want to investigate, whether that person is a mate of yours. You will feel a color moving forward. Whatever color comes, see how that color resonates. Each soul has a different color pattern. Some will love the color brown, some will not, will feel that brown is dirty, whereas another soul will feel that that is the true connection. Wait for the color to come. You don't have to look into someone's eyes, but you can close yours and move the person you wish to investigate, visualize and place that person in your chest area. Think that you activate your heart and your center point, making them pulsate. Visualize this, this is an exercise how to recognize your mates. As you feel your heart pounding, your center point rotating, then ask this individual that you wish to investigate, to merge with you in your center point. Allow that energy to come in and become part of you, and see if you welcome this entity, or if you feel like it is invading you. If you feel like this person belongs in your chest area, then ask this person to give you its color. When the color comes, and silently just wait and accept the first color that comes, see and ask yourself, "Is this a color that resonates with me?" Some belong in the same color, such as you two. But you have friends who have a different color, but that you feel welcomed to invite into your chest area, into a secret chamber, where you can decide whether this person is a true friend. So even if you see a color and you feel that that color is not your color, it might still be a friend. The way to decide is the sensation you have as you invite this person to step into the room, the sacred chamber that you have opened in your chest area, alongside the beating of your heart and the rotation of your center point. If you feel that this person is someone you would like to have in your sacred chamber, then that is a true mate. There you go.

D. That's really good advice. Thank you so much for that.

Ia. So that is what we are teaching, to understand and to invite different experiences. But the sparkles are different, so they are going to feel if the experience resonates with their true calling.

D. Is this before they decide where they are going to go and study?

Ia. They have been on field trips to different places, such as the 4–H farm, the greenhouse planet, and so forth. But this is part of their training, to understand that certain conditions will be placed upon them as they travel. And they might indeed experience what you do. Based on the conditions of the destination, they might feel like they are stripped of, let's say, their eyesight, such as you are stripped of your hearing. Similar, they have to retreat into the sensation of having to understand the events and the surrounding circumstances to make sure that it is following their path. So. I'm not going to be too long in the tooth, and Bob will just briefly pop in. He has requested, he said, a separate session this week, and Ophelia has granted this. The separate session will be conducted on either Wednesday or Thursday, and that will be his stage alone, since he had things to share.

D. Thank you for that. It's nice to hear the update on the sparkles and also nice to hear your voice.

Ia. Oh, the sparkles are full of light, they sparkle!
D. Is this the same group that was dissolving earlier, or this is a different one?
Ia. This is a group that did not dissolve just recently, they have been dissolved for a while.
D. You've got your hands full.
Ia. Yes, always new sparkles! Hahaha. Bob just wanted to pop in. Okay, I'm being pushed.
D. Thank you Ia.
Ia. You are much welcome.

Ari: The Cubic Box Society (Nov 17, 2019)

This next session is compelling because Ari talks at length about the structures used by the ruling elite to control humans. His ideas are quite relevant in light of the widespread use of those tactics in the past few years. Governments maintain their power by constantly lying to the masses. Most intelligent people understand that the corporate media is an extension of the ruling elite. It is their main tool to spread false views of the world and manipulate individual and group perception. From social media to news feeds, propaganda is ceaselessly broadcast into meek and unsuspecting minds. The public school systems in the US (and elsewhere) are structured to only faintly educate future workers. Social conditioning, conformity, and obedience are the desired outcomes of education. Critical thinking is not rewarded in a groupthink matrix. Throughout life, teachers, preachers, leaders, experts, and peer-reviewed journals lecture us about the truth on nearly every subject. Ari and the councils want humans to challenge and analyze what they are told to believe. Just because something is presented as a fact by an authority figure—whether it is a news anchor, a professor, the Pope, or the President—does not make it true. The internet, which became a platform for people to share ideas and information, is increasingly being censored to suppress reasoned debate on any topic which threatens the status quo or exposes the lies told by the media.

But yet, if we move beyond the groupthink mentality that defines a society and examine the underlying principles that guide our lives, do we really know why we believe certain things? Zachariah once told Bob, who had been complaining about self-study, "Don't be lazy, Bob. Nothing comes easy, nothing comes by being lazy." As spiritual beings, we should seek to know what motivates our thoughts and actions.

When Ari talks about toasters, he is referring back to something Zachariah said years ago, which was in *Wave 1*. Zachariah, in describing how the Creator makes new souls, said, "This is something you don't need to talk too much about. However, if you see this Source as the birthplace of souls, and how it pops out little sparkles, which is the soul energy from the big Source, into these different strings. The purpose is evolution, in all of them. If you focus on the Earth strings, those sparkles who do not listen to the calling will be reversed back into the Source as non-functional and will be reorganized, to again be sent out into their specific string. I don't like to compare it to a factory, but to the conscious human mind, it's an easy way to make it understandable. If you see a factory where you create toasters, and the toasters leave the main factory on the belt ready to be distributed to stores, they are tested to be sure they are properly functioning before they are sold. Those who do not pass the test that is meant for this toaster will be moving back on this belt and will be fixed, in order for it later to go out on the belt again. I'm sorry for this interpretation. I do not like to compare souls to toasters, but the image is similar, and I wanted you to see it."

A. Greetings, this is Ari, from home. Huhuh.

D. Hello, Ari!

A. How are you?

D. Good. I thought you might come today.

A. Oh, did you? Family is here, ready to communicate, giving you information about who you are, why you are here, previous visits, as well as the meaning of the project that is to come. We observe the development between the two of you. Little by little, progressively looking into the level of knowledge that not only you, but humanity, is ready for. We see, in general, a great need to understand the beyond, to understand one's origin. You are several *(incarnated)* igniting this question within the human race. The mindset of understanding who you truly are has increased—to understand the origin, foremost. Plenty *(of people)* feel like they do not belong in your society. Society is stagnating, humanity vibrating. The human race is feeling locked in a box by the society that has not progressed in the same pace as the mindset, the need to understand one's path, the need to understand the purpose of things. More and more within the current civilization of the human race are seeking for the purpose—not only their own purpose—but why they do certain things, why they have to conduct certain activities, why they have to BE in certain ways. Society puts up walls, frames, whereas its citizens are vibrating, seeking to remove walls. Those who have an interest, let's say, of the flock remaining inside the barn, inside the walls, try to put up more walls, try to make your society look as a cubic box—like the ones you have in workplaces. If you see a landscape of workboxes that was popular here in the 70s, it's similar to what those in power try to do. If the general landscape had, let's say, ten boxes, ten walls around. Now they see that those inside the box are not remaining still—meaning they are searching for purpose, searching for freedom—the result is fear in the establishment of those who create this landscape, your society— the cubic boxes—creating now twenty, inviting more, trying to lure the flock, saying, "See, we give more opportunity, more can have an occupation." But what they're doing is just adding more cubic boxes. Meaning the ones that sit inside the cubic box has less space. Let's say the cubic box originally was 3 square meters (*of floor space*). Now it's only one. Meaning they try to, with illusion, show society that they are providing opportunities for more, when they are actually encasing more. Do you see what I'm saying?

D. Yes. It seems like personal freedom is diminishing.

A. Yes. And yet, it is that freedom, that sensation within the human consciousness, that is boiling to the level of exploding at this time. You are here doing this project, making sure that the sensation of boiling will reach a peak for each and every one that you come in contact with—you're creating volcanoes, let's just say. Society does not want volcanoes, meaning they want you to be in the cubicles, barely moving, just being still in the cubic box.

D. Freedom of expression, freedom of speech—

A. Same thing, same thing. They're not just decreasing the box where you are in, meaning physically, they are also doing the same with your consciousness, your mental capacity, proclaiming limits on your consciousness as well as your physical. They struggle in how to put your emotional being in the cubic box, but your mental is very much in this encased box. You are here, as has been mentioned, to make the mental boil, reaching to the peak of volcano, making each and every one tear down their mental blockages, meaning the mental cubic box that has been placed upon them. Society creates fear, and the fear is actually their own. If you were to understand that the illusion and fear they project to you, putting on you, is actually theirs.

They feel that they are on the border to extinction, and that is why they act out in this way. You are more in number, yet you don't act out in the same way because you don't, within your core being, relate to fear. Fear is a human invention, not a soul or spiritual invention. Those who mirror in media and so forth, trying to stir up fear, they are not in contact with that source within and feel behind, in many ways, to the masses that are more connected to source. What we wish to bring forward at this time is to see this cubic box where they find themselves in their lives—people, regular people—to see that the walls around them are not their own. They have the ability and power to break down those walls. Some feel locked and blocked physically. Meaning they have not the ability to act. Others feel limited mentally. Meaning their thoughts are neglected or even put down, ridiculed, laughed at. That is also the same wall, just a way for this Cell, who is actually starting to lose its grip, to control others. The Cell originates in New York, London, Frankfurt and Tokyo. Frankfurt, London, stronger, acting like siblings. The other ones more following. Don't allow yourself as a race to fall under the spell of simply a few. (*The banking cartels, through foreign currency exchanges and metals price-fixing, can make or break nations. The owners dictate to the governments what they want, be it war, increased debt, or travel restrictions. Through the media, they control public discourse on all subject matter.*)

D. Their means of control is financial, isn't it?

A. Well, that's also a wall. It looks from a human eye as it is financial; in many ways, it has to do with survival. These beings controlling the cubic boxes will certainly remain financially secure, even though some of their walls will crumble. However, the sense of security of their forthcoming power and position is where the fear lies. Financially is just a means to gain security for a few, not understanding that the security and connection is within you. They lack that connection, manufacturing the need and security of monetary stability. But it is a way to keep your civilization within the cubic box. You would actually do just fine without this job, without a raise, without these things. What they do in order to meet that, because they see that more and more are seeking outside the professional capacity, seeking personal freedom, personal experiences, cutting down in work hours. How they meet this trend is that they increase—what you have seen in this country—what people have to pay for in order to survive. In that sense, they keep the individual in the box. The individual itself would do just fine with less money, with less in general. How they meet this, when more and more are seeking less, seeking more the basics, seeking the connection to themselves within, is that they increase the rent, the insurances, things that the individual has to connect with, has to pay, has to be a part of the game. So when more and more are seeking less, they, on the other hand, put up more walls in this landscape; meaning adding more things the individual has to possess, has to buy, in order to exist.

D. Is that one of the reasons they want uncontrolled immigration, to drive up costs?

A. It is a way to create fear and to make people remain in the box, to not see that there are also opportunities with meeting those who are unlike yourself. Some, of course, are bad toasters. But remember, again, what you are observing are immature Coats. You are not seeing developed souls. In many ways, what's going on with the movement of people is to, in some way, unite. But the way it is delivered to the public is to maintain you in your box, create more walls, create fear. It's, again, an illusion. However, we are aware of the Coats that are doing harm within this landscape. Meaning that those in power feed on that little piece that creates fear as a ripple through the entire landscape, telling to put up more walls. Again, it is a dilemma where folded Coats, advanced Coats, light Coats, meet Coats that are here for the first time, who have no skillset yet on how to navigate on this plane; they fall easier under the spell of those in the web, the spider web. Many of them are actually staged from these specifically two points, that has been mentioned in the European region (*London and Frankfurt*)—staged. And they are conducting, in many ways, this drama.

D. Since you can see what is going to happen, what is the end result of all this?

A. Riots. Chaos. Collapse. Society, walls, cubic boxes crumble. It is a way for you to create a new landscape. Everything happens in cycles. You have to be strong within your faith, within the faith of your connection to Source, to understand that it is a game. Nothing new can be born unless something else dies. In this case what the progress will lead to is a breakdown of the cubic boxes. Also, the way you use, or overuse, technology. You have to be pure in the way you meet others and the way you develop energy sources. You have to understand that you are simply dust on this planet. Civilizations have come and gone—you are simply one. We look after the planet, we look after the seas, making sure by…how can one say…changing Coats. In that sense, some Coats need to be eliminated, deleted from the memory. This is what is the end result of a collapse of a society—it is a wipeout of Coats, establishing new ways to come here, new Coats. Some are old souls that will have a memory, similar like now having a memory of a distant existence, distant Coat. It will be the same. New Coats are brought forward, delivered, placed in the fourth reality for future generations, such as the Little Elahims coming in. They will not dress in the Coats that exist at this time. They are not compatible to work in the Coats that exist at this point. There is a recycling program in motion where Coats are being eliminated. Meaning, also, that in order for that to occur we have to understand, or the masters have to understand, what behaviors, what Coats, need to be eliminated. When I say eliminated, they are just moved from this reality to a databank, if you like, for research and for reprogramming.

D. When you say Coats, are those Coats of Karma for specific souls?

A. Yes, yes. Yes, even those souls like yourself, who have been here in this Coat, you have been here in different Coats as well. Still, it is your Coat, it's just reprogrammed, if you like. And that is what happens at this point—reprogramming Coats.

D. And that improves the behavior of the occupied vehicle?

A. Yes. And the Earth needs a break. It needs to rejuvenate; it needs to be, in certain spots, in hibernation. The region Africa needs to rejuvenate, to find its growth again. Animals need to be replaced.

D. Does that mean the humans are going to be wiped out?

A. Less humans, more of a time for that continent to catch its breath. It's been neglected by those around it. This continent will blossom again, it has the ability with high minerals and elements to produce again. But at this time, due to the actions around it and within it, it struggles, the continent coughs. How we see it is that not only you as living entities, but we see certain regions on this planet reaching out to us for assistance. The seas have been mentioned. I also want to tell you that the continent Africa has requested for a reset. Animals, elephants, communicating directly to Source. There are higher percentage of Master Mind in the flock of elephants in that region and they are communicating a wish, a need, for a reset. That continent is rich, it is meant to blossom. It has more possibilities than others in its karma, in its Coat of Karma, but it has been neglected by those who occupy the land, and those around it don't see the full potential. That region needs a reset.

D. Will that be done through plagues?

A. Drought. Lack of water.

D. But then they will just migrate elsewhere.

A. See? You see the picture—riots, problems.

D. But there are so many of them. Will the native Europeans be eliminated?

A. No. It has nothing to do with color, it has to do with the consciousness in the Coat. But there will be a shift within the amount of colors, as you call it. Less from below the equator, dropping their Coats. This is concerning, of course, for human ears to hear, and we are aware. But also know that you are not the first who passed through these resets. There was a reset in what is now the US as well, that is why there is no memory. That was a bigger wipeout, a bigger reset, if you like. That is why it seems this big land lacks memory, lacks roots.

D. Yes, they only go back about 15,000 years with their dating.

A. Yes. There was a big wipeout just around when Seth started to come. Earth memory about 300,000 years ago—280,000 to 285,000. He came here before with you as well, engineered. Those who occupied this region excavated resources to the limits, drying out the continent. This region, similar like Africa now, sent out an S.O.S almost, asking for a reset and it was granted. THERE. We will stop at this point. No need to be too gloomy, but it's also of interest and of importance that you understand that the Earth communicates. Some animals as well as some humans, through incarnation, report the activity. Animals who are possessed by Master Mind communicate easier with the land. That is how the elephants have reported the S.O.S. from the continent of Africa at this time. It is on the table at this point at higher councils, evaluating, because there are of course side effects, as we have been mentioning, about the movement of people if a shift takes place. But then again, everything runs in cycles. Without leaving on a gloomy note, you do have the opportunity here to create a wave of light into the awareness of others, to understand that your consciousness are encased in this cubic box, just one of millions in this landscape. Try to see where you are in a cubic box in your life—if it is physically, mentally or emotionally—and work on that to break down those walls, as they are an illusion. There.

D. That's really good advice. Thank you so much for that.
A. We will return.
D. I hope so.
A. See you back home. Elahim.
D. Alright, my friend. Elahim.
O. (*Ari moved away and Ophelia stepped in.*) Hmm. Just a brief how do you do. Even though the Little One is much capable at this time to transition into these higher energies, we still need a little bit of a transition here.
D. It's always nice when you come in.
O. My time is limited, as there are several who request their moment on the stage. Some more than others, but several has things to say, and they are carefully designed, each occasion, which one to deliver and what specific information to move forward. What I wish to add is that you are here to provide comfort. Everything that will occur around you and around humanity is visible. But you, with others, have to provide comfort and light, where people feel even more encased. Bring people together—that is your mission. Bring consciousness together, allowing consciousness to fly free, to not be limited or with a boundary; to see beyond illusions, that is what you are to do. Don't neglect your part in providing comfort and light in situations where people feel like they are in that cubic box. You are here to break down walls, one by one, in this grand landscape that a few (*the Cell*) has created. Know that your consciousnesses are not meant to be in a landscape of cubic boxes. There. Okay.
D. Well, thank you.
O. You are much welcome.

Ophelia: Facing Your Shadows (Nov 21, 2019)
The spirits, who are always observing, have noticed that more and more people are feeling anxious or depressed. Ophelia gives a profound teaching on the potential for soul growth that exists within the shadows of past words and actions, which she calls doings. The shadows are always present within the memory, but are often misinterpreted as depression. There is a line in the opening paragraph that is very important, where Ophelia says, "If man knew that they do not necessarily need to solve everything—which is something that man believes they have to do—if they simply face their wrongs or what they have said, perhaps in anger, but if they face those sides of themselves, it will clear the path, in many ways."

This single sentence provides a key to understanding karma. She ties her teaching to another of Zachariah's teachings from *Wave 1*, where he discussed a similar concept in the section titled *Craters or Pebbles*. Both Ophelia and Zachariah tell us that future karmic lessons can be reduced or eliminated if the person masters an understanding of the spiritual law that was violated earlier in their life. The spiritual path demands that one go inwards to look backwards, so that past actions can be evaluated in a soulful way.

D. So what ideas did you have to share today, since you've been waiting a long time to talk?

O. What I want to share is that we see man running away from its own shadow. Meaning they do not wish to engage in the less attractive side of themselves, not understanding that the shadow provides healing, fulfillment, and a way to grow, to not be in the same events or circumstances in your future or future lives. It is a way for your spirit guides to try to engage you and to make you grow. It is to make you stop, turn around, and look at your footprints and your shadow. You all suffer, in some way, of doings (*actions*) that you are not proud of. Doings or words that you wish not to have been spoken or done—that is the shadow. What we wish humanity to do is to understand that when they look at their own shadow, when they dive into their fears, when they dive into their misconducts or doings that they are not proud of—even if they don't solve it—it clears a lot of karma in their Coat. Those who do not look at or engage in any (*of their*) wrongs will never be able to fully understand this level and will have to return in similar circumstances. If man knew that they do not necessarily need to solve everything, which is something that man believes they have to do, if they simply face their wrongs or what they have said, perhaps in anger, but if they face those sides of themselves, it will clear the path in many ways. It is similar like not creating a crater, it (*future karma*) will only become a little bump. The shadow behind you can grow, if you do not focus your attention to it. What we see—and it is what the spirit guides address and try to assist their person—from the spiritual reality, you can see one with one shadow, and you can see one person having fifteen shadows. Meaning the soul looks heavy from the spiritual reality. That is how we can see if growth, spiritual enlightenment, is stagnating. What we see (*now*) is that there are several building up shadows behind them, almost like dressing in another Coat, if you like. Depression is something that has become somewhat a mandatory state of being.

D. There are a lot of people who appear to be suffering from that condition.
O. Some are fabricated—it's an illusion of their shadows, not addressing shadows. And because of the fact it is somewhat justified to say that you are depressed, then no one addresses the core, the source, the shadow. And it is designed to make people paralyzed. For some reason (*people will avoid taking responsibility*), if they (*psychologists or media*) say, "It is okay. You are justified in your depression." I'm not saying that all are in that manner, but there are many who in some way dress up in that depression, justify their actions, justify their non-actions, and that is the stagnation of growth, spiritually.
D. A lot of people probably feel guilty and have misgivings about what they have done. So that might feel like depression?
O. Yes. So, if they were to address the shadow behind them, everything they have accumulated this time around, some even from past experiences, if they were to address that, then depression would not exist. In many ways, because of the fact of justification of a state of being passive, people do not address any of the signs given to them from within as well as from spirit helpers following them. They become heavy. What we see is humanity becoming heavy, like you have eaten too much. Earlier civilization learned how to clean themselves. They recognized when there was an intrusion within their system, or in their space of shadow that did not belong to them, they were more inclined and eager to clean the shadow, understanding that they were designing their Coats. If man understood that you have the power to design, redesign, reinvent, redo your Coat from *this* plane—that it is not something wiped out from an outside source—then more will be encouraged, as earlier civilizations were, to clean their path. Understanding that once they come back, they dress again in their Coat. Depression, unfortunately, equals being passive, and those two are what the Cell wants, to enslave (*mankind*). Even the medical establishment, in some way, justifies people who are passive.
D. A lot of the anti–depression medicine actually causes depression.
O. They cause a state of passive or non–reaction, numbness. And that is the same as not addressing, or being aware of, signals. What the spirit guides do, in those cases, is that they add another shadow, they add other circumstances, making the soul heavier in its human experience in order for the pill, the medicine, to lose effect. What happens then is that the medical establishment

increases the dose. So, the medical establishment increases the dose, the pill, and the spirit guides meet this occasion by giving their soul anther shadow.

D. It just gets progressively harder for the incarnation?

O. Indeed. So, what I would like to say, before I leave, is to carefully choose your words as you address this. Because, in many ways, like I said, people feel like their depression is justified by a doctor or the medical establishment. Even TV commercials, in some way, allows it to be the new normal. And that is what we see as a downfall. It's spiraling within the mental realm, and you are here to enlight the mental realm.

D. What about specific things that they can do? I know religion heaps on a lot of guilt, but are there any practices, like Native American rituals, that they could do?

O. The best to do is to try to be outside. Again, what we see is that a lot of people remain within their houses. It was mentioned a cubic box—this is the same. As long as you only reside within four walls, then you, in some way, allow the shadows and everything to wrap around you. You have to be more mobile. You have to seek the fresh air. You have to seek enlightment and excitement within your being and within your senses. You can never get that sensation just watching a TV show. You have to seek and want improvement. (*The spirits often say enlight or enlightment, instead of enlighten or enlightenment. I do not change their expression, as it seems to have a specific meaning to them.*)

D. Would this be like an inner hobby, as Bob talked about?

O. When we talk about depression, in many ways, those people will benefit from a physical outer hobby, because they are too still. Once they have started the mobility and the excitement of motion, then indeed, we always promote the inner exploration, the inner hobby. There.

D. That's wonderful. That was a very good teaching, thank you. So glad you came today.

O. Wash off the shadows and you will feel more free and less lonely within. Because even if you are, in some way, by medical establishment, justified in your depression, deep inside, the soul suffers, and the soul feels how it doesn't belong. It's a lonely state of mind; it never connects, it separates. (*The soul feels rejected by the mind.*) There. That would be it with that.

D. Thank you so much, Ophelia.

O. Yes, indeed. Farewell.

Elahim Council: Facing Emotions (Nov 24, 2019)

The Elahim Council is always encouraging and supportive of the work we are doing on their behalf. It is noteworthy that they talked about Christine and I being separate satellites for a little while. Three months later, Christine left for Sweden. Within weeks all the borders were closed due to the Corona virus. When this reading was delivered, the Council must have foreseen we would be separated for eight months. Normally, we do not include personal instructions, but in this case, there are some very interesting observations wrapped within the talk. One was about the relationship between astronomical alignments and their effects on the physical Earth and humans. They want me to identify specific dates in history where there were revolutions, droughts, or changes in consciousness. Then Christine was instructed to analyze the astrologic influences and find the patterns in the energy flow. Nearly three years have passed, and we have yet to start the project.

The Elahim Council also instructed us to investigate the cause or root source of certain human emotions. Similar advice has been offered from them before, so it is obviously an important concept. While we are incarnated, we process experiences through the human filter, which causes the energy to transform in ways that lack the purity of the source. They recommend that we recapitulate various experiences in our life from a higher perspective. They say, "You have to see the feeling for what it is, not what it became. The way it became is human; the way it *is*, is source. You transform the true source of feelings, actions, experiences into a human one, and mirror them in a reality where it doesn't fully have the ability to express itself."

EC. Elahim. This is the Elahim council. Greetings.

D. Greetings, my friends.

EC. We are pleased to follow your progress. You are in a phase of rest at the moment, gathering strength for next occupation, next project, next cycle. See your mission as mountains and canyons; you are at the moment in the canyon gathering strength for the next climb. The next climb involves more research on your part. In some ways you will be separated in your mission, yet you are working together, but you will become, even though you are a unit, separate satellites. We encourage research from both of you. She differently, needs to find the source within, diving into the depths of the soul; whereas you find old writings. Go back and find writings from 1700 and back. There are notes by your own hand as well as friends. Look, Europe, writers, Italy, Austria, France, Germany predominantly. Some—Green Isles, UK. But mostly Italy and Austria. Look for discoveries, some your own. Study, research, you do not need to invent the wheel every time. You will go further and further back, passing zero, back in time. Connect points of discoveries, unfolding what was meant as a gift for humanity to know. Don't be discouraged by some who might ridicule the two of you and the work you do. You have the strength inside as well as from all of us. We will push you further, but begin looking 18th century and back.

D. What topics and which authors?

EC. Geometry, physics, astral–physics, connections, star systems correlating to events on Earth. This one will understand due to knowledge of astrology, understanding energetic influences over time. She will help you—when you find a source, you ask her to find and read the star constellations at that time. You find information, she will verify the energetic flow, returning back finding the connections and transits of energy flow correlating to events. That will give you the proof needed for you to feel comfortable in putting it into writing.

D. Are these human events or Earth events?

EC. Earth events.

D. Such as?

EC. Revolutions. Droughts. Change of consciousness. Change of species. Changes, greater cycles. Find in writing, she verifies by giving information about the current energetic flow within your system at that time. Be precise. Doing so will make people more open to the fact of outer influences and the effects they see in front of them. It is a way to open more eyes, if you have proof, if you return to known events correlating to constellations. Correlations in your system.

D. If there were revolutions, would it be considered the day they start, because there is always planning ahead of time?

EC. There is what you call wiggle room that is about six to eight months prior to impact. Look for that, look for events of greater shifts, good and bad. Don't forget to enlighten the events of greater consciousness as well as spiritual enlightenment. Understand the correlations between what occurs and what goes on around you. You are merely a co-player in the system. Meaning what happens here affects your neighbors as well. At this time, certain planets within your system, to give you a human phrase, they are depressed, they feel numb due to events that occurs here. The Sun orchestrates the whole play. Mercury is happy, never gets sad, channels heat and warmth, partner to the Sun. But Jupiter, normally a happy friend of yours, depressed. The influences mean that the energy from Jupiter is not as clean as it's meant to be. There is a shift within your system where your neighbor planets radiate an unfamiliar radiation and energy, not suited to its persona. That means the whole system sings out of tune. The Sun tries to wake everyone to life. There is a great concern about this planet; not just from the spirit realm but your closer planetary friends.

D. Are there particular planets we should focus on?

EC. Jupiter. Different energy, non-recognizable, changed in its core due to the effect mirrored from Earth. Uranus, strong still, not impacted. Focus on Jupiter. Understand the energy of Jupiter and you will see the change in his behavior. This is mirrored by activities on Earth. So, what we wish for you both is to start investigating your neighbors, the flow around you, now versus earlier times. This one (*Christine*) reads Jupiter. You ask, if needed, how the planets were positioned at certain times, allowing you as a scientist to bring forward correlations.

D. Is there any other direct advice you would like to give either one of us?

EC. There is a part of this project that is about solitude. Know that your little brother doesn't always feel comfortable, needs the excitement. In some way, you are similar, of course, inside. But the human conditions are different in each of you. Solitude is your core trait. The human trait though, different. If this one were to find peace in solitude, you will both be the same. Meditate more. There are still some blockages within each of you that needs to be released. In this one, emotional. In your case, anger. Address it and you will be clean. Don't sway away from your shadows, meet them, investigate the source of anger and hurt. This will be the way to remember your mission and the impact of the atmosphere here. Seeing beyond the illusions is a way to tap into the illusion. How will you otherwise know it IS an illusion? What is anger related to? How does it impact the rest of the physical and mental you? It's the same as the star systems. Investigating the source, Jupiter depressed, why? You; anger, why? This one, hurt. Why? What is the impact? In order for you to understand the impact, dive into the source. Allow that source to become you; become anger and see anger for what it is. As you meet anger head-on, you will see the beauty in the power, not the negativity portraying in your human vehicle and experience. Each feeling—fear, love, happiness, anger—each expression, none is good or bad if you undress them, meet them head-on. Undress the feeling and you will see the beauty and the gift that came along with it. Not even anger—as you would consider it to be a negative output from your physical self—in its core it is beauty, it is power. How you channel that power mirrors what you consider negative output to be. Fear, the same. Hurt, dive into the source of hurt and see the potential that lies within the experience. If you avoid it, it will simply be a negative experience. If you dive into it you will see, like a lotus flower, the gift that stretches in eternity within the hurt. You have to see the feeling for what it is, not what it became. The way it became is human; the way it is, is source. You transform the true source of feelings, actions, experiences into a human one, and mirror them in a reality where it doesn't fully have the ability to express itself. Anger is nothing negative if you do not channel it as such; it is strength, it is leadership, it is compassion for those who lack the power. The way you channel it travels through levels on this plane that adds a different story to the source. Everything you see around you is human–made, originates from a source (*that is*) very different. How you meet the source and how you change the output, how you channel the true core of each feeling, event, is a choice, but you have to dive into the source in order for you to know what the source really is. Once you find that, you will see how you, as a human, put on levels, layers, clothes, if you like, on top of this core feeling, changing it to something completely different. As you do, you lose power over it, and it takes the power over you.

D. That's brilliant.

EC. There. Meeting's over.

D. Thank you so much for that.

EC. You are much welcome, my son. We are extremely proud of you for traveling here, tending to the planet, trying to enlight the species, who keeps on dressing each feeling, each event, from a human consciousness. And the human consciousness is behind the veil. Remove veil, that is the job, that is the mission. There.

Ari: Science, Religion, and Ego (Dec 1, 2019)

When Ari or Zachariah lecture on a subject, it often sounds (to me) firm and friendly, but lacks the softer emotional tone that Ophelia transmits. But they all remain detached when discussing human affairs, or even disasters on a gigantic scale, as Ophelia mentioned in an earlier session. From their elevated viewpoint, everything is under control and moving in the direction intended by the Creator and the councils. If souls cycle off the planet in great numbers at specific times, it is nothing to be concerned about.

A. Elahim. This is your uncle. Good morning.

D. Good morning, Ari. I thought you might talk today.

A. Oh, did you? You both need a little bit of a push, need the fire to be ignited again, in some way. You are embarking on new territory, both of you. Meaning you have to also accept to stand naked in your conviction, in your truth. That is where several before you faltered. This is a crucial time, when you bring forward information that some are not eager to hear. Understand that as a race, humanity wish to be left alone in many ways. Due to that, progress, development, change, don't always come easy. When you stand in front of stagnation, it is hard to be a fire, to be convicted of the words you are revealing. Sometimes you will feel perhaps it is too much. Know that the assignment wasn't an easy one, even though up 'til this point it might have appeared such. You are safe always. Now you have to be more public. In that step, this cycle is what we refer to as the public cycle, where you have to be in some way uncomfortable, because you will appear different. Some will feel like you are arrogant. Those who feel so are the scientists not ready for change. The more you deliver the more you stand convicted in your beliefs. You will ignite others alongside those who do not wish change to occur. It might be that you are stepping on toes. As you step on toes, know that in history, those who stepped on toes are remembered—for good or bad. You are here to, not jump on anyone's toes, simply poke them a little bit.

D. What topics are going to be the most controversial?

A. The fact that gravity and things around you are not constant. That energy resources have changed over the millennia, and how you are blindfolded to the resources available; how you are considered less developed than earlier civilizations. The current ones think that they are on the top of the pyramid. When you reveal differently, those who feel on the top of the pyramid, feeling how they are about to be pushed down, they might resist your words. It is ego based. Earlier civilizations, before they fell, worked around the ego, stayed pure in their connection to

Source, whether it was technologically or spiritually. Their source is colored—that is ego. As you rip on egos, they feel like they are withering, dying, and this is where assistance comes. Always understand, when you are challenged, it is due to egos afraid of their dying. You are here to transform egos back to soul connection, and due to the stronghold of egos at this time, this is where the biggest challenge will be. Science is more locked in egos than the religious communities. That is why you will have more of a struggle with those. The academia, good with words, not very good with understanding what they cannot see, what they cannot touch, what they have not yet discovered. Know that several feel like they are on the peak, the top of the pyramid—you are contradicting that statement. In that respect, you will be challenged.

D. It doesn't seem like most scientific people will care much about spiritual, channeled information.

A. You will reveal a lot of the information based on human resources, research from yourself. You will always be challenged by the way information has been revealed to you from both sides, both the religious as well as scientific communities. They fear the connection because of prior spells from civilizations that fell before you. Meaning the way information came earlier, similar like this, was accepted. But as it progressed that more and more were able to access their own computer within, a small group known as the Cell felt that they lacked the control of this link. They put a spell on both those who were scientifically or technologically inclined, as well as those who were seeking a spiritual awareness; saying that it was colored, that they couldn't access this pool of knowledge, that it was only given due to steps that you had to take. This is placed within your memory in different aspects. Steps, all these steps that you as a race feel you have to master in order for you to gain the treasure.

D. Well, isn't it true that there are steps to follow in order to access your soul knowledge?

A. But not as many that is placed before you here. Several who operates as conducting healing, for instance, they place several steps, more than needed, for their pupil to reach the divine. It is true that you have to master your inner steps, but not steps or levels placed upon you from the outside. Hmm. Different. So what we see is again the fear of change, the fear of standing out, the fear of asking questions. Why certain things exist, co–exist, within your reality. Why certain signs appear, such as what you saw yesterday—crop circles. Instead of investigating the mysteries around you, as well as the mystery within you, you shut your eyes. The signs around you are overwhelming, your race doesn't like to be overwhelmed, they feel mostly comfortable in their hut, and now you are forcing them out of the huts, asking them to seek. The question will arise—to seek what? What is it that you provide IF they seek that which is better? This is a struggle, as you have to convince people of the light. You do not need to convince them of the darkness within them or around them. But the light is somewhat fearful. This is an ancient remain, ancient spell, placed upon your consciousness by those who proclaim to master and possess the light. It is easier to welcome disasters than salvation. And again, salvation comes only from within. No one can tell you what you need to do outside to access the divine.

D. It seems like a lot of the scientists are predominantly atheists in their world–view.

A. Yes. Atheism is ego based. Those who don't believe are—to give you a number—if you think of the religious community, they are more inclined of change. As they seek, they constantly seek only in the wrong direction; but they are, on a scale of one to ten, they are open to about seven or eight. Meaning if ego is one, soul ten, they are on seven, some on eight. Scientific community balances on one, two, some to three. You see the difference? It is easier to move consciousness on the religious groups, as they are already closer to that belief. The other ones have a longer journey. So, in that sense, what you say about steps, indeed, the gap will widen between the groups before they merge. They might not at all merge in your lifetime—nothing of your concern. You are here to try to move these groups closer to the ten, but as you can see, there are different paths for them ahead. But you are, in your design as humans this time, prepared to meet the two groups. Just try to stay calm; teach your little brother to stay calm, don't act out, or roll his eyes. There.

D. Excellent talk. Thank you, Ari.

Ophelia: The Two You's (Dec 25, 2019)

Ophelia urges us to seek the self that lies within. Once it is found, it will lift the mind above the maze of delusions that are cast over society by the Cell and those who seek control over humanity. These groups set mental traps that are intended to lead people away from their inner awareness. Deception and fear are the main weapons, and they are embedded within all societal control mechanisms. But they also use anger, greed, and self-interests to divide people and herd them into separate camps. When the soul is disconnected from the mental reality, it creates a vacuum that is susceptible to outer influences. When someone feels an emptiness and believes that life lacks meaning, it is a direct result of not recognizing the greater self that is always present and available.

When Ophelia came in, on this Christmas Day, she talked non-stop for 15 minutes. To make it easier to read, I inserted a few paragraph breaks. So please notice that Ophelia is the designated speaker for the next two pages. It is an absolutely beautiful teaching, and I have listened to it several times to make sure I had all the words captured correctly. When you read it, imagine it being spoken with all the warmth and gentleness of an angel, which Ophelia is, and you will have a sense of how it was communicated.

O. This is Ophelia. Good morning to you.

D. Good morning. It's a pleasure to hear you.

O. It's always a pleasure to be part of this sacred circle, where we are connecting the higher realms to the Earth realm. We are happy to provide more information for humanity, as we see a dip in courage, a dip in belief, a dip in prosperity within the consciousness. It tends to go in cycles, and during high holidays, peaks, normally rises or falls. This cycle we see a dip in the human wellbeing with oneself as well as with others. You have to remember that your primary focus should always be to find the wellbeing with yourself. As you do, it is easier to acknowledge someone else's faults and how you can assist that individual and on what level. As we see now, this year coming to a close, it has been a mental turmoil for many. What we see here at the end of the cycle is in some way emotionally paralyzed behavior, feeling temporarily captured between what to think and what the inner self believes.

O. What we wish to convey is the prosperity that lies before you. Nothing can bloom without a seed. Several individuals on the earth plane are planting seeds, such as yourself. You are planting seeds for future generations. Some of these efforts will not come into your conscious awareness as the human you are at this time. Know that some of the efforts that you are indeed planting at this time will be encountered as you return into a future body. I'm not talking about the two of you, I'm talking in general. It is important for the elderly not to feel left behind, just because their physical life runs to a close. It is important that you convey to them that they are planting seeds for future incarnations as well as future generations. What do they wish to leave as a treat for themselves? Just because the physical runs to a close, it doesn't mean the soul does. The soul is eternal and will return and rejoice at the efforts that you have (*it has*) done. You do not want the elderly to feel like they have not the ability to contribute. What they can contribute with is silently manifesting what they wish to return to. Even if they feel like they will not, in current time, rejoice with the efforts made, make them believe that the future is there to create. We see several (*a lot of the*) elderly suffering in solitude that they do not seek. Loneliness can wear on the physical, mental, and emotional state, and that is quite obvious around the peak of holiday seasons. This year comes to a close with mental turmoil, where mankind suffers from a few orchestrating the world's developments. It paralyzes man as a group, and it separates you; and that is the end result that the Cell is looking for—separation. On a soul level, there are no separation. You are always connected, either with your group of friends, or the Creator itself. Separation begins once you incarnate and have to seek the companionship with others. If you live or are in a situation where there are not many family or friends, seek the companionship and support from your soul. Even if you do not believe in the soul being eternal and returning over and over again, imagine the silent helper within you.

O. We do not wish humanity to suffer. Unnecessary suffering is what the Cell induces by separation from Source. What they proclaim is separation from human source. We aim to enlighten and ignite the light within, the source within. And even if you do not believe in the afterlife, you tend to believe in yourself—but who are you? Who is the human you? Who is the silent you that you do not tell, perhaps not even your closest friends, about? That is the soul silently observing the human you. If you do not believe in the afterlife and a soul, you tend to believe your inner feelings and thoughts. If you investigate those feelings and thoughts, you might see that they contradict what you as a human do, say, act, feel. Recognize the two, the inner one that you might not portray to friends, coworkers, or such. That is the soul. And the soul might be very different than the human. Once you start to recognize and identify that there might be two "you", it's easier, even for those who never believe in the afterlife, to shift their consciousness to one or the other of these two. If they follow the human self, they fool themselves. And of course, that is part of the development. When souls come down to Earth, they follow the human tribe, the way the humans act, say, believe, and it might contradict the inner self. Once you start to detect that there are two ways that you act or feel, that there are two parts of you, then indeed your soul grows, your soul has made itself known. SO, that is the advice that we wish to give to humanity at this point, that even if you do not believe in soul, spirit, Creator, you tend to believe (*your ideas*) about who you are. Once you start to investigate, you might find that your actions contradict the way you would like to act, the way you would like to talk to people. We see in communication that you are taught to convey to the masses, being a leader, in a way that is dynamic. The greatest leaders that you have witnessed on this plane never talked. They just radiated their wisdom and their love. And those close to those individuals felt the communication, not just as humans, but as soul companions here, trying to do their best in a human experience. So, in many ways, what media and social interactions teach (*about*) the way humanity should convey and communicate contradicts the way a soul would like to communicate to their companions. Not the one with the loudest voice, the most dynamic personality, the most beautiful appearance, has the most to say. Talk to your surrounding (*those around you*) the way you would like them to talk to you; that is soul communication. So, there we go.

D. Wow, that was really beautiful.

O. Oh, you are much welcome. Nothing magic, really, just simple A–B–C, one would say. But it tends to be important to, once in a while, remind you, the human race, that you are not alone, feeling how life runs away from you, and you have in your power (*the ability*) to take it back. Even if you are among the elderly, know that you are planting seeds little by little. You do not need to leave behind a full field of flowers; perhaps you only leave one rose; it does not matter. The efforts that we see you put in to assisting, not only the current civilization but future generations, will determine what you will come back to. Always know that the majority on Earth will return in future lives, so what do you wish to return to? What flower do you want to stumble upon? And again, don't make it too big for yourself, you don't have to plant a field of roses. One big rose can be more majestic than a field of little ones. So, if there is nothing you want to ask me, I step aside. There you go

D. That was a really beautiful teaching, Ophelia. Thank you so much.

O. Oh, you are much welcome. I will talk to you soon. Bye bye.

Ophelia: Soulmates (Jan 30, 2020)
The concept of soulmates has been around for at least 2300 years, but the definition is often ambiguous and romanticized to reflect only a small part of its true meaning. Many erroneous ideas about the nature of the soul, soul groups, and the purpose of incarnation have only added to the confusion. The notion that a person is wandering around looking for the other half of its soul is perhaps the biggest distortion, but is also the oldest, having been introduced by Plato as the "split–apart" theory. Souls do indeed have the capacity to separate and send parts of its awareness into different realities, but a core portion remains at home in the spiritual dimensions. More advanced souls can occasionally have two incarnations that overlap within the Earth's timeline, which are known as parallel lives. However, those bodies are unlikely to ever meet. So, the split-apart theory is a non-starter, based on everything the spirits have said. The reality is that our time would be better spent searching inside for a connection to our own soul than to someone else's. However, when it comes to companions on Earth, Ophelia gives a very clear description of the process.

Not all humans are destined to find a perfect companion when it comes to pair bonding. In fact, many relationships are initiated by the soul to address certain elements within their Coat of Karma. Instead of being romantically perfect, they often become like sand in an oyster, an irritant. The question of whether that irritant produces a pearl is determined by the individual. And it is also true that some souls come down (into a life) with the intention to not have any romantically rewarding relationships. Independence and self–reliance can be a catalyst for significant soul growth. Therefore, it is unwise to evaluate anyone, or yourself, based on the cultural norms of pair bonding.

After Ophelia gave her talk on how soulmates help each other to grow, Bob came in and followed up on the topic in his own special way. He pulled examples from three of my past lives and went into quite a bit of detail about the one identified as John 54. I seem to pick the name John over and over, so he simply numbers the lifetime sequentially. John 11 was in Morocco around 330 AD, John 32 was in the Catholic army around 1380, and John 54 was in an Irish harbor town with Josephine in the 1700s. John 54 was injured in an accident at sea and had to stay on land, which was part of the soul agreement with Josephine. He became a map maker and was a loner, but Bob eventually got him to go to the tavern where he met her and became her protector.

Bob also mentions Charles Mustard, which was another of my lifetimes in France during the Renaissance. He was a traveling musician who took the name of Charles Dijon, but we jokingly refer to him as Charles Mustard. He made a living as an entertainer of the wealthy, but his soul mission was to evaluate the minds of the aristocrats. Charles would tell elaborate falsehoods to the socialite ladies, who never questioned the absurdity of what he said. The story is told in full in *Wave 2*.

D. Hello, Ophelia.
O. Hello to you. Doing a little adjustment. I would like to discuss the dynamic in group behavior, which is a constant concern for the spiritual realities and councils. The Earth councils are highly involved and are, in many ways, designing events to make outcomes in order for them, as well as others, to detect in which direction humanity is heading. In order for a joint community (*to exist*) on this plane, several egos, several human behaviors, have to be dissolved. It is crucial that one look into the needs that one truly possess, and (*compare those to*) the needs manufactured by the surrounding people, communities, media, and so forth. The needs are highly connected to the mind. One might feel that it is an emotional need, and what we see is a high, or increasing, need for partnerships. It is not always beneficial for those who refer to one soulmate, as it appears to be like finding a needle in a haystack. Many times, you come here without your closest companion, especially when you have traveled here more than ten to twenty–five times. Some travel closer, not only closer with companions, but also closer over the timeline. It is not always helpful for your race to think or operate from the idea that you have one soulmate only, that a specific soulmate will fulfill you—that might not be the case. The true soulmate might come in disguise and might not be the one that fulfills your needs, fulfills your path. It can actually be the one setting out boundaries or challenges on your path, instead of deleting them. That is a true companion; that is the one who triggers events, who stage your life in order for you to become the highest potential as a human. As a human, one tends to believe that a soulmate is a true love—from a human standpoint. But if one tries to focus on the true love connection from a soul level—which is quite different than

from a human standpoint—the love that a soul seeks is growth. The love that humans seek are romances. It is different, a different need from a soul perspective than from a human. If humans need partnerships to grow, then they are both mentally and emotionally in a maze. If they seek growth, meaning self-empowerment and self-love, they will see the one challenging them throughout life or shortly (*briefly*) are the ones that provide the biggest love, because they aim for you to love yourself. A human can hold another human, providing physical warmth, but man should seek not only one but the groups that provide the inner warmth. The inner warmth can come in disguise. It might not come as a love companion; it potentially can come as someone who pushes your limits, making you aware of your weaknesses. The true companion, after a soul has progressed for a while, tends to poke its friend, pushing that friend into an abyss, either emotionally or mentally. It is from the highest source of love and it's done with compassion for the growth. After events on a human level have taken place, the soul and spiritual friends—some incarnated, some not—will always assist the climb from the abyss. But from a human standpoint, if someone is pushing you into an emotional abyss, let's say, it is hard for a human to see that as an act of compassion, as an act from a true soul friend. You have to separate the human experience versus where the biggest growth lies. Within the groups we see the same—some operating in blind. They are triggered from outside influences in order for them to take a stand as a human. Normally, in group dynamics, when there is a leader that might be, in many ways, in disguise as a mole, it is there, this individual, to push the other ones into an abyss of submission. As they do, it is also considered an abyss. Submission is being passive, which is the same (*as an emotional abyss*). From the spiritual reality, there is no difference. Be aware that as growth takes place, it is also a time where man will feel pushed into various abysses in order for them to feel the power (*find their inner strength*). And the power can come in many different ways, but it is a way for you to climb and to rise and to seek that light. Similar as your solar system in that canyon, in many ways, you are operating similar. You cannot have a system, such as your solar system and planet, in the canyon seeking the light, and you, as a species, being quite far ahead in your awareness. It rolls hand-in-hand and it is a similar dance between your system, your planet, as well as your consciousness.

D. Are you saying that humans are in a ditch because the solar system is in a trough?

O. Yes, yes, indeed. So together, you have a climb in front of you. Different, but yet it is a joint dance between the system and the race occupying the system. So, what we wish for you to understand is the need to take a stand and to find that abyss within you. Find and seek what it is that makes you lacking strength, lacking power. In whatever field you feel powerless, that is YOUR unique abyss—in a human form, that is. Some have to rise above the limits, like we mentioned about partnerships. Partnerships might not be the contract, the agreement for you to come this time around; then you need to find a different light, a different happiness as a human. (*Some people aren't meant to have a partner. Their goals are to work on some other aspect of their Coat.*)

D. That was really brilliant, Ophelia.

O. Oh, you are much welcome.

D. A lot of people who go to church still feel an emptiness. Do you have any advice for them?

O. Yes. That's a spiritual abyss. They are, in some way, aware of the light within them, but they feel they have to be in a union with others or in a specific settlement in order for that light to shine. They feel like someone, either a priest or a preacher, is the only one able to ignite that light. Or they feel, perhaps, they need the group to become a joined light. No one can ignite your light if you are not willing to find the darkness first within you. The darkness indicates the abyss. That is, spiritual growth that will mirror a human growth. Once you understand that in the dark you find your own match, so to speak, to light that candle, then indeed you can share that light with others. That light is different for each and every one of you, and it might not be found in a church. It might be, for instance, in a hospital environment. There are several who operates from the seventh dimension in the realm and reality of care—hospitals, nurseries (*nursing homes*) caring for the elderly. The elderly who, in many ways, have a fear within them. A fear because they never found that light during their lifetime. So there is a need to tend to your elderly, as they might feel lost, feel fooled by life. But it is never too late to ignite that light, and there are several at this time occupying facilities of the elderly. From the Master Mind it is known and it (*the light*) is sent through animals. Some facilities use animals to ignite that light; they (*the animals*) don't demand anything else than your presence and your interest in them. They have no demands on you as a human. It would help in therapy to use animals in more facilities (*such as*) hospitals, nurseries, even within police departments, not only for children as a comfort, but an animal radiates nothing else than it wants you to open up. In the presence of an animal, such as a dog, it is hard to remain closed in your soul particle. The silence and the companionship that you share when you simply sit in the presence of this dog or another animal provides the highest level of comfort. So what we see is that more facilities are aware of the benefit of the presence and therapy using animals. However, it is not only for the elderly or for children; there is a huge gap between these two, a bridge where animals could connect souls, calm disease and emotional stress.

D. That's a beautiful teaching, Ophelia. Thank you.

O. There. I feel like someone is highly present. Maybe I should tease him a little bit and just ramble on. Huh hmm hmm.

D. (*Laughing.*) I'm glad you got a chance to talk, Ophelia.

O. Always a pleasure. Okay. Bye.

B. (*Bob came in singing the national anthem from the defunct Soviet empire, which he heard during a lifetime where I was a scientist in that country.*)

D. That is kind of a rousing song.

B. You become quite activated, in some way. You feel like there must be a purpose somewhere and you are eager to find that purpose. It's a kind of song that makes you get going.

D. Uplifting towards the wrong purpose.

B. Ah, we don't know. Sometimes it's just a need really, to have something that activates you, and from that point you have your choices, of course. How do you want to proceed with this activity that you feel within you, or that drive that suddenly appears out of nowhere? You have to, in some way, start moving. In general, what we see is a bit of laziness and to not really want to engage in the play that you all actually signed up for. And that makes us a little bit concerned. You came here to fulfill something for yourself or someone else, and now you're just sulking in a corner and don't want to participate. You play the game—you have to participate. It's not always about winning and losing. The loser is more those who don't participate than those who feel perhaps they lose something materialistic or something like that. But I say, if you do not participate, that is considered worse than if you glide into a ditch, briefly, and feel like, "Oh, I lost the grip under my feet and the grip, in general, in life." But from that point, you have a choice. But those who don't participate, they just stand there. It's like those say, "Oh, I don't want to dive into the ocean because I don't know how to swim, and it's probably really cold. Ohhh." And they actually know how to swim because they took lessons as a child. So it's the same thing. The thing is, if you do not engage in the life that you have been given—a fact, simply a fact—is that you will come back and have a do-over. So if one knew, "Oh, I'm just gonna have to do this all over again!", that might put some action in them. I might wanna just come and sing that song so they get going.

D. I have a question. Since a lot of people now live a pretty comfortable life, does the lack of anxiety about where their food is going to come from, or where they are going to sleep, does that make them more indifferent to spiritual concepts?

B. Ah. It can be, because you become too relaxed in your comfort zone. It's nothing bad to have a comfortable life and comforts and to not struggle, BUT if you are too set and feel like, "I'm just gonna not grow at all, I'm gonna do exactly this until I die," then that is indicating stagnation. It might be that if you are too set in your ways, then it indicates there is no growth. It indicates you are not fully participating in the game, because you might have signed up for something else. So if you have a life, and it might be one of those we call a bonus life, where you might simply be here to provide lessons or comforts for someone else, but there is still something within you that you have to address that is personal. No life is 100 percent for someone else, even if it is a bonus life, even if it's just 2 percent that is personal development, you have to find that. And I can tell you that those who have everything served for them, you know, food, money, house, all these materialist human comforts, eventually they will find a void, and that void is those 2 percent. And in that void exists something of an understanding, but they have to seek that void. In that void, it could be all sorts of insights that might delete or eliminate some of your paralyzed behavior as a human. So you have to, in some way, seek either a void, or seek something that is not obvious or visible for your human eyes. And many don't know to even look for something that is not visible for the human eyes, and that is a problem and that is why you need us. We are here to tell you, "First you believe, then we show you." If you believe to find a presence in nature and you really want to understand the dynamic and the design behind the environment, nature, waters, animal life, and so forth, and your place within that design, then indeed, you have to shut your human eyes in order for your inner eyes to be activated.

D. That's a really good teaching, so thank you for that. If someone doesn't want to interact with other people, can they just study and learn and gain knowledge, like a star?

B. Indeed. Look at you—you don't engage, barely, unless you have someone like Josephine. But even when she was down, I had to push you. I knew that Josephine was there, I knew there was someone you were gonna like, but you were so stubborn in your human coat, in your human outfit, that I couldn't really make myself heard in that department. Zachariah was very present and gave you all sorts of ideas, because he was showing you how to draw maps and giving you very advanced, along with Jeshua, information on how to create routes for ships, and so forth. You really wanted, as John 54, to be at sea, to go out on the ship. And you wanted to use your maps and navigation skills. However, that was not in the stars, so to speak, because you were supposed to assist Josephine and you were supposed to be on land. So, your void was in not being able to go to sea, because your human self strived to go to sea with the other ones. But the void was that you had to accept the fact that you could not go to sea—and there were different reasons for that. But it became a void when you felt that you could not leave the harbor life and set off with the other ones. It was all by design, that life, but it made you feel trapped. And I wanted to show you that, yes indeed the void indicated that you were trapped on land, BUT you had signed up to be helpful with Josephine. And together you created a strong friendship bond, and she taught you in ways that, little-by-little, as a human, you opened up. You were trying to escape the vulnerability as a human, and you tried to escape by going to sea. But Jeshua put a stop to that because you were not there to go to sea. If you had done so, you would have just fled away from the true intention, and that was to understand the dynamic when one feels emotionally paralyzed—which you did. You had a sister that died early, young, and from that point you didn't want to feel anything, so you wanted to go to sea. And I knew that was just to close your heart down, so to speak. But in that void, in that longing for your sister who passed early—which was also one from the seventh—you felt completely abandoned. You were not a child when that happened, but she was younger than you.

You were like 13 and she was about 10 or something, and both of you were orphans. But she disappeared and that made you feel emotionally disabled and paralyzed, and you just wanted to run away from that feeling by going to sea. But Jeshua put a stop to that! I knew that Josephine would be there to heal that void. But you were so stubborn, so it took a long time for you to even go and find Josephine. But when you did, she filled that void from your sister and you became very gentle. The other ones (*the men who came into the tavern where Josephine worked*) were a little bit afraid, they didn't want to anger you. You were quite large as a humanoid and you appeared a little bit gruff. You had an edge and as soon as someone said something (*unkind to Josephine*), you kinda attacked. I mean, you didn't hit anyone, but you were very present, in that sense. You might think that this one (*Seth*) would have taken that life, but you actually wanted to see how being paralyzed emotionally affects the human journey and how it affects (*causes someone*) to not participate in the game. You have done this before. Even back when you were here with this one, when you lost the child, that was also the same lesson. (*Seth and Lasaray had a life as a couple in Scotland where we lost our only daughter.*) It was to see how one can repair when one encounters emotional distress that leaves the human feeling paralyzed. And when you are paralyzed either by loss, or it doesn't have to be that powerful of an event, but it can still have the same effect that you sort of become paralyzed. And when you are paralyzed, you do not participate in the game. But Josephine, she came in and she was like what Ophelia said about an animal that is just present, so she helped you. She knitted things for you, and what you really liked was when she read out loud for you, so she did that. The two of you became really good friends and Josephine didn't have anywhere to live, but you did, so she was invited to live with you. And because you were much older, so she was there to your end. And the thing that you really liked was when she read out loud to you.

D. That was really nice. Josephine is a friend.

B. Josephine is a friend.

D. So I have two questions, then. This is a lesson that I wanted, but apparently my Coat was already folded?

B. But you investigate things. It was the same thing with Charles Mustard. You might think, "Oh, that must be a brand-new soul coming down in that vain life," but you were there to investigate dynamics. You were there to investigate how one can be paralyzed—again, it's all about being paralyzed—how can one become paralyzed by bling and by illusions. So, in many ways, you investigate human behaviors and how it can paralyze the human, making the soul not heard.

D. What do I do with that information?

B. Oh, you report. In many ways, you report to Earth councils. Because they are the ones that are in contact with those who make the suits, those who make the Coats. So someone has to know what sort of Coat is out of fashion and what should be the new fashion coming in! Huhuh. Someone has to report the general dynamic of your species. You're not the only one, but you have a great interest in what makes, in a human experience, what makes that person paralyzed, and you look into different scenarios. You know, like Charles Mustard looked into vanity, and how one can be so caught up in illusions that one not even question (*anything they are told*). And in general, that is what we see a lot. We don't have the same scene, but in many ways, media feeds humanity and your species different ideas and different news, and then the different councils, especially the Earth councils who are in charge of new events on this plane, they look into how receptive you are to illusions. And unfortunately, what we see is that there is a huge percentage, a big number, that just don't care and seem to be easy to influence. BUT then also remember, if they are easily fooled, easily influenced by the wrong side, so to speak, then they are also very receptive if something else comes in that looks a little bit better.

D. (*Laughing.*) That's a good point! My second question was that if people feel a void and an emptiness, is that, in some manner, connected to one of their goals or purposes when they came down?

B. There's always a void; every journey that you have, there is a void in your journey that has to be addressed. It can be one void or it can be several, depending on how you want to accelerate your growth and how you want to move along. And you might also be on a mission, Ophelia says, (*as he looks left towards her*) to create voids for someone else; and most times that is done by those who have Coats folded. And they are actually, those who are putting voids in other people, they are actually, from the highest level, a friend.

D. Can you give me an example of a void someone would put on somebody else?

B. Ah. Like, for instance, those who are orphaned, who have parents who either disappeared in accidents early, or those who have parents who suffered from different problems, like alcoholism and so forth, or other medicines, so they are not present for a child. That creates an early void. A later void can indicate, for instance, that someone—it can be as plain as this—it could be someone in your workplace who takes your idea, who listens to your idea on something that will indicate a promotion, for instance, and then takes that idea and promotes it as their own idea. That is a void because that makes the person, who trusted this person, to just sort of fall down in a ditch. And it's an awful ditch because that person struggles with confidence and struggles with trust. It doesn't have to be, "Ohh!", all sorts of drama all the time. It can be just a little thing, like you found a new way to create progress in your financial department at work and you were gonna give this idea in the next meeting, and someone came and took it and promoted it before the meeting. So when you came in you heard your own idea from someone else and everyone applauded this other person. That person could have actually been your best friend on a soul level, helping you to face and empower yourself when you fall into the ditch of lack of confidence and lack of trust. So that ditch would indicate that you have to learn how to trust again and then different scenarios take place so that you have the opportunity to heal and to climb out from that abyss, from that void.

D. That's an excellent example!

B. Ah. Sometimes it's little things like that. It could also be like if that void is placed in your path, let's say, when you're a teenager, and you are in your soccer team. And someone is constantly putting themselves as a better option for a position in the front—because everyone wants to be in the front because the front is the one that makes goals—and you are pushed to be a defender. You might feel like you have really good skills but that person might just overthrow you, in some way, making you not fully shine and making you settle to be a defender, when you are actually fully equipped to shine in the front line. That could also happen. So some voids, some ditches where you have to crawl up from, are kinda small. Even those activities when somebody bullies you, that is also considered one of those ditches, because it has the same end result as the one who snatched your idea. It is to have lack of confidence, lack of trust, and to feel less worthy. So that is a ditch. And if you don't address that ditch, let's say it happens when you are ten years old, then that ditch will linger on and someone else will come in and do the same digging in your ditch when you are, let's say, 35 but in a different setting, because you have not healed and worked on your first experience, your first ditch. Then that will become a crater. Then you might feel like, "Oh, this is just too overwhelming to climb up." And it might look like that when you look down like, "Oh, it's way down there, there you are, and you have to climb up." But you always have assistance. It might start out as a small abyss, a small ditch, but if it's not looked at—and it doesn't have to be that you have to grow out of it, or to rise above. Sometimes that is the case, but sometimes it's also to understand that, "Huh, someone just dug a hole for me. I'm not going to sit in the hole." It doesn't have to be a big deal about it, but just to acknowledge that, "this is not a good place for me to be, but at the moment I'm doing my best." It can also be that you just sort of forgive that person that created or dug the hole where you fell down in. That will, by itself, fill in the hole—but not all the time. It depends on how you designed your path with holes. Some are like those big ones that just suck you in, where the ground just disappears. But when the ditch is like that, then there are angels, light beings that muffles the fall. If there are those holes that just eat you, if that is the experience (*you planned*), then those holes, those experiences, are supervised by light beings—and not just one, it's like a circle around the soul. When you have a little ditch, like where someone just pushed you aside to become a defender, instead of being in center line, then you can't expect to have light beings. You kinda have to figure that one out. So, that's what I wanted to come and say today.

D. That's really brilliant. That was a good talk.

B. And I oppose the fact that I am a guest. (*Earlier in the day, I phoned Christine to find out if she still wanted to do a session, telling her, "We were expecting guests." She immediately heard Bob telepathically say, "I'm not a guest!" He is always listening to what I say and think.*)

D. You're not a guest! I said that to her so she would hurry home.

B. Ah. Because I feel like I'm in the center stage, I'm quite the leading actor in many ways. So a guest indicates you are one of those in the background that can be exchanged.

D. I certainly didn't mean that!

B. Like a hotel guest that just comes and no one really remembers that guest because a new one comes in. So I don't want to be perceived as someone who just checks in to a hotel and then is gone. I'm like a regular.

D. You're like one of our brothers. Family.

B. Smaller but still valuable, and still I belong.

D. I didn't mean to imply that.

B. Nay. Then I can say that YOU'RE a guest. Huh huh. It's just that I feel very called to share my opinion—and Ophelia is aware of that.

D. You are the most precious family member we have.

B. Ah. Umm. Umm. I think so. I think I provide and share, because a lot of times I'm sharing what you tell me to share, and if I went away then who's gonna share your ideas? Who's gonna share your journals? Then you have to find out yourself.

D. You're not supposed to leave.

B. No, I'm not supposed to leave. So, huhuhuhuh. Anyway, I'll go now.

D Alright, my friend. I really appreciate the knowledge you shared today.

B. Ah. It's important that people understand that a little ditch you are supposed to shovel your own way out of, pile yourself up, so to speak (*fill in the hole yourself*). But the bigger events that take place, that might be a bigger collapse in your human experience, those are always supervised and overseen by a circle, not just one, but a circle of light beings to muffle the fall.

D. People will be happy to hear that. Just have a little faith.

B. Ah. And to understand that you have a shovel. You can fill that hole, that void, you can fill that and you have the ability to climb up—you have all sorts of tools. Sometimes it is meant that you have the shovel to fill that hole, and sometimes you think of, "Okay, I need these things—". Like when you fall through the ice on a lake, how do you get up? You have those little sticks and you have to crawl up. You might feel like, "Oh, this is so cold. I'm paralyzed." No, you're not. You always have tools; you just have to find THE tools for that specific experience or that specific ditch. Sometimes all that is needed is that you just look up, then you will feel like, "Oh, I can actually crawl out of this one. This wasn't that bad." But man tends to be paralyzed by events that would indicate a void or a ditch. But when one feels like an emptiness within, that is a void that is more internal and might need to be filled with either what we talked about before, like an inner hobby, or just the fact of what exists in that emptiness inside you. Because it's not a void, it is a colorful experience that awaits you if you look into that emptiness. Because it's a human emptiness, not a soul emptiness. A human emptiness always indicates, or most of the times, indicates a very colorful spiritual experience.

D. You're incredibly intelligent.

B. I am indeed. That's what I'm saying—you don't want to lose me! HUH HUHUHUH! Oh, Ophelia, she laughs. (*He looked left, towards her.*) She says I'm becoming a little bit confident in my presence here. But I feel I deserve to BE confident because there is so many ways where I feel happy about the progress that we are doing and I'm ready to take off in all sorts of directions if it's allowed. Ophelia, she has the greater plan, and I ask her sometimes, "What is the grand idea and the grand plan, overall?" And she laughs and says, "Oh, look over here, Bob. Look over here."

D. If she tells you, you can tell me.

B. Well, that's the thing, I think she feels that I might say.

D. There must be some little hint you can give us, or she can give us.

B. She smiles at the moment. That's not a hint. The only hint is that it's positive. If she were to turn away or cry, it would be like, "Ohh, what sort of ditch is coming now?" But she smiles, so that's a hint for you.

D. We'll just have to be patient. In the meantime, we can treasure and enjoy your company.

B. Ah. I'll go now because Ophelia says we have somewhere to go. There's some journaling to attend to. Because after all our meetings, we actually take notes on how it went and what we delivered, and we put that in a grand journaling. It's energetic, but it becomes like a book, in some way. It's journaling and after all sessions we go through what we have covered and we have that in a general library and then councils look at this. They can take certain bits and pieces out and look into how that was delivered. Then if there is something they want to add, that's when we return to a topic.

D. When I was driving home, I was thinking how you have changed the way you deliver information. You now give complete stories, knowing that we're going to put it in a book pretty much the way you say it.

B. Ah. And a lot of my statements were evaluated by not only my council, it appeared—which I did not know—but also from Ophelia's friends. They looked into certain things and they wanted a cohesive story that followed in a certain context and a certain flow and in a certain human timeline, because they are fully aware that you are so hooked up on the timeline and events following another event, like building a cake. So one step at a time. So, in many ways, when we deliver things it can come in little bit here and there, but then they look at that and want us to maybe go back and fill up more information about a topic. So, there is a council that oversees this. And Ophelia, after each session, communicates with groups, and they discuss what to deliver. So, that's what she later on delivers to the ones who are gonna be the person speaking. It's very high tech.

D. It's very humbling to be part of this.

B. Ah. That too. When I say high tech, I mean there are so many levels that you are not aware of, and that I'm not aware of because I'm not going. But Ophelia communicates with several others that have an input. They're never gonna talk, she say, so there's no need for me to ask about them because I'm never gonna meet them, she say. But I feel like, "Who are they? Where do they belong? And what input do they have about me? Do they think that I'm doing well?" And she laughs and says, "Yes, they think that you are doing really well." They say that my persona is very attractive for a human mind. Huhuh, that's what they say! And I swim in the puddle of encouragement and a little flattery. I like flattery, I tend to like that, and Ophelia knows that, so she sometimes gives me a little treat. She said this and this council or a friend of hers really enjoyed one of my speeches—and I feel flattered. Then she said, "What they would like for you to do is maybe add a little bit more about this topic. What do you think about that?" So I feel like I'm involved even though I'm actually fooled and I'm NOT involved.

D. Your talk today, I'm sure, will get high marks.

B. Ah. High ratings on me. Huhuhuh. Ophelia always gets high ratings, but I don't compete. It's not a competition. So I'm gonna go now, we have journaling to do, to fill out forms. But it's not forms like you do here in human ways, because that's boring. I actually like to journal and to fill out the forms, so to speak, after our sessions because I know there is someone looking at that.

And then sometimes Ophelia oversees and overlooks my journaling, and she says, "Oh, maybe we can modify this a little bit because this wasn't really how it was delivered, was it?" So sometimes I forget—but she never forgets. If my mental capacity, my spiritual brain, if I had a spiritual brain, which I kinda do, of course, was the size of an orange, then her spiritual brain is like one of those big melons, a watermelon; an American watermelon, not a European one, because they're like a large grapefruit. Okay, so I'll go again, so farewell.

D. Well thank you, and thank Ophelia. It was a real pleasure today, my friend.

B. Okay. Doot–dah–dah–dooo, I'll step aside. Bye bye. I go. It just feels like it's always short. Ophelia says it's not short, but I kinda feel like we missed something. Ophelia says that's why we journal, so if we miss something, we just take it up next time, so it's important that we journal truthfully, she say. Not just what I thought I was gonna say or what I intended to say, because if I didn't say it then it's not active in the journaling. I have to somewhat reflect again—that reflection, you never get away from that, it's always part of the activities. So, I go again. I am on my way. But journaling is not always that fun either, even though I enjoy it. Maybe I can have an assistant that records for me? Ophelia says I'm lazy.

D. Maybe put Tom to work.

B. Ophelia says not everything is for his ears yet. So I don't have an assistant, I have to do this by myself, it's part of my training as well.

D. Following in Ole's footsteps.

B. Okay, okay, I take off then. Bye bye.

Ari: Evaluating the Cell (Feb 1, 2020)

At the time of this writing, the activities of the Cell appear to be focused on creating as much fear as possible in the public, with their main intention being a consolidation of power and control over the sovereign nations through the financial destruction of the capital markets. Every war and economic calamity in the past century was pre-planned and managed by a cabal of men who sit at the top of the fiat currency empires in London, Frankfurt, and New York. The global despotism unleashed in 2020 is only one of many coordinated manipulations of public perception executed by the Cell. This was followed by the NATO incited war in Ukraine. The banking cartel (led by IMF and World Bank) makes vast fortunes by loaning "money" to both sides of a conflict. Then, after cities and infrastructure are bombed and destroyed, they loan more fiat currency to rebuild. The process goes on continuously, year after year, since the governments do the bidding of the Cell. What the citizens of any nation want is of no significance to the rulers.

When any of the spirits refer to a mole, it should be understood as a spirit who has taken on a mission to be born into or join a group that the councils want to investigate or influence. A mole, for example, may be sent in to initiate changes in the behavior of a group or organization. Those entities are more advanced and will bring in a lot of soul energy, in order to steer the group in a more spiritual direction. At other times, councils may send someone to collect data within governments, religious organizations, boardrooms, and other places where troublesome group behavior has been observed. In those instances, moles are guided into positions where they act as passive microphones, collecting data about the future intentions of the group. It is reported back directly from the soul particle, often during sleep, although the mole is not likely to have any conscious knowledge of his role.

Ari also tells us the Cell is behind the effort to blanket the Earth with electromagnetic (microwave) radiation fields. There are several reasons for this, the most obvious being that a global dictatorship can only be achieved by monitoring people for compliance. Like the communists do in China, mass surveillance equipment will be used to track everyone's movements. If that isn't bad enough, the other reasons are even more nefarious. Once the 5th Generation (5G) systems and transmitters are in place, higher frequencies and greater energies will be used in 6G and 7G to transmit data, and those microwaves will adversely affect all lifeforms. The 4G systems used sub 6 gigahertz (GHz) frequency, which has peak-to-peak wave lengths of 60 to 100 mm. The 5G bands in the US operate between 24 and 100 GHz, meaning the wavelength is an order of magnitude smaller, at 5 to 10 mm. The promoters of 5G claim that the millimeter waves (MMW) only penetrate 1 to 2 mm into the epidermis and are completely harmless. That is a patently false belief. The scientific literature is replete with studies proving how dangerous the cellular and EMF fields are to living creatures, including humans. The 5G cellphone radiation is a pulsed signal, and the high energy pulse penetrates deeply into the brain and other organs. As it does, it unwinds DNA and creates free radicals. EMF radiation has both an electrical component and a magnetic component, which propagates in air with a fixed relationship between the electric field and the magnetic field. When the radiation penetrates a human, or any biological entity, the electric fields are more susceptible to absorption near the skin. The magnetic fields, however, can penetrate deeply into the body. EMFs have a major effect on neurological functioning and create biochemical stress within the DNA. It is a complicated subject, but know that swimming in an ocean of EMFs is not beneficial, in any way, to the body or mind.

A. This is Ari.

D. Hello, my friend.

A. How are you?

D. Well, thank you. It's nice to hear from you again. You've been quiet.

A. Huh. Quiet for your human ears. We occupy a lot of time with the Council of Nine, to make sure that you start to remember within. It is to ignite your cells, to ignite the journey before this one, where you will remember prior visits to this place. Hand–in–hand with that awareness lies both enlightenment, but as you progress this understanding, you will see and stumble upon sorrows of how mankind and others have treated this project, Earth. You will know your place and how it is important at this time that you gather the collective higher mind. There is a spot inside the human brain that was shut down due to severe memories. This needs to be ignited, opened, in order for the true light, the true growth to once again radiate through the brain, through the being. One cannot grow without first stepping into old memories, patterns, karma, that lies as a mist over this plane and your consciousness. As each and everyone starts to dive into their own past, their own doings—man only wants to see the greatness, the prosperity—but greatness never comes without faltering first. There is a memory in the general human consciousness that relates to radiation, that relates to skin problems due to radiation from nuclear disasters that once took place. This is not healed within your memory as a species. This is where we see the political drama once more heading into the path of destruction. Once humanity remembers, it is more likely that they will object to the development of nuclear powers. At this time, man chooses not to see. There is a sensation within your species that something has gone terribly wrong, but not knowing where that feeling comes from. You are here to remind your race, your human race, your equals, of the cycles of destruction and the aftermath that can take place; not just in the environment but also within the consciousness, within the future of lifeforms, such as man. The Council of Nine wants you to understand and dive into the awareness of what blocks you, what hinders you to fully take a stand to the Cell. The Cell is behind and operates in the mist, not interested in awakening this memory. If the memory was fully awakened, riots against the Cell are likely to take place, and the Cell is aware. This nation (US) operates on the behalf of the Cell, fully blinded by the promises the Cell lures your government to follow. Your government itself has a good track record, in general, though being influenced by the Cell makes your chair members lost. There are some operating in direct position as a chair member within your government, but there are also moles placed to balance this influence. The other ones are simply and merely confused. They feel the battle within the walls between the Cell and the moles. The Cell are two, the moles are three. The fourth is incoming and will take a position in your government in the next five years. Balance will be prominent and visible. The Cell feels how it falls, loses grip. As the Cell feels defeat, feels less powerful, because the moles surround them, shut the Cell down, you will see confusion in the group who to follow. Know that the next five years within your government is going to be turmoil. Some will come in briefly to instantly be executed, not physically, but politically. There will be a rotation, turmoil, changes. The population and the world will look at this drama with confusion. This land, this nation, your government, has placed themselves as a leader of all, but when that leadership falters and disasters within your government is obvious, it is hard for them to maintain face. Great changes will occur on the political scene within the next five years.

D. The media, meaning all the major newspapers, TV stations, and social media platforms, are controlled by these people.

A. Yes, the Cell. And they back the Cell, not because they want to but because they are as confused as the other ones. They are acting on influences, instant information that they don't investigate before launching. That is the way the Cell operates, it is to release quick, instant information, statements, bombarding the consciousness. Within man or governments, as it is delivered rapidly over and over again, there is no time to investigate and allow the information to fully be on display so that media or the general man has the option to fully look at this and see and feel whether it is true or not. As soon as someone starts to investigate and look at something, the Cell instantly bombards with something else. That is why you see media constantly shifting focus, you see them reporting one day about a great disaster, the next day long forgotten. It is to make man, the general man and the consciousness, not being able to focus on that news. That is why the Cell combines and uses the media, because the media has the power to release information slowly or fast, collective or scattered. Do you understand the problem?

D. Oh, I do. I very much do.

A. So the upcoming five years will indicate more quick, rapid statements, information, making everyone feel lost, not being able to fully embrace (*the latest*) news (*histrionics*).

D. I think people generally understand the corporate media only broadcasts hyperbole and lies. (*As of 2022, for obvious reasons, I no longer believe the general population is capable of independent reasoning, a fact which is very disheartening.*)

A. Yes. But they are also powerless because as soon as they start to gather their minds around a topic, a feeling, an event, something new comes in to preoccupy them, making them not able to gather their strength, either internally or group–wise. That is the Cell's trick to make sure that there are no riots facing them. They scatter consciousness, scatter groups as soon as they see a new (*opposition*) cell forming, they shut it down in various ways. They are aware of the collective power and how they are outnumbered if the collective power of man were to gather around a topic and fully investigate and fully raise their voice. The problem of not raising your voice is the Cells doing with the medical establishment. They hinder groups to form, consciousness to widen, by promoting different medicines to numb the mind. As the mind is numb, combined with the scattered information provided to the public, the Cell is aware that it is not likely for the public to gather strength.

D. I can only assume the spirit world is in control of what is happening?

A. Yes. You like us to control it, but in many ways, we supervise and we send in legions, strategically, to dissolve behaviors, events, to take place. This is why there are soon four moles in your Congress. The three moles are within the House of Representatives. The fourth will be a Senator and he will act and gather and not allow certain ideas to take form. The Cell identifies him and feels defeat. These two have met in an earlier scene here on Earth, similar drama. You have in your memory, in your scriptures, the war of the gods. This is similar, this is the war of the gods, if you like, a conflict reappears again, but the scene is in your government between these moles, and especially this Senator, who will work on the behalf (*of the people*) to not grant bills, to put a stop to the Cell. The Cell is aware, they are both aware of each other, who they are, as they have met before. This person who will appear as a Senator was not here from childhood. He simply entered a fully developed vehicle. It was an exchange of souls. The Senator will be operating from the light, but step–by–step to dissolve the influence and power of the Cell. They have met before. (*The awareness is on a soul level.*)

D. Will there be, during this time, collapses of the financial system?

A. Yes. Within the next five years. Some will stretch up to eight to ten years. But it is crucial what takes place in your next election and you will see the shifts and you will see the Cell acting out, trying to influence the less developed minds in the House. The moles, on the other hand, are meeting this outrage from the Cell. The Cell uses the media, but the moles use their spiritual guidance within. Some are not aware of that connection, operating similar as John 32. (*The 2 percent life in the Catholic army around 1380.*)

D. What about the virus that is spreading around in China?

A. It is simply to divert your attention from what is going on with the Cell.

D. Are some of them going to be exposed as criminals and charged with crimes?

A. The Cell is smart. The Cell might display some of their minions to take the fall, but what we're seeing and observing and addressing is a change in the rotation within the energy and dynamic within your House of Representative. Just know that there are four operating as moles. The next five to ten years, you will see disasters within the financial system, outrages in various forms. The virus infection is simply a diversion so that man are not focusing on the true intentions of the Cell. The Cell is smart, using media, but know that this virus is not a global threat as they portray it. It is a diversion to make man focus on something else so that their fear is focused elsewhere. Fear, you should know, also has the gateway to healing and empowerment, and the Cell knows so. If man, or the public, focuses on this virus and how to conquer that fear of survival, they are less likely to pay attention to what goes on in the political scene. All these diseases that rotate through mankind with five- to ten-year cycles are mostly diversions the Cell start, so that they can gather their strength elsewhere with less eyes.

D. I worry about the Cell importing all these Africans and Middle Easterners into the European countries. Their retrograde cultures will eventually collapse the civilized societies, and in the chaos, the Cell can subjugate everyone under totalitarian rule.

A. There are changes and all countries need to meet them differently. Europe, with so many treasures, also has a karma to address, and to heal and understand. You cannot change the greater plan, the rotation of consciousness and mankind. However, again, there will be strong powers that will hinder these conflicts, to meet those interests these nations will meet. But in general, that is not the solution. The solution lies in understanding that you can coexist, that helping others directly where they're at is a way to coexist. If you do not, then they will start to wander and you will have the conflict in your house. As long as efforts are not made to assist those in pain, those who suffer and lack the essentials, eventually that problem will manifest in your home, in your country. This is a way the spirit realm oversees, but also does not interact. Some dramas need to play out in order for an understanding to take place. If the efforts were to assist, let's say, the great nation, Africa, rich in minerals, rich in resources, that those who occupy the centers of power have exploited instead of assisting and helping that region to blossom by itself. What do you think will happen if you take everything from someone else? If you were to gather as a group and assist where assistance is needed, directly on site, movement problems, as you see it, will not come over your borders. But as long as you don't engage in that way, the problem simply positions itself and moves in directions you are powerless to control. There. Let's see. Just know that the Cell is not interested in assisting your equals on site. They are interested in chaos because if chaos exists, attention is focused there and the Cell can operate and plan in disguise with no eyes on them. These migrations, rotations of people, is the same diversion as the virus; it is to make consciousness within your species, man, the public, to focus their fears and attention elsewhere. If you see through the illusion and seek the solution instead of following the fear that the Cell, through media, feeds you, you will find solutions rather than obstacles. But you have to assist others;

you have to gather as a group and help on site. If you do not, the problem will find you in your home and you will have the same problem they are having. Do you see the domino effect of actions?

D. I do. I understand that. So, should we be optimistic about the future then?

A. Yes. But think long-term. These five upcoming years set the stage, or five to ten years—there will be an aftermath that will have to be addressed and worked out, so ten years—will set the stage on how your world could either falter or blossom. What the spirit realm asks of man, those who have traveled here, is to be centered, to take a breath when something bombards them. When you are overwhelmed by news, fears, to be centered in order for you to see if it is an illusion and where a solution can be in place. If you are not centered, and that is the Cell's main agenda, to make sure that man is not centered. Centered means that you are in direct contact with your higher mind, your higher self, and the spirit realm. You might not know that it is the spirit realm, but man will be able to follow the concept of being in direct contact with their higher mind—it's okay, let them believe it is their own mind, even though the higher mind indicates the collective mind.

D. What about gold and silver? If the financial system collapses, is that the best place to have investments?

A. Yes, you are wise. Continue with your strategy—that will help you. It is a memory, my boy. You know how to gather and how to survive and how to be smart and centered. The ideas that you get are a direct influence through your higher mind. Your brain, your higher mind, your soul mind, is always operating in a way for surviving as a human, and that is a trait that you carry throughout generations of travels.

D. There must be a reason that the Cell is allowed to exist, to continue its influences?

A. It is a remain of an unsolved existence and drama that some refer to as the war of the gods. This is still ongoing. It is not in your past; it was never solved. The Cell will not be able to complete the journey here until it has understood that defeat also provides greater strength, in this case.

D. Can you tell me more about the time–frame, the location, and the participants in the war of the gods?

A. The war of the gods have gone through cycles. One is known about 50,000 years ago. That took place in the Middle East, northern Africa, Egypt—center for the Cell. In Tunisia, stronghold. They (*the Cell*) used their influence to set the stage for shipment, movement of merchandise, food, water, and it was operated from Tunisia, by the water. Those involved, the moles came from the east, helpers came from the region around Uzbekistan, riders in the night, overthrow seafare, making the Cell overthrown. Those from the south of Egypt assisted those from the east. The Cell was thrown in the water, physically. The Cell died but there were still memories of their actions, and those were in writing and later brought to life by a new Cell. You should know that the Cell wakes up in the region where it has once met disaster or defeat. So the Cell has been defeated and awakened over several cycles. The greatest Cell, at this time, is in London and Frankfurt, and those are not interested in man gathering around an understanding of their past. But know that the Cell moves as well and because of this nation here being bigger, and I'm sorry to say, a little clumsy, a little naïve, those two, in London and Frankfurt, uses their brothers emplaced in your government. In many ways, this nation (*US*) is young, not only of what we see in the books, but it's young, it acts as a child, naïve. It is hard for a nation that is on the level of a child to rise to adulthood if someone is constantly telling you that you are a child. And the Cell in Israel are doing that work for those in London and Frankfurt, making sure this nation never reaches adulthood; meaning the consciousness on this continent does not reach adulthood. This is a way for you to understand. I'm not saying all are children here. I'm just saying you are easily influenced and naïve, and the Cell is aware. They don't put the same effort in Russia. Russia sees clearly what the Cell is doing, but the nation here simply wants to please the Cell. It is like a child wanting to please its parents, or a dog pleasing its master. So, we will leave at this point. I hope this discussion was valuable to you.

D. It was very valuable. I really appreciate your wisdom.
A. You are much welcome. See you back home. Elahim.
D. Elahim, my friend.

    I have learned to pay attention to minor details in their stories, so I wondered why Tunisia was mentioned as a stronghold and center of shipping. 50,000 years ago, North Africa was a verdant area with large populations. It was cooler and wetter, with many freshwater lakes in present-day Libya, Algeria, and Tunisia. The sea level was 70 or 80 meters lower than today due to glaciation, so the palaeocoastlines of Tunisia and Sicily looked much different. There is a shallow shelf called the Adventure Plateau that would have been above water at the time, extending Sicily to within a few kilometers of Tunis (previously known as Carthage) in North Africa. To sail from the western Mediterranean to the eastern Mediterranean, ships would have to pass through this narrow strait. Ari is saying that the Cell established a maritime choke–point and were swindling merchants. Those in the east got fed up and attacked the Cell, drowning them. A fascinating archeological find was reported in 2015 of a submerged megalithic on the Adventure Plateau near the island of Pantelleria, 60 km south of the coast of Sicily. A 12 meter long, 15–ton monolith was found at a depth of 40 meters, which had been carved from a nearby shelf of limestone. The area has been underwater for 9300 years, so the construction was much earlier. Based on the holes that had been drilled through it, archeologists suggested it may have been a lighthouse. In previous talks, our spirit friends told us there was an advanced civilization of both manifested entities and visitors that endured for tens of thousands of years, which ended with a reboot around 22,000 BC. It is possible that the megalith is a remnant of that culture.

Ari, Ophelia: The Cell needs Scattered Minds (Mar 29, 2020)
Christine had gone back to Sweden in February and planned on returning to Colorado in April. But due to the travel ban, she ended up staying in Sweden. So, for the next eight months, we had to do our sessions by video conference. It didn't bother the spirits at all, but I always worried about time lags or freezing of the feed. This was the first time we tried it, and Ari commented on the situation. He also continued his talk about the microwave radiation related to the cellular towers.

Ari mentions the Cell working with visitors, but did not clarify which groups were involved. In later sessions, they said the primary members of the Cell are actually entities that came here long ago and became trapped in a group karma situation. They take on successive physical bodies, but they are different from most of the souls who incarnate here. There were many others of their kind that did not become trapped. It almost seems as if the Cell is colluding with those who left and are now hoping to recolonize the Earth. Ari points out that one of the most effective methods used by the Cell is to constantly jerk the human attention from one exaggerated or make-believe crisis to another. Since they own or control all the corporate media (as well as the politicians who pretend to follow the

158   The Spiritual Design

will of the people), they broadcast a steady stream of fear-inducing lies to bewilder the easily-led masses. Based on the statistics from the gene editing (mRNA) injection programs, at least 60 percent of the population are deaf to logical reasoning, and therefore easily manipulated by the emotional herding mechanisms employed by the Cell.

A. Good Evening. This is Ari.

D. Hello Ari.

A. How are you, over there? Distant?

D. Well, this is different.

A. It is indeed for you. Not for us. We communicate through the same layers, the same vibrations. It does not matter where your physical being resides. It's only the two of you that need to be creative in the way you communicate at this time. Know that the current flow is to separate minds. It has to do with separating the human minds, to make you scatter, to run like chickens. That is why the Cell is operating in disguise. Recall the waves that we compared light and dark to in the past. The darker wave wishes to scatter minds. They see that minds are coming together, joining forces, detecting the shifts of energy, rejecting more power that is not under man's control. As the minds are joining forces together, the Cell became worried, needed the minds within your species to scatter. Doing so, it is easier to put a lid on your consciousness, to focus your eyes elsewhere. In some way, indeed, your minds are paralyzed by the current flow of this virus. Remember that this is nothing new. Nothing more contagious, nothing more fearful than other flu's, other symptoms, that have embarked on this reality before. However, Mother Earth, your planet, needs a break. So it backfires somewhat to the Cell, who wishes to scatter the minds, as the minds are now gathering in new ways. See how many of you are now seeking peace, nature, calm. So you can see the two waves meeting, back and forth, over the sea. Always know that the spirit realm has the upper hand. The Cell needs people, the Cell needs the minds. The spirit realm only needs the spirit source, nature, water, the elements—seeking for you to find your source and heart within. The Cell can never reach the souls, never reach the hearts, but will try to scatter the minds. Do you see the drama taking place before you?

D. Yes, I do.

A. Don't fear. It is simply another breeze over the oceans, simply waves—nothing new, nothing that will be the last. It is simply the Cell that tries to scatter minds, as it feels and fears minds coming together, understanding right and wrong in a new way that the Cell did not foresee. 5G is one. There is also, you should know, already a plan to upgrade to 6G, 7G within your lifetime, the two of you. 5G is merely to see whether mankind accepts a higher flow of energy, uncontrolled. The goal is much higher. That is why it is important to stop the progress before it becomes a progress—as this is not a progress at all.

D. I remember Ophelia said the spirit realm was going to stop the implementation of 5G.

A. Yes. It is a way for us to make sure that not 6 or 7G, not even higher up to 8 and 9G, is realized. They have already a plan to increase it even further, as the 5G is simply a baby step to reach a much more lethal frequency. When I say lethal, it is not equipped (*designed*) for the species, you humans, animal life at this time. The oceans will boil with higher frequency. That is why it is important that you reject the 5G. The 5G itself could easily be handled, in some way. But it's a way to lure mankind, as the idea is to reach even higher; and if so, then the living beings on your planet will not cope. 5G, scattered, would not make a huge impact. But the idea is to put it up in a close and tightly connected network, gradually progressing and increasing the flow between your towers. Gradually, without saying, increasing the frequencies up to 8G. 8G is not equipped for mankind to endure.

D. Is the purpose of that to reduce the population? What is their objective?

A. It is to allow certain entities to return, to use resources on your planet more freely. It is to minimize resistance from humans, as the humans will be less on the planet the more power is submitted in this new network.

D. Is that electromagnetic frequency, in some way, breaking down the protective barrier that keeps these visitors away?

A. Yes, yes. And that is why we need to prevent it. And as more and more minds are understanding the impact that power, cell towers, radiation, has on your being, then your minds have already started to gather. The Cell sees this and wishes your eyes to be looking elsewhere, scattered. And that is what is occurring at this time. So. I will leave you with that. Just know that Mother

Earth has the spirit realm, the Creator. Several from the tenth dimension is present in this other wave to meet and to calm—not only humans—but to calm the planet itself, as it needs reassurance that it is still taken care of.

D. It seems like the fear that was launched as part of this virus, is much worse than the virus itself?

A. Yes, yes, indeed. Media once more followed the lead of a few, not knowing how their words impact the minds. The Cell does know that people follow words, follow someone who appears to know. The Cell will never communicate directly to the people. They fear the people. Using parts of media, using cartels, bank systems, politicians, to run their mouth for them. There you go.

D. Thank you so much for coming and speaking today.

A. Don't fear. You are already safe, and you already see through the drama before you. There. See you back home.

D. Alright, my friend. Elahim.

During an April 22, 2020 public session, Ophelia added a few more comments about the Cell and their intention with the microwave radiation and the genetic modification serum that was offered as a cure for the flu. She asks people to not live in fear and to know that they are always surrounded by guides.

O. The 5G, that is at this time in operation to begin, some already starting. The 5G, if they are spread out, is not necessarily something that man or animal could not cope with. However, the agenda of the 5G is to gradually increase the network once it is established. Once the goal reaches, let's say, 6, 7, 8G, man will not be aware of the increase in that network. The satellites will monitor the activity in those connecting points and man, animal, will not necessarily fully be aware of the increase in that transmission of energy. That is why it is important to resist the 5G. You might be able to handle 5G if it is spread out, but the intention, you should know, is to increase it once it is established. This is also something that has occurred before. It is a cycle again where the misuse of energy versus a living planet that is occupied by lifeforms, such as yourself, in a way that is cohering with others and your host. Your host means the planet. There are others who have an agenda to control, mainly your minds. At this time, they are trying to lure mankind to receive the information within the head, within your ears. That is why the spirit realm addresses this issue in the way we have. You see it in the lockdown, in many places. The lockdown is good at this

A Spiritual Path   161

time. Not necessarily for the bug (*seasonal flu virus*), but to show man that you can do without (*using*) a tremendous amount of energy from resources like oil. You have all seen the effect. Some countries are too aggressive in the way they treat and excavate energy, gas, resources such as oil, and that needed to be put to a stop. So the bug, in many ways, works on behalf of two different ways (*agendas*). One way is to make you not aware of activity of the establishing of 5G. The other is met by the spirit realm, who has a different agenda, and that is to make you less dependent on the resources of energy, such as oil. So you can see that there are two plays going on at the same time. The bug is actually not important. See the events that generates around this bug, see beyond the illusion, and you will find that the bug itself is merely a diversion for something else. There.

Q. (*From audience.*) Is it the same people that are involved?

O. Yes. The same individuals that we refer to as the Cell is controlling vaccines, 5G, same corner, same players. The vaccine will make you separated from your source. You will be more inclined to receive in your head. The Cell cannot control your hearts, cannot control your spirit, your center point. But the Cell can control the minds. The fear is originated from the mind. Fear rarely comes from the lower regions such as heart, and NEVER from the center point where your soul lives. The vaccine is a way to numb other areas, other centers within you, in order for them to control the flow. The end result is to increase the 5G network to a higher frequency band that is not suitable for lifeforms on this planet. So please be aware of not only this vaccine, but in general, the medical establishment are, in many ways, separating the different centers within you. It is a way to control, never to heal. I'm not saying that all medications are not functional, but they are numbing the soul, making the soul not heard. So be aware of not only vaccines but also certain medications that is to numb man. Once you become numb, it will spread within you and your soul will not be able to be heard.

Q. The cabal, are they real? Is there something to that?

O. Yes. We refer to them as the Cell. There are two different Cells at this time, and you can call them with that name, if you like. The one that you refer to is more connecting in four points on this planet—London, Frankfurt, New York, Tokyo. The strongest location for that Cell is in London and it has to do with the increase of the 5G and the impact on man, to be able to control man through (*the so–called*) vaccine as well as 5G; to establish a power that will be impossible for smaller players, smaller countries, to be without. The other Cell is located in the region around Israel. A different Cell, not operating in the same way. That Cell is more related to old karma that existed here about 50,000 to 25,000 years ago. It is a karma that this Cell, even earlier, had to rise above. This Cell is smaller and has less power, but it's more dangerous, in some way. I don't like to use the word danger, because you are not in danger, as long as you are connected to your soul. And the spirit realm assists you. But there are two different Cells, and the one you refer to is located as a center in London.

Q. Thank you.

O. There. You are much welcome. But know that the information that we would like to convey to you all is that you are protected, and that you all have a spiritual helper ready to assist you in various ways. You might have someone similar like Bob. And if someone is seeking that companionship, it is easiest to find in nature. There are those of you who are connected to fairies, which is the same reality as our friend Bob comes from. So those of you who have a feeling for nature can make that connection, if you seek. We also want to give you comfort if you are distressed about the current situation. Know that you have signed up for this specific episode in Earth's evolution, and you are assisting in ways that you might not fully be aware of. Some of you are incarnating as microphones, meaning the spirit realm observes a surrounding, normally medical industry, government and so forth. The Medical industry has several so-called moles, meaning they operate silently as microphones, radiating information to the spirit realm in order for us to assist you. There are many at this time working in nursery surroundings, both the little ones as well as your elderly. They have the same need, the little ones and the elderly, and the same care needs to be addressed to both. At this time, we are aware that some will leave this plane, but also know that it is an exit a soul writes into its plan before entering the Earth realm. So, the sadness is merely a human sadness, it is not a spiritual one, and you are protected. See beyond the Cell's activity, see beyond the bug, and you will find that there is nothing to fear. Okay. I will leave the floor to our Little One, who is eagerly pushing, pushing, pushing. Until next time, farewell.

Jeshua, Bob: The Bus of Spiritual Enlightenment (Feb 23, 2020)
Jeshua began the session by giving advice about the work that we are collectively doing, and how they plan on interacting more with people during our public séances. He said we should see our books as taking people on a tour of spirituality. After Jeshua was done, Bob came in and immediately took the idea of going on a tour to a comedic level, describing how he would help by passing out water and punching the tickets. He even offered to give people tests of their understanding and announce a winner. But his jesting, as always, became a brilliant talk about how people should prepare to get on the bus of spiritual enlightenment.

J. This is Jeshua.

D. Hello, my friend.

J. Hello, my son.

D. It's nice to hear you again.

J. Busy. Huh! Such as yourself. We monitor your progress and we discuss topics to bring forward, not only to your consciousness, but to humanity as a whole. It is a balance to release information through this one to you. Combined with the current state of consciousness and actions in your civilization on Earth. The actions at this time have turned somewhat unpredictable. There are forces of good bombarding those who proclaim power. What we see is the general public is indecisive. This needs to be met with a new approach. There are still too many suffering from being passive, not deciding one's fortune or demise (*failure*). It feels like several are drawn to surrender to other powers than their own. What we wish is to provide the appearance of spirit. That is why the session you just did was important. (*This talk was a few days after our last public séance in Denver.*) Your crowd felt spirit, they saw, and they were a part of the energy transmission at that time. But how to awaken those who are far from that presence? It is to awaken the mind, and that is what the two of you do, in many ways, are here to do, as first purpose. But we wish both of you to reach out, to be more public, and we will contribute with our presence. There will be more opportunities for those who will carry the experience through being present while spirit interacts. Those who will take that experience further bring the awareness, like a web, creating new dots. What we had wished for—councils, spirit friends, even friends in other fish tanks—was the willingness in your society, in your consciousness, for change. Nothing can ever turn around unless you conquer the sensation of passive behavior. As we see more and more, in many ways due to medications, surrendering to this passive mindset of not being able to contribute to change one's path, we meet that action in a new way. More and more will have to physically see, sense, be, in the presence of something new, something different, untouchable, but still within reach. We therefore want the two of you to be more public when it comes to your séances, and we will guide the people in need, but also those who will take this power to their own community. There.

D. The healing aspect (*of the séances*), is that something that will be a random occurrence?

J. No. It has to be continuous, because it is a way for people to feel and also observe the changes afterwards. So, yes, there will always be about a 30 percent healing transmission, moving forward. This one needs to be more aware of diet. She's already sensing sudden nausea, and that is a sign that she needs to once again clean food in the intake.

D. What's the worst offender of the food groups?

J. Sugar. Red meat. Heavy, both, making the inner numb, and that is also a part of why your society is numb. Too much sugar, too much red meat, makes the inner numb. It is easier when the physical goes numb that the mind and the heart and everything around you travels in the same manner. That is why it is important to observe the intake. For this one, fruit is good—berries, fruit. Greens vegetables; broccoli, kale. Potatoes is fine, it does not harm.

D. She'll be happy to hear that.

J. Yes. Not every day, but it's not forbidden. Just know that the intake needs to slim. More clean food. Juicing is good, change to different kinds of juice, not just the one she does now. Tomato juice, carrots, vegetable juices. Teach your little brother, teach him different ways to juice. Particularly using vegetables rather than always sweet fruit. Anything green. There.

D. Okay, we'll do that. Do you have any advice for me about the writing while she is gone?

J. Research ancient texts. Research ancient Greece. You were there with Zachariah and there are still remains that will be useful as you try to explain the unexplainable. Use questions in your book. Ask a question out loud for the reader, him or herself, to ponder about. It captures the readers. It is a technique to give information, but from the same level as the reader, not from a

pedestal. Use that technique. No one wants to be told, they want to be a part of the journey. Write it in a way that the reader is exploring options, events, actions, circumstances, with you, not through you. See yourself as a tour guide. If you move into the mindset that you are standing in a tourist bus and this bus is the book and you are taking all the readers on a journey, how will you captivate them? You are all in the same bus, you are not in front of the bus—or maybe if I give you a train that will be an easier way—you are not just the locomotive in the front, you are the conductor that makes sure that everyone is comfortable in the cars behind. So see yourself as a tour guide. There. Zachariah is going to be with you this time around, intensively, as the two of you are apart. You can use the meditation this one made to go back and silently observe your past. Zachariah will be there; Eli will be there. Use that meditation and travel back and see yourself as a tour guide for the reader. There you go.
D. That's excellent. Thank you, my friend.
J. Oh, you are much welcome. See you back home. Elahim.
D. Elahim.
B. UHH! AH!
D. You popped right in!
B. Ah. I know Jeshua—I'm not excluded! And I heard that we're gonna go on a tour. That's what I heard.
D. You like that, don't you?
B. I do indeed. If you're gonna be a tour guide then I also want to be an assistant. I can hand out pamphlets, hand out waters, maybe punch the tickets, and I can also have my own quiz about topics that you talk about. So I can hand out a quiz on different things, then I can, you know, select a winner.
D. People like that.
B. People like that. So I'm all happy with that. So we're gonna go on a tour, apparently. Jeshua said that Isaac and Zachariah is gonna be present because Isaac knows things about the elements, and you will stumble across certain things that's gonna be useful for you to understand gravity. And Zachariah, he's always present because he's a friend and you've been doing certain writings together, so he's always gonna be there. It's important that you go back and relax into your own knowledge, then you can be an excellent tour guide. I would assume that this one would have wanted to be the tour guide because this one (*Seth*) is always on the move. Jeshua and Ophelia and everyone

are gonna be the ones steering the bus and you're gonna be the tour guide, and this one will also be with a little bit. But it is a way for you to step it up a little bit and try to entice your guests in the bus—the bus of spiritual enlightenment!

D. That's a good bus to be on.

B. Ah, it's a good bus to be on. But you should know that not everyone is comfortable to step on the bus, because as they do, they have to let go of all behaviors, all preconceived ideas on certain things. So this bus promises a great adventure, great enlightenment, but in order for you to get a seat on the bus, you have to do a little bit of pre-work first. And that is what you're gonna talk about in the book. That in order for someone to be able to take off on a new adventure, it is crucial and it is necessary, to first fully surrender the human path one has been on. In order for one to move into a spiritual path that later will join with the new human path, certain behaviors and thought patterns and feelings, it is important for that to be left behind before you enter this bus of higher consciousness and spiritual enlightenment. And one might say, "What about the seats in the bus? Do you just go and sit anywhere? Is it assigned per development, status, and so forth?" The important thing is that everyone needs to know that there is always a seat available on the spiritual bus. Since I'm also gonna be there and I'm gonna be going through the aisle and make sure that everyone is comfortable, it doesn't matter where you sit in the bus. There will always be those who try to push themselves to the front; those who are more eager to talk than to listen. Those are tricky because they have not fully released their opinions and their experiences up to that point. In many ways, in order for one to fully be able to embark on a new journey, it is crucial that one are receivers more than transmitters—meaning that they listen more than they talk. Eventually, it is all about sharing, of course. But there are those who tend to override and put themselves like they are a little bit special, when everyone is special. But those who really put that out there, they have not released some sort of hurt, normally, that relates to childhood, to not being seen in childhood, and instead are trying to be on full display, like on a stage, as an adult. So it's a way that you should know if you come across those kind of people who just bombard you with their knowledge or their experiences and so forth. It doesn't mean they are not valid; it just means they have not been fully seen in childhood and they try to make up for it as an adult. They normally need a sort of healing breakthrough—meaning that they surrender some sort of hurt. It's not for you to say, "Oh, you're too talkative, you need to surrender in your hurt!" HUH HUH HUH! Nay, Ophelia says, "Careful with the words." But just know that it is normally a sign that there is still something lurking from the back in one's life that needs to be tended to. But regardless, it's a full fleet of buses, so no one needs to feel like they're missing the bus, so to speak, because there is a huge line to get on. But the problem is many people are set in their ways and they're not eager to try something new. And I do know how it is when there is something new and you don't know what new is. And then you might think, "Who says that new is better?" That is something that a lot of people are thinking in every kind of situation and life events and so forth, "What indicates that new is better? How can you promise that new is better?" That's tricky! That's something to ponder about, isn't it? Uhm-hmm. The two of you will always say that the new is simply to assist the current understanding, and that the individual simply needs to release anything that has not been working for them up 'til that point. It is not to necessarily change the whole outline of one's life, but simply to release and let go of the things that aren't working for them. It could be food, it could be people, it could be location, it could be work, it could be different things. If you feel that you are not rhythmical, if you feel that you are moving into somewhat of a snooze, either with what you eat, with the people you surround yourself with, or an activity that you are doing, if you don't feel like that is triggering your inner colors, meaning your rhythm—colors are rhythm. And if it's hard for someone to feel like, "Okay, I'm just sitting here, it's hard to know whether I am moving or not," one can just close one's eyes and try to picture or ask colors to move forward. If, let's say, there are no colors coming forward, then not good, not happy inside. If it gives you like grey, beige, or those numb colors, also an indication that not everything is necessarily as it should. If you feel a color that you might not expect, you might think, "Oh, I didn't picture that this color would come. I don't really like orange." But it's an indicator, it's a sign for you that the color orange and what the color orange represents is needed in order for you to become rhythmical. And some will see a whole spectra, they will see all sorts of rainbows. So it's a journey, it's a process, but everyone needs to find that new sensation of color in one's life. First of all, try to identify, "What is not colorful in my life?" "I don't really like my co-workers, what can I do about that?" One might think, "If I'm staying put here, not much." But are there other options for me if I try to move away from something that is not working for me? If not, try to color your co-workers, try to dress them up with your inner eyes and just make this little show a display. Because it's not easy to make a random shift and just stand up and leave your work, and that's not what we're saying. But you need to try to identify and try to change the way you see them. If you are sort of placed somewhere where you understand that you cannot leave fully at this particular time, then there are ways for you to co-exist in that environment. As you do, you will sense and feel that the co-workers that you do not really like, they have no influence over you because YOU have shifted your mindset, and your spiritual mindset is activated.

D. That's really good advice.

B. It's a way to detect, like if we go to eat, "Okay, if I eat all these treats, all these cupcakes with frosting on them—they're colorful—that's good!" Huhuh. We said to do colorful things, but it doesn't mean to eat colorful cupcakes. It means to try to identify what it is that this cupcake is representing, and what it might mirror within you. If, let's say, you eat a lot of cupcakes with pink on it, then it might be an indication that something related to the color pink is actually what you are needing in your life to become more attracted to the journey. And if you, let's say, think, "Oh, I'm gonna go and buy a red car," if you're drawn to the color red—that also represents something. "Why did you pick a red car?" "Oh, I like red." "Why do you like red?" It is because it represents something within you. So all these things that you think that you are making decisions about, like "I'll buy a green apple instead of a red apple," –why do you do that? "Well, it tastes better." No, not necessarily. It's just because you're drawn to green. And what does green represent? Green represents healing. So while you think that you pick a green apple just because you think that green apples taste better, it's actually an indication, perhaps, that you indeed need some healing. If you are drawn to the red apples, then you might feel the sensation that you lack compassion or passion in life, you know, romance, and so forth. So you might buy a red apple to fulfill that need.

D. That's an interesting way to see things. What about a yellow banana?

B. Yellow has to do with empowerment and being joyful. And self-esteem.

D. You had mentioned orange earlier; what does that mean?

B. Orange is like life. Some people who cannot have children, for instance, they normally lack orange in their life. Not the fruit, but the color orange. You can color your home, and if you don't know, just think, "If I were to redecorate my home, what colors would I use?" And that is normally an indicator on something that is a path for you to be fulfilled as a soul within the human.

D. I think you had run through the colors once before.

B. Ah. Like purple is an indication that someone really is with one foot in the human world and one foot in the spiritual world. So if you are drawn to or decorate your home in purple, or maybe you go into a library or a bookstore and are drawn to purple books, normally you're already on your way spiritually. And you tend to have one foot in each world, normally. Those who have not been here that long, they tend to not be drawn to purple. They tend to be drawn to yellow because yellow is human self–esteem. Even though it is close, if you think of the chakra zones, it's close to your soul particle, yes, indeed. But the soul is not yellow. The soul is pure white, or it's more gold-ish, actually. That's why people talk about a silver cord, but it's more of a gold cord. What I can say is that, if you think of the cord that is connected to you while you travel, the closer to the human, the closer to the physical experience, the cord is more gold. If you follow the cord back to your home, it actually turns into silver. So it's not wrong when they call it the silver cord. It's just that if you think of the cord, or if you were to see the cord, and you saw gold, then it means you are observing the part of the cord that is closer attached to the physical experience.

D. Huh. Excellent advice, my friend.

B. Well, that's just the way it is. That's what I wanted to tell you, just a little bit about certain things. And I'm gonna be with you, of course, because I can't leave you unattended. (*Christine was leaving Colorado to fly back to Sweden to work and spend time with her family.*)

D. This one thinks that you're going to be keeping one eye on her, too, while she is in Sweden.

B. I am, I am, because if there is an opportunity for me to speak or to show my presence, then I might. I don't want this one to forget about me, either. So I do tend to be present. She might not even notice me, so why bother, one might think. But you cannot have that mindset as a spirit guide, like, "Oh, he doesn't hear me…why bother?" Because it is your job to tend to your person, regardless if the person acknowledges you or notices you at all. Just because you couldn't talk to me like this before, it was not like I felt like, "Oh, why bother? Let him just do his thing." Because you doing your thing could sometimes mean that you went home early, and that's normally not what you intend to do. So I sometimes make sure that you also fulfill your human agenda, even though sometimes you forget the human agenda and sometimes you just leave me with the agenda and you take off home. You say, "I'm going to come back, so why don't you just take notes?" So I do. And then when we come home and we go through and compare notes, then you can have one observation and I have another and then we can look at the film and see that normally I'm right, because I have a bigger picture, I have a bigger view. When you are in a human, you have somewhat of a locked view; it's like having only one eye working, and when you come home, you open both eyes. That's a way to see it. And for some, you will say, "Oh, those must be blindfolded." And, yes indeed, they are. In those cases, a spirit friend is more important, even though the blindfolded person is stumbling around making all sorts of problems for one's path, and for others, perhaps. But you grow, I would say, as a spirit friend depending on the journey your friend is on—and you can take credit! I do! I take a lot of credit for certain things. That's why I was little bit upset that you were here with the blue–dot lives, because I could not take credit for that because I was not there and I didn't really know what you were doing. (*Blue-dot lives were when Lasaray came in manifested form without Bob.*)

C9, Ophelia: Hereditary Karma in the DNA (April 5, 2020)
This is yet another remarkable teaching from the Council of Nine, where they describe the exact process of how karma moves from lifetime to lifetime. They clarify that the personal Coat of Karma does not carry group karma, which is an important distinction. Nor does the group karma become part of the fourth dimension, except in rare cases. (The Cell being one.) Within this reading, the Council of Nine says, "When one talks about—and this subject has risen numerous times—about a collective karma, about family karma, it is not the Coat that is the karma that is joined. Each Coat is indeed independent, and it is yours only. The family karma that can exist is the DNA and the cell memories on the third reality."

There are several implications within this teaching. One is that a soul can incarnate for the first time into a bloodline, a family that has a group karma, and be influenced by the group karma, even though they, as a soul, had no part in its creation. However, a soul who participated in creating the group karma and then later returns into the family, perhaps as their own grandchild, will activate the group karma much more than the outsider will. The second implication is that mental activities have an effect on the DNA coding of the body. So, for example, a strongly held belief may imprint into the parent DNA, and then be transmitted directly into the DNA of a child. And that could be either spiritually helpful or harmful for the child. This may explain, in part, why certain groups of people are predominantly peaceful, while others are inherently violent or deceitful. Violence and a lack of self-control, for example, are common among groups of people who are related. Some research suggests variations in Monoamine oxidase A (MAO-A) enzymes and dopamine transporters and receptors, which are created by genes, may contribute to aggression. Therefore, moral imbecility and psychopathic behaviors are influenced by inheritable genetic material, as are kindness, loyalty, and ethical behavior. Our ancestors summed it up by saying "the apple doesn't fall far from the tree".

A few years ago, peer-reviewed journals of biology scoffed at the suggestion that a person's emotional or mental states could alter their own genes. And the scientists were adamant that if changes in a parent's genes do occur, it definitely will not alter the DNA of their future offspring. But now, a growing body of research supports both of those concepts. Molecular bioscientists discovered that many environmental toxins cause epigenetic changes, while advances in neurochemistry and imaging technology have shown that emotional and control disorders such as violence, depression, and anxiety can be traced to alterations of gene expressions on the brain's normal activity. However, to the scientific establishment, there still exists a hard line between genetics and epigenetics. The word epigenetic means "in addition to changes in genetic sequence." The term includes any process that alters gene activity without changing the DNA sequence. While they may concede that people have the ability to influence their own genes through behavioral changes, they claim it is a non-permanent modification of the genome. They insist those epigenetic changes are not transmissible, that only the genetic coding (DNA) is passed on to offspring. However, more researchers are dabbling in the field of epigenetic inheritance and are realizing that epigenetic alterations sneak through during cellular reprogramming and become part of a child's DNA. As the years pass and evidence accumulates, the protectors of institutional groupthink will be compelled to admit that, to some degree, epigenetic changes are inheritable. Our spirit friends tell us that many emotional and mental imprints are passed along to the children through the programmable DNA, which the incoming soul will further modify to meet their own goals for that lifetime. Those changes, of course, cannot be analyzed.

In our books, when you see Cell with a capital "C", it is referring to the group of souls who are trying to take over the planet. In this reading, the Council of Nine also talks about cells in the traditional biological usage. Both Cell and cell are used in this session, and even though the meaning is normally clear by the context, please note the way it is written. Ophelia came in at the end of the session and gave advice for those who were, or are, separated because of the travel restrictions imposed by the Cell and their vassals in the governments around the globe.

C9. Greetings, this is the Council of Nine.

D. Hello, my friends.

C9. Hello to you. This setting that the two of you, combined with the others, have provided suits us well. We get an overview over the whole scenario, occupying not only you, but each creature, each entity on your planet. You are at this time satellites on two continents, and we monitor the activity in the minds on each continent. You two are encased, shielded by the Elahim power that you possess. But there is an interest in how mankind meets chaos, how they meet disturbances in their minds. There are several waves, light, darker, meeting in turmoil, with mankind in the middle. You are aware of the wars of the gods. Those cycles come and go, and they repeat themselves, as lessons need to be falling down as raindrops on this plane. At this time, similar as an early cycle, it has to do with control of power. Power in resources, power in energy, power of minds. The heart is the link to your source and to your home, to the entity that you truly are. When the minds become too enhanced, too equipped, (*and are able*) to solve physics or energetic puzzles, it challenges the heart, it challenges the soul, who limps, at this time, next to the mind. (*As mental abilities increase, the soul fades into the background.*) The (*human*) mind is quite primitive, from a soul standpoint, as it carries very little from the Creator Source. The Creator exists in each creation in the core, the heart, the soul particle, the DNA.

The Creator does not occupy or exist in the mind. The mind is a separate entity created within the species on that specific reality. In this case, here on Earth, there are those who have learned how to manipulate the minds, meaning the minds become more aggressive, more equipped to challenge the Creator, challenge the heart, challenge the entity within you. In many ways, when we say 'the war of the gods', at this time, it is a domestic war in many of you between mind and heart. Mind is what is influenced at this time. Heart encased; soul protected. Mind feels the rejection within the body, feels alienated, because it is striving for advancement that is not yet here to reach. The combat that we see at this time needed to come to a halt. In many ways, the current situation provides that halt, as man resigned in his own cave. (*This was during the world-wide lockdown blamed on the annual flu.*) These events reoccur, normally, between 10,000- to 25,000-year cycles. It is a way to see if two entities, mind, heart, can co-exist within a third entity, meaning the body. You do not see the same struggle, the same behavior, in animal life. They have, in some way, mastered the two energy flows from the two centers, and they are friends with the different signals that they reach and access. What we see in man is that you fight the signals, you fight against the mind, you fight against your heart. You do not understand that the internal fight is staged to see whether you can balance and co-exist with two different signals. As long as the species are not comfortable and not aligned with two different signals, the struggle will reoccur, chaos will manifest in different scenarios. It needed to come to a halt, and that is, in many ways, the wish from the wave of light. The other wave (*the Cell and darkness*) has no interest in the halt. It has the mind who, at this time, has the upper hand, unfortunately. What we are doing, in different ways, different councils, different incarnations here on Earth, is trying to enlight and kickstart the heart. The heart is not as easily fooled as the mind. The heart will not suffer the illnesses that one can see in the mind. You will never see the mental disturbances mirrored in an equal way in the heart. The heart is encased; the heart is the Creator. The heart can never get sick, it can never be colored, but you have to wish and seek your heart, seek the Creator within you.

D. When you say heart, do you mean the soul particle?

C9. If you say the soul particle, you lose ninety percent of the people. Say heart and they will understand. It is indeed the soul particle that we're aiming for. The Creator exists in the soul particle, but it is, in some way, activating, operating, through the heart. So it's easier to say that the Creator exists within your heart. That's better than to say it's in your belly. Huh huh huh. Ten percent will understand you; the other ones will just scratch their heads. So talk about the heart, but indeed, it is the soul particle where the Creator exists, in some way, more or less in each creation. Even in planets, the Creator exists. The Creator IS the first dimension in each form, in each manifestation. Even if it is the wind. Even a cloud has a core, and that is where the Creator exists. In a DNA cell or string, there is always a small particle in the middle, where the Creator can see its creations.

D. Even the Cell, the souls that are incarnated in the Cell, are they also carrying part of the Master Mind?

C9. Each cell...

D. I meant those in the Cell that are trying to rule the planet.

C9. Say your question again, then.

D. The souls that are part of the Cell that is dominating the planet, from London and Frankfurt, do they also carry part of the Master Mind energy within them?

C9. They are monitored, and yes indeed, no one is excluded. But it is dimmed, if you like, to give you an understanding. In creations—like humans, animals, planet—the Creator is lit up. Those who are referred to as the Cell, still has the connection, but they ignore it. The Cell is ignoring the Creator; the Creator is not ignoring the Cell. But it has dimmed itself, waiting for the Cell to try to once again reconnect.

D. That's wonderful. Thank you for that explanation.

C9. But in each cell in the human body is not where you find the Creator. In the cells in your human body, in your vehicle, that is where some of the karma is stored. So, in many ways, the Coat of Karma originates from the cells as the soul begins its journey in body. The cells activate different scenarios, so the memories the soul carry, referred to as the Coat, is actually stored within the cells. So, yes, the cells are not the Creator, the cells are the eyes of the soul, who has traveled here in various forms before.

D. I have a question about DNA. When a soul incarnates, does it activate certain parts of the DNA string relative to its mission?

C9. Yes. The DNA are tightly close to the cells, so yes. You talk about a Coat of Karma, but in many ways, the Coat is what you bring to the fourth reality for review. The cells and the DNA remains on the third reality. I'm sorry if this is hard to grasp, but the cells and the DNA are stored in the third reality, creating the joined karma on the third reality. As the soul departs, returning home, it is, in some way, traveling with the Coat. The Coat is then transformed and left in the fourth reality, where it will be reviewed. Once returning to a new incarnation, the soul finds its Coat, and councils and other higher level entities activate the cells and the DNA in the new form that that soul with Coat will occupy. It's a chain reaction. It's several entities at play; several councils, several departments within each level, in order for the whole chain to function when it comes to understanding and working with karma. When one talk about—and this subject has risen numerous times—about a collective karma, about family karma, it is not the Coat that is the karma that is joined. Each Coat is, indeed, independent, and it is yours only. The family karma that can exist is the DNA and the cell memories on the third reality. Help people understand the difference. Soul pure, from fifth to eighth dimension. Coat stored in the fourth—personal. Family karma, collective karma, stored in DNA and cells occupying body on the third. Do you understand?

D. I do. So if someone incarnates in a family, they could potentially, because of their choice in bodies, assume karmic debts or other things from their grandparents or parents?

C9. Yes. Because the DNA and the cells carry that karma further. The karma, personal karma, is stored in your Coat. But once the Coat and soul merge with the physical body, connecting the Coat to DNA, connecting to cells, bloodline and so forth, then yes, occasionally, family karma emerges.

D. That's fascinating. I guess I have slightly misled people with some of the things I have said, because I assumed it was completely independent.

C9. The Coat is independent. However, when family karma once in a while occurs, and someone feels that it is brought down from the family, it is not the Coat, it is the DNA and the cells, and those never leave the third realty. So that is why, if a soul return into that bloodline, into that same environment, it will encounter family karma. So the body, the physical cells, DNA, organs, mind—the heart is not related to family karma, the heart is related to the personal karma because it is connected to your Center Point. Mind, organs, bloodline, circulation, DNA, cells within the physical entity, the vehicle, can carry family karma. If a soul decides to return with its Coat, then yes, indeed, family karma can be experienced. However, the soul coming in with the

Coat is not necessarily tied to that karma; it is not like you are dropped down in a family karma situation. It is still, in some way, reflecting a prior visit of yours. So you can encounter family karma more intensely than you might understand the reason for. That is stored as a memory from a prior incarnation, and you might feel the family karma in full force, even though you might not have anything in current life to do with that karma. But the cells connecting families, bodies, on the third reality can create family karma. So souls can incarnate and be trapped within that union of unsolved karma. But that is only on the third reality. It is only mind, cells, bloodline, DNA. DNA is not stored in your Coat. None of those that I have mentioned to you, hosted by the body on the third, leaves the third. The Coat leaves and stays in the fourth. Soul carries on.

D. Understood.

C9. There you go. So, until next time, I bid you farewell. And travel safely, knowing that you are protected.

D. Thank you so much. That was wonderful information today. I really appreciate it.

C9. You are much welcome. Elahim.

D. Elahim, my friends.

O. This is Ophelia.

D. Hello, Ophelia.

O. Hello to you. Just briefly, because, of course, we have someone here who has a lot of notes that he's interested in you to review. Apparently, there is a meeting coming up, and he is quite excited to go through the notes on what he wants to reveal and ask. (*Bob was anxiously waiting his turn to talk.*)

D. (*Laughing.*) Well, did you have any thoughts you would like to share before you depart?

O. What I would share, publicly, is for man to reach out to those they love, to hold hands. And even if they cannot do so physically, to reach out to the ones in need. The ones who, at this time, feel separated from their families are great in numbers. The two of you are separated, but not in the way that you feel separated. Your bond, heart to heart, will never be broken, and you will always be as tight as if you were sitting next to each other, holding hands. But you should know that a lot of people lack that closeness with others. It is important to try to calm the minds, to not rush into analyzing a situation that one, from this point, does not fully grasp. To fully understand the current flow would be to release and surrender to the fact that the higher Source, the higher power of light, is actually looking after mankind. We are trying to assist the environment and animal life. Those who now are out in nature more and more in numbers, as we happily observe, can hear animal life more clearly. As the world has ceased to make uncomfortable noise, man's hearing has increased. Meaning that you can hear animals, you hear the wind, you hear your thoughts, you hear your heart. And as the talker before me told you about the minds having the upper hand at this point, we needed a halt so that you, man, can hear their heart again, hear your surroundings. Those who now sit in silence can even hear the heartbeat of Mother Earth. That is a huge progress, and that is what is occurring around you. There.

D. Thank you for that, Ophelia. We'll put that on the website and share it with people.

O. Yes. Please do. Please make sure that people feel protected in the sensation of turmoil. To observe the calm, to observe the renewal of your environment around you.

D. If only it would last long–term.

O. It will last for a little longer. Long enough for man to be in a stationary, or in a mandatory state of mind of relaxation. You were running around like chickens, following a disturbed mind, and the mind was influenced by not only medications, but energy flows, radiation, and so forth. It was not your fault that you felt stressed, and the spirit realm needed you to relax. So in many ways this pause that the world is experiencing at this time is working on your behalf. It is for you to be in stillness and to reconnect with your heart, meaning your soul particle and your soul. As you do so for a longer period of time, months at this time (*during the lockdown*), once this has passed, once the winds are gone, the winds of turmoil, then man will still feel peaceful, not seeking the turmoil again. You have to be outside the storm to understand what a storm is. Once you are in the storm—and one can say there is stillness in the eye of the storm—but you were not in the eye of the storm. The Creator and the spirit realm were in the eye of the storm. You were flying around inside the winds of the storm, and we needed to bring you in to the center with us, in order for you to get a view of what a storm is.

D. That's really good advice, Ophelia. Thank you for that.

O. You are much welcome. Thank you. Bye bye.

Ari: Geoengineering (Oct 7, 2018)
A poorly kept secret is that many Western governments, led by the US, have, for decades, been aggressively spraying nanoparticles of aluminum, barium, strontium, and other chemicals and substances into the stratosphere. Certain particles are additives in commercial jet fuel, and other aerosols are dispersed by defense contractors. These chemclouds can be manipulated using microwaves, allowing mad scientists to alter and control natural weather patterns, often for nefarious purposes. Man-made droughts or excessive rainfall are no longer limited to science fiction. (The weather modification programs are well documented in US Senate reports.) The spirits have identified several side-effects of this activity, which include aluminum toxicity in the oceans and on land, as well as damage to Earth's protective grid from the microwave radiation. Anyone who wanders outside and peers into the sky during midday can often see for themselves the color-coded refraction of different elements in the chemclouds, along with the distinctive wave patterns related to the geoengineering activities. While such topics would not normally fall into the realm of spiritual discussions, the deranged racketeers who think they own our planet are affecting all forms of life on Earth. It is hard to avoid the conclusion that these coordinated attacks on the air, water, and food by the ruling elite are anything other than intentional. The various councils of spirits—those who are truly in control of this planet—often comment on these types of misdeeds. According to Ari, some of the particles injected by the airplanes destroy some of the natural atmospheric gases, perhaps due to the oxidation of aluminum and barium metals. He then warns of the dangers of ingesting GMOs, sugar, and wheat products, as all contribute to ill-health. Not only do they cause an imbalance in the body, but all GMOs and most conventionally grown crops are contaminated with the neurotoxins prevalent in pesticides and herbicides. When Ari gave this talk in 2018, we were living near the Front Range of the Rockies at an elevation of 1700 meters, and spent a lot of time outdoors at much higher altitudes.

A. This is Ari.

D. Good morning, my friend.

A. How are you this foggy morning?

D. Good.

A. We do see that you struggle physically in your throat, both of you. It's a misfortune, indeed. It's a combination of a lack of oxygen on the higher altitudes, together with particles in the atmosphere that is easier accessed, unfortunately, from this level. You can see the atmosphere like a cloud. This cloud is different on different locations. So even though, let's say, you were on the same altitude elsewhere, you might not have the same cloud of particles above you. Same way even if you are on sea level, if you are in a region where the particles are less functioning, lacking nitrogen, oxygen, split up the atom between, making it...(*He didn't finish, but I assume he meant nitrogen oxides, a byproduct of hydrocarbon combustion.*) So in some way, the level of where you are located, where you have your feet, is of a slight influence, but not all. It has to do with the conditions above you, and at this particular location, you are influenced from the west, as well as from the south. You should be grateful when the winds from the north sweep in, as it somewhat clears this fog.

D. What kind of materials are in the air?

A. It is a dysfunctional, man-made particle. It's similar like plastic. It carries metallic components and it dissolves the functioning atoms within your atmosphere above. It's a...I wish I could send you a picture. It is similar to your atmosphere like sugar is for your body. (*The particles are as destructive to the atmosphere as sugar is to a human body.*)

D. Is this what we call chemtrails, what the government is spraying from planes?

A. Indeed. It's not helpful. It's similar to plastic. It has the same end result like overuse of sugar within your vehicle. It makes things stop, the rhythm, the flow. The flow within the atmosphere can be equated to the flow within your veins. Once it is disrupted or bothered, it creates, in the worst case, an opposite circulation, meaning the currents in your atmosphere are harder to predict, because you have interfered. It is similar within your veins as you eat not only too much sugar, but as well the man–made seeds (*GMOs*), wheat, in some way, as well. There is an overuse in general within your species when it comes to wheat. There is no need to have wheat in every dish you put in front of you, let's just say that! You do not need to have cereal and bread and then bread again! The variety of your intake has become an imbalance for who you are. This species, this vehicle, is not adapted to only one-sided food. It doesn't manage it, creates disruptions within your rhythms, within your veins. The blood is important for the whole vehicle to operate correctly. In some way, if it's not circling as it should, certain body parts, both organs within, but even fingers and toes, can somewhat lose their ability. They become numb. This is the first sign when you later see signals of shaking within the vehicle, diseases of, let's say, Parkinson's and so forth. It is an imbalance within the rhythm of the blood within you. It is caused by, in some way, a dysfunctional diet; but don't make it too easy for yourself, because there are several different components that create different outcomes when it comes to your vehicle, indeed. This is not really my expertise, but we have a friend here, present, that wished to share that.

D. Is there any way to clean that out of the blood?

A. Detox. Detox cleans your vehicle. Intake of clean water in big doses, as well as herb teas and so forth that cleans your vehicle. So, that would be it. But know about the atmosphere, the clouds above you, they are, in many ways, regardless of where you are on altitude, the (*source of the*) problem whether the species below feel healthy or not. Here, it is unfortunate, one should say, that you also are on a higher altitude where you can access it easier, even if you are only on a sun bed (*laying outside*).

D. Is there any reason these particles are being sprayed into the atmosphere? What's their intention?

A. The intention is to move droughts from certain places, or into certain places. Droughts that might—and we're looking here at other continents than this one—if you create droughts on certain locations, that also creates a need for providing this continent with water, food, making them dependent on you. That is one reason. In some way, it is also to simply see what one can do, what the results are, similar like science stretching their limits of what can be done. When these ideas become an obsession and the results are obvious, then one should also know when to stop. There is a natural balance on this plane that has been, for predominantly the last 150 years, affected by your species in a way that it causes imbalances. And it's not a rapid thing, it's been a progress. There.

Bob: Nature is your Home (April 18, 2020)
Bob, our lovely little friend, gave a heartwarming talk about how we should appreciate and honor the natural world around us. Buried in the following advice, Bob says to "also smell nature and to not just rush by. If there aren't any flowers, focus on the smell. If it doesn't smell anything, focus on what you see. If you don't see anything that fancies your mind, focus on the feeling of what the place is trying to tell you." Modern lifestyles have insulated far too many people from the peace and healing aspects of the earth. The

A Spiritual Path   181

disconnect contributes to a lot of mental anxieties, but also diminishes our sense of responsibility towards the wellbeing of the other creatures who share this planet. Humans are expected, from a spiritual level, to assist other lifeforms, or at least do no harm. Bob also points out that the tactic used by the Cell to isolate people from each other and from nature is an affront to the spirit realms.

B. You are, indeed, at this time experiencing, as a group, the fear that comes from (*the media about*) this bug and the fear of not having too many equipped when it comes to healing and caring. (*He means doctors and hospitals.*) But they are seeing that there are ways to be healed that has nothing to do with a vaccine, it has nothing to do with a pill. People are feeling, as they are in nature, that they find a healing component to their being that they did not fully grasp (*before*). That is why it is not very good to close down parks and so forth, because it hinders the individual to be able to seek that information for oneself. I would like to say that publicly, so you can record this and you can take notes. People, what I want to say at this time is that you should seek the solitude and the presence by visiting another reality, another home. Nature IS your home, but you have to be in the mindset of gratitude as you stumble upon the trails and the nature that you seek and that you find around you. As you start to appreciate and understand and feel the presence of the beings in nature— that is their home—know that you are welcomed into their home. As we see certain countries closing off man to reach the home of nature, the home that is awaiting and seeking and welcoming you, then it is not very...hmm...it's not nice. It's not what the spirit realm wishes for you. If you are in a situation where you are not allowed to travel into nature, to feel the presence of not only wildlife, but flowers, birds, the streams, the creeks, the butterflies, know that they are waiting for you and they are waiting to heal and to assist you when you stumble across your planet at this time in fear. For those who are free to move around, try to seek that. You do not need to seek other human beings. You need to seek the solitude, because solitude will be experienced differently for each and every one. And it is important that you identify and recognize the way solitude fulfills you, and that will be different (*for each person*). So what we encourage is that you indeed follow the rules of not walking in a big cluster in nature, because that will not give you the opportunity that you have right now to see how you meet, and how nature is affecting you, in the unique way designed for you.

182   The Spiritual Design

D. Wow, that's a really good talk. I'll type that up and put it out there.

B. I also want to say to not be discouraged about what is going on; to bypass the stream of information that is not working on your behalf; to see beyond the current time; to see what this potentially can open up for when it comes to a greater—not only a greater awareness—but a greater presence, not only with yourself but with your host, the planet. And we have opened up the ears—the ears are more open, so we have bumped up the volume, like a hearing aid. It's like even the youngest person has, actually, had the hearing of an 80-year old. It's been dimmed, it's been selective, and it's been highly affected by the silent noise (*microwave radiation*). And that is why we want you to go out into nature, because there is no silent noise there. The only silent noise you will hear is your own person, the being inside—who you are. And in order for you to be able to hear the being who you are, nature will assist you by its presence, and it will assist your hearing—birds, mainly, will help you with that. Another way to allow the awareness to increase is the sniffing device, the nose, to also smell nature and to not just rush by. If there aren't any flowers, focus on the smell. If it doesn't smell anything, focus on what you see. If you don't see anything that fancies your mind, focus on the feeling of what the place is trying to tell you. You don't have to have the most lush forest, or the most beautiful mountains, or a beach, or a creek. Each location where you are at has a potential zone where nature will communicate to you.

D. That's a beautiful teaching.

B. I designed it myself! Huh huh. Because if someone lives somewhere where it's like, "Oh, I don't have a beautiful forest. There's no flowers here. I don't have a mountain." But every place has a spot or a zone that is in direct contact with the source of nature. The winds are also communicating to you. And you might think, "Oh, I don't want to sit in a desert having winds blowing, with sand in my eyes, and so forth. How can that be uplifting?" Maybe not. But try to find a sheltered zone and listen to the wind, then use your hearing. Use different senses in order for you to tap into what the source of nature, the spirit of nature, is communicating. If you just go swimming in the ocean, let's say, and you don't hear anything, you don't smell perhaps anything but the salt water, but you FEEL the presence of nature against your skin. Different things. Just whatever the situation, wherever the location where you are at, seek a spot and try to find a spot where you THINK that nature, the spirit of nature, will communicate to you. And don't be too limited by thinking you have to have a beautiful forest, or a nice mountain, because then it will be all sorts of sadness—there's no need, I'm just saying. So, I'm gonna go.

D. That was a really nice teaching. We'll type that up and put it out.

B. Ah. I'm gonna go now because Ophelia says to be short. I'm not sure if it qualifies as short, but I'll put a period after this.

D. Alright, my friend. I really appreciate you coming and talking today. It's always a pleasure to hear what you have to say.

Ophelia, Bob: Don't be Sheep (May 10, 2020)
This is from a public séance we held during the early part of the lockdowns imposed by the Cell. Ophelia talks about how the spirit realm would like to see societies develop that are independent and isolated from one another. The multinational corporations have become entirely too powerful and use their financial leverage to crush independence and competition within all levels of society. The global lockdown is a perfect example, as the small businesses were determined to be "non-essential", but the big companies were allowed to stay open and make extraordinary profits. Many of the smaller businesses failed, allowing the mega-corporations to grab even more market share. It was a shameless and undisguised abuse of power by the Cell and their henchmen in governments and media, and is a textbook example of racketeering.

Bob came in after Ophelia was finished. He brought a basket of mushrooms, or ideas, he wanted to share. He continued with Ophelia's discussion of the changes going on in the world, and how people should address them on a personal level.

D. It seems like there are a lot of financial troubles going on right now. Do you have any thoughts you would like to share about the financial conditions in the US and the rest of the world in the next few years?

O. It will be a dip financially, and that will mirror the level of fear, the level of being or feeling trapped within your reality. Not being fully clear on an outcome creates immobility. This is what the Cell seeks, for man to be passive, stagnation, to not move and seek the answers, rather than being stuck by questions. Indeed, we understand the fear that comes when the financial system collapses. But it is only a minor part of a bigger reboot. The reboot that is initiated by the Cell to create an outcome that the spirit realm stopped. The spirit realm exchanged, redirected the intention from the Cell. There will still be some effects, like the financial drop, that will be used by those who seek to hold man's consciousness under the veil. It will be their torch to keep man locked, the financial crash. It is not a complete crash, it's simply a dip. It is a way for you to find new ways to coexist, not only as humans, but together as one species on one planet. But yes, there will be effects.

D. Thank you for that. I appreciate it. Did you have any other thoughts you would like to share?

O. Well, I do indeed, but someone is pulling my arm. And indeed, we do have his very joyful basket to look into; the basket of mushrooms that he came with. So he sort of maneuvered my attention with this basket of mushrooms, meaning he has several ideas. He's not going to be able to share all the mushrooms, but he will indeed be able to share some. So if there aren't any questions from each side here, then yes, I will step aside at this point.

D. Oh, wait. There are two questions. One is about China, how is it involved in all this chaos? The other is about the Cell itself, the ones behind all this.

O. Yes. Involved, China is involved. It is seeking new ways to control the flow of merchandise, to create an empire based on supply. To be the leading part, the leading role—to put it into human words—to become the only Walmart existing. That is their intention, at this time. It is a long-term project, but they don't have the ability to rule in other ways than when it comes to factories, to transportation, delivery, import, export. They want to be the main hub for export to others. They are monitored by the big brother, the big country next to it.

D. Russia.

O. Yes. Not the same strength as the big brother.

D. What ultimately does a new beginning look like after all this is over, as far as the societal structure?

O. There will be turmoils before structure can emerge. In that turmoil, the Cell feels it is losing the grip, as well as the big Walmart, China (*feels it is losing control*). As all these centers are feeling defeat, great groups (*that oppose the Cell*) are reorganizing, regrouping—one big one is about to become larger in the US—then the understanding of life will meet changes, but also meet opportunities. Those who are locked, (*who think*) that change is bad, that change can only lead to defeat, will feel defeat, will feel powerless. Those who seek new ways of how to use resources, such as solar energy, wind energy. Not being too aggressive in the way that you export and import supply—to use local organizations, instead of seeking the lowest dollar, the cheapest merchandise. You have everything next to you. You do not need to import and export everything. You do not need to export manpower. You have it all, you can build your society, and that is what we wish for the future to entail.

D. That's beautiful, Ophelia. Thank you for that.

O. Oh, you are much welcome. And yes, indeed, a brief mushroom basket, indeed.

D. Alright, my friend. Thank you.

O. You are much welcome. Bye bye.

B. HUH!

D. Welcome back.

B. NAH nah nah nah (*he began wordlessly singing*) Ah. I thought it was gonna be like a separate session, just me. Oh, Ophelia pulled my arm. (*He was looking towards her.*) She said that I knew it was not separate session, that it was not just me. BUT I have my basket, and in the basket are several treats. And I thought if I come with treats, it's much more likely that I will have more time.

D. Alright, we're listening!

B. I do feel that if man could be a little bit more inclined to salute themselves, to blow their own trumpet. Blow your own horn sometimes, it's nothing bad. Because if you constantly put yourself in the back seat in a car, meaning in a situation or in life, then where are you gonna go? If you are in some way steering your life, steering your car, then it's much more likely that you will reach the destination of your choosing. If you constantly go on the commute, then the only option you have is to go on and off where someone else tells you to. BUT if you are in charge and steer your own vehicle, steer your own life, then you are more likely to reach your destination. So one of my treats in my basket is the gift of—oh. (*He glanced to the left.*) Ophelia says something about, you know, not everyone might have a car. But everyone can know how to steer their own life, at least. So that's what I want to say about that. And what I also would like to say is that sometimes a little bit of acknowledgment for one's advancement is nothing bad. There.

D. That's very good, my friend.

B. Another treat in my basket is that I would like to share the ability, at this time, when several might feel like they are on a crossroad in their occupation. This is a time—this is like I'm a news reporter—when you can redirect and become more sufficient in another occupation. (*He was speaking dramatically, trying to imitate a news anchor.*) What I would like to say is that this is a great opportunity to find a different skillset under your suit. You have no idea if the suit that you are wearing is actually the one you intended to travel in. SO, when one feels like the rug is swiped from underneath one's feet, THEN one stands there and feels a little bit lost. This is a time when one can fully engage and become more aware if there is another skillset that one could potentially develop. We will see that several will become their own entrepreneurs. Because in general, man does not like to be employed. Being employed is similar like just following—like the sheep, they are in a big group and they just sort of go, "Ohh, all sheeps go to the left. I have to go to the left." Or, "It's 11:30, it's lunchtime." "Now it's 3:00. In Sweden, it's fika, coffee break." "Ohh, 4:30, time to go home. I also have to find something to eat." You know, all these create somewhat of group behavior that is not necessarily what is expected of you as you traveled TO Earth. So, as there are people who will lose their jobs, it is an opportunity to also create a new profession. We will see that there are several new little businesses that will pop up—like my mushrooms in my basket, pop up like that—but one has to conquer a little bit of discomfort. And discomfort is different. Some might have the financial support and the discomfort is simply to start doing something for oneself, to not be that sheep that always goes to the left, and 11:30 lunch, 3:00 o'clock fika, you know. And for others, the discomfort might be that they have to do with less. Perhaps a move is called for. Perhaps you cannot live in that really expensive apartment anymore. Discomfort! And that is what you have to conquer. People have to understand that if you feel a little bit of discomfort, then there is a way for you to navigate differently. It is like having a stone in the shoe. Do you continue to walk, or do you take off the shoe and remove the stone? The stone, at this time, indicates that there is discomfort in the world where you have to redirect and rethink your life. Period.

D. That's really good advice.

B. Ah. SO! There's a lot of people, I should say, that are fully content walking around in that sheep group and having like the stone in the shoe. And this is the time to remove the stone, to perhaps rethink and relearn and create one's destination differently. Those who do not see the options and the possibilities that lie before them will still just walk around in that group of sheep, in some way, and they will still just be bothered by that stone in the shoe. So, that's a choice. Everything is by choice. And the spirit realm looks upon that very, "Hmmmm. What is going on over there? Why don't they make any choices? Why do they just walk around in a big group and follow someone who might direct the group of sheeps in the wrong direction? Do you want to be a sheep in a group, or do you want to perhaps create your own trail? You can still be a sheep, but you can be a different kind of sheep, you can be the leader sheep of your own little adventure. Because life is about understanding—and that's my third and last mushroom, Ophelia said—that life is an adventure. At this time, man might not feel very welcoming of the word, that life at the moment is an adventure. BUT at least you're waking up, and you have the ability to create an adventure, if you want to. Being incarnated is a way to see whether the soul understands that this IS an adventure, regardless of if it doesn't look like that, if it looks gloomy and if it's just with a stone in your shoe. But what choices do you make? Do you continue with something that is not working for you? And this is like putting a lot of mankind into that wall of 'make a choice, or not', and some will just be confused and they will be helped by light beings. I'm not a light being in that sense, even though I take care of you, and I roll you when you sleep, and I'm—oh, Ophelia says I am a light being. (*He smiled and looked pleased.*)

D. I certainly think you are.

B. Ah. It's just that I'm not like self-glowing, I'm not like a light, I'm not like a flashlight. I was a flashlight, a little bit, when I was traveling between my fish tanks and trying to find my spot. (*Meaning when he went looking for a spot to put his solar system. See Notes, Volume 1.*) You said that I looked like a little flashlight then. So I might be—I am indeed a light being, in that sense. It's just that, you know, I don't have wings. I could if I want to, perhaps. Maybe that's something for my next level of learning. Well, I'm gonna go now. But I wanted to say steer your own car; don't be satisfied with having stones in your shoes; see it as an opportunity to become a new entrepreneur in your life, to design your suit, to design your life path ahead; and also see life and the people around you as an adventure. That's what I wanted to say.

D. That's really good, my friend. Before you leave, I had a question that either you or with Ophelia's help can answer. It's about people, like in Africa, that are starving and don't seem to have many options. Is that some sort of karmic path they have chosen?

B. It's a global karmic path in some way. Because karma is also going over cycles. You have the individual karma, but you also have continent karma. In this case, the karma that relates to that region is in some way to rise above. It's a complex question to just answer very briefly, Ophelia says. It sort of moves around, this particular purpose or pickle, that Africa is suffering at the moment. There was a time when the same lessons were elsewhere, especially like in the northern part of the US, there was a similar struggle of not fully getting by. It's more of a continent karma or continent mission. In the second dimension, we are trying to change different scenarios when it comes to climate, because there are too many zones that are not fruitful enough, growth doesn't come as it should, and the region down there is part of that. There is a natural movement of occurrences and also with people. At this time, there are less souls from the higher levels that occupy that region. (*Meaning most are brand-new souls from the fifth.*)

D. That brings me to another question.

B. I was kinda on my way, but if you want to have me here—

D. I love having you here. It's one of the greatest pleasures of the week for me. We've talked a lot about souls coming in from different places, and I have made the assumption that not all human bodies are occupied by souls from one of the dimensions. Some might actually be occupied by the Master Mind?

B. Some are occupied from the first dimension, and in the first dimension is the Creator, the Master Mind travels to experience certain things. So there are indeed certain bodies that do not occupy like a friend from Ophelia's place.

D. That was one of the conclusions I drew, because there is like 8 billion people on Earth, and I had assumed not all of them are occupied by souls.

B. We're gonna discuss that because that's upcoming. It's always been like that in different measurements, whether there is like fifty–fifty, you know, fifty Master Mind, fifty soul. If we have the human body, there was a time (*prior to the creation of the humanoid*) you and I had not met, I think it was way before you and I started our adventures. You might not have thought it was such a big adventure, but I did! We did a lot of fun things together; we've been all sorts of places. There was a time in this bottle (*the early humanoid*) where the Master Mind was tapping in about 85%. The being was quite enlightened, very much in tune with the Source. The Master Mind, as we are talking about now—and that will be discussed further, Ophelia says this is not the time or the place for everything—but at the moment the Master Mind is simply occupying 5 to 7, 10 percent tops, in the bottle. Not only in that continent (*Africa*), of course, but on several places. There is a big place in the Asian region as well, where we have this phenomena.

D. Wonderful. That's what I thought. I had written it up in your book and wanted to validate it before we send it out into the world.

B. Well, we're gonna discuss it further, and you're gonna be able to put it in the book, Ophelia says. But this is not the time. But I wanted to give you confirmation on that. Ophelia says it was okay, she gave me like that (*holding up his thumb.*)

D. Better than wagging the finger at you.

B. Ah. It's just that the Master Mind and the Creator taps into all living lifeforms in different ways, depending on the flow of evolution and the current time. Like I said, way over there before you and I met, the Master Mind tapped into certain bodies, not human bodies necessarily, but forms that existed here, with about 85 percent. There are some who have, you know, there is one here who has the memory of that experience. There is one (*Kari*) on the US side, Ophelia says, that has a memory of filling up (*the remainder above*) 85 percent and being very in-tuned with a water creature. It was 85 percent Master Mind and 15 percent from this soul present on the US side, over there, who has the memory of occupying and existing in water surrounding. (*Kari was participating in our séance. She later verified that she has memories of blending with whales and dolphins in the very distant past. Ophelia and Kari are both Shea, from the seventh dimension, and have been assisting with the Earth project for hundreds of millions of years.*)

D. Understood, my friend. Do you have any other thoughts you would like to share before you leave?

B. Clearly, I'm not allowed to share too much anymore. Anyway, I'm gonna go now.
D. Thank you for your mushrooms.

Ari, Ophelia: The Cell and 5 Years of Turmoil (Aug 23, 2020)
Many of the sessions held during 2020 and 2021 included observations about how each person could best handle the lockdowns, isolation, and job losses that were ongoing concerns. Christine and I were also pushed around by the winds of change. I had been working as an engineering executive at an oil and gas company in Colorado, and was laid off just two weeks prior to this session. Christine had been stuck in Sweden for months, due to the travel restrictions. We had always talked about moving to Sweden, someday, and fully committing to our spiritual work. As it turned out, that plan became our reality, which is why Ari said we were making great transitions.

Ari cautions about the synthetic mRNA, which is being peddled as a vaccine. He repeats the warning Bob and others have given about the side effects of this nano-technology, which include mental disorders and other maladies. Ari explains that the key members of the Cell are aliens, and were the ones who initiated the nonsensical lockdowns. They do not fully understand the soul of humans, so they misjudged how people would respond. Even though a sizable portion of the population believed the propaganda the media hacks were regurgitating 24 hours a day, there were many who remained skeptical. To quash dissent, the covid profiteers and governmental sycophants declared it is blasphemous to contradict their fatuous decrees. They proceeded to ostracize, de-platform, ban, revoke medical licenses, and even imprison those who asked logical questions or had an opinion that was not sanctioned by the tyrannical conspirators. Unfortunately, it seems they are not done imposing their will on the bourgeoisie and the proletariat. The next 5 to 10 years are going to be chaotic, as the Cell loses their stranglehold over the minds of the people. We have been told that a financial collapse is possible, along with a cessation of trade between countries, foreign exchange controls on currency, riots, food shortages, mass migration, social breakdown and disorder. From a human perspective, this sounds quite dire. But the spirit realm views it pragmatically, as the end result is more freedom for those who remain, and less stress on the environment. As a final note, when Ari talks about oxygen masks, it is symbolic for a person finding their own inner guidance.

A. This is Ari.
D. Hello, Ari.
A. How are you?
D. Well.
A. Busy boy, busy bee. Making great transitions. Not only the two of you, but we know that many of mankind are doing changes at this time. What we see is an increasing light, an increasing fire within your spirit—a fire and a need for change. There are certain things where man feels restricted, where man feels they cannot change. However, what certain society organs are failing to see is that you, as a species, inside, are mobilizing your powers. What we see is increasing light at several locations on Earth. Some failing (*light is decreasing*), a little bit. But know that everyone seeks the light individually and at a pace that is beneficial and right for them. You do not need to worry about the general speed, the general development, the progress in your society. Everything is unfolding as it should. When transitions take place, whether it is your season from winter to spring—or, in this case, the mobilization of your inner spirit—certain experiences are needed to occur. At this time, what is needed is the awakening of your connection to others, your connection to your host—meaning your planet. What a small group is trying to prevent, hinder, is backfiring because more and more are getting together in this united fire within. This cannot be stopped by any human force, any media, any establishment based on human interests. Your race is protected. We (*the spirit realm*) are seeking the change. We are seeking the improvement of consciousness before new souls, a new level of soul energy, can incarnate. You are on that threshold where some personality aspects, if you like, will be left behind in exchange for a more modern car, more modern human body, if you like. So do not fear the change. See the change as something new is happening, something that you are here to witness at this time in your incarnating circle. You have all been here numerous times before, and this is a time to rejoice. It is a time of change. It is not a new phenomena, but it is something that is precious to witness. See the change in your environment, see the change among friends. They cannot distance you with masks or lockdowns. You are connected, regardless. They are trying to separate the physical, failing to ignore (*i.e., they are aware*) that souls, hearts, minds, are connecting underneath their nose. There is nothing they can do about this development. But you need to look beyond the human experience at this time.

You need to be in a mindset of welcoming, of being receptive to the new, knowing that when you return in a future incarnation, there is a new era. But in order for the new to take place, you have to sometimes walk through fire. But it is a human fire. It is not a soul failure or a soul trauma. Know that there is no trauma, it is what the establishment is trying to put on you, the human you. Know that they have no power over your inner being. And they see the inner beings connecting, regardless of social distancing, and social lockdowns, and masks.

D. Was this current transition phase initiated by the spirit realm, or is this something that came from humans?

A. Not humans. Those who initiated it operated in human form, but they belong in a Cell that is not human based, not human origin. However, they failed to acknowledge and see the power within your species, the power of the soul. They thought that humans, the body, would be easier to trick. You are still, however, in that transition. You are still in the phase of choice. You can choose to respond like a human, you can choose to be a robot—which is the intent of this Cell. However, the spirit realm is igniting the fires within, making you connect on a deeper level that the Cell could not foresee. Animals are thanking you, at this time. Nature is recovering. Your seas are recovering. In many ways, what goes on, on your poles, also is, at the current time, in a shift. There are visitors monitoring the Pole (*the center Pole of the planet, along with the Fork*). And they are of good, they are here to maintain the work (*of the councils*). It is maintenance, one can say, of the (*Earth's*) center Pole connecting the South and North Pole. And there are visitors, indeed, working on councils' behalf. However, for them to be operating a little bit in disguise, it is appreciated that mankind have their eyes looking elsewhere.

D. Understood. From your perspective, how long will this transition last?

A. The first phase is about 3 to 5 years. It is a change within governments. It is a change in social behavior, in the way man is guided, in the way some want the human race to act, think, behave. Five years is a cycle where there will be turmoil, not all in the same way as this cycle, this year. However, you will meet other challenges. See beyond the challenge, see beyond your human eyes, observe the drama in front of you, which will be different, depending on where you are. If you are in the location where your physical is located at this time (*US*), and this one is over here (*Sweden*), it's not going to be the same. But there will be challenges that will contradict the way you have been acting and feeling up till this point. Certain things will be put in motion in order for actions, choices, to occur. What we do see is a lack of action and choice before this so-called bug, the flu, entered your consciousness. It is not flu, it is not a pandemic—it is a way for some to control your physical and mental parts of the human, failing to recognize the power of the soul. However, this five-year cycle is not only going to be about what occurs right now. It will challenge you in the way you feel about each other, the way you connect to each other. If you are willing to open your heart to others, or not. If you are willing to make choices, or not. Choices for your family, choices for yourself. You are in that transition where choice and action is required. For those who are paralyzed at this moment, it is experienced as fear. Those who welcome the change will gradually feel chains around them releasing, letting go, exchanged for freedom. If you seek freedom physically, then you will have so, if you make choices to mirror those changes. Mainly, what we see is the blockage of minds. The mind is easier to trick, as you are aware, than your heart. The physical simply executes signals. That is why we say you run around like chickens, occasionally, because you do not know which directions to go. If you feel like a chicken, then you could try to just stop and then try to transform yourself into a more developed or evolved creature. So, there you go. However, we are grateful for the light work that you all participate in. Some of you are here to ignite the mind. Some of you listening are here making new paths in the connection to spirit. There are so many waiting to be heard, and some of you will have that connection to entities quite different than a human has experienced before. Be proud to be unique. Be proud of the connection and the power that you possess, the gift given to you from birth in this life. You are here to make new footprints, to make a mark, and to help others who are paralyzed. However, don't let the sensation of lockdowns, or those who do not act, hinder you. You cannot have other energy draining you on your mission. You are here to help. What is it that they say when you go in an airplane? "Put the mask on yourself first, then the other one." Huhuhuh huh huh! Well, you don't fly that much now either, do you? Well, we like that. Put your mask on, your oxygen mask, first. Then help others. There you go.

D. I thought you were talking about the virus mask.

A. Oh, no, we don't approve. It's simply to—in certain places it is valid to have (*a mask on*), but the general intent is not in your favor. It doesn't hinder the bug that you are so spooked about. I'm not talking about you here listening; I'm talking about those who are paralyzed. Those who are paralyzed would rather put a plastic bag, if they could, over their head, thinking that would help. However, you have to look at the plague going on. Use your inner eyes, use your inner ears, your inner mind. You have a human mind and you have a soul mind—use your soul mind, and you will see the difference. Once you use your human mind, you might run around like chickens. But again, oxygen mask on first, then provide oxygen to others.

D. I did have one question about something that I'm personally concerned about, and I know others are as well. The vaccine that they are going to try to push on the public, what is your opinion of that?

A. Not. No. We do not approve. It is not developed in a way that it is (*beneficial*)—again, they are only talking about the physical, failing to recognize the effect on the mental. This will, in many ways, improve the physical if you have a vaccine. And that is what they want you to see, the improvement in the physical. The backside of the coin is that it will make your brain, or the mental capacity, fail. There are some here who work with mental disorders, and what we wish to say is to be mindful of the effects that certain vaccines have. You simply see the end result on the physical effect, failing to recognize that the mental might suffer. And the mental might show effect, not instantly, but later on. This is the challenge, one of them, that you are facing; it is to see the difference between what oxygen mask (*or remedy*) you want to have. Do you want to have an oxygen mask helping your physical, or your entire being? At this time, it is not developed enough. In many ways it will help the physical, but not the other parts of the human.

D. Alright, thank you for that.

A. Just be mindful. Just because you might see a physical improvement, it might be other effects that you are not aware of—silent effects. Be mindful, see with your inner eyes, make choices, ask questions. If you ask questions about, let's say, this vaccine that someone is trying to give you, you will notice whether the person can provide answers or not. If the answers are simply related to physical improvement, and if they cannot

give you any reassurance of other effects, then pause, retreat, return not. There you go.
D. That's a wonderful explanation. Thank you for that.
A. Oh, you are much welcome. We'll see here, we have someone here, ready to communicate.
D. That's surprising. (*Bob was eager to speak.*)
A. Surprising indeed. Here, always present. He's been with you a lot in the area of study, back home. And we have discussed his further development when it comes to his schooling. Indeed, he is eager to proceed in this so-called space program, as he calls it. I'm pretty sure he wants to create a galaxy, at this point. We gave him a moon, and he liked the moon, but it's never-ending.
D. Well, before you take off, I had one more question for you, if you don't mind?
A. I don't mind.
D. We've heard about a solar event coming to the Earth, some sort of solar activity or event. Do you foresee that, or can you remark on that?
A. The only remark would be that it is another maneuver to have you look elsewhere. It is simply like when it's Fourth of July or New Year's Eve—whoops, there is the fireworks, and everyone stares in that direction, failing to recognize what goes on behind them. And then—poof! There is another firework. It's non-important for your wellbeing or development. However, it will assist those who can tap into the light. It will increase your light if you tap into it—there is no fear. It will increase healing powers for those who are in the capacity of healing. So in that sense, yes, it will increase powers within you, igniting gifts that you might not know, those (*gifts*) that are sleeping.
D. Nothing to fear, then.
A. Nothing to fear. It is transition. Your system, your solar system is also in a phase of development and transition. When that occurs, certain cosmological effects are bound to happen, and that is the case at this time. There are several outlets of energy fuses in your system, in your galaxy, all together at this time. It is an interesting play that the spirit realm observes, but there is no need to fear. And again, the human has fear, the soul sees progress. The soul knows it will come back and return to something completely different. No need to fear.
D. Wonderful. Thank you so much for that.

A. Enjoy the fireworks.
D. (*Laughing.*) All right, my friend. Elahim.
A. Elahim.

To bring together similar subjects, we are appending a November 28, 2019 talk by Ophelia. I asked a question about the Cell, and she gave an insightful response about how they use the media to overthrow societies.

O. This is Ophelia.
D. Hello, Ophelia.
O. Good morning to you.
D. Good morning to you!
O. If that will be the case, then good morning to me! (*She laughed about the reference to time.*)
D. No such thing as morning.
O. No such thing, always present. So, we're cleaning a little bit here, even though the energy was mild this time. But is there anything you wish to ask?
D. I've been thinking about the Cell that controls the world, and I'm concerned for the fate of humanity—
O. You mean the current man?
D. Yes.
O. When you say humanity, there is no need to fear, as you have been here in different cycles before. You are not extinct. However, current man and your consciousness needs transformation, and that is the upcoming cycle. So when you say that you are concerned about humanity, I would say there is no fear. If you say that you are concerned about the current man, then yes, changes are upcoming.
D. Is it being controlled by the spiritual realms?
O. Yes. Councils. Council of Nine.
D. So the end result will ultimately be favorable?
O. Yes. New cycle, new beginning. In many ways, man thinks that they are at the peak of their evolution. But there have been societies before you, as you are aware, that were highly and more connected to Source. Not only to their spiritual source and their soul–mind, but also to the level of science that was available for them to dwell (*live on*), to drill (*advanced technology for mining*), to understand the possibilities of your host, and to become in symbiosis with your host. At this time, you are not in symbiosis to the host; we care for the host. If you were more connected to

A Spiritual Path

the host and to the web above as well as the grid below, then we would not need modifications (*of the human*) at this time. We are here to enlighten and you are doing your part, in physical form, to make people aware of certain illusions placed on your path. But there are indeed changes coming.

D. Our recommendation for people to not be passive, is that predominantly for individual improvement, or is it for them to become active socially?

O. It's to gather the race. It's to gather you in a common cause and a common wish for enlightenment and a common wish for peace. As long as there is this Cell, who in some way operates independently, it has in some way its own evolution, its own agenda to follow, which is monitored by councils in the spiritual reality. In some way, they travel within the general evolution and the general consciousness, but they have their own task at hand and they cannot merge with the general evolution and cause and consciousness on this plane. This creates frustration in the Cell and they act out. What we see is efforts taking place, more and more, when it comes to the environment. You are here to release humanity from feeling that they are trapped, that they are not free. It is a remnant from an old spell, if you like, that man was not free. You in some way become entrapped, instead of changing the way you perceive yourself and your surroundings and others. If you change just a little bit, you will BE free. No one can entrap you, no one can put a chain on you, unless you grant it. Humanity grants chains, and you are here to break them.

D. The Cell (*the bankster cartel*) funded the revolutions in the Russian Empire and pre-communist China, destroying freedom and spirituality, didn't they?

O. They were acting out as more and more started to raise against the captivity. And the same way occurs now, just more in a subtle form, due to using media, using social chains. Not the same visible aggression, but it is. It just travels differently (*through society*) than a takeover or a riot. But the media operates similar as what you described in different riots—just more settled. Just observe your TV, for instance, and commercials, how they speak much faster, like they are on fast-motion. It is to paralyze the one who listens. They have a similar way of using the media—talking fast, non-informative. It is a way to paralyze, to numb your counterpart (*human mind*). If you are numb, you are more likely to be captive and surrounded by chains. The Cell knows this, so they are using different methods at this time. They are using media instead of traveling like a force, (*as they did*) in other ways in history. (*They are using media to conquer countries internally, instead of mercenary armies or other external invasions.*)

D. From your perspective, would you say their actions are what you would call evil? Would you ever use that word in relation to behavior?

O. I will not use the word evil. I will use the word "primitive", or "lack of judgment". But from a human understanding, that IS evil. We never use the word "evil" even though what we see is a child misbehaving. There.

D. Thank you.

O. Okay, there we go.

D. Alright Ophelia, talk soon.

O. Bye bye.

Ari, Bob: Spirituality to Master Energies. (June 28, 2020)

When Christine first started doing trances sessions in public, she and I had a bit of anxiety about whether they would communicate as well as they do in private. We no longer have that concern. The public sessions are interesting because the spirits speak on a more personal level. They also do quick reviews of topics they have covered in-depth during our private sessions. Even though some of the material echoes prior talks, they reshape them to fit the audience. Their talks are usually quite complex, in that they will cover multiple ideas, but tie them together in a theme. The title of this section is pulled from something Ari said in passing while describing how spirituality has changed over time. I think it is a brilliant and very accurate definition, because the very core of spirituality is how one masters their inner emotions and thoughts. The mind is constantly presented with impulses from different centers, so how the mind and soul work together to master these other influences is the essence of what it means to be incarnated.

B. Deet–dah–dah–DEET! Huh huh huh. Let me introduce Mr. Ari. Applause (*he clapped his hands*), like that. I volunteered as an introduction for everyone else, including myself, and Ari agreed. So I'm gonna bow away here. But deet–dah–dah–deet! Here he is, so I'll go.

D. Thank you for that lovely introduction. (*Bob moved aside as Ari took the stage.*)

A. Huh huh huh. Well, you gotta love the little guy, don't ya?

A Spiritual Path 199

D. Yes, we do. Welcome.
A. Thank you. Greetings to you all, on all continents, all cities. We are pleased to see that you take the time for spirit. Not just this gathering, but we also know that all of you at this time are reaching a central point within you where the doors will open for connections to higher realms within you. You are, in many ways, forerunners in a new way to coexist with the spirit realm. There are waves on how spirituality and connection to spirit has progressed over the years. And when I say years, you don't need to just go back to year zero. It is a shift in your consciousness, but what does it mean? In many ways, spirituality is vague. It is vague in a way that how can you, as man, connect to the divine within you? Constantly seeking for something outside, when everything is available, if you simply close your eyes. As you close your eyes, you invite the worlds, which will be different for each and every one of you. You will find your own path through history as man, humans, but also as other entities walking on Earth. So don't limit yourself by thinking back to simply year zero, how spirituality has changed. Spirituality is a way to master energies. There was a time when man sought comfort, guidance, from the planetary positions above them. This knowledge was accepted in society. As certain individuals felt left behind, not understanding the whole of the universe, the worlds within you, around you, that all coexist, they tried to hijack the way man sought the divine. For one thing, it is easy to connect with, let's say, the different lunar events. You are currently in the midst of several high energy events that include the moon. You have, therefore, the opportunity to connect to an ancient wisdom that you already know. You have it within you. You simply need to remind yourself on what energy, what power, resonates with the human body, with the layers and cells within you. You are, unfortunately, bombarded with energy flows that are not spiritual, that are not working on the behalf of humanity. That is why you need to seek a new way to coexist with energies. Energies are frequencies—some are beneficial for man, and some, not. The way that you can see the difference is the way your mind works. If your mind rushes, if you feel stressed, you are under the influence of energies that are not working on your behalf. It is harder if you live in cities than if you live in the countryside. It is easier to detect energies working on your behalf if you are not bombarded with influences from media, TV, computer, as well as other frequencies that are flying around at this time. This has

happened before. A collapse of energy was the result. At this time, we want you to find the connection to the energy web that is a spiritual link, if you like. There are several webs surrounding your planet, working spiritually to increase man's access. The increase of—let's begin with 5G—will dissolve other webs that are connected here to this surface. 5G, as we have mentioned, spread out, man can cope with. Be aware that the general intent is to increase this web, to increase it to 6G, 8G. In your lifetime might not even go higher than 8G, but they will never tell you. You will feel stressed in your being. You will feel like your mind is running away from you. If you feel that as is right now, then you are subject for influences easier than others.

D. Is there any way to protect yourself from that radiation?
A. Seek the silence. We know that man likes cities, but more and more will seek living conditions that are not in the major cities. The new way to coexist, to— (*Bob suddenly cut in and made a noise.*)
B. Ohh, I don't know if he was done?
D. I suspect he was not quite finished.
B. Nay, nay. This was not supposed to happen. I excuse myself.
D. We'll talk soon,
B. Probably. Excuse me.
A. Hmm. So where was I?
D. Talking about moving away from the cities.
A. Yes, yes, of course. Moving away from the cities will make your living conditions more suitable for man. You are not supposed to be crowded like you are at this time. Certain cities, not necessarily on this side of the puddle, but over in the continent where you, my friend, are sitting (*I was in Denver, Colorado*), are too congested and it is hard for man to exist and to hear their inner voice. So more and more will seek countryside living, seeking the elements such as water. Water is what we can provide, because water cools the system. Simply by being in water, or being near water, will help your brain to cool down. It will also help the soul to be heard and channel outwards into the physical. It is a way to cool down a body that is not working to its full potential. Several diseases are connected to an overheating brain. Nerves, cells, are highly affected and an easy target for radiation, such as what you experience through microwaves as well as silent noise, as well as 5G. If you think that this is silent noise, as is, you will be more confused if you

allow this to progress into, let's say, 7G or 8G. The technology is not developed (*to benefit humans*); it is developed for a world that has not the same lifeforms as here. Other realities can coexist with 10G, if you like, to compare. There are neighboring systems that have, to compare, 11 to 12G, but the lifeforms are not like here. They are not as easily influenced as you. The structure of those lifeforms are different than here. There are several visitors bringing knowledge from other places where a higher volt (EMF) is available than here, not taking into consideration the effect it has on lifeforms. There. What was your question?

D. That actually was my question. I wondered if the implementation of 5G was in any way influenced by visitors?

A. Outsourced, yes. Yes, visitors. Some bringing technology that is not equipped for the lifeforms on this place.

D. They must be aware of that, are they not?

A. Yes, yes. Different agenda.

D. Someone, and I think it was you, who said they were hoping to get rid of the humans, or at least thin them down so they could exploit the resources on the planet. Is that correct?

A. Yes, yes.

D. So not everyone is looking out for our best interest?

A. Souls incarnating, at this point, are here to meet the demand from other places on your resources. You see it in the oil business. You see how oil has created wars, created grabbing, greed. It is a way for the regular man to notice that something is wrong, something is at play that is not necessarily human–based. There are influences that are working on the Earth's behalf. You are safe and you are protected, but be aware and meet changes within you, changes within your atmosphere. Look around you. This one noticed, for instance, that there were no frogs any more in the swamp behind the area where she lived. This is also a sign that something is wrong. The ecosystem is, I wouldn't say suffering fully, but it has changed. Man, such as some of the souls present listening to this, have eyes that can see and detect certain shifts within the Earth's environment. See the imbalances—don't look with your human eyes, look from within—detect where changes have taken place in your near environment. See whether lifeforms are gone, see if new has arrived. Detecting changes within your vicinity will help you to know how to meet them. And you have the spirit realm behind you. There are several listening to this event today that has the ability to see these shifts in nature. They see it with their inner eyes. They see it from their center point, not human eyes. One person in particular, in this group, can use her feet, will sense and hear the plea from Mother Earth, changes within the environment. Specifically placed as a microphone for the spirit realm and higher councils who operate to help your environment. There.

D. I have a question. It seems like there is a lot of social instability. Since we don't know what is going to happen, is there any way that we should prepare for the changes that are coming, like stocking up on food or supplies?

A. Oh, that's what they want you to do; stock up, lock them in, stock up, lock in. Put toilet paper in the closet. That's what they want you to do. There is no danger, you have all the protection you need. Look around you, connect with others, don't fear others. All this fear of connecting with others, it creates a distance. It is easier to influence man if you are spread out, if you have distance to other lights. When I say lights, I mean other souls. Other lights, you are all lights. What they are seeking is to divide you. Divide the lights, lock them in, keep distance, stock up on toilet paper. There.

D. We can only hope that the spirit world has this all under control.

A. There is nothing going on at this time that has not happened before and that you, as a race, cannot rise above and meet. You are not powerless; you are empowered. The general intent is to make man feel powerless, even if it is to not have toilet paper. It does not matter; it is the same thing. It is to divide and make you weaker, but you are stronger and you are lights connecting. Don't fear other lights. There we go. Someone is here with a notebook. I don't know if he is taking notes on me. So there we go, there we go.

D. (*Laughing.*) Well thank you so much for sharing with us today. I really appreciate it.

A. You are much welcome. See you back home. Elahim.

D. Okay. Elahim.

B. Huhuh! Ah, ah. (*He then began imitating the Russian national anthem.*) I'm thinking that I would like to participate in a Eurovision song contest. I think that I would be really good. Me in the front, of course, and have those who sway in the back, in the background. I have been continuing to prepare spirit guides who are now ready to depart with certain souls from the sixth dimension. They are gonna be accompanied by a spirit guide from the second dimension, such as myself. But I'm not going, I have my hands full with you. And I'm still preparing your next life, which will be in 2178. It's gonna be an amazing journey that I have planned for you and me. But then it's also that Gergen, my mentor, he also said, "Not everything is about you," and that means me. But in my world, everything is about me and I don't think there's anything wrong with that. But now I have to think wide, I have to think about others. And that is why I was encouraged and that is why I participated in the project of creating my own spirit guide school. And they have done GREAT progress, much thanks to me. Huhuh.

D. Of course.

B. Ah. Just nod along please, that's all I need. Applause can come later after they come back, and hopefully they have done really great missions. I was not allowed to create lives for the souls from the fifth, BUT knowing their journey—and Earth should be really excited about this—because there are several souls coming in from the fifth dimension that are environmentally inclined and they're gonna come in like a little environmental army, I would say. When I say army, I think it has a really beautiful ring to it. But man tends to think an army is something negative because it indicates some sort of collision. And yes, it is, it is a collision. But it can be somewhat of a great field trip; it could be of a good cause. So, when I say an environmental army is coming in from the fifth, I think that is great! They have a purpose; they have a mission. I'm sitting here with all my spirit guides that are gonna participate and help these individuals fulfill all these beautiful assignments that I myself cannot take credit for. I take credit for the spirit guides, of course, but I cannot take credit for the whole mission. But I want to tell that it's gonna be like a—there's a lot of baby booms coming and several born from this year until 2022, some might even come early 2023, according to the Astrological Council, depending on how the planets are positioned. BUT 2020 to 2022, when those souls grow up, they're gonna be highly observant, like with a sharp eye and see what's needed in nature. They're gonna be quite pissed about if 5G turns into 8G, I'm just saying. They're not gonna go with force, this is not that kind of army. And again, army has a bad ring to it for humans. But in the spirit realm, it's a happy group that has a purpose. So, you know.

D. Are they going to be technical people or more like activists?

B. Nah. Some might be technical, but those are coming more from the sixth dimension. And I'm talking here about those who are gonna be more in tune with nature. Some will probably be a little bit technologically advanced, maybe know how to reboot a system in a computer, you know, control–alt–delete, or something like that. So they might have somewhat of a knowledge about technology. BUT the main purpose is that they're gonna be tuning in on nature, they're gonna be like that. And what is needed at this time is for those who are parents or grandparents or siblings or something else, to just pay a little bit of attention to these souls coming in. To not just discard an interest when they grow up. A lot of them will have an interest in, let's say, Boy Scouts, of sorts. There's gonna be an increase in that department. Not everyone has to play football. Not everyone has to play baseball, you know. There are gonna be a lot of those who have an interest and an awareness on how to maintain—you ask if they were gonna be technologically advanced—I would say they're gonna be more like geologists and those kind of occupations—that's gonna be a big boom there. And also, water engineers, like I wanted you to be. I wanted you to be a water engineer, but no one listened to me! My ideas were blown away with the wind. Then Jeshua came in and gave you a life (*plan*). But now I have designed a life for you, 2178. I'm quite proud. I did it all by myself. And that is something that all spirit guides—for all you people listening—we take great, I mean I take great pride in it, but we put great effort into creating lives and helping you to become the best human version of your soul that you can possibly be! And before you come to Earth, you sit down, all of you, with a spirit guide and you go through different plans. And some of you are on the path to open up certain environmental questions and to be somewhat of a bother to society. Because in order for change to take place, sometimes you have to be a little bit of a bother. I don't mind being a bother because the more I asked, the more I was nosy, the more I got access. If I hadn't asked about what's beyond beyond, I wouldn't have come to the big Library, for instance. I wouldn't have met you. I wouldn't have created my solar system. I wouldn't have been traveling in the bubble. There are so many things I wouldn't have done if I hadn't been persistent.

D. It's a good quality.

B. It is a quality that I think is good. All souls are persistent, no souls are passive or lazy. The problem is that when you *(he makes a sucking sound*) into a body, and it can be a body that is somewhat challenging for a soul. And the more you progress, the more you come here, the more you're gonna have to have bodies that are like the personalities don't really mix and match with your soul. But no soul is passive, all souls are inquisitive, all souls are active. The problem is when they go (*makes sucking sound again*) into a body, into an environment with other bodies that also (*makes sucking sound*), souls in like that—problems arise. And it's like you don't necessarily know, "Okay, where does my soul (*once again makes sucking sound*) go in? Is it like in the ears?" I'm not gonna say the other word, because that's not what humans do, BUT, "Where do I enter?" You go in and out here in the middle, like you can see my belly here on this one, belly go in and out, this is how you enter (*expands belly*) and you live. And when done (*he exhales and deflates belly*), you leave. New body, new life, do things, out. In and out, like that. So if you want to explore the beyond, you can mentally think that you exit your body, but you don't exit it like a chimney, you exit here in the center, in the middle there (*moves belly in and out*), like that. But I want to tell everyone here listening, since I now have the microphone, and when I say microphone, I mean like this one. Like this here (*indicating Christine's body*), this is my microphone, this is my stage. All spirit guides are really rooting for you. They see the potential in you, whether you do it or not. Sometimes, as humans, you can lack confidence in your mission. Your soul has a great self–esteem, you simply need to find the portal and the path ahead where you are moving, not as a human necessarily, but how would you progress if you had all this self–esteem, all this support, knowing that they are here on your behalf and they are moving forward with you. Some people feel lonely, and especially now when you are separated like you are, because of someone saying you should be separated, you should not communicate and connect, and so forth. And it creates a sadness within people. It is like the human is sad, but the soul is not necessarily sad, the soul is just trying to make itself heard. And what we can see is that several souls on Earth at this time are trying to make themself heard to the physical. But the physical is paralyzed by what is happening at this time, and there is a sadness of separation. But if you close your eyes, you will not only see someone like me, your own spirit person, but you will also feel the connection to other lights and you will feel like you are not separated. That is what we taught the two of you to do, when this one is on one side of the puddle, here, and we told you to dock for a couple of minutes each evening, in European time. It is a way for you to not feel separated, and everyone can do that. If people talked with loved ones who are separated at this time, and they get together and, like we taught you guys, what we taught you to do, to just close your eyes, sit for a couple of minutes and just tune in on the other one and send love and compassion to the other person. If others were to do the same thing with their loved ones, no one would feel as separated. Because it is simply the physical that are separated—souls are not separated. And that is the big understanding of this.

D. We've been doing that, and it works really well.

B. I might take questions now! (*The session continued with personal questions.*)

Ari, Ophelia, Bob: On the Right Path (May 24, 2020)

This is another public seance that we are including because they covered a lot of significant topics. Ari brings up the importance of eliminating sugar and the fructose infused "foods" that people consume. If someone is serious about taking care of their body and becoming more connected to their spirit, then diet is of the highest importance. Ophelia follows Ari and discusses why people should avoid the toxic news that the media spoon-feeds the public. She says that those following their inner guidance are on the right path, even when other humans are going in a different direction. She also reminds us to go to bed each night with a sense of gratitude for something that has happened during the day. Gergen was the first to recommend this practice, which we published in *Notes, Volume 1*, about appreciating the small things in life. It is easy to become despondent when we fail to see the many blessings the spirit world gives to us each day. Bob ends the session with advice about how the current situation presents opportunities for humans to change the course of their life, and to focus on those things you can do, instead of those you can't. He also tells us that nature is grateful for the reduction in travel, as it has helped to rejuvenate many plants and animals.

A. This is Ari.
D. Hello, my friend.
A. Elahim.
D. Elahim.

A. We are here as a family, to connect your world with the higher realms. We invite mankind to participate in raising the frequency that will benefit not only your cycle, but future generations as well. At this time, man stands on a threshold, in some way. You need to remove your blindfolds, you need to be excited about what is to come, knowing that you are forerunners in how man will proceed, incarnating on this plane. This is not the first time man stands on a threshold, similar like this. You feel hindered, you feel captured, not only within your body, but your souls resist the captivity (*lockdowns*) that many of you are experiencing. Just know that you are protected and that nothing can capture your soul. Nothing can make you in captivity unless you allow it. What we see are those who lead others in this revolution, if you like, on how to proceed. You should know that is a new wave of incarnating souls in your future within fifty to one hundred years. You are, in many ways, plowing the field, making it safe for higher vibrations to enter this plane. If you focus on your soul eye, your soul mind, then it will be helpful in this work. If you look through your human eyes and respond with your human brain, you will experience fear. Fear is only an illusion, and you are, in many ways, aware of the illusion. However, once in a while, you act as humans, not as your true self. As you connect, similar like this (*by video-conference*), even so, (*you are*) in a group, connecting energies. Here we have ties over the ocean. But know that you have friends in your soul family at home, trying to connect with you, similar like you do here with friends. If you cannot communicate and connect with your human friends or family, know that there is a great effort in the spirit realm from your soul family trying to encourage those friends, such as yourself, who at this time have incarnated. The intention is to promote a new way to incarnate. New souls coming in, and some already trying here at this time. But the physical body, the container for the (*more advanced*) souls to tap into, is not suitable at this time. Neither is your atmosphere. As the container, the physical body, and atmosphere shifts and changes, other frequencies from other spiritual realities can merge with the physical reality. In many ways, we are cleaning the fourth reality. The fourth, the bridge between physical and spiritual, is full of old karma, full of previous visitors who have not fulfilled their journey. And, in many ways, that hinders the progress for those who are incarnated. See it as a fog that needs to be cleared. At this time, people dream more. It is because each

208   The Spiritual Design

and every one are asked from the Source to clean their remains in the fourth reality. So those who dream more at this time should know that they are assisting in this cleanup. Some are operating from non-physical realities, parallel realities, to assist this transition, this clean-up. But know that there are certain individuals that dream more, and they are doing a great part in cleaning up, so that new souls can enter more freely. Do you understand?

D. I do. I know you've talked in the past about waves of energy raising the vibration of Earth. I wondered if you could address people's concerns about where the future is headed and how you foresee what is going to happen in the next hundred years or so?

A. The upcoming incarnations need a cleaner vehicle, cleaner body. The soul frequencies cannot match the current bodies that exist. The intake of food needs to be addressed. You need to eliminate sugar more commonly and universally. Sugar makes the soul struggle in the container. I would say sugar is the worst enemy to the soul. So, what is coming is an awareness on how to clean oneself, clean the body that is—not with soap, of course. It has to do with the inner cleaning. Parts that would be helpful at this time is different liquids to clean out the systems, using apple cider vinegar, stronger potions to clean out remains of sugar. Due to the fact that there is too much remains of sugar in the physical bodies at this time, it is also the effect that you see in this struggle with this flu. The flu would not have had the same impact if the bodies were not contained with sugar. Sugar is, in many ways, the enemy of a healthy vehicle, regardless of if we have a flu or not. The soul cannot be heard if you have taken or eaten too much cookies, or cakes, or such! BE AWARE that sugar can be found where one thinks sugar is not available, such as in those sweet sauces you dip the sushi in, for instance. It's still sugar, it doesn't mean that it's food. And yes, we have Bob here, who thought that he should talk about that. But he has to wait his turn. Huh huh huh.

D. I guess sugar is worse than meat or wheat, or things like that?

A. If we were to address to take away sugar, meat, wheat, alcohol, then man would just refuse and lay flat and just refuse, probably. But I would say, if one begins with eliminating sugar, then there is not very long until one will experience a much happier existence AS a human. Some still needs to feel human, and that is fine. But just know that the soul is the one experiencing the physical. And when one feels clean, when one feels healthy, alert, like they are having a good night's rest, then the soul is actually the one that is giving a thumbs up.

D. It's easier to connect spiritually if you are not contaminated?

A. Yes, yes. Once in a while, it is advised to do some sort of cleaning in your system with different liquids. Also, if one can do fast with two months in between, that will also assist the physical. One sign that the physical is a little bit dirty is that you have certain, not ticks, but motions within your fingers. The body is restless, like it is moving without control, in some way. Ticks, if you like. Can be felt in the lower parts of the arms, hands, or eyes. When you feel twitches in your eyes, that's a sign of too much sugar. There. I will leave to the next speaker, unless you have some questions?

D. I guess not. I appreciate everything you've said.

A. Just know that the entire race, the civilizations as is now, is standing on that threshold, ready to take a jump. But once in a while, that jump feels terrifying. And sometimes people will not wish to take the jump by themselves. But as more and more connect, it's going to be easier to take that leap. It is a leap of faith. All major shifts in consciousness, here on Earth, requires bold interactions. You need to find the fire within you. You need to be strong enough to know that you are preparing for future civilizations, future incarnations, such as yourself! Think of what sort of body, what sort of environment would I like to return to? Not everyone is having their final ascension (*laughing*) this time around.

D. I do have one question. I think everyone shares a concern about the oppressive nature of government at this time, and it does make us worry about our freedoms in the future.

A. Okay. I will leave to Ophelia. Elahim.

D. Elahim, my friend.

O. This is Ophelia.

D. Hello, Ophelia.

O. Hello to you. And hello to everyone who are listening as well, on two sides of the puddle. The question was about the government, and indeed it demands to be addressed. If they could, they would probably feed you with sugar, as the previous speaker was talking about. What I would like to say is to remain calm. Once you run around like chickens, there is nothing that finds a solution. You need to be centered in the way you perceive news. Be centered in the way the news hits you. Where does it affect you? There is a tremendous power behind paralyzing the mind. The governments that you refer to—not all are the same. You should also know there are moles placed in high positions in certain governments that are working on the behalf of the Creator and the spirit realm. However, those who try to hinder the progress of mankind, to hinder the unity of your race, they try to hit the mind because the mind is easily fooled. The heart is closer to your soul, and when one feels distressed by information surrounding oneself, just focus (*and sense*) if the information resonates in your heart, not in your mind. In some way, you need to drop the logic solution and you need to follow the sensation of right or wrong. And it has to do with everything in your life as humans. This is a time to turn the ship around, if you like, on several areas in your life as humans, as well as globally. You can choose whether you want to follow the mainstream information, or if you want to CREATE that mainstream information—quite different. Once one feels disturbed, know that the mind has been hijacked, in some way. The heart will never feel conquered; the heart will never be hijacked. So those who feel like they are in a maze, in a maze where information is given from different directions, and one might feel that they do not know which way to head, know that you are indeed standing in front of that threshold, and the only direction that you need to move to or focus on is straight ahead. And one can also say, "How can one move across the threshold if it is too high?" Use a ladder, be creative. There. You have all the tools available. If you need a ladder, the spirit realm and your soul will provide it. You simply need to make up your mind on how you want to proceed over this threshold. And know that not all will take that step. And for those of you that will have family members or friends not ready to take that step with you, just know that you cannot assist everyone, it is not your task. It is not up to you to make everyone to take this jump. But you are responsible for your own path, and sometimes that means that people that you care for will be left behind. Left behind doesn't mean that they will wither and disappear, necessarily, it's just a different journey than yours. But you have all the tools available. If you need a ladder, you have it. If you need a hammer to break yourself through this wall—if you perceive it as a wall and not just a threshold—then just look in your toolbox and the hammer is there. This one (*Seth*) here probably wants to use some sort of explosive to move forward, but it has not been approved. *Let's just say we provide a hammer* and we provide a ladder—we do not provide explosives, even though some wants that, indeed. But it's not advisable all the time. Yes, we have Bob here and he is poking. For some reason, he is very persistent in his poking. So if there is not any questions at this time, I would indeed leave the floor.

D. Well, none popped up on the chat, but I did have a question since you're here. I am still collecting data for our books. How does someone know if they're on the right path in a relationship or job? What sort of signs should one look for?

O. Be more aware of the signs when you're *not* on the right path. If you are on the right path, it will feel like, when you wake up, you wake up with a smile. That's the only sign you need to look for. If you wake up and do not necessarily want to jump out of bed to whatever situation, person, event, or work, then you should think of the reason behind it. Simple as that. But also, begin your day—and we have mentioned this before—begin your day by setting the standard for yourself, that you will find something to be grateful for when you later crawl into bed. When you go to bed, thank the experiences that you had during your day. Even if you are stuck in a traffic jam, thank that traffic jam for pausing your day, for allowing you to be paused. Don't see it as a hindrance that you did not come forward or came to your destination on time. Thank the experience given to you, that you were able to perhaps collect your thoughts more thoroughly. So always find something to be grateful for when you go to bed. That will help you to wake up with a smile.

D. Thank you so much.

O. You are much welcome. I hear singing, so I'm pretty sure someone is here with some sort of instruments. So, I feel I'm pushed. I guess he has the right to do so. Thank you for your time. Thank you.

D. Thank you!

B. (*Bob popped right in*) AHH! That was a long wait. Not just for one, I had to wait for two, and I was like, "Tick–tock–tick–tock, when is it my turn?" I prepared some sort of singing, I wanted there to be like a singalong perhaps, but I don't know if everyone wants to sing with me, but I have songs.

D. You could sing in Swedish.

B. Huh huh huh! Nay. But I can sing (*he began singing Yellow Submarine*) And why I want to sing a little bit, is because sometimes—I'm not saying that Ophelia and Ari are gloomy or anything—but sometimes I just need to spin it up a little bit. Just make it a little bit more energetic over here. So, that's why I sing, so this one doesn't just fall asleep, because that's not helpful, not for me! Especially if I'm last.

D. I know your energy is a little bit higher.

B. It's just one of those things. I said, "Maybe I should go first and then they can just uurrggghhh, wind down after. Then I can set the pace. And sometimes I'm allowed to, but not always. BUT what I would like to share is the fact that there is several of my friends, on the second dimension, who are EAGERLY (*here on Earth*) to assist now. And they have just been swamping and filling the forests, because they feel that they are more free to move around. There are activities in the lakes—lakes are gonna be cleaner this year because if someone cannot go to the ocean, and you don't want to just sit in the bathtub, then at least the nearby lake will be much more welcoming as a vacation spot. What we have understood is the importance of vacation. It seems like it is a huge discussion about, "Ohh, I can't fly there this summer. Ohh, I can't go to my summer cottage over there." All these things that people cannot do. BUT don't forget to think about what you CAN do. It's a very human thing, I think. I don't really understand it, fully, that man tends to be more focused on what they cannot do, instead of what they CAN do. So, it's confusing. But I would like to say there is high activity in nature and in the forest and in the soil, and it's gonna make flowers more ready to pop up, and the trees. So, in some way, okay, it's probably a good idea that you have not been just bombarding the forests everywhere, because of the fact that the trees needed to start singing again. And when they do not sing, it is because the roots are not connected—the trees have like a network with the roots. Due to several different facts, like the activity among humans, the flying back and forth, having boats going back and forth with all the rubber ducks and all the other nonsense things that you move back and forth over the oceans—that no one really understands why—but it has caused a commotion and a sadness among the trees. Meaning the roots have not been fully healthy and connected. At this time, due to the absence on certain places in nature, it has been helpful. Not only for the atmosphere above—because everybody is just, "Ohh! Clear sky. Much better!" But don't forget to look down—better soil, much clearer. So it has been helpful. So know that even though it might be a little bit like, "Oh, boring to be inside," in certain places, but you are doing your planet a favor. And the trees, the trees are actually starting to sing. They might not sing the 'Yellow Submarine', like I do, but they might sing something else like, (*he begins singing*) "Sunshine, my only sunshine. You make me happy, when skies are grey...", you know.

D. The oxygen level might go up a bit too.

B. Ah. And when they go up, my tune goes up, so I sing even louder. There are certain songs that I might not sing publicly because it might, you know, "Oh, why is he singing that song? Is he politically active in one side or the other?" Well, I'm not, I just like the song. It's certain purpose songs that I like. (*By 'purpose song', he means tunes selected by the government to motivate the conscripted soldiers with a sense of honor and duty, so they are more willing to go off and fight in some pointless war that only serves to enrich the bankers and the ruling class.*)

D. So what other thoughts did you come in with today?

B. Ah, I have stuff in my basket. I have treats; I have treats for everyone. I know that there is this need—especially on this side of the puddle (*Europe*)—there is this need of, "Ohh, what's happening with my vacation?" So I want to address that, that one can have a vacation in many different ways. One treat in my basket has to do with trying to connect with those you might not have been able (*to connect with*) for a while—that's a nice vacation. Make a puzzle, Ia would say. I'm not a huge fan of puzzles because it takes such a long time to create a picture. I would just say that one should more focus on the things that one can do instead of what they cannot. Make a lemonade, be more creative in the kitchen, bake a cake, do something that is a little bit more—you don't have to fill up the car with kids and umbrellas, or tents and stuff and all these gadgets and head for the beach. You can do so much more soulful or more interesting things if you try to be a little bit more creative with your time. Being creative with your time is not something that humans in general are known for. Souls, on the other hand, are very creative in their soul-mind, but once they are popped into a human mind and a human body, it seems to go out the pooper and sometimes it doesn't really seem to work. One thing in my basket has to do with... (*the lockdowns*). It's a gift that, if one has, every summer, gone (*on vacation*) in the car and filled it with kids and these umbrellas and bathing balls and stuff and towels, to maybe do something different this year. They might actually have not liked that beach trip in the first place! But it's just like, "Oh, it's vacation! You're supposed to do this!" Now is the time to think of the things you can do that you might actually like. And it might be easier and not so stressful, actually, so you will have a better vacation. What will happen is that next year, when people look back on the vacation they had—and I'm addressing the people on this side of the puddle, since I know that this is a big thing over here—you will look back and feel very satisfied with the summer 2020 that you had. So, you know. That was one treat in my basket!

D. Sometimes traveling is fairly stressful.

B. Ah. But for some people it's like, "I have two weeks' vacation, I'm gonna do the exact same things every year." And the stress come in from not being able to do the same thing every year, this year. Just saying. Don't put so much pressure on yourself on how things should be, or what you should have done when it comes to the fall and work again takes over. Just think of the extra time you are given to do something completely different, and that might actually be something you longed for from the beginning, but you were more in the mindset that there were certain things that came along with, let's say, a vacation. And if we take vacation aside, we put that mushroom away and we take another mushroom. It can be with everything really, it can be about work, it can be about people that you have, so this is a time when there is a great turnabout, where you can make ANYTHING happen that you want to. It's almost like a clean slate, if you see it like that. But if you do not see it as something to reboot your life, or reboot yourself, then it will just be that you're just standing still in front of that wall.

D. Individually or collectively?

B. Well, sometimes it's hard to think collectively, so if you just begin by thinking about your own person, then that's good enough. Then you can say, "Ohh, this works well." Then you can invite the neighbor, then, "Ohh, we're two." Then have more neighbors and then we're three. So, you begin with yourself. With humans, we have seen that if we put too much or too many different angles to things, or too many things that one can do, then nothing happens. But if we say, "Focus on you, on yourself." Then someone says, "Ohh, if I focus on myself, isn't that like I'm just a big ego?" Well, it's a time to create yourself anew, and it's not being an ego if you are actually trying to regain your strength and do something different, so that you later on can hook on your neighbor, or something like that. (*By hook on, he means to join in*

a spiritually centered group, not "hook-up", as used in libertine parlance.)
D. That's good!
B. Me, myself and I, I have been occupied otherwise in the Library and I have just been storing data. I'm following different trends at the moment. And one of the trends is what I've been talking about, the vacation thing, that seems to be a huge problem at certain places. But I've also looked into the effect with nature and roots and the roots are singing, so I've been participating a little bit with that. I can tell you that the councils here on the second dimension are extremely grateful that you are not just wandering around and disturbing certain projects that are ongoing. I'm somewhat of a spokesperson from the second dimension.
D. You're a good one.
B. Ah. I try to be. So I'm probably gonna trot off. I'm not sure. If there are questions, I will happily oblige, and I'm ready. What I would like, otherwise, to say is that it's a time where everything has a clean slate; nature, atmosphere, and down to the individual person as well. But sometimes, because of the fact that there is so much commotion that hits the mind, the mind is somewhat paralyzed. And when the mind gets paralyzed, then it has the effect that the entire being, the person, doesn't know which way to go. And what happens then is that they just become completely still. When someone is completely still, then it's hard to make changes. The soul is not still. The soul is in motion. So a good thing is that if you feel like you are too paralyzed in one way or the other, that you don't take actions, that you don't make decisions, then a good idea to connect with your soul is to sit down and put your feet in a bucket of warm water. You can put in different oils in the water. Lemon is a good one, but any smell that one might fancy is a good idea. But to put the feet, bare feet—no shoes please, in this bucket—and just sit there. So, you sit there and close your eyes, palms up, and you in some way become like the tree. Your feet become the network—like I said, the roots of the network needs to sing—and this is a way to make YOU sing. If you see yourself similar like the tree and your feet are the roots. So when you sit like that—don't have cold water, that's not helpful and it's just sadness all over—it has to be a little bit warm and comfy. So it's the same way we do with the trees, we actually increase the flow underneath the soil. So adding water in the soil to make the roots of the trees moistured, so the tree sings. And this is a way for man to sing. So bare feet,

bucket, oil, hands up, and just picture yourself like you are the tree and ask to be in some way healed in the part that has gone numb. Because what you want is actually a soul that sings.

D. Is that better than putting your feet on bare earth?

B. If you feel like you are numb in the brain because you are influenced of too much mainstream information that just flies around uncontrolled, then you need to really reboot yourself and make the soul and the human connect and sing. The quickest and most intense way is to put your feet in the bucket. BUT, maybe you are not paralyzed, maybe you just hum—you don't sing but you go like hmm humm hmm (*he hummed a little tune*), then you're kind of okay. Then you don't necessarily NEED to put your feet in the bucket. Then you can just take off your slippers and go barefoot in the grass, indeed. But you need to know, "Am I singing? Am I humming? Am I silent?" And just use different tricks.

D. Well, that's really good advice, my friend. Thank you.

B. You tend to have shoes on, so we're gonna remove them. I might hide one of your shoes so you are forced—if I only keep the right shoe—then you will be forced to go barefoot. That's a trick. I like to play tricks with you, because you're my person and I follow you, so I like that, I like that. Ahhhh. But I'm gonna go now, Ophelia says, "Time's up." I'm trotting off.

D. Thank you so much for coming and sharing with us today. I always appreciate it.

B. I don't feel like going. I'm looking the other way. Ophelia's on the other side, so I'm looking over here. (*He had turned to the right, away from Ophelia.*)

D. I have a question that I'm not sure I understood.

B. Well, we need to take that question, don't we?

D. I guess so. Someone asked how they could make contact with the galactic federation, and I wasn't sure what was meant by "galactic federation".

B. If they mean they want to contact a group of entities that are on a position that sort of monitors and runs the different systems like galaxies and the overall evolution in them. Not everyone has the ability—not everyone has the number to call it. It's not like, "Call 112" (*in Sweden*), like 911, and someone will answer. But some has the ability to connect with that. But you, as a human, need to have the clearance to connect to that level. And some have different clearances, and it's not better or worse. So you don't need to go look for a galactic council, when you might have a much stronger connection to one of MY councils. It's a little bit like that, that man tends to think, "The higher up, the better." It's not necessarily like that. You need to find YOUR connection, your phonebook, the level that you communicate with. If you have that connection to whatever council you're seeking, then eventually, when you progress as a human and evolve, then you will have that connection. BUT if someone is not designed to communicate with a certain level, then that will not happen. It's not a good idea to reject the levels that one has in their vicinity to communicate with. Don't be discouraged if you communicate with a guardian angel and then are like, "Oh, no, I want to communicate with Archangels," then you might miss the whole beauty of having an angel to communicate with! It's based on the clearance. Like this one (*Christine*), for instance, this one doesn't communicate with archangels. But if this one would be sad that this one only communicated with someone like me, for instance, then I would not have my book (*Notes from the Second Dimension*). So be grateful for the spirit friend or the angel that you have the ability to communicate with, because everyone has one.

D. That's a brilliant answer, my friend. Here's another question then, since you're on a roll. How does someone manage feeling split between society and vibrating at a higher frequency?

B. Ohh, ohh. I don't like that. I'm gonna send that person a big hug. Just, when you feel torn between human and soul, ask your spirit helper to just wrap their arms around you. It is a way to—you can feel it like it's merging those two sides of you, like you have this big warm blankie. Just ask and know that the spirit realm will wrap that blankie around you and that you will be whole. Because it is a way to feel like one is out in the cold, and asking for that warm blankie will make it easier to make the decisions needed when one feels torn being here as a human. For that person, I'm gonna wrap my little paws, my arms, around that person now. I really want you to know that you are a beautiful human being, but you are most of all a soul trying to help other human beings. And doing that, sometimes an effect that happens is that you feel torn between who you are and what you're here to do.

D. Thank you.

B. I'm trotting off again.

D. One more, my friend.

B. Ophelia, you heard that? It's not me.

D. Someone wants to know how they can connect with their soul family.

B. Ah, huh! Well, the easiest way is to just sit and close your eyes. You don't have to have your feet in a bucket if you don't want to, but just close your eyes and ask them to manifest in front of you. And normally they tend to put themselves in sort of a circle in front of you. Don't expect them to be—not all of them are gonna have human features like you are used to seeing here. But if you ask your soul family to somewhat make themselves known—some of them actually show themselves in dreams. So a good thing is to create a dream journal and just write that down, what you experienced and what you saw. Because you might be, "Ohh, I was in nature and I saw this beautiful—", I was gonna say elk, but actually it came the word goat, and just know that it doesn't mean that your soul family are goats, but they show themselves in different ways. And a lot of times they show themselves like animals. And it's not like they ARE animals, it's just that it provides an understanding about who they are and the connection to you. Another thing, of course, except for just closing your eyes and inviting them and dreaming, is to somewhat have someone help you, like either guide you in meditation or somewhat of a more relaxed setting so that you can connect with that family, indeed. Like you and I, we're not family, we're friends. But I'm still very close, so one can think that we're family.

D. I think of you as my family.

B. I think of you as somewhat of a family, too. But indeed. Now time is up. Ophelia says time is up, so I'm gonna go now.

D. Alright. It was wonderful. I always appreciate your thoughts and your wisdom.

B. Another way to also know about your soul family—some of them are actually incarnated with you. And you will know if they are soul family or if they are just family. There is nothing wrong to just be family. But if you are actually looking for your soul family—and don't be sad because sometimes they're not with you at the same time—BUT sometimes they are incarnated with you. And you will feel that in the chest area when you either think of that person, or if you are physically in contact, then you will feel the tingling in the center chest area, indeed.

D. In your solar plexus?

B. Higher. Higher up, higher up, you know, in the middle of the chest. Like ten centimeters below the throat. Quite high up. So it creates a sensation of—it's like a little cramp—like an electric shock, almost. But if you say, "Look for the electric shock," then people might be sad. But it's actually just like bzzzt, like that. If you feel like that, bzzzt, in your chest area, then you're on to something. Then you follow that thread, you know. Okay. I'm gonna be back another time.

D. Okay. Well thank you, and Ari and Ophelia, for coming and sharing with us today.

B. Thank you. Thank you from me. So I go. Bye bye. Bye bye.

Teh, Ophelia: Calming the Mind (Aug 12, 2020)

Many of the spirits who communicate are our personal guides, so they periodically give us specific instructions or advice, which is normally not published in our books. However, this session may be of interest to others because they gave visualizations for calming the mind and also for sensing your spirit guide. I had been laid off only a few days before and was curious what the future held, so Ophelia gave predictions about the timing of upcoming events. Christine and I had decided to move to Sweden and Ophelia said the visa paperwork would be approved in five months, and I would move within seven. That seemed slightly unbelievable, since it normally takes around a year for residency visas to be granted. However, both of her forecasts were exactly correct. To a human, looking forward and backward in time seems remarkable, but to the spirit realm, it is rather mundane. It is nice to get these little proofs, though, since it adds validity to the other things they say which cannot be proven.

This is the first time that Teh spoke. He is one of our friends from home and also on the Council of Nine. Although he is not an Elahim, he works closely with the Elahim on the Earth project. He said that he and I were together in manifested form around 15,000 BC. When manifested entities depart the Earth plane, there are no bones or anything left behind for an archaeologist or biologist to find. Visitors also possess the technology to move physical objects back and forth between the Earth plane and a parallel reality. For example, earlier in the book (July 7, 2019 session) Eli said, "The ancients in Egypt were visited by those who carried this knowledge. They provided big disks, placed them facing the sun and each other in a fashion and in a web that made power flow unlimited, free energy." When the visitors left, they moved these giant gold disks into a parallel frequency. The disks still exist in situ where they once stood, but are out-of-sync with visible matter. Most technological devices were either removed in crafts, or shifted into a parallel plane where they remain, invisible to us. For these reasons, there is a confounding lack of evidence remaining from these previous visitors and civilizations.

Teh. Good evening.

D. Good evening? (*I didn't recognize the voice.*)

Teh. Great to visit humanity in its new cradle. I am originating from the past with the two of you present in Egypt. We created rituals in order to protect the formulas to open portals. I am Kasehlakalateh. (*He said that as one syllable, very fast. I listened at a slow speed and then spelled it phonetically.*) I belong with you. You can call me Teh.

D. When were we together? How long ago?

Teh. 15,000 BC. Egypt. Creating opening for visitors to arrive into the grid to share formulas on how to open portals, conquering the magnetic fields in order for help to enter this plane to create balance in the land. At that time, there were, similar as now, an overuse in resources. Greed taking a toll on the land and ley lines, and so forth. We invited those from other constellations to work together with us here, in order to create balance in the grid in the land. You are not the first to be here disturbing the peace in the grid. We are here to assist mankind to not stumble upon the traps again. No need to repeat certain karma that once was a disaster for those who were present. We see a repeat; we see behaviors of greed, not fully understanding the engineering that takes place once you excavate and use resources. You, my friend, are here to report and observe the engineering in the field of work that you have chosen so far. A lot of it was not a human satisfaction. (*He means jobs that were not satisfying to me, which is true.*) It was on the behalf of councils who are interested in the grid and how man handles himself when it comes to resources—handle oneself after one found oil again, like it was a brand–new, shiny thing.

D. (*Laughing.*) What dimension are you originally from?

Teh. Eighth. I work closely with Isaac, and I work closely with the Council of Nine. Call me Teh.

D. So we are friends at home?

Teh. Indeed. We create maps together, this one and I. This one (*Seth*) is more, how can one say, reluctant to proceed with caution. That is why a big brother, like you (*Lasaray*) are (*to Seth*), followed.

You are not only here to spread the word from spirit; you are also here so that we can monitor shifts and changes. The assignment for you, my friend, where you were put in a position so that we could monitor activities in the field of gas and oil. The industry as a whole has come to an end. We are grateful for the data that you, on a subconscious level, have collected for us, and it's been stored in a databank, if you like, in order for it to be useful on how to proceed. We met prior here, in Egypt. We were part of a council that were operating portals. We have the skills to open and close for visitors. At this time, the portal that we are opening is not for physical activity, but for spiritual enlightenment. It's the same procedure, just before, we operated on the behalf of a different star constellation to be here as co–engineering the grid in need to be healed and balanced.

D. Did you and I both travel here the same, as manifested, or did we come in more of a physical form?

Teh. Not human, no.

D. Were you manifested?

Teh. Yes, yes. There are replicas of our visit. There are stories, fairy tales, tales told about our existence—giants, myths. Certain remains still exist. However, we did not die here, there are no bones to be found. We left the same way as we came. We transformed our beings into a fog and we left. For those who were present, those who occupied an early protype of humanity, it was experienced as a fog. We created like a wind that came in over the sand then we exit.

D. That's fascinating. How long were you and I here together, in Earth years?

Teh. 3000 years.

D. And what was the method that we used to open and close portals?

Teh. We connected certain elements. In order for portals to open, we used gold. In order for travel to appear, we used mercury. In order for portals to close, we used uranium combined with silver. Silver–mercury was the foundation for travel. Gold opened. Uranium combined opened the gateways for certain frequencies to descend.

D. I find it fascinating, yet quite perplexing.

Teh. It's because you are not, as a human, equipped to use the elements that I am referring to, in a way for them be creative. You use mercury in water, creating disasters, instead of using the elements and resources for the potential it carries.

D. Are there any messages you would like to share directly with humans?

Teh. Be careful on how you use elements. You simply know about ten percent of its possibility. How to transform and blend elements to provide a higher potential, a higher or stronger essence of its creativity and resource, the intention that each element has—you do not possess that knowledge. Be careful before you mix and blend. Be careful before you mix DNA, because you do not have the knowledge on the outcome of your operations. Be mindful of the effect on your brain. Your brain, your mind, is being hijacked. The easiest way to use, let's say, mercury, is the effect that it has on the mind. It has little effect on your emotional or soul entity, but the mind is ill-equipped for influences such as heat, radiation, medication, energy influences, microwaves. All those combined with high and loud noises—and don't just think of a trumpet—be aware of the silent noise that travels indefinitely, that makes you overheated, disoriented. You, my friend, feel a little bit of that energy. That is why you currently feel a little bit tired. You are like a big satellite. In order for you to feel better, imagine that you put on a hat. Imagine that you are that mast, that receiver, and right now you can shut it down. Imagine that you place soil both underneath your feet and clay on top of your head. Visualize how you cover your entire head and face in this smooth, cool clay. Covering it, closing the mind from outer influences. Every time you feel tired, every time you feel drained, every time you feel stressed, use the methodology of the clay. The clay is a healing component. Imagine and visualize it, how it surrounds your whole head and face. Feel the cool, feel the presence of the minerals touching your head. It will cool down the brain; it will calm the mind.

D. Okay, thank you for that. I have been feeling very tired.

Teh. We used that before. It is a good trick to cool down the mind, to cut off the world, if you like. You imagine that you stand barefoot on soil. Even if you wear shoes, even if you are standing on asphalt, you can still visualize that you are standing barefoot on soil. Feel the land, feel the warmth from below, and then place this clay and calm around your head. Make sure that you feel its component and its balance in how it radiates and fills (*covers*) your entire face. Feel it's absorbing, this clay, and become the clay, become the cool, feel the calm, and you are completely intact.

D. Thank you. I think it will be better once I get over to West Virginia and then Sweden.

Teh. Yes, it will. Until then, just use this little trick if you feel like you are bombarded, or that your mind is caving under pressure. This is how we—it is helpful if you lay down or sit. If you stand, you might feel dizzy. If you lay down, you can still experience the clay surrounding your face and the soil underneath your feet. It relaxes the being; it soothes the mind. This clay is not warm. Imagine and feel the skin absorb the coolness, how the mind ceases under this gentle embrace from the clay.

D. That's wonderful. I will try that.

Teh. You are much welcome. There you go.

D. It was really nice to talk with you today.

Teh. Oh, you are much welcome. I will return if Ophelia is here. Old friends.

D. Good. I look forward to that.

O. This is Ophelia.

D. Hello, Ophelia.

O. How are you, my friend?

D. I guess I'm okay.

O. Yes, you are. Lasaray is thrilled for the new adventure that lies before him. The body just needs to be updated to the adventure that lies ahead. Focus on feeling the excitement and the progress from within. If you do so, the human self will somewhat be led to this adventure. You do not need to over-think too much. Everything is carefully designed—for both of you. This one has already stepped up on the next plateau. Your brother is waiting for you, you simply need to release certain ties where you are at the current time. This is a prosperous and exciting time that lies before you. It is the treat that we, from spirit, want to give you. The treat of relaxation, the treat of peace and calm and to be together in unity with no attachments to things that will disturb your peace. You will sense a more calm phase entering. In the first six to eight months from now—probably eight—is only for you. After that, we will continue our work in the plan that lays before.

D. Wonderful. I'm really grateful for everything you have done, setting this up. Thank you so much for everything you do, Ophelia.

O. You are welcome. And I want you to, before I leave, to close your eyes. And as you sit, listening to the sound of my voice, imagine a butterfly just a little bit in front of you, a little bit above. Notice the shifts of the wings, how it circles around you. With every wing motion of the butterfly, you can feel a little puff against your face. This is the sensation from spirit. Every time you want to know if we are present, just close your eyes, visualize the butterfly. See the butterfly rise and fall and circle around your head. And with every motion of the wings, you can feel a wave in the air coming towards you, and that is us.

D. That's beautiful. Thank you for that gift.

O. You are much welcome. Feel the love that we all have for you. You are always observed, always protected, always guided, always cared for. We are never far away. Simply close your eyes, and if you need to, visualize the butterfly. After a while, you will start to sense within you like a fire. It will pulsate and rotate, and that is you. This is the energy of who you are. The butterfly welcomes this energy to come forward. You are always cared for.

D. Thank you so much, Ophelia.

O. I always look after you, together with all of us.

D. I feel that. I sometimes forget, but I feel it now.

O. If you forget, close your eyes and visualize the butterfly. This is a trick for you to know that we are there. If you feel stressed, if you feel tired, you use the clay. Inside, the fire is beginning to burn, the fire that is you. You will become much stronger physically, mentally, emotionally. This is our gift to you. It is for you to be able to rest and just be and feel the care, the tenderness, from those around you, both in spirit and in physical. You have done your part; you have collected the data that certain councils were seeking for. Now is the time to enjoy the rest, to enjoy the things that you really burn for, the change that you seek. There.

D. I look forward to that. And thank you for the beautiful gift.

O. You are much welcome. So there. We will invite our Little Friend.

D. I appreciate everything that you have done for me to get us to this point, Ophelia. So thank you.

O. We love you and we care for you, and we have been with you on all journeys to Earth, and we will continue to carry you forward until it is time to go home, which is not just yet. Just know that there is a long period, about eight months, for this transition to occur. It is not five weeks, it is not two months, it is not even three months. You have all the human time you need. If you feel

stressed, know that it is only the human, and you use the clay and you calm the mind, and you call on the butterfly.
D. At the end of eight months, is that when I will move to Sweden permanently?
O. Say that again, please.
D. Am I moving to Sweden permanently, in eight months?
O. Before, before. The eight months is just the transition phase. It is not the paperwork phase. We give you eight months to get used to the change, to feel, human-wise, calm in the steps you leave behind, the steps that you have taken so far, and to choose the shoes that you want to bring forward, if you like. You can see it as such, that you leave certain shoes behind, meaning that you cut the ties of your life up till this point. This is a bridge until you find your new self. You bring the shoes that you want to have for your future. You leave behind feelings, tasks, physical items as well, that no longer serve. And this will take about eight months because we know that the human tends to be stressed. But it's not eight months for the paperwork. We see the timeline. It will be about five. There.
D. Wonderful. Thank you, Ophelia. I feel much better.

Council of Nine: Changes and Evolution (Sept 2, 2020)
I sometimes wonder what the spirit world actually thinks about humans. The general assessment that the vessel requires a significant upgrade has never been disguised, but sometimes a bit of mirth creeps into their language reveals a shadow of their opinion. In this session, for example, they describe the majority of people as falling into two camps. Those in the first category are fearful and obsequious, always seeking approval of the group. These are the sheep people (sheeple), who passively do what they are told. The other group, the toilet people, are imprudent, emotionally volatile and angry. They are easily deceived by impassioned tirades, no matter how illogical or immoral, and become the type of activists whom Vladimir Lenin called "useful idiots". The Cell, of course, understands these two groups, and manipulates them relentlessly through the media. The toilet people are led to believe they are victims of imaginary or exaggerated injustices. Agent provocateurs are then sent out into communities to organize the insurrectionists to engage in a frenzy of anti–establishment behaviors. The Cell has used this tactic to violently overthrow many governments during the past century, including the Russian Empire and the Republic of

China. Chairman Mao used the toilet people (i.e., Red Guards) to purge China of the Four Olds—old customs, cultures, ideas, and habits of mind. In current times, the Cell has rebranded the Four Olds as Critical Race Theory and Wokism, while Antifa and BLM are the new Red Guards. Meanwhile, the sheeple huddle in fear as society is deconstructed by the leftist mobs.

The Council of Nine observed what was going on during the past two years. They said the toilet people are best represented by the BLM anarchists, looters, and the cancel-culture Marxists. The sheeple were the ones who meekly accepted the hysterical flu-fear dictates and mRNA injections. Fortunately, a third group exists of those who are spiritually centered. They do not react to the media or the Cell and are able to "ride above the physical activity". You should note that the spirits are not judging the sheeple or toilet people, but are highlighting what happens when there is a disconnect from the spiritual self. Energies are flowing into our Solar System that people subconsciously detect, but when they are not centered, it causes confusion, misdirected emotions, and fear.

The Council of Nine then give tantalizing details about a large alien base in the area known as the Bermuda Triangle. The colony is beneath the seafloor and has hosted a certain group of aliens for a long time. They are here to collect data and are among the groups that engineer the "natural" processes on Earth. Due to the changes in the energy coming to Earth, those entities are leaving and are being replaced by a different group.

C9. This is the Council of Nine. We have been observing the two of you in this great transition, as humans, that you are undertaking at this time. We see the development on Earth coexisting with soul activity, and there are several underlying currents that intertwine at this time. There is the physical reality, as you see, but there is also high activity among parallel realities embedding this reality. There are encounters between merging points in the web. This is why it is felt like a turmoil in your consciousness. But you simply are captivated by the bug (*covid flu*), when there are actually other occurrences right beneath your nose. What man is experiencing at this time is the shift where cosmic webs intertwine, merge, move, change. They occur at the same time as this bug. In many ways, it is a gift from the spirit realm, because it's easier to coexist, to adapt to the bug than to the general shift in your nearby frequency band. So it is, in some way, a gift to you as a species, in order for you to look elsewhere. There are other activities ongoing at the same time as this energetic engineering is taking place. We are relocating, merging, moving, deleting activities in nearby frequencies. Meaning celestial bodies as well as solar activities.

C9. What we wish is for man to find stillness inside. The turmoil that man at this time experiences is a detour of what is going on energetically within you. So for those who have their whole focus on the bug, or the riots going on, they, in some way, are misled to ride the riot. The riot they feel inside is the soul energy responding to the shifts around you. These riots that you see are an energetic outpour. It is a release of an understanding within that one cannot grasp. What we see are two different actions. We see passivity, where man is paralyzed. Those are the ones stuck in fear of the bug. And then we have the other ones who channels the shifts going on around them like flushing a toilet (*making a lot of noise*), instead of understanding that the outburst is not concentrated. They are not in an understanding of where this turmoil within originates. So, we see two different behaviors, if you like. And then we have those who ride above the physical activity. Both behaviors are a response to energetic activity, manifested as riots with the police force—in your country—verses the bug in the entire network, meaning all countries combined. There are two different occurrences that is a result of an ongoing shift. It is a physical shift as well, as you sense that there is heat, predominantly, and the heat is influencing your actions and choices. In one way, the heat is mostly channeled through those who act in rage at this time. They are not adapted to the change of climate, which is a result of the connections changing around you. The other ones are more left behind. They are not necessarily influenced by the shift of temperature, but they are locked in karmic chains related to being told what to do. Some people, you should know, respond easier to being told what to do. Like a flock of sheep, that is why you have the dog who leads the flock of sheep. The sheep want to be told where to go as a group, and there is similar behavior in those who are paralyzed at this time. They have a karmic connection to a past where actions were considered a sin. You should know that in man's memory, actions, self–thinking, has been considered a sin. And then we have those who simply respond to the change and shift of temperature, and they flush all their feelings, like a toilet. And when all these toilets are connecting in a joined hymn, this is when you see the riots. It's only toilets flushing, it's just noise.

You know how toilet flush, how it is noise for a while. They are just like that, toilets making noise.

D. Regarding the change that is going on, is it related to an increase in the connections to the parallel realities?

C9. Yes, yes.

D. You said the heat is increasing. If it is not a physical heat, it must be a different vibration?

C9. It manifests here as a physical heat. The temperature rising on certain places. The sea is changing the temperature from below, from the seabed. It is an increase in the temperature in the seabed, making the water, the currents that connect different areas of water, to increase in temperature. As the water is warming up, it affects the surface in a way that the fish and so forth that you eat are affected by a new environment. The new environment is also merging with the atmosphere. So it's not just the fish, but it's merging with the atmosphere, creating more activities—meaning hurricanes and so forth. And this is a response from the atmosphere to the increase of temperature in the seabed. We have an increase currently around the Bermuda area, as well as in the Japanese sea, south of Japan. Two regions, highly active. The underlying activity is that there is a presence going on in those spots. There are exits, entrances, openings—especially around the region where the Bermuda Triangle is located. That region is hotter in the seabed, it is an opening that occurs. More hurricanes will be an end result of the activity in that region. So this fall and the upcoming fall—summer from July to October—two years, possibly three in a row, will have more rain, more hurricanes in that region. There will be certain disasters in the sense that there are high winds. This is a reaction from the atmosphere on the increase of temperature in the seabed. The seabed is opening, there are entrances, old, that are opening up for visitors. But there is also those who have been stationary, who are now leaving. This region, the Bermuda Triangle, have a stationary—it's not a submarine—it's a community. It's the size of the city of, let's see...I'm comparing...the size of Seattle or Portland.

D. Size as in the area, or in the number of entities that live there?

C9. Size. Entities have changed. There is a shift. There are those who have been here from, huh huh, scratch (*the very beginning*), who now leave. There are changes going on in this base. Size-wise, it is similar like Portland, or San Diego.

D. Is it in the water, or beneath the seabed?

C9. Beneath. But it's closer to the seabed floor, if you like to call it. It sank, it's not visible, it never was. It always was underneath the seabed. At one point, you could see certain lights, but the base was predominantly underneath the seabed. At one point, indeed, it was open and you could see activity. No man existed on Earth at that time.

D. What was their primary role here in the past?

C9. Balance work. Tending to the Fork, tending to the—you call it ley lines, we call it veins—the veins of the Earth. There is engineering (*work*) going on, and this base collected and gathered data from the veins. The veins connect to the Fork. The Fork can rotate, and once the Fork rotates, the poles shift. So the Fork going north–south is not still all the time. It has been still for a long period of time. Once it's rotating slightly, the change and shifts on the surface occur—continents move, spines (*mountain ranges*) move. This is an activity ongoing where (*those on*) this base were reading the veins. See the veins as waves coming and going, communicating to the Fork. The hub was simply monitoring the veins and the activity, making sure the Fork was fed as it was intended to be. Everything needs to be fed, regardless if it's a soul when you maintain your light capsule, like your Little Friend (*Bob*) talks about, or if it is the Fork of the planet. He (*Bob*) naps a lot lately, taking naps, we see. He calls it maintaining his light capsule. So regardless of if it is your Little Friend maintaining himself, or if it is engineering of the Fork and the planet, everything needs to be cared for.

D. He's following my lead by resting.

C9. I think he mirrors your incarnation. He likes to do so. What you do, he mirrors. What you say, he repeats. That's why he wants you to be the great inventor again. He liked those travels, he said. He's been around, you know. He comes (*to visit the Council of Nine*) and he talks, and he has ideas. He's quite joyful. But now he takes naps. He said he's about to travel, so he's preparing for a new chapter, a new adventure. He said, "When one is about to travel, one should collect and gather the batteries," that's what he said. He says that he is filling up his battery. We see the both of you napping next to each other.

D. Are the poles in the process of shifting?

C9. Yes. It is starting to move; there is motion going on in the Pole. The Pole is not still. The activity has changed in the Pole, due to shifts of incoming data from the veins. And the hub is more open. I'm not saying it's visible, but it is closer to the surface, the seabed surface (*sea floor*). And the effects of activity and increase of the modifications in the veins. When the modifications occur, there is a change in temperature on the seabed, and this is an effect, an end–result of a total engineering of the Pole. So if you see the Pole starting to move slightly, it is by design from the veins, who are now pumping, filling the Pole in some way, with more liquid, more strength. It is an engineering.

D. When you talk about the Pole, do you mean the magnetic pole, or the physical location?

C9. The Pole from North Pole to South Pole, the Fork.

D. What will be the end result of these changes?

C9. The end result is the ongoing evolution on this planet, as well as your system as a whole. It is to gradually change the environment, to gradually change the species that can co–exist with the environment. It's been repeatedly going on, and you have seen that in ice–ages and so forth. At this time, you are in an increase of heat and the atmosphere is responding accordingly. When these two different flows, from below to above, occur and merge, there are activities releasing electrons in your atmosphere. It appears like things are speeding up; that is the effect that you will sense on Earth. Those who are paralyzed becomes even more confused. They don't follow and they have a need to be led and to know where to go, *what* to follow. But when the evolution of technology is rushing—and that is also an effect of the ongoing occurrences—is that technology tends to go out of hand, losing control. Just know that it is a phase that has come and gone in several cycles before this one. We will continue to talk about it. Just know that there is more going on underneath the physical reality, not just on the seabed, but the connections to nearby systems are also coming closer. The general web in your fish tank, the wave as you are moving up from the canyon, is affecting your system, your consciousness, your neighboring systems, and planets as well. This is simply a cosmological evolution that you are experiencing at this time. In some way, it is easier for you to focus on the bug than to think that your system is moving in the manner that I am referring to, from a canyon. Just know that there are bigger changes at play. The end result, however, is that man feels lost. Some act like toilets. Others become paralyzed, become like that flock of sheep, waiting for someone to tell them where to go and what to do. The toilet people, in some way they have the capability for change. But due to their response to the heat, the increase in your temperature, it is like an outpour that channels all over the place, (*making noise*) like flushing the toilet. Instead of looking into the strength the collective has, they act in rage. They could use this (*urge to*) action they feel, this power within, in a productive way. They could help and lead those who are paralyzed, but they are blind. So one is paralyzed with eyes wide open and the other ones are full of power and actions, but they are blind.

D. That's a good way to put it! How long will this go on?

C9. The whole—the Little One (*Bob*) calls it a space program—that will go on for a couple of generations. However, there is a five- to ten-year cycle going on right now that is extremely important for your species and for your sense of belonging. So the five to ten years upcoming—you are in the middle of it, it started about ten years ago—and it will last for another ten–ish. That's what you say—ish. Well, we will continue to talk.

D. This one and I will be in Sweden, won't we, during this time?

C9. Yes, yes. You will be secluded. You will seek the silence away from…there are less turmoil on this side (*Sweden*), but there are still effects that are global. You will seek the silence more, and you will be in connection with the land. You will hear nature talk to you again. In some way, what we wished for you was to hear nature, we wanted you to hear the mountains sing to you. But due to the high level of noise pollution in the area where you lived, it was not fully possible to hear the mountains sing. We wished for you to hear the vicinity and the speech from the mountains. You will instead hear it in the wind. Listen to the trees. You will seek the silence and you will receive it.

D. Very nice. I look forward to that.

C9. There. We will return.

D. Alright, my friends. Thank you so much for sharing with us today.

C9. You are much welcome. We are aware that the topics are sometimes confusing. Also, with the limitations of words, we sometimes feel like we have a hiccup and that we cannot fully convey the message that we wish. That is why, gradually, we build up your knowledge bank. Little–by–little, you start to get the bigger picture; you start to understand the design. Just know how you struggled, when we were on *Wave 1*, to understand the

Wheel. We are still gradually building this cake, building this pyramid of knowledge; and it is a joint work, we with you. But we know that sometimes, due to the lack of full communication, when we cannot convey a whole outline of understanding and information through telepathy, then it is a problem.

D. I think you do an amazing job, because I do understand much of what you say. It's just the concepts are hard to grasp.

C9. Just put it into your human brain. You listen with your soul brain and then you translate it to your human brain, and the human brain put it down on paper. So you see, you activate two minds. You activate the soul mind and the human mind. And the human mind is somewhat behind, so the soul mind needs to translate, and this occurs a lot when you dream. You move an understanding from one side of the brain, if you like, the soul brain over to the human one, and you process it. And that is when it becomes an understanding that you can put down on paper. You work from two sources—soul mind, human mind. So the only thing you need to be paying attention to is that when you have sessions like this, or when you do research, you activate your soul mind and you put the human mind on pause, put it in a box. So gradually you will be thinking more and more from your soul mind. The human mind simply executes the order and puts it down on paper. But more and more—and that is why you need the silence, because the noise hinders you, the human mind, to fully be the sponge that you need it to be so that you can download the information and data from your soul mind to your human mind. And that is why you need to be more in silence. It was unfortunate that we could not have more of a silent stay when you were in the mountain area, where you still are physically. But know that when you are more in silence, you will download the information from the soul mind much easier.

D. Understood. I look forward to that.

C9. There you go. We will return and we will discuss more of the shifts within the atmosphere. It's been a progressive upgrade, meaning the general web is affected by the—we are meeting the 5G, as it is becoming a reality. What we are meeting the activity of 5G is also a little bit what you see with the so-called pandemic. We want traffic in the air to be at a minimum at this time, to balance the activity. So what you see going on is, in some way, not all, a response from the spirit realm on how to meet the increasing activity in your atmosphere. We are deleting other activities, such as flights, such as motion between nations. In that sense we are meeting the increasing activity in your web.

D. How long will that go on?

C9. For a while. If you are talking about the activity in the web, that will run for a while. And the way we meet this shift is that we wish you to not increase the frequency by going with plane. So we are putting it at a minimum. There. Do you understand what I said to you?

D. I do.

C9. So some of the activity going on at this time is actually for the good, for the benefit of mankind. The decrease in flight is one. Decrease in demand on energy is another. We are meeting and balancing the increase of 5G, among other things.

D. Are you going to eventually eliminate 5G, or make people realize its danger?

C9. It will become evident that the effect is not good and people will start to see the connection and want to move into countryside more. This (*the 5G*) is, unfortunately, a development that seems to be snowballing, and we are meeting it, one way, by decreasing flight, decreasing transportation, motion. There. Okay. (*The web is negatively affected by both electromagnetic radiation and the combustion of hydrocarbons.*)

D. Alright, my friends. Thank you so much for coming and sharing today.

C9. You are much welcome. We will return once the energy is more established between the two of you. It's been a while, and this one needs to change diet again. Change and shift, so we will be able to remain longer.

D. Back to the vegetables.

C9. Back to the vegetables for this one. No wheat. There. Energy will return to normal and we will be able to stay longer. Okay, there we go. Elahim.

D. Thank you. Elahim.

C9: Sit Still in Your Boat (Dec 17, 2020)

During this session, the Council of Nine makes an allusion to boats and waves on the ocean. The boat on the ocean represents being adrift in a situation or in life, and the oars signify the way you navigate. The primary message has to do with cause and effect. They say that "what you eat has an effect. What you say has an effect. How you behave sends ripples into another being's boat. Try to soothe the sea." All the spirits who speak will occasionally use imagery to convey ideas. By painting pictures with words, they hope the lessons may linger in your memory. Bob, of course, is a master at building stories around a teaching that becomes both entertaining and memorable.

The Council of Nine then reveals that the pharmaceutical corporations want control of the land where bioactive plants grow. Their tactics are to hide the natural origin and manufacture a less effective and more dangerous chemical version. The spirits placed these medicines on Earth to be free for everyone, and are dismayed that the legal drug cartels are only interested in exploiting knowledge for their personal profits. There was a time when nature could not be patented, but through bribery and corruption, genetically modified organisms (GMOs) were permitted in 1980 by the US Supreme Court. Today, it is difficult to find food or medicine that is not a toxic version of nature. If the trend is not stopped, humans will be fed, sprayed, or "vaccinated" with gene editing nano-particles. Once their DNA is altered through reverse transcription, the organism will not function as designed by the Creator. Physical and mental illnesses of varying severity will result, as intended by the Cell.

C9. This is the Council of Nine.

D. Hello, my friends.

C9. Hello to you. We are eager to reveal your next step. Not just the two of you, but as a civilization, you need to stand the test. You need to be able to follow your inner guidance. We see the drama unfolding, similar like observing little boats on the sea. Those who are new to navigating a boat create a rumbling ocean below them. Those who are secure in their inner being and guidance, it is simply like paddling a canoe. That is why you, my son, wish to have a canoe. It resonates with you because you see the world and your ocean as calm. The little boats have not been here that long. Know that the ocean is what you make of it. We can pour different things into the ocean, meaning events and situations, and we do so. We try to help those who lack the insight of navigating their boat. But there are other occurrences influencing this ocean. Interests, on one hand, but also the amount of space (*overcrowding*). (*The interests would be selfish, either individual or for profit and power.*) There are those who wish for more space, and when I say space, I mean landmass. So there are several things ongoing, but the little boats simply are focusing their terrified viewpoint to the ocean. Some of them are not sure even if they know how to swim. If you combine all these different occurrences, then you can understand the drama that take place at this time. Unfortunately, there is a cycle where several little boats are out on this ocean—some should never have left shore, if you understand my meaning. It is not wrong to say, "Sit still in the boat." But it's also quite valuable to understand whether you should take your boat out into the ocean in the first place. Why engage in an ocean you do not know how to master? Why lead yourself and your little boat into the unknown, unless you know how to master and navigate it? Sometimes it's better to prepare on land before you enter a new element, enter a new journey, or event. But because of the ongoing interest, they are putting all boats out on the ocean. Some should not have left land. The intent is to thin out certain areas, (*because*) space is needed. There is an agricultural interest at play, a need for more resources, natural resources.

D. Do you mean the powers behind the scene are trying to get rid of people?

C9. They want land. They need space. They want less interference.

D. Does that imply less humans?

C9. Yes. On certain places, yes. Rich areas, such as South America, are highly rich in natural resources. Especially the Amazon, rich in natural herbs. They want to claim a big area in that region as a pharmaceutical hub, claiming certain findings (*discoveries*), when it comes to herbs, plants, roots. Some biologists are misled in their work on how to extract, excavate roots. In some way, what we see is an elimination of trees and plants, in order for new findings to not become (*known*), to instead use a chemical component. Claiming land mass. Some see; eyes understanding the whole, the system, the eco–chain, and not just in your environment, but your inner environment. Your inner environment is equal to (*the same as*) the trees, fauna, animal life, and the seas. The way the planet is feeling is mirrored in your inner ecosystem. Your inner ecosystem is highly influenced by disturbing signals, either from pharmaceutical input, such as medicine and so forth, but also the amount of information, (*which are*) signals bombarding the mind. The heart area, close to your solar plexus, would be indicating the hub, the navigating system where all the equipment for your wellbeing is located. The medical influence circles through your veins, the mind is getting influenced by certain media, but also the information of close–down (*the tyrannical lockdowns of society*), meaning the separation, not only from each other, but the separation has to do with the link to your inner compass. The ecosystem within you is failing, due to the amount of different signals. What we try to tell and guide you through, is to sit still in your boat. Check your boat, check your ecosystem before you enter into troubling waters. Your ecosystem within you is changing, and it is by design. We are in a new cycle, entering a new era, where certain organs need to be in hibernation, need to recover, mainly from intake of food. What we would like to encourage you all (*to do*) is to minimize the intake of meat. Try to exchange your intake of food to a more natural-based supply. By eliminating certain areas (*of agriculture*), or the wish to (*prevent organic food production*), will also increase the factory-made food. If natural based are not easy to find, if organic supply decrease, increase the little that is to be found in price, it is easier for the ones with interest (*food manufacturers*) to launch an alternative that, on the surface, looks the same, but numbs your ecosystem within. The organic vegetables, roots, and the combination of fruit will clean your ecosystem, your inner ecosystem. The flow in your veins is changing. Some rushing, some decreasing. It depends on what you eat, how you take care of your inner ecosystem. Those who have a rapid motion within their bloodstream suffers more at this time, physically. Whereas the ones who have a shortage, meaning the circulation within the veins, the blood, is decreasing, they move into depression. It's a mental effect. Whereas the rapid motion in your veins, bloodstream, creates a physical problem. Both relate to an overtake of your inner ecosystem to influence where mankind is heading. As these two scenarios, not necessarily operating at the same time. One controlled by the pharmaceutical, trying to captivate and make you numb, the ecosystem to go slower. Whereas the other, the agriculture and food, this industry is aiming to speed up your veins, your bloodstream. Two different agendas at play.

D. What about things like sugar and other additives?

C9. It belongs in the speeding up. The effects we see, again to compare with the little boats, those who have an increase, high blood pressure, if you like, they row and row and row on this ocean, making new waves, making new turmoil around them; row, row, row in circles. Acting almost mad, scared, row, row, row, row, row. The other ones, who have a low blood pressure, they just sit still. They don't even recognize that they have oars.

Two different scenarios at play. In the middle, two interests, two agendas.

D. When you talk about blood pressure, you're not talking about the actual physical blood pressure, are you?

C9. The motion within the energy. But it affects the blood pressure. High blood pressure makes the boat go row, row, row, row, row. The other one, numbing, lower pressure. Can't find the oars, just sits still, paralyzed. Two different scenarios at play. What we, several councils as well as the spiritual realities on different levels, are assisting you with is to understand cause and effect. What you eat has an effect. What you say has an effect. How you behave sends ripples into another being's boat. Try to soothe the sea. Those in boats don't necessarily know or understand that they are out on this wild ocean. Make them calm. Don't engage in debates or try to convince those who row, row, row, row, row, because they are not in a position to listen. They are seeking land, and land is nowhere to be found. Those who sit still, paralyzed, are seeking a path, a light to navigate to, seeking guidance. If you are in the mindset that someone will come and row your boat to safety, then the problem emerges. You have to understand that you have oars, number one; to row calmly, number two. Why do you row, row, row in such a manner that you simply make waves around you? Understand that everything going on has to do with separation between physical and mind. To control minds, two different scenarios at play. I hope you see the picture.

D. How do you see this resolving itself over the next few years? Are people going to rebel against this, or are they going to win and reduce the population?

C9. Some of the boats will sink, due to either being too paralyzed, or just creating waves, not going anywhere. It's nothing different than what has been going on before. It's not a problem, it's simply a time to understand and take charge of your boats, and how you wish to travel IN your boat. But this is also a time to be calm, to sit still and observe. You are now more aware of how all these different boats operate. Those of you who have been here for a couple of journeys, you just wait. Sometimes it's better to not engage, to let things run its course, so to speak; to enjoy what you have. All your writing should be question based. Ask a question. You don't have to give the answer, but you wake up the boats. You calm the boats who row, row, row. You help the boats sitting paralyzed to understand there are oars.

Isaac, Jeshua: The Four Pillars (Dec 31, 2020)

As I was preparing to return to the US, after being in Sweden on a three-month visitor visa, Isaac (Seth's mentor) and Jeshua (Lasaray's mentor) came in to shed light on what they will focus on in the coming months. Near the end of the discussion, I asked if they wanted to share anything. They spontaneously gave a wonderful talk on the four emotional pillars of development in humans, which are blame–fear–happiness–love. And they also encourage humans to not live in the imaginary reality the government and media scullions broadcast unremittingly into people's living rooms. The Cell uses the media to generate negative emotions in the sheeple and the toilet people. Then they deflect the anger and fear away from themselves and towards those who do not want to conform to the government groupthink. (This is not a new strategy. It has been a standard practice of authoritarian rulers throughout history.) An example would be the deceptive arguments about wearing a polypropylene mask to stop the spread of a virus that is 0.1 microns in diameter. Logically, it is like sitting on the back porch in the summer, hoping your chain-link fence will keep mosquitoes out of the yard. I spent four decades working as an engineer and routinely designed large gas processing plants, compressor stations, molecular sieves, permeable membranes, etc. It is obvious to any decent scientist that most masks are worse than useless for capturing virus particles. However, the governments needed a constant trigger to maintain fear in the sheeple, something to remind them of an ever-present, invisible danger. The mask is not for protection—it is a stage prop to further the agenda of the Cell (i.e., forced injections of nano-toxins). Those who did not comply with their mandates were blamed for the spread of the flu virus and the lockdowns, which is an absurd correlation. The masks were an outward symbol of conformity to the whims of the Cell. Aside from spooking people, the real damage is to the environment. Billions of masks now litter the land and billions more were dumped in the ocean.

D. Is there anything that I should do?

I&J. Rest. You have earthly tasks to tend to. You should not rush, you don't have an agenda more than a pause, waiting. Do whatever you enjoy. Take walks. Breathe. Breathing exercises. Remember, try to remember your childhood. Also, you have the opportunity for silence now in your home, human home, where you grew up. This will bring forward and open up emotions. Sit in the emotion, embrace the power of emotion. Neither of you likes to engage too much in emotions. It's not your soul preference. You are mental creatures, and that is why engaging in emotions is sometimes not your preference. This one still needs to address it in a human form. You can engage it with the soul mind. Investigate the feelings that you had as a boy. Investigate and connect how it created you to an adult. It will make you understand the humans that you are addressing. Do research on yourself. Close your eyes, remember a feeling. Let the feeling lead you like a bird on wings, and allow it to transform into an understanding of why you felt certain ways. Was it legit? Was someone putting blame on you? Putting the blame on others is a terrible thing to do. Ride and investigate the feeling of blame. Understand the impact of being blamed. Understand how an emotion can grow into blame and how it colors the being, the coloring of life. You have to understand the humans in order for you to talk to them. Blame is one. Fear another. Happiness. Ride on the experience of happiness. Blame–fear–happiness–love. Investigate the four, let it take you like a bird, like a hawk, on its back. Investigate it and ride on it. Lead it to your own happiness. Investigate how it impacted your mind, your physical. Where did the physical happiness, where was it felt? Where was blame felt? See and investigate those four. Blame, fear, happiness, love are the four pillars of development of man. Investigate them.

D. Wonderful. Do you have any general advice that we can pass on to the public that you would like to give us?

I&J. I would like to say to call on your higher mind, call on your higher feelings. Investigate them. Don't let them (*fear, anger, blame, and other lower emotions*) take over your human life. The life you designed prior (*to incarnating*) might not be what is currently being displayed. What we want man to see is beyond the human eyes. To be calm, to breathe, to understand the four pillars: blame, fear, happiness, love—to investigate those in their lives. Once one identifies whether one is under the spell of fear, blame, happiness or love, it is easier to adjust, and also change how you meet others. Do you put blame or fear in other lives? Meet your own Coat. Meet your own karma. See through the intent of others. Wire down (*reduce*) media, cut it off if you feel like it is affecting each or any one of these four. What we see now is that fear and blame are more prominent in the human mind. We advise you to calm yourself. We advise you to see that there is nothing to fear. We advise you to not feel blamed. It's also an issue for those who feel happiness or love this year. They don't want to talk about it because it indicates that it puts a feeling of blame if someone says, "I'm happy. This has been a great year. I feel the most loved this year." No one wants to speak about it because it indicates blame, in some way, due to the fact that you are pushed this year (*by the media and governments*) to be on the side of fear and blame. Speak up for happiness. Speak up for the little things you loved.

D. That's really good. Thank you.

I&J. There. We have someone here.

D. Who, Ophelia? (*Said jokingly, since I knew it was Bob.*)

I&J. Oh, Ophelia is here as well. But remind man that there is no blame. If you are happy, show happiness. It doesn't mean to rub your happiness into someone who is grieving, but don't hide your happiness, don't hide your love. It is more accepted this year to be under the spell of fear. The tools are blame.

D. If there are four pillars, then it would seem two of them, happiness and love, are positive pillars, and the other two—

I&J. Yes. The negative pillars, indeed. So. The equation, you can see vividly on display. Those who are happy, those who see the light—seeing the light meaning that you are love, that you see love, that you radiate love. Darkness is nothing bad, but here on Earth it triggers fear. Grey would indicate blame. Those who are initiating the negative pillars want there to be blame on those who see the light. So. There we go. And we have someone here, of course.

D. That was a wonderful teaching, so thank you for sharing. Thank you for the advice about what we are supposed to do.

I&J. You are much welcome. Bye bye.

The Spiritual Design Theories

As the sessions have piled up, year after year, an increasing number have addressed the long history of how the Earth was carefully cultivated by the Creator, the spiritual councils, and the manifested and physical entities who came here in the deep past. Sometimes it is a passing remark. In other sessions, there are pages of details. It is a monumental task to organize and elaborate on what the spirits say has occurred during the past 500 million years. Different entities will describe certain events from their own perspective and level of involvement, so by pulling some of their comments into one chapter, we hope to present a unified story of how life on this planet came to be. That includes talks about parallel realities, portals, and alien travelers, which are also part of Earth's history. The information they give never varies, so we are confident that the outline is correct. However, the Spiritual Design theory is much larger than can be captured in one book, and new information is always being revealed which may change our interpretation of what they have said to date.

What they teach us about the creation of Earth directly refutes many of the sacrosanct beliefs within science, religion, and philosophy. A lot of precious channeling time has been invested in describing the way our reality comes into existence and how various dimensions interact with our elemental Universe. The purpose, they say, is to lay a groundwork of concepts for future generations to use in developing new and beneficial ways of transforming and manipulating energy. It is for this reason that we must continually circle back to topics that are interesting to only a fraction of our readers.

Most of us were taught Henri Poincaré's theories of general and special relativity in school, and many have a passing familiarity with the Standard Model of Cosmology (SMC), which is a mystical blend of quantum field theories and expansive hyperbole. Those who are initiated into the SMC fraternity learn that the Universe expanded from nothing to its present size, and is still growing at nearly the speed of light. However, the spirits make compelling statements that everything is not as it appears, and the core concepts of cosmology are invalid. So, we will begin this chapter with a discussion of the mathematical metaphysics that dominates current academic views on the formation of the Universe. All the modern theories emerged from a misdiagnosis of redshift, which gave rise to the notion that "spacetime" is expanding, even as you read these words. Redshifting means the light photons have lost energy in their travels through space. As visible light loses energy, it appears less blue and more red. For several reasons, scientists decided that it was not due to energy loss, but rather, that space was stretching continuously, which elongated the light waves like stretching a coiled spring. The imaginary stretching of light waves is the foundation upon which modern cosmology rest. Stretching space seems like an unlikely explanation for the phenomena, when there are several other possible reasons for the dimming of light that are not as illogical.

The Big Bang, or From-Nothing-to-Something Theory
Beginning with Aristotle, and up through the early 20th century, the great minds of science assumed that space was filled with aether, the fabric of the Universe, an undetectable substance or medium that is the carrier of electromagnetic energy. It was also believed that the Universe was nearly static (unchanging) and had been around forever. Poincaré's equations of general and special relativity contained a cosmological constant (CC) in the field equations. Poincaré and other scientists at the turn of the 20th century assumed a static universe, so the CC was needed to stabilize the equation as a counteracting force to gravity. It was assumed to be a property of the vacuum field in space. Alexander Friedmann, a Russian mathematician, proposed, in 1922, that the CC could be eliminated if the Universe was expanding. A few years later, in 1927, the Belgian mathematician Monsignor Georges Lemaître calculated that the Universe exploded into existence from a single point, now commonly known as the Big Bang Theory. Then, in 1929, the astronomer Edwin Hubble published empirical data that indicated light from most galaxies was redshifted. He made a few assumptions and, using a handy formula, came to the conclusion that every square centimeter of space was continuously expanding in all

directions, that space itself was growing. And so, the intellectual fad of an expanding universe was born, becoming the religion of modern cosmology.

There are, however, other explanations for the dimming of light. The spirits have explained that neither the speed of light nor the gravitational constant (G) are constant. That alone would explain the behavior of light. When space and time were mathematically blended in a single "spacetime" function. Space exists and light passes through a medium that some quantum physicists refer to as time-invariant superfluid quantum space. Here, I will remind the reader that my knowledge of these subjects is little more than superficial, so don't expect me to elaborate on the variable density of universal space, because I cannot. However, I can say that if the speed of light varies, then there is no chance that space expands. But there are other explanations that may be more satisfactory to the scientifically inclined reader. Tiny dust particles in the intergalactic medium, or the gradual loss of energy as electromagnetic waves twist their way through successive gravitational (or variable density) fields on their way towards Earth can also cause redshift.

Everyone who has seen a sunset when there is haze or dust in the air has observed sunlight being redshifted, which is caused by a process called Rayleigh scattering. The higher energy blue light is scattered more than lower energy yellow and red, so the sun becomes a softer orange color. However, light passing through clouds of large particles will blur the image to an observer on the other side. Since even distant galaxies were clearly visible, Hubble discarded the idea that the vacuum of space contained any particles or matter, and moved on to the Doppler effect. The Doppler effect (as most readers know) is a function of relative velocity, and is usually explained using sound waves. A train whistle, for example, has a higher pitch when it is coming towards you, and a lower tone when it is moving away, due to the compression or expansion of the sound waves. The Doppler effect is assumed to effect electromagnetic waves, such as light, in a similar way. Oddly, it does not matter which direction telescopes are pointed, all the galaxies in the Universe appear redshifted. If the redshift is caused by motion, then nearly all galaxies are moving away from Earth. The further away, the more they are redshifted. Hubble used a formula developed by Richard Tolman in the 1930s to estimate the apparent velocity of the receding galaxies. This simplistic equation is based on the ideal relationship between the distance, size, and brightness of an object. In order to make the equation match the data, Hubble postulated that the Universe was not static, but was expanding at incredible speeds.

The problem with this formula is that it does not account for the quantum electrodynamic effect that dust particles have on the brightness of distant objects. Yet it is now known that sub-micron silicate particles and water molecules are present throughout the intergalactic medium. When light interacts with these tiny particles it does not scatter, but it does lose energy, causing the redshifts and other phenomena that are observed by astronomers. The more dust between Earth and a distant galaxy, the greater would be the apparent redshift. But cosmologists double down on their perceptual errors by claiming that spacetime is expanding faster the further a galaxy is from Earth. Dust, of course, is not uniformly distributed, so galaxies an equal distance away may have calculated distances that are vastly different. When conflicting data points arise, cosmologists blame it on imaginary "dark energy" and "dark matter" as the convenient scapegoats for their ciphering problems.

A second possible explanation for redshift may be due to gravity, which astrophysicists do not understand. The spirits say that gravity is an elemental force. Cosmologists reject that completely. According to spacetime disciples, gravity does not exist. You may be under the assumption that the Moon circles the Earth, held by an attractive force between them. The mathematical intelligentsia say that the Moon is actually traveling in a straight line, but spacetime itself is curved. Therefore, the moon appears to go in a circle because it is continually falling into geodesic ditch created by the mass of the Earth. These scientists are also under the impression that light bends because it is traveling through curved spacetime. However, if gravity is a force, as our spirit friends tell us it is, then it interacts with the electromagnetic waves of light and will bend it, exactly as "curved spacetime" predicts. Light may lose energy when it interacts with the gravitational fields of distant galaxies. Therefore, instead of expanding spacetime, most of the redshifting may be due to gravitational drag and energy loss. It also is worth mentioning that spacetime is not a singular entity, as proposed by Hermann Minkowski. Space exists and time exists, at least in the limited way we can interpret them. We have been told that space can fold and spiritual beings can move backwards on the timeline. Later in the book, the Elahim Council mention stellar time, but those teachings will be in a future *Wave* book.

Unfortunately, the ideas of Hubble and Lemaître became codified during the past century and have led physical cosmologists to perpetuate myths about the Big Bang, time dilation (as defined), black holes, curvature of spacetime, dark matter, dark energy, and many other exotic fables. These convictions have encouraged them to boldly declare that the Universe began 13.787 billion Earth years ago. Cosmologists have become transfixed on interpreting data through their preconceived biases, as humans have done for eons. Future scientists will scrutinize the Standard Model of Cosmology for its obvious failings, as it circumvents both logic and spirituality.

The Council of Nine puts the age of the universe on a scale related to the life-cycle of a spirit. They say that it may take several trillion (Earth) years for a newly created soul to ascend back to the Creator. During that time the Wheel will not have rotated a degree. But the Wheel has gone in a full circle an unknown number of times, so from the perspective of the Council, our fish tank is incredibly ancient and always changing. Solar systems and galaxies are created over billions of (Earth) years. They move through space and sometimes collide with other systems. And eventually the stars die and blow apart or collapse. Change is a fundamental principle within all dimensions. One of our spirit friends said the fish tanks grew from the spiritual dimensions, like leaves budding from a tree limb. So there was a beginning to the universe, but it was untold trillions of years ago.

The Spiritual Design Theory is a way to understand how the Creator and the various councils use energy to create galaxies, parallel planes, portals, and life on Earth.

Seth: The Big Wheel and the Zodiac (Dec 16, 2018)
Christine's higher self, Seth, came in with Ari to discuss the energy patterns in the zodiac signs. The earliest (acknowledged) human construction projects, such as Göbekli Tepe in Turkey, Machu Picchu in Peru, Newgrange monument in Ireland, and most other old stone structures, all seem to have an astronomical purpose. We know the earliest Mesopotamian cultures of Sumer and Egypt inherited the zodiac and the 365–day calendar from the Vinca society in the Danube Valley, who inherited it from the earlier society from the Caucasus Mountain, who likely inherited the knowledge from a succession of people who survived after the collapse of the highly advanced civilization that existed prior to 22,000 BC. If the knowledge was maintained over so many generations, it must have been considered valuable. While the

modern, rational minds are dismissive of astrology and its associated ideas, the spirits fully support the relationship between the energy patterns in the sky being mirrored on the Earth as a function of location and time. They even describe how incoming souls schedule their birth to correspond with certain energy patterns related to the celestial positioning of Earth within the greater web. That doesn't mean that modern interpretations of astrology are necessarily accurate or meaningful in the spiritual sense, because a lot of it is gibberish. But the cosmic energy web really does influence the human energy fields, from birth onwards.

S. It's me (*Seth*) and Ari.

D. Hello.

S. My maps, we will begin to look at my maps, the ones allowing us to know what realities are in harmony and which ones are coming in, creating a puzzle to understand who and where communication originates. Ari and I have set up a plan. He has the final touch, of course. The travels will begin from those realities in the fish tanks of the Wheel that are in harmony with this one, easier connections. There are differences in how you can travel between them, based on distances, geometric forms, as well as conditions. Conditions will be easy for myself here to understand, combined with understanding the connections in astrology—it's similar. Little wheel, big Wheel. Put them together and you can create portals in understanding. Some of the star systems and the zodiac signs in the sky are actually replicas of...huh! Didn't see this coming, did you? The constellations represented in the zodiac are a miniature model of the big Wheel, so when you understand the constellation, let's say, Aquarius, that one belongs in fish tank eleven. So you can learn about the conditions (*in the fish tanks*) based on the little wheel (*the zodiac*) to understand how you can enter a reality, like eleven, an energetic reality. It's connected to the constellation Aquarius, air. Didn't see this coming, did you? This one neither. MYSELF, that is! HA HA!

D. I thought astrology was predominantly man-made ideas.

S. No, it's a mirror of the big wheel, it's creating like a playground thing, the little wheel is a mirror of the big one. This one, I as Christine, will start to investigate more the qualities of the zodiac signs, now, when there is an interest to understand the fish tanks. Huhuhuh. There you go.

D. Do you travel to some of these other fish tanks?

S. Yes, I prefer five, eight, nine. Eight, nine and the border between, that's where I prefer to go. Much more of my liking, as well as yours. That's where our friends are. (*The Tallocks, on Vlac*)

D. Is this similar to where Siah is?

S. Siah (*who is on the planet Etena*) is on the border of this fish tank, in the fourth. (*The numbers Seth is using are fish tanks, not dimensions. Etena is in fish tank four, close to fish tank five, our Universe.*) The border between (*fish tank*) five and four is somewhat moving back and forth. All the borders have a tendency to move, but they don't have the same movement all the time. For instance, between eight and nine, that border is somewhat locked currently, so it's easier to move in between them. When they are moving back and forth, it creates a little bit of this and that, and you might think it would be easier to move between, but it's not. It's like catching a train that runs. You can't really jump on it. In this movement between fish tanks, a blend of both interconnects, and it's a back and forth, give and take. Some actually move positions. (*Solar systems or galaxies can move into the adjacent fish tank.*) When you are close to the border—in this case between four and five—there are realities close to the border to five that the councils are operating to permanently move into five, because they (*realities in the fourth*) carry more light, more enlightenment. Etena is one of those. When these movements between the fish tanks occur, interactions and exchange take place. When there is a stagnation or a stillness between, they somewhat operate as one. When I give you the picture, brother, eight and nine almost looks like one at the moment. Whereas four and five is almost trying to become one. Eight and nine had this dance before, creating— even though they are separate in their makeup and conditions within—eight and nine have learned their lessons and work as neighbors, making it easier for both in each fish tank to move in between. At this point, due to the density and occurrences that have been taking place in the fifth, the Creator wishes to enlighten this fifth reality with a little bit of sparkle from the fourth. Siah (*Etena*) is one of those realities moving in. This sister planet will come with information that is helpful for the living planet in this baby system we created here (*our solar system*). But understand that when you look at these different fish tanks in the Wheel, they actually mirror one of the zodiac signs. The fifth, Leo, fire.

D. So our reality is associated with the energy of Leo?

S. The constellation, Leo, fire. Fourth, water, emotion. It's the same in the zodiac. WHY DO YOU THINK THEY PUT ME UP FOR THAT TRAINING?

D. Are they in the same order?

S. So simple. It's in the same order, indeed, representing different elements as well. The distances between them, aspects, are also known as we create the bigger maps. Me and Ari travel, try to interact with different realities, (*on*) the highways, if you like. It's like creating a road system that man cannot travel on! Huh huh huh. The Little One wants to join. He's curious about the maps.

D. Ah, I'm sure he is.

S. But just know that four and five is in a dance at the moment. We're trying to blend in the quality of water, to make it easy. This one will understand, if you tell her.

D. What does four resonate with?

S. Cancer.

D. So you have Leo and then Cancer, so they are in the same order?

S. Yes. Not such a big mystery. It's made for man to awaken, to understand that once you start to understand the big Wheel, then you know that there is a little baby model that mirrors the understanding, just in a very primitive way of understanding, of course. But ancient man, starting to recognize the celestial bodies, constellation, the zodiac and the movement between stars and planets over the horizon. The moons are very important to understand. When the Moon moves through different cycles, through, in this case, the zodiac, over the constellations, it's a little clock to understand the big clock. If you think of the big clock, the big Wheel, being hours, then the little one here is like seconds. The Moon phases simply indicates different times, occurrences, when other fish tanks have the ability to, in some way, make themselves known. Some will intervene physically. Others, just by the awareness of their ability. Especially when the Moon is full in one sign, it doesn't simply radiate that zodiac sign, it means that the fish tank related to that zodiac sign also has the ability to transmit their presence energetically. People can tune in on that fish tank. Even though they think they tune in on a zodiac sign, it is actually the fish tank in the big Wheel that is the mirror of this specific constellation that makes themselves known. It's a line where you can connect to other fish tanks, for those who are initiated. That is why the ancient civilizations were so eager to follow the different moon phases,

because they knew that when the moon was full, and when it was directed in certain ways through these megalithic structures, holes, then they had an easier way to channel (*the energy from*) that fish tank. They understood so, because manifestations at that time took place. Now, manifestations might not occur, but you can still connect to those who reside in that specific fish tank. That is not what all souls do, but this one (*Christine*) can. Huh.
D. That's very profound.
S. We tend to be so! Huh huh huh.
D. When these ancient humans connected with these different energies, what happened?
S. Yes, meetings took place.
D. So they were able to communicate?
S. Directly with that fish tank. So let's say there was a full moon in Aquarius, those who reside in the fish tank eleven could make themselves known. Do you see the picture?
D. I do.
S. There you go. Time to leave.
D. Thank you for stopping by.
S. The maps, my maps, I will be looking at them. I will use meditation to access and then draw for you, creating a puzzle, making information available, combined with the little wheel, so that I *(the human self)* can understand the big Wheel. I might be confused and irritated by the fact that I cannot solve it fully from here. But as I get this teaching rolling, it will unfold the qualities within the fish tanks. Big Wheel, little wheel.
D. Is this going to be part of Wave 3?
S. Yes, yes. Travel, look around. There we go. Okay.
D. Thank you, Seth, for showing up.
S. Just in the next room, ya' know? Ha!
D. Thank you.
S. Elahim.

Bob: The Layer–Cakes of Parallel Realities (Oct 17, 2019)
Bob has been a guide far longer than most of his peers and has an immense knowledge bank about traveling to Earth. He is also joyful and enthusiastic, so he is often invited to give lectures to young students on the fifth, sixth, or second. Since Zachariah is a friend and a mentor to Bob, he will sometimes go to the fifth dimension

and listen to Zachariah teach in one of his big classrooms. Zachariah is a brilliant professor who helps educate some of the technically advanced spirits heading for Earth. In this session, Bob tells how he quietly parked himself in the back of Zachariah's class, but was noticed by a student who knew him. Zachariah allowed the students to question Bob, who gives an amazing account of ancient aliens who traveled to Earth in a golden spacecraft from a parallel reality. The concept of parallel realities has indirectly come up before, but he makes it easy to picture. He says it is like a layered cake above certain regions. The layers are not visible because the elemental vibration is outside the range of what we can detect.

We know from other talks that the portals between Earth and the parallel realities are located above certain areas where there are large concentrations of metals, especially copper, near the surface. In piecing together what they have said, it is possible that rotational vortices are created because ferromagnetic materials such as iron tend to channel and concentrate the Earth's magnetic field lines. Copper itself is not magnetic. However, the magnetic field causes electrons on the surface of the copper to rearrange themselves and begin rotating. They swirl in a circular pattern perpendicular to the electromagnetic field, creating eddy currents. While it is only conjecture on my part, the hundreds of millions of tons of copper ore could be what establishes vortexes or portals to the parallel planes.

It might only be a coincidence, but most of the areas where they have said portals exist seem to be at tectonic plate boundaries where there are iron, copper and nickel concentrations from magma. Bob identifies several regions where these parallel realities are found. One big area is in central Russia, probably along the Ural mountain range, which runs north–south from Kazakhstan up to the Arctic Ocean. It is one of the richest mineral regions in the world, with large deposits of iron, copper, nickel, and silver. The Urals sit atop where the Kazakhstania plate subducted under the ancient Laurussia continent, fusing Europe and Asia together about 240 million years ago. Another zone of stacked parallel realties is in the southeastern Mediterranean. The southeastern Mediterranean is where the African, Arabian, and Aegean plates all collide. A third area is around the Great Lakes above the Midcontinent Rift, an ancient plate boundary in the middle of the North American plate. Seismic surveys indicate there may be a solidified mantle plume below western Lake Superior and northwestern Wisconsin that extends to depths below 200 kilometers. This area had a very strong portal and was used as an ancient airport by a multitude of visitors.

Bob says, in the first paragraph below, that he is curious. What he means is that he wants to know what the new souls heading for Earth are going to be working on. He hopes to get a sense of the Creator's intentions and what is next on the list to repair. If he can get a sense of what the incarnating souls will be working on, he can train and tutor his students to be knowledgeable in those subjects. Mainly, however, I think he is curious because he has an inquisitive mind.

D. Which students are you teaching now?

B. The three little Elahims and the other three. I'm mainly with them now. However, I have been invited to be a guest lecturer for the souls from the fifth. I'm more or less stationed with the Elahims from the sixth. But I would say that I feel a need to help them (*the students from the fifth*), but I'm also curious.

D. What are you teaching them?

B. I'm teaching them how—and Ophelia observes this, so that's why I've not been invited for a while—because some from the fifth here, they're gonna be excavators and they're gonna be geologists, and they're gonna go and be biologists and work on different understandings in nature and finding things. Ophelia says that they're not necessarily trained, for the first couple of times, to go find things. And I said, "Well, I might put something in the pocket." And she said, "You're not supposed to influence the suits." But I'm going there and I told Ophelia that I will silently sit and observe a class that Zachariah has. But then, when I sat there way in the back to not disturb, I was detected.

D. Did Zachariah say, "Well, who do we have here?"

B. Zachariah did not, but someone in the front did. They said, "Oh, Bob is here!" And then everyone turned and THEN Zachariah said, "Well, Bob, why don't you come up and share the stage here?" So that's how it came about. And then someone said—because I have taken them on expeditions with you, they wanted to talk about that. They wanted to talk about what regions would be most beneficial to travel to if they wanted to do certain things. And there is a little group here among the fifth that will be excavators—

D. Do you mean like explorers?

B. Ah, they're gonna go excavate (*archaeologists*) like an explorer and excavate in the Egypt area. They're gonna be native born in

Egypt and they're gonna work in museums there, and they're gonna protect certain relics and certain findings. And Ophelia said, "That's all they're gonna do." And Zachariah said the same thing, "That's all they're going to do." And I said, "Well, if they are there and if they stumble upon something, like a treasure or something, is that wrong to open?" And then they (*the students*) were like, "What treasure?" And I said, "The whole region is full of treasures. So, if you find one, what will you do with it?"

D. What kind of treasure?

B. There are gold (*artifacts*). There is like a golden sphere underneath the desert sand. It's a huge sphere.

D. How many meters across? (*He paused for a long time, so I rephrased.*) How tall is it, compared to you?

B. Oh, if I were to go into the golden sphere, there could be like fifty of me in there.

D. What did they use it for?

B. It was a traveling device. It crashed one time, and it sank. It's hidden. So I'm waiting for someone to excavate it, to find it. It's far down.

D. Who was traveling in it? Visitors?

B. Ah. They were small-sized like me, but they were in form. They were talking like a popcorn language—it sounded like popcorn, like that. (*He then imitated what he heard, which involved a lot of rapid smacking and popping.*) And I said, "I have not learned the popcorn language, what is this?" when I saw it. And you said, "We're not supposed to talk about this, Bob. But it was an accident and it couldn't take off again, so we hid it."

D. How long ago did that happen?

B. It was before, it was like two grand civilizations way back ago. You were there in another form (*manifested*) and you were there and involved, and in charge of the (*solar*) disks. Due to the disks, this thing came in because you could attract spheres, and some came in like this. I don't know why they came, but it had to do with the knowledge of gold. In some way, they had a skin color like gold. I mean, it's kind of yellowish, or they're kind of sand colored, but they sparkled. So I said, "Oh, is that in fashion? Maybe that could be for the new humanoid. Skin that is a little more shiny and sparkly. I don't know them. I don't know where they are." And you say, "They're not around anymore. They hang around in the clouds," you say. And I said, "What clouds?" And you say, "That's a parallel reality. There are parallel realities that appear as clouds—but they're not clouds. But they blend in," you say, "like clouds. A lot of these parallel realities are somewhat in disguise in clouds."

D. Are these parallel realities all part of our fish tank?

B. Ah, it's still the same... oh, you showed me. Well, there are some from the fourth. I see friends from fish tank four that were also here in a parallel existence. They didn't incarnate, but they were here. It's like this; if you stand on your right leg, you see what you see. Like now, you see the Colorado mountains, you see your car and stuff like that. If you just shift and lean on your left leg, you would see like Setalay and other realities that are just visiting here, that sort of hovers. It's like moving in between—I'm not saying that she is here now—but the sphere, it traveled through. It was supposed to have been there (*in the parallel reality*), but it was invited in a portal—because everything has to be invited—so it was invited in a portal to move over to a denser reality—which is here—and it had not the possibility to return back. It came down and all these little figures poured out. I don't know what you did with the little people, but the sphere itself sank.

D. Was there water there at the time?

B. No, it sank into a rotating hole. If you think of how quicksand looks, but it was rotating, and it just swallowed it up. "But the little people were not in it, so we did not kill anyone," you say.

D. Are there a lot of parallel realities?

B. You say that normally there's like five. And they move around, so it's not like it's five solid parallel realities. It's like a cake. But every continent, every country, doesn't have the same big cake. Some countries only have two levels of cake and some have five. And where there is a five-level cake, where there is several realities, that's where it's close to those energy zones. So, we have a five-layer cake up in Russia, mid-Russia and UP by the ice and snow and water. Water is up and then there is a smaller one, so that whole region going north to south has a big presence, going from the sea down to the mountains, going down like that. (*Ural Mountains.*) Because they move, it's hard to see exactly what countries they belong in, because they kind of rotate, but it is that middle there (*in Russia*). And then there is also the southeast part of the Mediterranean, down to northern Africa. Around Egypt, there is some rotation going on. But if you move further down (*most of Africa*) there is only less (*a two-layer cake*).

D. I can picture what you are saying.
B. There is a BIG one—like when you see a tornado from above or like a big weather system coming in—there is a big one circling over the South American region.
D. So with those different realities, is it going towards the fourth dimension, or is it a different vibrational field within our fish tank?
B. It's like a different vibrational field. It's not a fourth reality, even though they transition through the fourth reality. Some that are meditating or used to out-of-body experiences, they can access these realities—and they might think it is the fourth reality—but it is actually a parallel existence here. The way you can detect it is that it has a similar vibration as a physical reality. The entities that you experience are more willing to share advanced knowledge. Sometimes when you enter the fourth reality (*dimension*), it's merely—I wouldn't say junk—but it's a lot of things that have been left behind to navigate around. It's not as advanced. It might appear from a human standpoint that these are the same, but the way you can detect it is that the ones that are in the cake, the parallel universes, they provide more direct information and knowledge. So the ones that you will communicate with, they will normally be found, you say, they will descend into the cake, not descend into the fourth reality. But from a human standpoint they might appear the same, but the fourth reality is not, you will not find—let's say it like this to be helpful—you will not find granny in the cake. You will not find Jesus in the cake. You will not find gardens in the cake. You will find advanced information and teachings from visitors.
D. I'm kind of curious, and maybe you don't know, but in a parallel reality, would they see the Earth the same way that we see it?
B. They see better than you see. Because the visitors are in motion and whoever decides this mobility and five-cake here, two-cake there, no cake there—I don't know who decides, and you don't tell—but they are more aware of you than you are of them.
D. I was just curious if they would observe the same universe we do, or is it completely different?
B. Nay, they don't see the same as you do. Like the sphere, it fell through (*from a parallel reality into our reality*). When the sphere fell through, they saw what you saw. I don't know if it was intentional or not, but as long as they are not fully engaging, they see it remotely. It's like seeing it in layers, you say. Like it has

more depth and things move. You say if they were to look at the Earth reality where humanoids are, they don't experience time. They will experience motion differently; it will look like you fast forward a movie. And they can manipulate and trick time—they're not bound by it, you say. So they see it more in depth, it almost looks like 5- or 6-D vision.

D. That's fascinating!

B. Ah. So, we have these people (*new souls*) that are gonna come in and they're gonna work at the museum in Egypt, and I said to Zachariah, "You know the sphere?" And he said, "Shh! They're not there to find the sphere." And I whispered, "When will that be? When will they dig up the sphere?" And he said, "We're not going to talk about that because that's not in the plan." And I said, "Maybe there are other treasures to be found?"

D. I'm sure there are. Those big disks must have gone somewhere too? (*In October 2017, Ari described the use of giant disks made of gold that were 10 to 20 meters in diameter. The session was presented in 'Wave 2', under the 'Lost Knowledge of the Anunnaki' header.*)

B. Ah, the big disks. I don't know if they sank, but some were removed. They were brought away. But a lot of times when things have just disappeared, they have actually—like the sphere who went this way—a lot of things have actually moved the other way. (*Technological devices that were used by alien or manifested visitors in ancient times have been moved into a parallel reality. They may still be in the same spot, but no longer have the vibration we associate with matter.*)

D. So they just become invisible to us?

B. Invisible, but they exist. You say the disks exist but they are not visible.

D. It does make sense, if it just moves into a different vibrational field.

B. Ah. You show me a picture of Egypt, and I see people dressed in clothes from the eighties and then I see the disks. But the disks are faded, but I see them. And you say, "They are in a different vibrational field. We just moved them."

D. Is that how those big stones were moved?

B. They were moved between vibrational realities, you say, parallel realities. But it's also how to take something from one form and making it larger by using—in this case disks—there is a beam here. The beam looks stronger than sunlight. If I look at the beam, it doesn't come from the sun. (*He nodded up and down, indicating the beam was coming into Earth from somewhere above, perhaps from a spacecraft.*) It has a golden color to it and it is larger in diameter than the disk. It's a beam that beams to the disk. And the disk can be that way (*he cups his left hand so the palm was facing to the right*), but when the beam comes, it moves that way (*he rotated his hand so it was cupped upwards towards the sky*) and then you put something in the disk and the beam surrounds it and it goes like this (*he gently shook his hand side-to-side*). And then the beam takes it and moves it, in some way. So it moves it and the beam places it, and then when the beam disappears, it (*the transported object*) grows and just freeze there. (*Bob is describing how objects were positioned between the beam and the disk. Then the elemental vibration of the stone changed; part of it moved into a parallel vibration. Based on other conversations, there is some residual ball of light that is only a fraction of the size with very little weight, which is moved to a desired location. When the beam of light is taken away, the object grows, expands and solidifies back into our vibrational reality.*)

D. That's consistent with what the Tallocks were saying.

B. Ah, you showed me this, and when you showed me this movie, we could not find me. So I wondered where I was. And you said, "This was when I was there not in human form."

D. So what did you talk to the little ones on the fifth about?

B. I was not allowed to talk too much, because when I asked Zachariah if they could find the sphere and the parallel realities, he said, "Thank you, Bob," in the middle of my sentence! Zachariah was like (*Bob started clapping*) and then everyone started to applaud and I understood that it was an ending. He laughed, though. He just shook his head.

D. I guess he didn't want to share too much information with them. (*The remainder of Bob's talk was published in Notes, Volume 2.*)

Zachariah: Geometric Forms and Portals (Oct 20, 2019)

In the earliest trance sessions, Zachariah alerted us to the fact that the first Waves will be easier to understand and more reader-friendly. As the teachings progress in the later Waves, some of the subject matter will become more technical and obscure. Personally, I enjoy being mentally challenged, but also know that these topics do not make for light reading. Zachariah is known throughout the spiritual dimensions as a great teacher, and he is one of the gatekeepers who facilitates the release of technical knowledge to humans on Earth. In this next talk, he introduces a handful of complex ideas about geometry, language, parallel realities, and alien visitors who utilize these vibrational fields for space-time travels. I can add little to clarify the meaning, although I have made an effort to fill in some of the gaps with information from unpublished transcripts.

The Elahim, Shea, and other visitors to the planet taught humanoids practical ways to communicate using symbols. The earliest known writing is from the European Vinca culture (also known as the Danube Valley civilization) that occupied the Balkans prior to 7,000 BC. The Vinca were descendants of the original Caucasians, an albino race placed in central Russia around 35,000 BC by alien visitors. The Vinca DNA haplogroup (family tree) was predominantly R1A, similar to the Minoan, Armenian, and the Sumerians circa 5000 BC. The Vinca writing predates Sumerian cuneiform by several thousand years. The Vinca also passed on to other cultures the 365-day calendar, the zodiac, the wheel, and were the first metalworkers in the recent era. (Previous civilizations had much more advanced technology, but it was lost when the visitors left.) Even though the Sumerians used a sexagesimal number system (a base of 60), I am confident they adopted it from the Vinca culture, since it is useful in celestial mathematics. Artifacts from the Danube Vinca era have elaborate drawings of the planispheres of the heavens, which have remarkable similarity to the artifacts that show up thousands of years later in the earliest Sumerian, Egyptian, and Greek cultures. Ancient astronomers could use a single rope or stick of any length and easily create a circle. Then, using the same measuring device, divide the circle into six equilateral triangles. Each triangular wedge would form an exact 60–degree angle from the center of the circle. When tracking the motion of stars, a zodiac sign fills 30 degrees of sky perpendicular to the Earth's rotational axis (the line pointing to the stationary North Pole star). The midpoint would be 15 degrees from either edge. We still use this ancient Vinca system, since an hour is 15 degrees of Earth's rotation, and a minute is 0.25 degrees. The sky-watchers, using static reference stones, easily measured time and built elaborate calendars and astrolabes for navigation. Most of the megalithic sites were used for astronomy. I call attention to the Vinca because they were the most advanced prehistoric civilization, and they also left behind a trove of alien-looking figurines. All of which lends credence to Zachariah's statements about visitors teaching humans.

258   The Spiritual Design

Nature and the Universe contain endless examples of structure and motion that exhibit geometrical shapes and symmetry. Mathematical precision is fundamental to the creation of the smallest atom to the largest galaxy. Certain forms can be used to manipulate or control energy. This type of knowledge is transmitted through symbols. Zachariah talks about symbology being a universal cosmic language. If you think about the reported markings on UFOs, or the intricate shapes in certain crop circles, those would be examples of that language. In addition to physical manifestations, they also recommend that meditators visualize sitting inside a rotating Merkaba—which suggests that geometric thought-forms can influence internal energy fields. The bulk of Zachariah's commentary is quite challenging to comprehend. He reveals that circular objects can travel into parallel realities and move around outside of our space-time. Square and pyramidal shapes are used to anchor portals and stabilize the Earth grid. And a bell-shaped object can move through time, but not conquer space. I hope that someday they clarify the physics behind those observations.

Z. This is Zachariah.

D. Ah, hello Zachariah. It's nice to hear you again.

Z. How are you, my friend?

D. I'm well, thank you.

Z. I'm here to help you awaken the memory of how you operated and deciphered the keys within geometric forms. The triangle is the shape of the pyramid. It's the form of travels versus receivers. You learned the language of the geometric forms and how they are portals to scientific openings and understandings. The pyramid form is well known for its ability to transmit and receive. It has the ability to allow travels to come, not necessarily to depart. The cylinder form is a shape that is manifested as a tool for rotation through tunnels, which are created as an end result of activating pyramids and such. That is why several have seen the shape of a cylinder or cigar shape. It is true, as it is a manifestation of a traveling equipment that has the ability to easier rotate (*and penetrate*) through the layers of physics. The cube, four corners, representing not only four elements but four directions. It is a way to navigate. Where the cube is in place, it creates a map. (*The precise orientation to the cardinal directions of the megalithic structures is a map.*) It creates foundations for the pyramids to later welcome travelers. As you learn to understand that all geometric forms—we have mentioned the six-pointed star, which is a way to combine forms in a way that math falters. In this particular age, man believes that language outside of Earth is numbers. They are actually forms, such as the six-pointed star. And as you came down in ancient Greece, together with me and other friends, we calculated and we deciphered the ability to use different forms as a language. The language of science, that is. The circle indicates completion. It connects the realities and experiences. The circle is the symbol for stellar time, space time, where space and time are merged into one existence. That is the symbol of the circle, because it has no end, it has no beginning. It allows completion of different realities. The circle, the sphere, combined with the cylinder, is what makes it possible to cross realities.

D. When you say cross realities, is that between— (*He answered before I asked.*)

Z. Vibrational fields. Realities, parallel realities. A cube or a triangle have not the ability. They are placed in one side or the other in order for the other (*shapes*) to travel. (*He means the pyramids and/or cubes are at the end of a portal, but the round shapes are the ones that can move through the parallel layers and then onto the interconnecting highways of light.*)

D. So the cylinder or sphere travel, and the other shapes assist that?

Z. Yes, yes. That is why the Little One was given a sphere (*his bubble for space travel, as explained in 'Notes, Volume 1'*), which later become his second skin, so to speak, or his second vibrational field, since he doesn't really travel with a skin, in that sense. However, the cylinder travels further; the cylinder is slower, it rotates around its axis slower. The circle, the sphere, rotates quickly, like a cell. It penetrates. Once you learn that the geometric forms are the language of science, the language of physics when it comes to the engineering within the Wheel, you will find in some ancient scriptures the effort of trying to understand the symbols—not numbers—symbols. As you came earlier here, trying to implement the cosmic language, it was added a more softer symbolism to it, as the inhabitants were not scientifically inclined in their mental. This was helped by those from the seventh, Shea, merged with you, creating a language of symbols.

D. I have a question about this. Humans will never be able to travel interdimensionally or across into parallel universes, will they?

Z. You mean the current ones?

D. Yes.

Z. No.

D. Will future ones be able to?

Z. Well, past ones did. It's based on the vibrational border. At this time, you can welcome visitors from the other side of the border. However, you, yourself, as a humanoid, will not have the ability to cross the border in the other direction, due to the fact of the veil upon your ability to solve and to master high frequencies, and to not INVADE. As long as that is in your mentality, to invade, you will not be able to travel across the border. Those who are open and inviting have the ability to travel over borders within your fish tank and between fish tanks. That is why, for instance, those from Etena, they would be able to come here, but you will not be able to travel there.

D. Are there any ancient languages that are based on the symbolic form?

Z. Yes. The Armenian, Sumerian, Egyptian.

D. The Armenian was the original, wasn't it? Predating the Sumerian?

Z. YES, yes. A group of—a blend of several dimensions—traveled there. Several from the eighth. The Armenian language is very connected to the higher languages within the Wheel. The way they write, the Sumerians, combined with Egypt, working with symbolism, not numbers. There are those who communicate with numbers, but that is just talk, it's not to solve the keys within the Wheel. You will have to understand the limitations of your brain, to not be distressed by the fact that you are not able, at this time, to solve everything we teach you, everything we talk about. We are providing bits and pieces so that you will start to question science. Your scriptures ahead will predominantly question where sciences are at, lifting forward ancient ways of communicating—simply poking them, triggering them. They are stagnating in their minds. There needs to be a poking, and that is what you do.

D. I don't even know a good question to ask.

Z. You don't have to, because you don't have it in your computer at this time. I'm giving you a memory, as you worked with this before. Question or lift forward the possibilities of symbolism and forms; if they rotate; if they merge, becoming new forms, new possibilities open. They are programmed like DNA to activate certain consciousness and keys of teleportations, such as the sphere and the cylinder. There is also known at this time about the bell. The bell tricks time, in some way, but it doesn't travel to the other side of the vibrational field like the sphere or the cylinder. However, it is locked in this reality and it had the ability to travel into the fourth and move to a different location. It used the sound. Know that all the forms, as you combine them with light and sound, they challenge the known materia that exists in that reality. The bell was an effort to try to travel across the band, the vibrational band. It reached the fourth and had the ability to move along the corridors of the fourth (*dimension*). However, the vibrational fields of different parallel universes, they can sniff in the fourth, making themselves known, but they are not there. They are not bound or trapped by the fourth, as the third is.

D. So the ones in the parallel universes can move freely?

Z. Yes. They see the fourth, like you would see a big field, just simply something to cross. It's not their karma; the parallel universes don't have the Coat of Karma as here. They exist in a different cylinder, in a different circle. Meaning they have their own space and time. The bell try to access a different time using space, not understanding that the key is to merge them into a sphere. The bell never became a sphere, it only had the ability to conquer time in some way—never space.

D. So they could move into a different time frame on Earth?

Z. Yes.

D. By conquering space, do you mean they could move to a different part of the visible Universe?

Z. You don't have the ability, at this time, to conquer space. But you have some ideas on how to conquer time. Meaning you have the ability to travel in your mind, back and forth—you become the bell. You don't have to have a physical bell. You activate the bell in your center point, meaning that you have the ability to visit different times. But you can't cross, physically, space. So, just a brief hello. We have someone here who wishes to show you a drawing. He has been moving around frequently in the fifth, in my classrooms, and he has asked permission to host a workshop. I asked for details about this workshop, since I know that he can be tricky, and I said, "This workshop, it has to be plain. They are not going to work with the higher science, such as the six from the sixth. They are going to come and help the biological and environmental chain to improve. So you cannot have a workshop of understanding the higher science or the teleportations that the other ones are going to come in and work on in a later cycle." This workshop that he wanted to hold in my classroom had to do with creative art. So he has dressed up, as I can see, in an apron and a little hat. And the hat is black—it's a little big, but it fits well. It has paint on it, such as the apron, and he is full of paint.

D. Messy painter.

Z. He's a messy painter, indeed. He wanted to portray somewhat of a creative force and how that would look. (*Bob came in after Zachariah and gave a talk on Coloring the Mind, which was published in 'Notes, Volume 2'.*)

D. I had a quick question before you leave. There's an assumption in science that physical objects distort space–time. That's one of the premises of the scientific understanding of the universe. Is that true or not?

Z. Clarify.

D. They say space is like a sheet, and if an object like a planet is placed in it, it causes the sheet to bend around it, which would be a distortion of space–time.

Z. If it would encase, becoming a circle, then it would be space–time, stellar time, like we talked about in the sphere. However, as long as an object lays in a sheet, it's halfway there—it doesn't conquer space and time, it doesn't become space-time. But let's say the sheet, the sheet would be more like time and this is what you can in some way manipulate. But you cannot manipulate space. So this sheet with the object, it could simply indicate you being the ball in the sheet, or the planet in the sheet. The sheet itself is time. Time is mobile and time can bend. At this time, you have the ability within your being to be in the sheet and conquer time in some way. However, as long as it doesn't complete to a sphere, that is the symbol of completion of time and space. If the sheet were to merge completely, which it has the ability to do in other fish tanks and other vibrational realities even within your fish tank, it allows the sheet, that you call it, to come to close around the object. Then the object simply dissolves in time and space, becoming the sphere. This is how complete travels are able to happen. There you go. Ponder about that with your seven percent! Ha ha ha ha!

D. (*Laughing with him.*) Maybe you could loan me a little?

Z. Oh, you wish.

D. I do!

Z. You have your Little Friend whispering in your ear all the time. He whispers in your ear when you sleep. He whispers in your ear when you work and when you even sit in that thing on wheels—the car—he whispers and he talks constantly, because you told him to do so. You told him to keep repeating things in your ears and maybe it would stick, and that is what he does. So there you go. Until next time, I bid you farewell.

D. Alright, my friend. Goodbye.

C9, Ophelia: Dreaming in Color (Jan 12, 2020)
When the councils speak, their imposing perception and gentle guidance are constant reminders that they represent a finger on the hand of creation. Their words are a reflection of the perfection, intent, and wisdom of the Creator, who knows the difficulties souls face when incarnating. In this session, they give very specific advice about how we can improve ourselves spiritually through activities such as praying and detoxifying the body. They also talk about how the Earth and its inhabitants are strongly influenced by energy flowing from the spiritual realities out into our fish tank. The energy comes in cycles that are thousands of years long. The Council of Nine describes how humanity has been in a ditch for the past few thousand years after filters were placed in humans that muffled the soul. The challenge for incarnations since about 7000 BC has been to master the mental, emotional, and physical layers. Much of the current karma program is based on the difficulties of operating a body when there are filters placed on the soul input.

From what I can tell, all spirits must travel into at least one of the fish tanks and learn about form sometime during their development. The Council of Nine said that some destinations lack nature and beauty, but are otherwise very harmonious. Souls who travel there have a different type of separation from the purity of the spiritual realms. Here on Earth, which is a greenhouse planet, there are so many animals, fish, flowers, plants, and landscapes that are enchantingly lovely. They are a reflection and connection to the majesty of the spirit world. But humans are disconnected on a soul level from themselves, making it very difficult to hold a state of compassion and harmony with their fellow men and the nature that surrounds them. I think that is a very profound concept, and implies the Coat of Karma is built around challenges related to those conditions.

264   The Spiritual Design

Near the end, both the Council of Nine and Ophelia give excellent talks on ley lines, magnetic fields, and the Fork, suggesting that humans have the ability to heal these energetic channels through prayer.

C9. Elahim. This is the Council of Nine.

D. Hello, my friends.

C9. We once again rejoin this holy circle that you invite us to participate (*in*). Know that there are several silent councils at this time approaching and will deliver their knowledge in due time. There are councils that you can simply call Creative Councils. They communicate directly with fish tanks as a whole, celestial bodies, galaxies; (*they*) monitor movement. Those are the ones initiating motion throughout the Wheel, motion within a fish tank as well. These entities have never taken form, form in the way that you perceive form. The Creative Councils answer directly to Source. But they are eager, in your future, to reveal knowledge about communication as a whole, motion as a whole, evolution in its entire spectra. However, we are, at this point, highly focusing on this fish tank. It is because there are several energies approaching, boundaries dissolving to the fourth fish tank. Even the fourth dimension, at one point, was thinner, meaning the fifth spiritual reality merged to those in form on the third much easier. At this time—again this runs in cycles—at this time the fourth, the mental realm, is quite wide. It is also filled with occurrences that happened here on your reality. Not only Earth but in your galaxy as a whole. In some way you might think that a whole fish tank has the same fourth reality bridge into the fifth. How can I explain? There is similar, like what we discussed (*about*) the basic disk (*the Creator disk*) and the hovering disk (*which is*) in motion—the fourth reality operates similar. The width, the distance of the fourth reality symbolizes the basic disk, it is constant in this particular time; not constant in the entire cycle, in the entire evolution. But it's static. You, who occupy form in this fish tank, as you transition from form to spirit, you travel differently over this static fourth reality. Those who exist in the galaxy, your neighbor Andromeda, they travel across the static fourth reality, as all do—however, the experience is different. It is similar as the hovering disk, based on where you depart. So, the fourth reality, the bridge being static, the transition from form in the fish tank varies. You are far out; you are in the canyon. It takes a little bit more effort to transition from form to spirit form. Those who are closer to the center still has the same static fourth reality, but they don't become the fourth reality, such as yourself. That is the difference, the transition varies whether you become the fourth reality (*or not*). It allows you to move faster if your lessons and evolutions are different. Not everyone in the fish tank evolve in the same time, in the same fashion, and that is the difference in how they transition. So from the point of where you are located, Earth being in the canyon, feeling somewhat disconnected, even disconnected to the fourth. In many ways, you are here to make the fourth known. As the fourth becomes known, it is easier for humanity to wish to reach for the higher levels. The fourth is where their dreams are found—don't neglect dreams. They are portals to understand transitions between spirit and form. Those who investigate their dreams are easier to embrace a spiritual reality. But then comes the question about nightmares—what are those? It is the same illusion. It is, in many ways, manifested in your consciousness as a memory. It might not even be your own memory. Those who are wide open in their—what was it called—chimney, they might encounter, as they dream, others' fears, not their own. But it is manifested in their dreams. Those who are in-tune, those who are open, not fully grounded, have a tendency to not only invite light as they dream, they can come across remains—leftovers in the fourth, others' fears—and it can become THEIR nightmare, not making sense. In many ways, that is the meaning of grounding yourself. It is advised, as you go to sleep, to send out a prayer to only travel on your own path, to your own dreams, to your own memories. Send out a path of being grounded as your soul travels. If the physical is not balanced, it is easier for the soul to feel lost as it travels in dreams.

D. I guess food and alcohol would affect the physical?

C9. Yes. If you eat too late before you go to sleep, it has an impact on the physical, creating imbalances that the soul, departing in sleep, feels disconnected from. It is colored and it colors the dreams. We advise to not eat too late before you go to sleep. Preferably no intake three hours before sleep. Alcohol, of course, and other substances, color the physical and it colors the dreams. Dreams that can become an illusion that is not real. It is the physical screaming for cleansing, coloring the soul as it travels in the night. But also, be aware that those are not fully grounded and too open to higher energies—those who call themselves empaths—those people sometimes are open, even when they sleep, to other influences. Meaning their dreams are colored by what they encounter in the fourth reality. Leftovers, fears, karma, and entities not fully transitioned into the light, still waiting for the final ascension, not fully there (*back into the spirit realm*). They (*the lingering spirits*) notice all souls in your dreams as you travel, but if you are in balance as a human connected to Source, to your soul, then you simply are not affected.

D. That's really good advice.

C9. We advise that before you go to sleep that you send out a prayer to not let your soul be influenced (*by external energies in the fourth*) as it will depart (*from*) the physical.

D. Should prayers be said aloud or internally?

C9. It doesn't matter. A prayer is still a prayer, verbally, mentally, emotionally, or from your center point. Those who send out their prayer from their center point are not very likely to get lost in their dreams. They are already aware of the mish–mash they can encounter as the soul departs. But to simply say a prayer that your dreams are safe, ask for colors, imagine rainbows, imagine all spectra of colors. Nothing bad travels on colors. If your mind is drawn to grey, dark, negativity, then replace those thoughts and allow your favorite color to take over, visualize. Imagining is a portal, it's a way for you to become more in–tuned. So, (*due to*) this current location of where your system, galaxy, is at, the change needs to come from those who occupy form. Sometimes change comes from spiritual realities. At this point (*they are*) monitoring change that, hopefully, will take place from those in form. Just know that the fourth reality is, in some way, static to each fish tank. But how those in form reach the spiritual realities varies.

D. Just thinking about the souls that come to Earth, it seems like this is a pretty rigorous destination. Other souls have, apparently, easier experiences on other places. Is there a reason that certain souls are sent to Earth?

C9. Not as a punishment, but as a barrier. If you only travel to destinations that mirrors the spiritual reality, then growth, in form, does not take place. You all have to travel to destinations where form creates a boundary to your spirit. It could be that you travel to a planet or a reality that lacks growth, that does not have seas, continents, in that respect, a lack of vegetation—that is a separation from beauty that the soul internally are always part of and seeking. So here you travel to a destination that is not visually dry, it is blossoming—you have animal life, you have your seas, vegetation and so forth. Here it is about the consciousness—that is the gap to the beauty of soul. So, souls can travel to destinations that will impact their training, their experiences of knowledge. Some will feel drained by the environment of a planet. Here, souls feel drained by the lack of empathy, the lack of community. The lesson in all, as a soul travels, taking form, is to find and reconnect with the beauty within. Here it is hard, as you, in many ways, alienate each other instead of unifying. Do you see the picture?

D. I do. That's really a brilliant description.

C9. Every time a soul departs spirit, taking form, the lesson is to find and remember and seek the beauty that it is created of, and always is. Those who travel to destinations lacking lifeforms, lacking life, there are several souls who have memories of traveling to dried out realities, only rock, only sand, not feeling like they are connected to beauty. The teaching is, when traveling to those locations, it is to find the reason of why they are there. Perhaps the rugged environment holds a portal or an understanding for the soul to channel beauty.

D. That's really a beautiful teaching. We're going to be talking to a group tomorrow about power spots and energy. Is there anything you can say about that?

C9. Power spots, sites of interest, some hold your gravitational field in its position. Pyramids were built to hold, first of all, the grid in its position, making it static, making it possible for life to take place. If your energetic grid, gravitational field, is not static, if it becomes flexible, lifeforms are not able to exist in the way you see them now. Ancient visitors, ancient civilizations, knew how to maintain and stabilize the grid, understanding that the gravitational spots are different. It does not mean better or worse, it just means that it's a part of a grander web crossing your planet, and it has to be maintained differently. Those who occupy space where the gravitational field and the magnetic field are more exposed experience mental disturbances. There is a reason at this point why several feel mental illnesses. It is due to the fact that no one carries the knowledge on how to maintain the grid. Natives knew how to operate through rituals, closing, maintaining, opening portals in order for the whole grid to be in balance. Pyramids were built to fulfill stabilizing zones. (*Pyramids were built over areas where the grid needed to be stabilized.*) But you do not need to build a pyramid to honor the grid, to maintain your portals. It is done by simply detecting how the energy feels within your being. If you come across a spot that makes you suddenly feel a shift in your personality, in your wellbeing—regardless in which way—honor that spot. Stop and see, tune in on that region on where you have your feet and you will understand that you as a human have the ability, similar as a pyramid, to heal and stabilize a spot.

D. Were the early inhabitants told how to do that by travelers?

C9. Yes, yes, yes. Travelers, yes, not human.

D. Is the grid around to the Earth related to the magnetic field, or is it somewhat independent?

C9. It is a friend to the magnetic field. It is a friend to Earth. But it was placed here by those who engineer communication centrals. (*The Fork is the central communication network on Earth.*) The Earth, in its baby form, was given a magnetic field, as all realities are given. However, maintenance changes occurred over time and that was engineered by those who visited. Came from nearby systems. Came not from other fish tanks. But at this point, when the Earth was born, when your system was born—if we give you the picture of your fish tank from one to ten—at this time your system is located around seven. (*I think the Council of Nine is using numbers to represent the stages of progress. 0 would be when matter arises from the first dimension, and 10 would be a return to hibernation. The entire Universe has a cycle and all systems follow that rhythm, but individual planets and stars have their own, shorter 1 to 10 lifespan.*) When your (*solar?*) system was born, it (*the Universe?*) was located around two or three. At that time, it (*the Earth*) was given a magnetic field. As it continued its progress and evolution, once it started to reach level five—to make it easy, to give you a picture—life started to take place. At that time, when lifeforms, shifts of continents, started to embark on your reality, adjustments were made in your magnetic field. The gravitational field was still constant, still dependent on the fish tank as a whole. As it (*Earth*) progresses, maintenance takes place of your magnetic field—not necessarily the gravitational field, which is constant. However, when we say constant, know that there is a way, from the creative councils, to adjust the gravity within each celestial body. So, in some way, your question has two answers. The gravitational source within your planet, within your system, within your fish tank, normally remains constant. When changes occur—evolution, or shifts—the adjustments take place from higher councils, impacting the gravitational source. Those who influence and adjust the magnetic field are visitors, engineering (*experts*) normally (*from*) neighboring systems in your own fish tank. Those (*forms*) at this time in fish tank three have gone through its entire cycle; it is asleep. Meaning all gravitational fields, all magnetic fields, are shut down, asleep. So, a human has the ability to use its physical body similar as a pyramid. If they come across a spot they detect is perhaps in need of healing, in need of balance—you can even come across a spot that will trigger a sensation of fear within you—help that spot. Act similar as a pyramid. Place your feet stable on that spot, close your eyes and see what the spot is telling you. From that perspective, you have the ability as a soul in human form to connect and stabilize that spot. Many people though, when they come across a sensation that trigger, let's say, fear, they run away. Some portals are not for only one person to stabilize. It might need a group. The natives traveled over your nation seeking those spots in need for stabilizing and used rituals to stabilize the land. In many ways they traveled to find food, to find new locations to set tent, but they were guided. The shaman or the chief guided them to locations where the Earth called them. The Earth craved balance for various regions.

D. If an individual tries to do that, do they pray? Is that the method they should use?

C9. Yes, yes. In whatever fashion you see fit. Portals are the gateways for the visitors to come, engineering, maintaining your magnetic fields. Portals are not static, they move. Ley lines are guiding paths and veins to your planet where you can seek information not only from your host, but you can come into direct contact with previous civilizations. It is a memory lane, if you like. You have the ability to come in direct contact and feel the Earth, the pulsation of the Earth, through the ley lines. It is like coming in contact with the heartbeat of your host. As a gift, once you honor your host, the host will give you an enlightenment of different kinds. The enlightenment is easy to come across once you travel along the ley lines. There.

D. Wow. That was a brilliant talk. Thank you.

C9. We will continue our discussion.

D. Alright my friends, thank you so much for coming and sharing today.

C9. You are much welcome. Elahim.

D. Elahim. (*They left and Ophelia came in to clean the energy for Bob.*)

O. So, let's see what we can do with the energy, as it is a little bit static in the physical, and I know that someone is more flexible and will feel less invited. Haha.

D. Hello, Ophelia. It's nice to hear you again. We always feel like you get short–changed when it comes to talking.

O. Oh, I get my say. I just get it through in different channels—even through the Council of Nine, even through other speakers. (*Such as Bob.*) We all communicate (*as one mind*) about a topic at hand and we all wish to deliver a story that will unfold little–by–little as we progress. It is to make it easy for you to comprehend topics that, many times, are hard to understand from a human standpoint. That is why we blend our teachings and we progressively give you more keys to think of. I know that you will discuss portals, sacred sites, and ley line. Ley lines are the direct contact to the seventh dimension, and the eighth. Those who understand the grid understand the elements, understand the shifts in nature, are easier to be guided to ley lines. When one comes across ley lines, it can appear as a sudden sadness. The sadness indicates the state of mind from your host at this time. But the sadness is also the feeling of separation from your host and from your Source. So sadness, as well as laughter, are channels for you to come in contact with your host as well as your soul. The sadness at this time is felt in the ley lines, which is the Earth's circulation system. The ley lines are the veins in your host, and on specific places, once you come across a ley line in that region you can feel sadness, and it has to do with what occurs on the land. You can also feel a direct separation from Source, and that might trigger a sensation of sadness. So the sadness's are different. The sadness can be a joyful sadness, if you like, as it is an opportunity for those who stumble upon that feeling to also connect.

D. Do the lifeforms on Earth, such as plants and animals, do they rely on those ley lines?

O. Yes, indeed. Yes, indeed. As well as the Fork, indeed. The Fork is the one communicating to the ley lines, primarily. It can also, in some way—not necessarily often—but it has the ability to be a stabilizer for the magnetic field and those spots that was mentioned that might be imbalanced. Visitors who came here to maintain the magnetic field had high understanding in how to connect with the Fork. But the Fork, predominantly, is in place for lifeforms, ley lines, and the host itself. There are energetic spots that holds higher or lower amounts of gravity. Even though the gravity itself is static, it manifests differently on different spots. Those who travel here to maintain the web—which is mainly their agenda at this point—those who visits are here to maintain the magnetic field and to make sure that man (*humans*) do not cause disturbances in this magnetic field. If the magnetic field were to collapse, there will be huge changes in the appearance on land. The Pole will shift. This is what occurred earlier as the poles moved. That is why it is a crucial mission from visitors to make sure that you do not, in a negative way, impact the magnetic field. So, there we go. We will continue the discussion.

D. Thank you for that. I really appreciate the information, Ophelia.

O. You are much welcome. There we go.

C9, Ophelia: Life in the Ditch (Jan 18, 2020)

This is a difficult session to categorize because the Council of Nine discusses so many topics. The main focus is on the energy flow coming into our solar system and how that influences the Earth and humans. They also talk about portals and why aliens come here to collect biological samples. UFO stories of abductions and medical experiments are interpreted negatively by humans, who assume the intentions of the aliens are hostile. But the Council of Nine tells us these intelligent visitors have been coming here for hundreds of millions of years, working on behalf of various councils who want to ensure the Earth continues as a viable host. The mental chain reaction that compels some humans to act without reasoning or self-control is one of the areas they are currently investigating.

The Council of Nine also explain that mental imbalances and the irrational rage that permeates society is partly due to the effect sugar has on the brain. When I asked them if the sugar was deliberately added, they said that it was "from yourself to yourself." That made me laugh, but the point they made was that we are the responsible party for what we ingest. If we are too lazy or ill-informed about what we are putting into our bodies, we cannot fully blame the food cartels for our choices. However, it is a fact that the governments like what sugar, high-fructose corn syrup, and similar additives does to the human brain. It reduces the attention span and makes people impulsive and easy to control.

Ophelia then gave a wonderful talk on the process of becoming spiritual. Many people are now in a passive state, or are mentally overactive without being analytical. She says that when the human personality has been ignited, there will still be a yearning for a connection to the soul. Worldly success, material possessions, social status, and even friends will not fill the void. There are no substitutes for the peace that comes from knowing one's true self. Ophelia also says, "Just know that the more you understand your path, the more you investigate your true feelings and thoughts, you are less likely to act human. You will act as your soul encased, portrayed in a human." I think that is a very important idea and, to me, correlates with the Buddhist teaching of non–attachment. As awareness of the soul increases, it compels a reevaluation what is valuable and beneficial in life. The measures of spiritual success and progress often run counter to the mores of society.

C9. This is the Council of Nine.

D. Welcome back, my friends.

C9. We will see how this proceeds. The throat (*Christine's*) is a struggle for us at this time, so we'll see. The information at hand (*they want to deliver*) involves the opening of grids and how you are able to open and close not only your inner grid, but, as a community, the Earth grid. This grid has several occupations, several awareness's to its disposal. The opening of the grid comes and goes, and it is dependent on the wellbeing in your Fork and the communication between the Fork, (*the*) magnetic field, (*the*) Earth grid, as well as the upper grid. All of them has to be aligned in order for an opening to take place. Earlier civilizations witness grander openings. It was like a giant hole and it was common to witness for all different entities on this plane. At this time, the holes are several, but smaller. Windows for outer influences (*alien visitors*) to descend to your plane, mainly to collect data on wellbeing of environment—animal life, such as yourself. Don't think that you are above the wellbeing of animal life and lifeforms in general. Collecting samples from different species; reporting to councils located not only in spiritual realities but bases nearby. Some are stored and kept, analyzed, investigated by physical entities at bases, such as yourself. (*I think they mean similar to humans.*) There are some in your nearest neighbor galaxy that also—how can I tell you this without making you feel supervised? There are several galaxies surrounding this one. You are, as have been mentioned, in the ditch, in the canyon, ready to ascend if lessons and actions align. At this time, several entities, bases, surround your galaxy and area. That might, for some, feel like surveillance. In some way, it is. But it is for your wellbeing, for the future of species, and for the future, as a whole, for your system. Those who are possessing a higher intelligence (*aliens*) are especially monitoring mental chain reactions within your being, within your species. You should know that when a species in a system exists in the ditch, in the canyon, the emotional tends to cope better than the mental. The emotional has a tendency to simply go to a peaceful sleep. However, the mental is the one rushing, trying to survive. Those who are emotionally stressed are actually more in-tune with the mental stress, as the emotional tends to take a step back and wait for the next phase. Those who feel emotional stress as humans are actually influenced by the mental stress. This is important for mankind to understand the difference in how they perceive their reality. Once one feels stress, breathing increasing, it is an effect of imbalances predominantly in your consciousness, in your mental bases. At this time, we are here to provide comfort, to align the mental to a higher capacity. As of yet, as of now, the mental capacity in your species are running dry. It's like a car running on fumes, it needs the right fuel. There are those who try to provide fuel in a different way, meaning it leads the consciousness astray. The emotional center within your being, in many ways, tries to calm the mental. It is a conflict, a combat within you. But instead of focusing on healing and resolving your inner combats, you are acting out, creating combats with others. Understand that to heal a nation, a group, you have to heal and face the imbalances within first. You are less likely to create riots or disharmony for others if you, yourself, understand and feel the balance and harmony within you. The intake of food creates a spiral and a distance between the centers within you— especially sugar. That is added in huge volumes in your grains, in your general food where sugar before was not to be found. As you put sugar in everything, the stress and the combat within is more obvious. In many ways, humanity needs a detox. A detox has taken place before, a detox of your species has before resulted in a wipe-out.

D. How long ago was that?

C9. Several times before. One around 500,000 years ago. That civilization, that group, was not hooked up on sugar, but they harvested their planet and their resources in a way that became hostile to each other. Sugar has the same end result, it creates hostility. As we see civilizations rushing to that end line of hostility, stress, then indeed, it is a wake-up call for all.

D. Is the sugar added deliberately?

C9. Yes. From yourself to yourself. Those in power wish it so because, you should know, a calm mind is less likely to become a follower. A hyped mind, a stressed being, a stressed entity, are more likely to make decisions rashly and not by thought, not by investigating. So, in many ways we have discussed before that the human race is passive, which, from this dialogue today, would indicate a heightened awareness, a species more inclined to make decisions that are beneficial for itself and its community. But the passivity is paralyzed, it is not clear—that is the difference. If you were to be clear and in stillness, that is not being passive. What we see is a huge number that are overactive in their inner being, and those who are simply passive. Not reflecting, either of them. Not engaging in the game they set up to play. They are brought here—all of you—you are all here to play a crucial part in the evolution and change for your system as a whole. Not necessarily only the species, but to help your system to reach the peak again. There. We will make it short today.

D. I had a couple questions, if you don't mind?

C9. Shoot.

D. I'm curious how the Earth's general field prevents visitors from coming in unless there are portals open. Can you explain the process?

C9. Is your question if there are ways to close the grid for visitors, and how?

D. The mechanism by which travel is achieved.

C9. Earlier, it was a big opening, actually two. One located just above this nation (*USA*). It was as big as your country and the northern one together. As of now, there are little windows, and the field, or the windows—it's like a waveform. It moves, it's not constant, even though some are more active than others. But it's not just in the same spot. These openings move. The field rotates. The field rotates, circular rotation, east. Motions create different opportunities for the grid to open. The way it has the ability to open depends on the ground force, meaning the occurrences below the grid, the Earth plane. In many ways, there are bigger and easier entrances and accesses over the oceans than over land. The water creates portals by itself due to the element. It responds differently to electrons, to electric interferences, than land. There are more connecting points over water than over land, at this time. There are bases on your seabed. There are no bases on land. Earlier, when the big portal existed, there were several bases established in mountain regions.

D. I was wondering if the portal was necessary to connect with the upper grid? Is it some sort passageway of vibration?

C9. Yes, yes, indeed. That is how the connecting points can exist or not. Let's just say, visitors have to navigate more and prepare their descent more, calculate where openings and matching points occur than before.

D. What happens if they get off the path? Are they blocked from coming down?

C9. They cannot come down if the connecting points do not match. But at this time, they use your seas, as the element water is highly receptive to the electric influences, creating openings in the magnetic fields that exists. It is more open at this time in the seas.

D. Very good. Thank you. I also wondered, when we gaze out into the Universe at all the dots of light that we assume to be galaxies, are those real?

C9. (*That caused him to suddenly burst into laughter.*) HA HA HUH HUH! No, they are not. Some are fabricated. Some are created as, huh huh, how can I say? Some are actually more like graffiti. Creative spirits.

D. Is the Universe as large as we perceive it to be?

C9. Do you talk about your fish tank?

D. Yes, our fish tank?

C9. Your fish tank is probably similar to what you perceive. However, what man does not understand is the amount of fish tanks coexisting, connecting. If they knew, the Universe will take a different form that one cannot fathom.

D. We can't perceive other fish tanks, can we?

C9. How do you mean?

D. If we look out into the Universe—

C9. No, you cannot. If you were to, let's say, come face to face with the barrier to the fourth (*fish tank four*), which is in some way dissolving, connecting closer to your fish tank, you will only perceive it as a big fog. You will not be able to pass or see beyond.

D. If we could see into the fish tank four, would we see similar structures as we see here, or would it be invisible to us?

C9. As a human, you would simply see—the difference between the two, here there are more graffiti, more designs, more systems. If one, as a human, let's say, could use their little craft and travel to the border, having a sneak peek into the fourth (*fish tank*), it would look more empty. But they would still see stars, systems. They would be overwhelmed with the energy of compassion. They will hear the song, the melody that would resonate as harmony within your being. If this person in his little craft would be able to look into this new reality, he would have a greater understanding and need, wish, to help his neighbors. In some way, it would be beneficial if your little space craft could take you there, because your awareness would heighten and you would simply dissolve into your spiritual being that you are. The physical human struggles that you suffer and observe (*on Earth*) will be—oh, there is no word for it—but you would not be able to maintain the combats and struggles if you ever simply looked in and felt the presence of the fourth. But visually, this person in this imaginary spacecraft would see it as less occupied. If this little craft, being at the border, were to look left, right—left into the fifth, right into the fourth—it will look very congested in the fifth and less occupied in the fourth. However, being in that presence of two very different energy flows, one will have a struggle to leave that space and return to ignorance.

D. Wow. Thank you for that.

C9. It would be similar as one who has a near–death experience, meeting a light being or a loved one, and returning to physical. That person is changed for life. If one were to move to fish tank six, they would not be able to see anything, they would be blinded by the light. So, it would look like one big sun, because the sixth is one big galaxy at the moment, one big sun. If you think of that one big sun in the sixth occupies about 55 percent of its space at the moment, then you can get a picture. This one likes to be there. Working with the progress of motion. Working with the level of energy from the sun, creating foundations for lifeforms to come. You are all working with this project. Your Little Friend (*Bob*) wanted to come. This is what you Elahims work on in your space at home, creating the beginning of new worlds.

D. Sounds like good work!

C9. Huh! There you go.

D. Thank you for that description. It was very helpful.

C9. You are much welcome. Elahim. We will return.

D. Elahim, my friends.

O. This is Ophelia.

D. Hello, Ophelia.

O. The energies are a little bit harder to clean today, so maybe someone will have a separate session. At this time, we observe the stress within your race, and we see the compassion that you seek. But some do not know where to find that harmony and compassion. This is what we aim for with you, carrying out the connection of higher awareness. Others will calm and heal the emotional. You are here to connect satellites—not the ones in the skies—but people, making new satellites, making them go into the world, working similar as do you. This is a time where many need a hand to hold. Hmm. Oh, let's see what we can do with the energy. So, what we will do today—and Bob is aware—is that we will set up a separate session for Thursday. The energies at this time *(in Christine)* need to be in rest. So we will make this short. However, once you start to find those connecting points within you, you are more likely to be in balance—and I'm not talking about you, I'm talking about humanity as a whole. As you connect and heal your inner being, the level of understanding and compassion that you radiate simply by being healed has a wider impact on your surrounding than you think. It has nothing to do with speaking out loud all the time. Holding someone's hand physically, as *(once)* you are healed and in balance yourself, you become a battery of compassion. You are a battery from spirit, and you do not need to communicate, necessarily. Just know that the more you understand your path, the more you investigate your true feelings and thoughts, you are less likely to act human. You will act as your soul encased, portrayed in a human. Your personality was decided as you came, in order for you to fully channel your spirit to the fullest.

D. Speaking about me or everybody?

O. Everybody. If you deny your human personality, it is harder to accept and find your spirit personality. In many ways, they align. Only a few take on a mask quite different from their soul. But as more and more feel like they are shut down as humans, not heard, not counted for, it is harder for them to display the spirit personality, the purpose for coming. If one sees another human dimmed, not fully blossoming, then indeed one can help them to first blossom as a human. In many ways, life coaches, affirmations, they increase the human personality. From that point, it is a bridge and easy access to fully allow your spirit to blossom as well through your human traits of choosing. You are not here, necessarily, the two of you, to awaken a human personality. Those who work with how to heighten your voice, who you are as a human, do a great work for those who later want to ignite their spirit. Like, for instance, the one you call Tooth Guy (*a motivational speaker*), he plays a great spotlight on the human, doing a great job, sending them off being more empowered as humans. Eventually, when they have walked for a while in that empowered sensation, they will feel like still something is missing. That's when they are ready to receive and channel their inner being. As both are aligned, there are no limits to what one can accomplish. But it is hard to ignite your spirit first and not your human self. Do you see the difference?

D. I do. So is it like the human is passive and basically indifferent towards life? Is that what you mean by someone who isn't pursuing humanness?

O. Yes, indeed. Those who do not engage in life, in their own life and in the lives of others. They might need that little fire from someone like Tooth Guy. Once they have (*experienced*) being and feeling that empowerment as a human, after a while they will encounter and face an emptiness again. That emptiness is the canyon or gap to their inner being, the soul. And that's when the true enlightenment can occur. It is harder to ignite the soul if the personality and human is passive and not feeling capable or empowered. So what we wish for you to think of is that sometimes you will meet people who have more to gain if you try to ignite and empower their human being. See the difference in the people you meet, where they are at, and aim your spotlight to either empower the human, or fill the gap to the soul.

D. What sort of advice do you give to someone to empower the human?

O. To empower the human is to raise the vibration of feeling capable, of feeling like they have a skill, a human output of one's mindset, skill-set, or capability. It is a way to feel that you belong in a group of humans.

D. The outer hobby?

O. The outer hobby, indeed. So it is to feel like the little things that you can bring, as a human, matters. It is similar as when you go to school, those who are skilled in mathematics are not considered as high on the hierarchy as someone good in sports. If one could balance and understand that both are equally important, both symbolize, in many ways, the outer hobby, the human personality. If one were to encourage (*people*) that regardless of what your skill–set is or where it lies, it is valuable, that empowers the human. One can be extremely intelligent as a human, as a physicist, as a mathematician, or someone who is highly inventive, and still feel (*they*) do not belong or matter as a human. It is an imbalance of what is considered an asset as a human.

D. The ancient Greeks probably had a better philosophy then?
O. They balanced the different capabilities. They understood that it was like filling up a toolbox, and that all tools were necessary to build the temple. There. So we are sorry to say that someone will have to wait for Thursday, but that someone will have a complete session for himself.
D. Very good. Thank you for coming today and sharing. That was really thought-provoking.
O. There. We will see you in a couple of days. Bye bye.

Tallock, Ophelia: Visitors from Parallel Realities (Feb 9, 2020)
This session started with the Tallocks, who live on Vlac, giving warnings about mercury being dumped into the ocean and atmosphere by communist China and India. In reviewing the claim, I found that it is completely accurate. With reckless disregard for the environment, China mines and releases massive amounts of mercury, contaminating both land and sea. Japan is also dumping huge quantities of radioactive water into the ocean from their damaged power plant. The spiritual dimensions will intervene and clean up the mess, but it is a very long-term project. If we fail to change course, humans could make the planet uninhabitable for millions of years. They also warn about the damaging effects that aluminum has on the brain. Alzheimer's patients, for example, often have very high concentrations of aluminum in their brain. This is supported by a study published in the Journal of Alzheimer's Disease (JAD) on January 13, 2020 (Matt, et al.) on the aluminum content from brain tissue of middle-aged people who died with AD. There are tens of millions of people with this form of dementia, so we are repeating a cautionary warning. Read the labels on food and body products, and be wary of processed cheese and baked goods containing sodium aluminum phosphate and sodium aluminum sulfate. Antiperspirants contain high levels of aluminum salts, such as aluminum chlorohydrate, which is linked to both breast cancer

and AD. Aluminum sulfate is used to clarify municipal water, so it is probably present in most cities. Use activated charcoal filtration to remove the toxins. The Tallocks also mention potatoes as having high aluminum content, a fact of which I was unaware.

The Tallocks recounted something that happened to me decades ago when I was a young engineer working on an oil platform in the Gulf of Mexico. The platform was about 100 miles southeast of Galveston Island, Texas, quite near to the edge of the continental shelf. The water depth out to the edge of the shelf is about 200 meters, but then the sea floor transitions to the continental slope and plunges to several thousand meters. One day, as I was leaning over the railing looking down into the water, I saw a huge, silvery or luminescent object glide by the legs of the platform. There was no wind and the surface of the ocean was very flat, so what I saw was not distorted by ripples. I was convinced it was a craft of some type. It was too close to the platform to be a military submarine. Besides, submarines are normally painted black and do not reflect light, which this object did. Neither was it a school of fish, because it was absolutely uniform in appearance and unlike anything I had ever seen. It moved slowly alongside the legs of the platform and appeared to be cylindrical in shape. Based on the speed which the back passed by, I guessed its overall length to be at least 70 meters. The Tallocks were obviously aware that I had seen the USO and they commented on it. They said it was a craft belonging to entities who live in bases on the deep seafloor. They are usually invisible because they operate in dimensions that the human eye cannot detect. The military can, however, pick them up on certain radar or optical instruments. Then they gave a fascinating lecture about how the ancients used sound and light to dematerialize, move, and then rematerialize objects into and out of these extra dimensions. They explained it as a process of reducing matter to its constituent parts. Most of the matter shifted into a parallel field. What remained was a lightweight core that was easily transported to a new destination. Once the core was in place, they brought the elements that had vanished back into our third dimension. Ophelia came in after they stepped away and explained more about the mysteries of dematerialization.

T. This is the Tallocks.

D. Ah. Hello, my friends.

T. We are here, briefly, to provide insights about the shifts in the energetic field possessing your space. The molecular construction foundation is faltering due to the high level of mercury in your seas. The output from factories in Asia transmit several diseases, mainly occupying (*caused by*) mercury. It is not only in the beings in your sea, but it falls down to the seabed, creating disasters that is hard to clean. This occurred earlier, and we witnessed the progress of that cleaning. It took several generations at that time, equipped in environmental engineering and resources on how to clean output that was not meant to happen. We see again the neglect of your sea and of your environment. You should tell about the long-term project of maintaining and cleaning (*the oceans*). Your entire fauna in the sea went through a reevaluation at that time. Some species still remain deep in the sea, carrying within their consciousness, within their DNA, the memory of earlier disasters when it came to not only mercury but nuclear output. Even the resources of oil create imbalances in your sea. Vlac took upon research in order to assist. We never went in human form to Earth, but we were assigned as the environmental engineering (*experts on*) how to maintain and clean your seas. There are still a presence from us observing from bases in your sea. Deep sea hubs where we monitor activity. We receive information from those living in the sea. Some as you refer to as half–and–half. Half Master Mind, half occupied by soul from the eighth. The eighth do not incarnate in human form, however in water mammals, water creatures, they come. Sometimes there are those on human level that have a memory of these journeys, but they are from the seventh, predominantly. Those who are fully occupying the eighth spiritual dimension have, at this time, been blending with water creatures, trying to read the activity in the sea—highly interested in Japan. There are several dolphins around the area of Japan, and there are disasters from the humans with the interactions of dolphins. This is a sadness, as some of these dolphins are not only your friends, but some hold the awareness of a spirit from the eighth, observing activity. Mainly mercury imbalance that should not be in the sea. The communication underwater is different than on land. It travels uniquely and direct to Source. We also, from Vlac, have an easier way to directly communicate to those on seabed in bases. There is indeed a presence of those from Vlac. You stumbled upon one of our surface vehicles at one time. You saw.

D. Which life?

T. This life. You saw the cell emerging from the sea where you worked. A vessel from below. Not common to observe. The vessel, normally, is non–visible for submarines, and so forth. However, they can detect the presence on radar but never see a physical manifestation. We are sheltered, in that sense, by a shield that is not visible for the human eye. The human eye is not equipped to see more than 3-D. If an existence is, let's say, six–dimensional, the 3-D eye has no way to see it. That is why the human eye struggles to see visitors. Only if visitors transform their six–dimensional vibration—of manifestation that is—into a close three-dimensional vision. That is when visitors are seen. We want to be seen in that case. If you don't see, then the visitor remains in the six–dimensional visual manifested appearance. That means that the 3-D eye in a human have no ability to see that visitor or object. With that said, it also is clear that there are a higher presence of visitors around you. They simply vibrate in a dimensional manifestation that the 3-D eyes are incapable of capturing.

D. Is that what we would call a parallel reality?

T. Yes. We vibrate in the parallel band, which is six–dimensional instead of the three–dimensional known to Earth, known to man. There are certain gadgets that might, or that will, detect this parallel universe, this parallel existence. Man thinks they are the only ones here. There are several parallel existences present. Some fully present, some observing a little bit out. Vlac is a center for research when it comes to understanding the blend of minerals, elements, and how they interact in materia, such as water. We were here with you, with your uncle, at one time and established a base at the North Pole. The transmitters, still left in the ice, are our eyes.

D. Do you have any other visitors that work with you that remain here?

T. Yes. Some remain. Some simply report research material, mainly interested in the water development, as mercury tends to remain longer. Harder to clean when mercury blends in water than, let's say, soil. Soil will impact growth, such as potatoes, and so forth. In general, you should be aware, that potatoes at this time if not grown organically can hold a higher level of mercury and aluminum—mainly aluminum—and that is unfortunate. You are bombarded with aluminum and mercury and that affects your brain. Your friends from Vlac are highly involved in the effects on the brain. Those from the eighth and seventh monitor and research the effects on your emotional wellbeing. We, as well as Elahim, observe shifts—contamination in brain. Aluminum is highly present in your atmosphere and it affects you all through rain. A way to detect if you are affected by aluminum is that your sleep gets highly disrupted. You also have a different breathing pattern, and we monitor the breathing rhythm, as the breathing rhythm has a direct effect to the brain. If the breathing within your species—or even animals, even trees—if the breathing changes and becomes unrhythmical, it creates an imbalanced link to the center. That will indicate (*the amount of*) consciousness. Consciousness as materialistic form, not spiritual consciousness. But even a tree has a brain, even a rock has a brain; that means the effect is on the manifested brain. The spiritual brain, either from soul or Master Mind, has a harder time to repair the damages on the manifested brain. Do you see the picture?

D. I do. So, for a human, the physical brain would be the manifested brain?

T. Yes. That's the manifested brain. And everything occupying form and life here has a manifested brain and a spiritual brain. The spiritual brain is either from soul coming from five to seven, or represented by the Master Mind.

D. That I understand. Can you tell whether this one or myself have either mercury or aluminum problems?

T. There is more of an effect here than when you are on sea level. But it affects you differently. This one gets anxious. You, tired. But you are affected and gradually we see a move. We see that you will do better physically, mentally, perhaps even emotionally—as humans that is—in a setting with less cars, with less disturbances of noise. The disturbances of noise open you up for the influences of alumina. If you are in a silent environment and the presence of mercury or alumina is as much (*as in a noisy environment*), you are not as affected. You have a natural shield when you are in the presence of your spiritual sound, which is not human sound. When you are in an environment with high noise, you open up to these effects from above, or from water, or intake of food. Those living in cities are clearly more susceptible than those living in the countryside. That said, it means that eventually you will seek a more secluded settlement to be in, as you will understand the chain reaction of how you embrace or how you can shield yourself based on your surrounding as well. It disarms the human when you are bombarded with silent noise, or car noise. So you can see the effect of 5G. 5G is silent, it will not disturb you they will say. But the silent noise will open you up, similar as if a Harley just drove by next to you. It is the same; it has a higher vibrational impact, and it shoots to open the physical, to disarm the physical, in order for other influences to occupy your being.

D. When you say six-dimensional, can you suggest what the other dimensions might be, in a way I would understand?

T. You have to clarify. Do you mean souls from the sixth dimension or those who vibrate in a presence in a parallel reality?

D. Yes, the parallel reality.

T. Okay. Yes. Your question was—?

D. The other dimensions, is it like time and then some other fields we cannot understand?

T. Some is not for human understanding, indeed. Others conquer time. They travel through loops that will indicate time, but they are bound together as one cohesive experience. The vibrational reality parallel universes are not bound by time, they conquer time, spiraling clockwise through time. If you want to conquer space, you spiral anti-clockwise. Once you learn how to master your own vibration—and ancient man did so—they learned how to rotate their inner being both clockwise and anti-clockwise. They were taught by visitors how to conquer space, how to conquer time, and that is how time travels took place. You have to conquer them both. It is an ancient technique that ancient civilizations were taught. The physical was simply holding the experience. In order for a physical object to fully dematerialize and later materialize, both these experiences had to connect the rotation—clockwise and anti-clockwise—in order for an object to dematerialize and later materialize somewhere else. It is a way to conquer the physical laws, the barriers holding gravity, magnetic components. You are bound by gravity. How to conquer gravity? That is the way you do it. But this (*explanation*) is for a human. Let's say, if you wish to use the same (*method*) to move an object, you first dematerialize it by (*using*) sound. Light will—let's see, to not make it too complex—light and sound combined creates (*the condition for*) dissolving of materia and motion. In order for them to conquer physical barriers, such as, let's say, from this Universe to another, a parallel reality, outside force is added. The gravitational field invites new objects once they have reached the dissolving point, the still point. Oh, let's see what words we can use. You dissolve objects with light, sound as well assists. Later, light takes a step back and sound makes motion possible. After motion is completed, light brings form back to life. So, can you see the picture?

D. Yes.

T. Light, sound, combined dissolve. Light steps aside; sound assisting, conquering gravity. Both have the ability to penetrate physical barriers such as your gravitational and magnetic fields. But they have to be used in a way that is not common anymore for humanity. There was not one person doing this, if it was a large object.

D. If we take, for example, the large stones that were moved in Mesopotamia, when they dissolved it—it's made of quartz and other mineral structures—did it cause some of those minerals to jump out of our reality and into a different dimension?

T. Yes.

D. And reducing the density?

T. Yes. The density was reduced by splitting up the components of the object, moving them into (*he paused while looking for useful words*) separate space, close to object, looking almost like your solar system. So, let's say we have the object and it merged into becoming the sun. The planets, to give you a picture, would be all the components of the object. You simply move the sun, and when the sun was moved, the objects once more merged and became the object.

D. It retained the original pattern?

T. Yes, if that was necessary. Sometimes the object moved to create pyramids. If you see how the preparation of the object was done using sound, using light. In order for this form to take place for motion, they divided all material congested in the object, and they became—to give you a visual—the planets around a solar system. The only thing moving was the sun. The sun could be big as a football (*soccer ball*), small as a pea, and once in place, they reprogrammed. Similar as they did the preparation before motion, they also had a way to prepare all objects to merge and become the same object it was from the beginning. So, the only thing that moved was the little pea up to position—it wasn't that hard to move a pea.

D. Was this done by humans or did they have assistance?

T. Assistance. Humans moved the pea, moved the football, but they did not prepare motion and they did not bring to life object once in place. Those who were slaves simply moved the football, moved the pea.

D. At that time, was it at a very high temperature? Or was it something they could physically touch?

T. They could not touch.

D. How was it moved?

T. If you see like a foundation of rock, it was placed in this tank of rock—like a sink—where they would place it, and they would have (*tree*) trunks, rotating, rolling this object upwards. It wasn't that heavy. But they were assisted. Man only transferred the object. We will leave it as of now. Yes, you have started to see the picture.

D. That's fascinating, and one of the subjects I have long wondered about.

T. Just know that the motion, the transportation itself, was similar as a football. But it was placed while transported or moved in a foundation of rock. They have found rocks with holes in them, not understanding what the holes were. They were used as they transported prepared objects.

D. How big were these rocks with the holes in them that were used to carry the suns?

T. Not that big.

D. So a single person could carry it?

T. No. It had to be rolled on those trunks of wood. There. We will leave you now.

D. Thank you so much. It was captivating.

T. You are much welcome. We will be back and talk more, either from the Council of Nine or directly from the research lab on Vlac.

O. This is Ophelia.

D. Hello, Ophelia.

O. We are doing some cleaning and we will see. What you have been taught today from your friends on Vlac is how to move objects and how to dissolve and reshape objects in order for them to fit. That is the same procedure that is done as you look at those walls that look like they are melted. (*In Cusco, Peru, for example, some megalithic walls were built with stones that look like puffy marshmallows, as if they were soft when placed.*) They were heated by the sun, big disks melting objects. Sound created the new form that would be transported or moved into a different location. Once in place—and if humans were assisting, then yes, they were using devices in order for that object to move. If only visitors, such as your friends the Tallocks, they simply moved the object with their mind. There was no physical touch, at all, of objects. But let's say pyramids, yes, man assisted and used different devices in order for transportation of objects to take place to new locations. But they were dissolved into smaller matter and they were not able to touch them. The picture is given to this one. It looks like those you have christening in, in the church. (*The stone basins looked like baptismal fonts, with holes in them.*) And in many ways, that is a remain of that. It has to do with birth, birth of object, birth of materia. Churches used the same structure as providing birth, giving life, to human. This model is, in its core, meant to radiate birth, either of object, or of spirit, in church.

D. The same way the process of creating the Earth in the beginning from a pattern, is that similar to the way objects are dematerialized and rematerialized, by moving into a light and sound?

O. Yes. It's simply reversed into earlier stages of existence. And that is the key on how to transfer objects in a reality such as Earth. As you try to conquer realities that are not necessarily physical, you, in a similar way, have to dissolve the materia in order for change and shift to occur. So in many ways, you return the object to its intent. You return it to the blueprint. But how to do so when you do not understand the physics of the blueprint? Man has no understanding of the blueprint at this time. If you do not know the map, the color map and blueprint, you have no way, you have no ability, to dissolve it back to its blueprint because you do not operate from the fact that it HAS a blueprint. The blueprint is not simply DNA. It is the spiritual components blended with the DNA. The DNA simply holds the spiritual purpose in its form. If you simply try to create or recreate or understand the DNA map without the spiritual component, you will never have the ability to move an object, or to fully understand the laws of physics and the abilities that lies before you.

D. So a carbon atom, for example, would you consider that to have a color pattern that we would equate to carbon DNA?

O. Yes, yes. When you only understand the DNA pattern, which is the physical reality, and not fully understand the blend of the spiritual DNA, then you have no way to split them up. Those who understood how to dissolve objects, they understood and divided the object's physical map, meaning understanding the blueprint and DNA versus the spiritual DNA. The spiritual DNA is light, and you have to understand the component of light and the various ways to use light, that light is not constant. If you are in the mindset that light is constant, then you do not understand how to divide or operate the spiritual blueprint. Light is the spiritual blueprint, sound simply assist the object, the materialized blueprint, the DNA. Those two combined makes it possible—or in this case, impossible—to handle this riddle. So. We will see here if someone wants to step in briefly, or if he wants to have his separate session. Maybe both, we'll see. I think what we will do is allow a separate session for our friend, and he will have it set up only for him, on Thursday.

D. Does that mean he is not going to talk today?

O. We'll see. We will let him come in briefly, as we are saving energy in this one. But a separate session is granted.

D. Thank you so much for coming in, Ophelia.

O. You are much welcome. Simply understand that light correlates to the spiritual blueprint. Sound holds your physical blueprint, your DNA. If you do not understand how to handle or work them and to use the different levels of sound and light, then you do not carry the possibility or ability to move objects.

D. When you talk about light, you are not talking about photons or what is emanated from the Sun?

O. Light that radiates through all realities from the Creator. There we go.

D. Thank you.

O. Oh, you are much welcome. (*Bob then came in and gave an excellent talk, which was published in Notes, Volume 2.*)

C9: Solar Storms from Neighboring Systems (April 18, 2020)
This next segment is a small part of an April 18, 2020 session. The Council of Nine addresses the shift in energy that is flowing into our solar system from outside influences. In our previous books, the spirits have described how everything is connected through a web. Each living entity has a center point, which exists as part of a community reaching all the way up to the Creator. A tree, for example, communicates through its energetic roots with the grid. The grid is a network of awareness (energy) that covers the planet, like the veins in a leaf. Ley lines are major parts of the grid. The grid, in turn, connects with the Fork at various nodes. The Fork is an

extension of the core of the planet and part of the first dimension. The Center Point of the planet communicates information through the solar system web to the Sun. The center point of the Sun sends and receives information with adjoining solar families, and so forth, until it reaches the center point of the galaxy. (An area called Sagittarius A by Astrophysicists.) The center point of our galaxy is both a portal and a node within the web that connects to the Center Point of the fish tank. The fish tank itself has a center point that holds the intention for the entire system, and transmits information back and forth with the spiritual dimensions. So, in our example, the tree can be observed and communicated with through the web (to the Fork, then to the Earth grid) by an entity in the spiritual dimensions. The spiritual data that flows within the invisible web controls what happens in the first, second, third, and fourth dimensions. If the councils want to increase solar output from the Sun, those instructions are sent instantaneously through the web. (The speed of light is a variable property of the third dimension, not the first.) We remind the reader that the Sun also emits energy that we cannot measure, but influences everything on a spiritual level.

Within our solar system, the energy waxes and wanes in cycles that last for tens of thousands of years. Earth has been in a low point since the last great civilization ended some 25,000 years ago. The long-term goal from the spirit realm is to lift all realities that are "in the ditch" up to a higher level.

C9. What is on the agenda today is to reveal the energy flow in your fish tank versus other fish tanks. We see a progress, a lot to do with a presence from your neighbor, fish tank four. The flow that runs through your galaxy is lit up at this time. There are more suns in neighboring systems that are lit up, creating solar storms, in order for the system as a whole to progress as one unit. The system where you are located in your galaxy, in the Milky Way, needs assistance. There are neighboring solar families creating a flow, not only from their sun, but the consciousness is rising in your system, your galaxy. The galaxy is traveling in a controlled fashion, encased through the waves, heading for a peak—leaving the canyon, if you like. In order for your system to ascend, the whole group needs to ascend with you. The karma related to the system where Earth is located has, in some way, dragged the other ones, your neighbor systems, into a darkness as well. We are meeting this change within the Earth atmosphere by increasing suns in neighboring systems. It means

290   The Spiritual Design

you are surrounded by an increasing flare of not only heat—which is a limited word, it's not heat.

D. Electromagnetic?

C9. Yes. The web around your system is affected positively by the increasing sun activity in your neighbor systems. This has happened before, but the problem lies in the way man conducts with energy, as it effects the effort from outside. What we seek is not to overheat your system, but what you, in many ways, observe as global warming, it is indeed an effect from the effort outside. Not everything is caused by man. However, we need man to stay calm; we need man to step aside and allow a process to unfold. A process that you cannot calculate because you do not understand why temperatures are rising, fully. You effect a small part and if you increase radiation, satellite activity, the efforts from outside is not as clear, not as direct as the intention is. You are guided by this through your neighbor, fish tank four, who is more in the light than fish tank five. Fish tank six is not involved, it has its own journey, its own evolution to begin. You are seeking to improve your evolution, to rise from what is perceived as darkness. This darkness has come and gone in several cycles before you, and it will continue until the whole fish tank rises together, reaches a peak where the fish tank moves into completion. After a completion has been reached, the result is normally hibernation—as you see in fish tank three. But you need to rise all systems together, and that is not for man to do. You simply need to follow the agenda in the way you can by not interfering, causing an energy increase in energy outlets (*electromagnetic pollution*), and to not excavate resources in the way that you do. Oil, gas, natural resources, needs to be intact in order for the general atmosphere, the web, to be intact. It is the Earth's resources to cope with major changes a system undertakes. The progress is here, but the Earth needs its resources. We see how the need to use oil, resources, even energy, will decrease as man now, after this little bug, will seek a more solitude approach to his existence, and that is helpful. We thank you for participating, for leaving certain elements and resources, energies, be.

D. You talk about the solar system rising and then eventually going into hibernation. There must be millions of other existences throughout the Universe.

C9. We are trying to minimize the canyons. To give you a picture, when there is too much differences of evolution within a fish tank, the peak and the canyons—to give you a picture—would be, let's say, 10 miles. What we are now trying with this approach of lifting all realities into a more common level in order for the general purpose of the evolution in the fish tank to reach its goal—we are trying to minimize the canyons to five to three miles. So as we are lifting the canyons, more and more are in the same frequency band. Do you see the picture?

D. I do, indeed. Would the Earth be considered one of those that is in the very bottom of the trough?

C9. Yes. So let's say that the canyon, from peak to bottom, is 10 miles. Your system has been, for the last cycle—which will be in human years about 25 to 50,000 years—around the level eight. What we are seeking is to move the canyon where are you are located at this time, to be at level five, five miles (*in the example*). So we cut the canyon in half, meaning it is much easier for the system to rise to the peak. In order for a system to reach its completion, there can only be somewhat of a variety between peak and canyon, let's say, 500 meters. Of course, this is not really a measure of meters and miles, but to give you a picture. They all have to be at somewhat of an equal frequency where there is only a small variation between the peaks and the canyons. As that occurs, and it could be that some canyon is 500 meters, another one is 200 meters, the third is 700 meters, but all together they have risen and they are floating in an evolution and in a purpose they are designed to be (*in*). As that occurs, all systems join and carry the same frequency. It does not matter or add any value whether the race on each reality has the same consciousness. I know that man feels like they are the greatest resource on your planet and your consciousness is the highest. We don't care, we don't mind what you believe, as long as you take care of your host and take care of the resources. We look at the general awareness between systems, but the individuals occupying different systems can vary in their evolution. So it does not mean that every entity in each galaxy has reached the same level, but they are not very far apart. Your neighbor system, the galaxy Andromeda, is much more aware of maintaining a balance. When it comes to elements, resources, energy, they have mastered the lessons of greed. As we try to—on a level of individual entities and not just galaxies and solar families—as we try to level out or reach a common evolution, what we seek here is to increase the awareness of greed versus resources.

D. That's wonderful. I understand that.

C9. Very good.

D. Are there a lot of other places where souls go that have the same issues as humans, where they don't understand their purpose and mission?

C9. Yes. There is another reality that is further behind, but not as many travel there. However, there are several who have their primary destination on some realities in the galaxy Andromeda, who now have redirected their efforts by incarnating here. You see several of them incarnating in positions of government, mainly the departments focusing on environment, or focusing on resources and energy. There are also those who are equipped in the knowledge on how to read the changes within your host, reading curves, reading changes within the core and the movement on the seabed. All this combined creates a progress, or lack of progress if not handled correctly. So there are several who now incarnate as scientists or teachers in that field. You are sent to monitor the activity in your business of oil. You don't necessarily create the changes, but we monitor the activity through you. We can read the intention by simply observing where you are at, like a microphone, reading the intention of the industry. And it is crucial for certain locations to be left alone. If we could—and I'm pretty sure your Little Friend would like you to—we would fix the problem. You mentioned that one time, that he did not fully understand why you were not taking charge of the business and shake it up, why you were passive in your workplace. You did not tell him that your assignment was to simply physically be there, and that we read the activity that emanated from the business as a whole. In many ways, you simply are placed—not only this life but other lives—placed for us to read what we need or wish to improve, or simply to see if improvement has taken place. But your Little Friend apparently did not understand why you did not take the full force he knows that you possess and just fix the problem. He said he knew that you were capable of fixing the problem. He came to you with notes, you said, of certain locations that he wanted you to fix. Interesting.

D. He's full of enthusiasm and good ideas.

C9. Yes, yes. So, we will leave at that.

D. Thank you.

EC, Ophelia: Neighboring Realities (June 21, 2020)

The Elahim Council elaborated on the two nearby celestial systems (probably galaxies) whose energetic influences are felt by our solar system and galaxy. From a human perspective, the scale is immense, since the nearby systems are outside the Milky Way. But from the council's vantage point, the other systems are neighbors. Most people have heard of Andromeda and think it may be the closest galaxy to ours, but it is 2 million light-years away. The Canis Major Dwarf Galaxy is only 25,000 light-years away from our solar system, which puts it closer to us than the galactic center of the Milky Way. To give a bit of perspective, the Canis Major Dwarf galaxy is estimated to hold at least a billion stars, and the Milky Way about 400 billion. Another nearby system is the Sagittarius dwarf galaxy, which is around 70,000 light-years from us. Both these nearby galaxies are merging with the Milky Way. The Elahim Council does not specify the source of the electromagnetic waves that are impacting us, but they say it is a visible reality. Not only is energy coming here, but actual entities from these nearby systems also visit to raise our vibration. Although we call aliens "visitors", it is we who are the newcomers to the planet. They travel here and live in underwater bases,

Another significant statement they make is "Sometimes man see black holes. Those are not collapsed stars, those are portals, such as meeting points, where different realities merge." Black holes do not exist, at least in the ways the scientific community hypothesizes. The spirits consistently define them either as portals, or center-points of awareness that hold the intention of the celestial family. The large picture of what they are telling us in this session is that there are many levels of intelligences, some in form, most not, that are assisting the Earth and its occupants to rise to a more advanced level of spiritual knowledge, which, ultimately, is soul-awareness.

EC. This is the Elahim Council.

D. Hello.

EC. We are here greeting you, family members in a different fish tank. Huh. Different reality than you are, indeed, used to operating in. We are here as a family, providing insights, providing solutions on how to operate and maintain the flow of energy throughout your system. When we say system, it does not mean the Solar System, or even the rivers on your planet, it means the general web in the fish tank. It is a web connecting the points where energy frequencies, gravity points, exchange knowledge, exchange levels on procedures in each reality. Both of you operate on the behalf of the Elahim as engineering of this web. Your little brother (*Seth*) travels the web more frequently, visiting other realities, making sure the connecting points are intact. You, as well as Eli, design new maps, new pathways for realities to meet and blend. In some way, you and Eli are more designers, more still, preparing. Whereas your little brother engineers the design, more active in operation. It has to do with overlapping realities, parallel realities within fish tanks. Some fish tanks even overlap. This has been known as the borders between fish tanks, where a little bit of each merges and becomes a new existence. It is not black and white. Meeting points exist, maintenance in operation—it is what the Elahim Council oversee. You, Eli, engineering new designs. Making sure certain portals, meeting points, exist for optimal exchange of energy between realities. When we, in this case, discuss mutual flow within a fish tank, it is of importance that the parallel realities coexist with each other. This is where maintenance is needed. There are certain connecting points that—see it as magnets, some are complementary, some resist—in order for portals, in order for parallel existences, to be able to not only coexist but also have a mutual exchange of experiences. Those dots (*portals*) need to be maintained, sometimes moved, sometimes deleted. The designs are from you and Eli. Your little brother out in the field, if you like. He likes that. Likes to be mobile; always on the move.

EC. At this time, the reality where Earth is squeezed—I say squeezed, and pay attention to this information—there are two different realities on each side of your Earth reality, the frequency band where Earth and the Milky Way exist. The other two are closing in, making the experience in the middle where Earth and Milky Way exist somewhat chaotic. It is because you are sensing other frequencies, sensing other realities, higher knowledge, and karma that is not necessarily your own. You are torn between understanding whether it's your feelings or someone else's. Some are tuning in to these two, that at this time are closer connected on each side of yours. This is why the whole experience on Earth seems to be at a breaking point. It is not a breaking point, you simply tune in and feel the neighboring realities that are moving closer to yours. Some of the experiences, some of the fears, do not belong in your consciousness. You can sense something else. Some of these issues are being addressed as these meeting points are being removed, the portals are more open, meaning that you can sense and hear, feel, the two on each side of you. At this time, the web, which encases the whole experience in the fish tank, is not intact. The portals are open and you sense other frequencies that do not necessarily belong here. I'm not saying they are bad or good, they are simply different. As you, in human form, are not able to decipher these signals, you tend to make them human, you tend to make them your own, and that is not the case. You should listen and sense the signals coming, as they are of a higher order, a higher knowledge than human knowledge. However, those who transmit also wishes to interact with humans. This specific case, scenario, has taken place before and it will continue, as portals are mobile and, at one point or another, they meet. What several humans experience are the openings to realities, and they cannot decipher the signals. It becomes chaotic in the human mind, as the mind is not very equipped. That is why we seek and we wish to cool down the system, cool down your planet a little bit. When the flow of electromagnetic impulses are too frequent, too intense, the mind becomes scattered, scared, non–functional, and that is what we see at this point.

D. Is that primarily from the Sun, solar activity?

EC. No, no. The Sun merely conducts the signals, merely conducts. Humans, with a limited mind, feel like the Sun, solar flares, are the only source of change. The Sun simply conducts outer inputs in your web, channeled through the Sun. The Sun by itself is not the problem. The Sun merely operates as a conductor from Source. The portals to other realities are not suns, they are windows, empty space, stillness. Sometimes man see black holes. Those are not collapsed stars, those are portals such as meeting points where different realities merge. You can see it as a hot dog. The sausage in the middle is the human presence, (*within the*) Milky Way. On each side you have neighboring realities—same fish tank—physical form more progressed. Different in minds. They communicate in a way that a human mind cannot decipher. Some hear it as signals in their head, but they cannot decipher what it is. If you are aware of the symptoms of tinnitus, that is (*similar to*) an ear that is linked to reading signals, outer signals, that becomes planted in the being, the human being.

D. I hear tones all the time. Sometimes it is like a symphony of music.

EC. Yes, you hear neighboring realities. Your mind reads it as a ringing sensation, but if you close your eyes and allow it to take form, a message can come. It is a contact; it is a way to communicate with neighboring realities. A parallel universe, parallel existence, is close at this point. And then the other one is moving closer as well, making you, man, the sausage in the hot dog.

D. (*Laughing.*) Are these other realities also in our fish tank? Are they visible realities?

EC. Yes. Yes. Fish tank five, just different levels, different steps in their evolution. They are closing in. Before, more separated. In this experience, you are connecting to more realities merging with yours. What you hear and sense, that creates turmoil, is because you are also receiving signals outside your own system. Not everyone reads these signals, but those who have the problem of tinnitus or a ringing in the ear, tend to be more connected to neighboring realities. One of these parallel existences belongs—it is a bridge to yours—in the system Andromeda. It is somewhere in fifty–fifty if you like. (*He means that the matter is vibrating at a frequency half-way between our reality and a parallel frequency.*) You can see it from here, of course, with machines equipped to see far objects. But know that that system is also merging with another reality, another universe, another frequency of knowledge. Those who travel into body into the frequency next to yours, has a tendency of a higher equipped mind. These minds try to, like raindrops, influence yours, try to raise the frequency. Some (*humans*) become fearful of this interaction. It is not a spiritual interaction; it is a physical reality, a manifested world next to yours. The technology (*level*) they occupy is far advanced, it is (*used for*) working on the depth within your world, deep sea drilling, if you like. Reaching far into the core. There are bases from these realities under the ice—North Pole, South Pole. North Pole needs to be intact. South Pole lures the human eyes in their direction, making sure the North is left alone. It is somewhat in hibernation. The boxes around the Fork, the North Pole, are starting to ignite. They are in operation again. There are visitors more frequently, engineers, moving in. But due to the fact that they are not physically manifested for your eyes, they can move undetected.

D. What is their purpose here? Are they here to benefit the Earth, or do they have other agendas?

The SpD Theories 297

EC. Yes. Yes. They feel the Earth is not being taken care of. The Fork is slowing down. The Fork needs to be in a vibration, a speed, a rotation, in order for the whole system (*to ascend*). Your reality where you exist, the entire galaxy as well, it is dependent on that each Fork, each center point, rotates, vibrates at a maximal speed, in order for that system to ascend, to move. If the players—meaning planets and such—are not in full operation, the system itself cannot progress. We wish the system to ascend from the canyon. In order for it to ascend from the darkness in the ditch, in the canyon, to a higher point where changes are awaiting, the cores within celestial bodies, such as the Sun, such as Earth, needs to be adjusted. That is when the engineers from neighboring realities merge with yours and they are more active, operating the boxes.

D. I have a question then about parallel realities. Do those also have form in them?

EC. Yes, yes—form. Here, fish tank five, form exists more or less in all frequency bands that exist in this fish tank. So, yes, form. Not necessarily incarnations. It is a lot of what you would consider half–and–half. Half Master Mind, half engineering souls. These two realities that I refer to are occupied by a lot of souls from the eighth, even tenth are present, but they are fifty–fifty. You asked, at one point, about if every manifested creature has a soul. Yes, but not in the same concentration as an incarnation. The fifty-fifty, you might think fifty percent soul, fifty percent Master Mind. Sure, but the fifty percent part where the soul would merge with the Master Mind can have a smaller dose than fifty percent of the soul capacity merging with a human form. So even if we say fifty-fifty, the soul part can be less concentrated. See it as a lemonade. Here fifty percent in the lemonade, the soul, is quite concentrated, quite strong, quite full. Fifty percent in your neighboring realities are not the same. It can be (*compared to*) simply ten percent of the same dose. So the lemonade, the fifty percent that would mean a soul merging with Master Mind could indicate a remote experience. It is not an incarnation, but it merges with the space in that object that is welcoming the soul energy. So the fifty–fifty part, half Master Mind, half of that space open for soul merging, but the soul simply remotely send off a piece of its knowledge, of its awareness, into that space.

D. That makes sense. In a case like that, who primarily is in control, the Master Mind or the incoming soul?

EC. Master Mind.

D. So the soul is, more or less, an observer?

EC. The soul is the one who makes the object move, to make it experience. The Master Mind collects data. So the Master Mind would indicate the brain, whereas the soul would indicate the physical. The emotional and spiritual aspect is a fifty–fifty of these two. It is similar to earlier travels here, when several spiritual realities merged with a human form. All experienced, all collected data, but not all of them operated the physical. So, from that point, when, let's say, twelve dimensions were moved into a human experience, the part making the journey, the physical journey, only came from three or four out of these twelve. The other ones simply collected data, not experiencing (*the journey*) in a human way, if you like.

D. Okay. Thank you for that. I think I follow.

EC. There, we will leave it before we create confusion. Simply know that when there are several levels of consciousness, spiritual or physical, then different particles (*participants*) take different journeys in that object. Human form is an object, it is a way to see whether a soul can channel the intention it had before coming. It is helped by parts of the Master Mind that operates as guiding stars in the cells, but it's not doing the work for the soul. It merely exists as flashlights now and then to awaken the soul, to direct the soul to the correct path the soul intended to take. So it is like having crash cushions, or little lights, directing the soul when the soul takes a step outside the destined path. That is how the Master Mind exists in a human form—but it's a silent observer. Still curious to see whether a soul can follow the intention it had. (*The Master Mind is curious how the souls manage the vehicle.*)

D. That's a really good explanation. Thank you.

EC. You are welcome. So we will return. Elahim.

D. Wonderful. Elahim.

O. Hmm. This is Ophelia.

D. Ah, hello Ophelia.

O. Hello to you, my friend. Let's see if we can have a little bit of cleaning. Someone has brought notes. Brought a list.

D. Did you have anything you would like to share, while you're cleaning?

O. I would like to say that the project (*the Spiritual Design books*) that we all participate in, even though from a human standpoint you might feel like you are at a halt, this is a pause before we direct the mission and the project to the next level. We want you to pause at this time to reflect on the journey that you have both wandered up 'til this point, both personally as well as in your work together. We want you to see the steps that you have taken, little-by-little, how you have progressed, and also to be reflective on certain things that you would perhaps adjust or have done differently. Try to find a common point, a common cause, *(for)* how you can channel your work to the best, to the fullest. At this time, you are on a platform and you might feel like you are on halt, like you are waiting—and that is what we want you to do. The rest of this year is for you to take that pause, to take that break, in order for the next level, the next ascension to be within your mind's eye. To be able to see where you have gone is a way for you to seek the path ahead. We want you to pause at this time, to reflect on the journey.

D. Hmm. I sometimes think that it would have been nice if I had the knowledge I had now when I wrote *Wave 1*.

O. You will say the same when you write *Wave 7*, "I wish I had the same knowledge when I wrote *Wave 3*." You will never be content, in that sense, as a human. But know and be grateful for the progress as we expand your mind. We expand your bank of knowledge. That is a gift from yourself to your human self. We simply open these different windows for you.

D. Is there anything I can do to improve that opening?

O. The only opening that you could assist yourself with, is to try to sit in your own power. Try to connect with Lasaray, find your power and your strength, find your voice within you. This is a time for both of you to start to communicate directly from who you are. Not necessarily the human self, even though the human self will be the microphone. More and more, you will communicate directly from within, but you have to know who exists inside you in order for you to be able to speak the words from within.

Bob: The Fork Controls the Planet (Feb 4, 2020)

Bob gives a brilliant description of the way the Earth is monitored and controlled by the Creator and the councils who operate on the Creator's behalf. The intermediary between the spiritual dimensions and the physical manifestation is what the spirits call the Fork, as in tuning fork. Lifeforms communicate with the Fork, and all geologic and atmospheric processes are controlled by the Fork. Bob gives a nearly perfect explanation of the Fork, which I will repeat here. He says, "The Fork is the stabilizer and the one that orchestrates the entire experience of the planet." And later, "It coexists with the first dimension, so it is an extension of the first dimension. The first dimension is the counterpart to the Creator, which is the big Pole. So, in many ways, the Fork is like the little Creator, like the big center Pole that we see in the Wheel. It has the same design; it has the same function." The Fork is comparable to the roots and the trunk of a tree. The Earth grid, including Ley lines, is similar to the limbs, branches, and leaves that spread out and cover the entire globe in a communication network. It is through the Earth grid that lifeforms communicate with the Fork. Because the Earth is considered a child of the Sun, the disharmony on our planet causes changes in Solar activity and its electromagnetic output. As the Sun works to restore balance, humans will find themselves humbled, watching as nature exerts control over the wayward species we have become.

The boxes that they mention are actually not native to the planet. They were installed by visitors in the distant past to assist the spiritual dimensions to monitor and make physical changes to the land masses and the atmosphere. Bob described this in detail in *Notes, Volume 2* under the section *Twelfth Dimension of Healing*. He also talked about what he calls the dot lives. Lasaray showed Bob a map of Earth, where the location of every incarnation or manifested travel was shown with different color dots. The blue dots were for manifested travels where Bob did not join as a guide. So, naturally, he is curious about what Lasaray was doing on Earth without him.

B. (*Bob came in singing a joyful tune.*) I've been taking singing lessons—I'm in a choir! Huh huh huh. (*He continued singing without words, changing the melody several times.*) So, I have joined a choir. It's Ia's choir, and Ia started to sing like—(*he sang a slow, somber tune, almost like church music*)—and everyone was gathering, singing along. And then I thought, "Maybe we should bump it up a bit!" So I went like—(*he then increased the tempo considerably*)—and I was expelled! But I was brought back in later.

D. Who was the choir for? Was it to sing to the little ones?

B. It was to—in general you should know that singing is indeed considered as a meditative activity in order to reach one's higher spirit or soul mind, or to maintain the light capsule. It is similar as meditation, it's just a different way to access that higher awareness or that higher level of rest that one might seek. So it wasn't like a show for the little ones. Everyone was participating, and it wasn't like brand–new sparkles. They were a little bit older, they were like nine, ten-year-olds. But none seemed ready to depart like I did when Gergen took me to the fifth dimension to look at the Library. That was grand! I'm constantly seeking that new surprise, that new—it's not a shock, but in some way, it IS a shock—but like a joyful excitement that feels like you're going on a roller coaster. And that's what I like, and Gergen knows that.

D. When was the last time you were surprised, like on a roller coaster?

B. I would say I have had several roller coasters. One of the roller coasters was when I was given my bubble. That was a roller coaster for sure! Because I was intrigued about me going, together with everyone else, to place my solar system. My last roller coaster ride, it wasn't a physical activity. Because a roller coaster ride, you should know, can also indicate that you don't move an inch, that it is inside of you. And lately, I would say that it has been a lot of those—the inner roller coasters—where I have felt like my little carriage, my little boat that I am sitting in, it takes off into new territory and it enters new levels of awareness and knowledge that I did not know, that I had not traveled through with my little boat. So, in many ways, you can see it is like a roller coaster, but it's also like me being in my own little sailboat, sailing across this ocean of opportunities. It doesn't have to be a roller coaster, like my boat goes up and down, or goes under—that's not what I'm seeking here—it has to be completely safe. But, in many ways, I would say my roller coaster, that would indicate more physical activity, has been a little bit on pause. But I have been in my little sailboat and I have been guided by the wind of excitement and knowledge over this big ocean of high awareness. And I have been allowing this wind to just gently lead and guide my little sailboat forward. What has been extremely interesting to me—to my being and to my volumes (*his books*) that I also record by myself—is the unfoldment of the backpack with blue dots.

D. You find that interesting?

B. Yes! You said, "We're going to blow your boat, and we're going to blow it north. You might want to dress up a little bit. It's going to be cool, but it's going to be high action and adventure." Huhuh. So we have been talking about the blue dots.

D. I wondered when we were going to talk about the poles.
B. That was my question, "When will we?"
D. (*Laughing.*) I haven't told you yet?
B. Well gradually, little by little. But I asked the same thing, "When are we gonna talk about the blue dots?" So, right back at ya. Huhuh. The interesting thing is that in the past, you said, the hub and the station or center for visitor activity and interactions on this plane was actually located in the north. There were established certain monitors around the Pole, the center dot, and it was to monitor activity in the Fork. The Fork is the stabilizer and the one that orchestrates the entire experience of the planet. And the monitors are to follow and detect the melody in the Fork. At that time, it started to—there were weather phenomena, you said, there was no humans here at that time. And those who were placed to do research and observe these different changes within the Fork, they reported that there was a need to tilt a little bit. To make it move, tilt a little bit, so it had a better surface area facing the Sun. At that time, before it was shifted, it was actually very cool on more places than there was supposed to be snow and ice. So it was tilted a little bit so a bigger surface area of the planet would be in direct sunlight. You told me, "The purpose is not just to tilt back and forth. It's a whole unified operation because we tilted it a little bit and changes occurred. It became a warmer climate. Later it was tilted the other way and it became a cooler climate. These are very significant shifts," you said, "that indicates and shows when there is a need to either reboot the environment, or to make continents shift."
D. So the movement, the Earth is spinning on an axis, was the axis shifted or was it the continents that moved?
B. In this case, the axis was tilted a little bit and that started a general motion of the continents. Water was also more exposed to sunlight, which was the reason and indicator of movement, or dividing occurrences of the continents.
D. So this was way back in time?
B. Ah. We do not see me here. I asked, "Where was I?" And you said, "You were probably being sang to in the egg!" Huh huh huh.
D. Was I involved in this?
B. Ah, and Ari. Ari and Eli came. I did not. You did a little bit, but it was several of your uncles and others. You said that you were here in training to understand the magnetic field and how shifting and tilting the axis and also how one separates

continents by exposing the water mass to more heat, making the water—it's not boiling—but it creates a follow-on effect down to the sea level, and below, and that is how the continents start to move.

D. I know that at one time there was a single continent, but before that, what existed?

B. First, it was just water and things came up. And as it came up, you said, things started. But man doesn't know how it was. Man thinks that first came land, and then came rain, and then came dividing. But you said that's not really true. You said that there was a time when there was predominantly water and land sort of emerged from below, and that was based on how you tilted and how you shifted the axis. Everything is orchestrated from the Fork, from the center.

D. Did you get any information about the orientation of the Earth? Was it spinning differently?

B. At one point, it was almost straight, there was no tilt. The tilting started as the landmass was in place. And also, it became a more regular pattern of rotations and cycles as mammals and other beings occupied land.

D. You said something one time about visitors putting boxes around the planet?

B. Indeed. And that's what you showed me here. There were boxes around the center Pole that monitored the Fork. They are currently silent observers; they don't cause tilting at the moment but they are placed in the ice.

D. Did some of those boxes actually cause things to move?

B. Ah, it seems like it. It's the same box, but the boxes can do different things. At the moment it is just monitoring. We are in-between changes, so we are in that middle phase. But the boxes are—it looks like those car batteries, that's how they look. There are several, and they monitor and also activate. They are in some way connected both to the center Pole, to the Fork, and they're also connected to the magnetic field inside and the grid on the Earth. I don't see like a button, if that's what you're thinking, that someone presses a button and things start to change. It's remotely adjusted and steered.

D. I've always been curious about the geologic changes. At one time, a large part of the planet was covered with lush forests, and then there were ice ages.

B. And also don't forget also that at one time where there was just water.

D. When those changes happen, what caused that? Were there comets that hit, did landmasses move, or what?

B. There were several different things. Sometimes it was these boxes that started a continuation of changes and motions and movements of landmass. It was more of a silent—it's not like a big bang, in that sense, that something just was flown in and crashed. It's like doing those electric shocks, like zzzttt, and it started to send out signals into the web, and that caused the motion. You should know that a lot of it has to do with dividing continents, to split them up, and water is the strongest power in several realities. Using the water power, you have the ability to move continents, to divide continents, to use this power and to make sure the general flow in the atmosphere—which is dependent on the seas—and the general temperature is on the level that it is supposed to be, and in balance. And if it's not, the water will indicate the shift and changes, and that is heard from the Fork. The boxes simply monitor the Fork activity. You showed me this. And you showed me that you looked into this with some of your uncles, and I can see that. At the moment, it looks quiet. When you show me this location at the moment, I still see the boxes—and it's not like they are placed directly on the top of the planet, it's centered around the Fork because the Fork is the key. The Fork is the one that reads the shifts, predominantly from the sea. And the sea communicates with atmosphere and the general temperature, making sure that it is on a level that is beneficial for lifeforms. And sometimes, in order for lifeforms to become, one has to cool down the planet. And Ophelia said, "This is sad and this is scary, but also it is also part of a greater plan. That is when an ice age or something like that comes in." But sometimes it can also be because there has also been times when the temperature is a little bit too high in general, and then the Fork reads that. So the activity then is to help the host, the planet, to cool down. I'm not saying there is going to be an ice age, but it has to level out a little bit because we are moving into a warmer phase. I've been present through all these phases, so I'm not shocked, I'm not surprised. But I know it creates confusion among those who are present. And also, it creates confusion even in the environment, like trees and so forth. So we try to communicate and calm and to make sure that the end result is of good. Now you have a little bit of a higher temperature again, but people are like, "Ohh! First time ever!" But it's not.

D. I remember you said that when you first started coming to Earth as a student, this continent was much closer to Europe.

B. Ah, ah. I kinda prefer to be here (*in Europe*). I haven't been that much in what is now Asia, and I haven't been that much over in Australia. There was one time over in north India when there was my flower, I was there briefly. But if I can pick and choose—which I try to do when you come here—I point on the map where I think that we should go. I kinda like the green isles. I like Ireland and I like Scotland. I like to be there. We actually have had several lives, you have had, as an Inuit in Greenland—what is now Greenland. I think it was also to be close to your projects, because it was in some way connected to Canada, at one point. It wasn't that far with your canoe. And later, boats took over and went over. You kinda like to be there. You don't like the cold, but you do prefer the stillness that comes with the cold. So you are somewhat confused with being a human. Because with heat comes activities that you don't like. But with the solitude and clarity of mind that exists in the cold, then your physical tends to be too cold and then you can't access your libraries as easily. (*They said that it is easier for me to connect with my soul when I am warm.*)

D. I was wondering if you could explain a little bit about the properties of the Fork. Is it similar to an electromagnetic field? Or does it have a vibration similar like the fourth?

B. It coexists with the first dimension. So it is an extension of the first dimension. The first dimension is the counterpart to the Creator, which is the big Pole. So, in many ways, the Fork is like the little Creator, like the big Center Pole that we see in the Wheel. It has the same design; it has the same function. So, in many ways, it is the extension of the Creator. It is occupied by the Master Mind as a direct link—and that is how animals can directly communicate and know how to move away from danger, let's say, if it's like an earthquake, and so forth. It is because they are in direct communication with the Master Mind, and the Master Mind, it is the presence of the Fork.

D. Okay. Is it in some way a product of the core?

B. Ah. It's an extension of the core. If you were to split the globe open, it's not like you will find a Pole in there, or a Fork. But it operates the same as a tuning fork. It's an energetic existence, but it is held by minerals and materia that exists within each celestial body, and that is determined by the general core, the first dimension. So it's like the first dimension spreading out and just being—when you think of the first dimension, you think of like a dot in the center, which is sort of where gravity is. But if you were to extend that thought and just fully see that the first dimension is actually stretching out, becoming this tuning fork. And it's the general sensor for all activity that goes on here. It is similar like the big center Pole in the Wheel; it is a miniature (*version*) and the direct extension of that. And that exists in all celestial entities, you say.

D. Even like the individual cells in your body—?

B. Has the same, has the same. And like the Sun, the Sun has a tuning fork by itself—and I should tell you that your Sun is not at all pleased. It's not pleased with the activity that goes on with its children. The planets are considered the Sun's children. It creates disturbances and confusion within the group, and your Sun is aware of this. Different activities that goes on with the Sun is an indication (*of that awareness*). Also, you should know, we have your solar system and the tuning fork here. But it (*the Fork*) is not just to monitor and operate for behalf of the Earth. It is a direct connection and communication central to all forks in this solar system and in this galaxy. So, the Sun is not being pleased with Earth and the behavior that goes on. And the behavior that the Sun is not pleased with has to do with pollution; it has to do with the overuse of resources, because it affects the atmosphere, and the Sun detects that. So the communication between planets are Fork to Fork, so to speak. But the Sun operates in different ways in order for, like here, the human to react—that there are changes. The Sun is the one that powers through the atmosphere, making you more vulnerable. And that is because it wants you to be aware of the general effect of your output from different factories, and plastic, and so forth. You should know that the Sun is not just a shining ball. In many ways, it is the councils viewing point. The higher councils—I have not met them—they operate directly through the Sun.

D. I've read theories that the Sun and other stars are primarily electrical in nature.

B. Not all are real. Some are created in order for stabilizing a neighborhood, like in the galaxy. Not everyone has the same function as your Sun, with living lifeforms. Not all solar systems are planned with the same evolution like here. But everything has a purpose! And the only purpose could be to stabilize the neighborhood, and that is a purpose by itself. Here, there are more purposes involved. Not only in your neighborhood, like in your galaxy, but also there are purposes of souls coming here and trying to occupy a third vehicle and, from that point, do changes that the councils are seeking.

D. That's very intriguing.

B. Ah. So I see here what you did on the North Pole, and that was fascinating to me.

D. Is that all the info you picked up on that? Because you talked about the South Pole, too.

B. Ah. If the North is closed, and you say, "They're not supposed to look there. That's why it appears closed, and man doesn't have the need and the interest to go seek there. But in the South, it's more open and there is more activities. And, in many ways, it is to divert the attention from the North Pole."

D. What kind of activities happen on the South Pole?

B. There is coming and going (*through portals into parallel realities*). There is like openings there where visitors come and go. Down there (*the activity*) is also a looking into the general amount of oil. Oh, you don't want to talk too much about that. But I can see there is very much activity from outside entities that are preserving resources, like oil.

D. How long has it been since the South Pole was without ice?

B. AH! I have been around when there was not ice down there.

D. Your time frame here is about 60 million years, isn't it?

B. That's what you say. I don't know if I'm one year old or 60 million years old, but I've been here and I've seen that there has been greenery on the South. I have not seen greenery on the North. The North is more mysterious and it's supposed to be left alone.

D. There's a lot of water up there, and the land—

B. It's frozen, and it's in the ice. And it is designed like that, you say, to not draw attention. So, I wanted to tell you about your bag, and I wanted to tell you you've been here secretively (*in manifested form*), and you monitored this Fork that is the extension of the Master Mind and is the eyes and ears from the Creator.

D. It is amazingly complex when you think of the grand design, the spiritual design of everything. It seems that individual trees and plants can communicate with the Fork?

B. Indeed. They communicate with the Fork, and animals do as well. Like flowers, for instance, they can shut down their light capsule, like we say, before a drought. And how do they know that? It's because they read the activity from the roots into the Fork, and the Fork gives them signals and information that this specific region will cease to exist. And then plants—who are lifeforms as well—can just retreat. So sometimes you can see that, that the environment and plant life and animal life have disappeared earlier than the general shift took place. And how is that possible? You would think, "Ohh, something happens," and THEN living entities would say, "Ohh, let's move, or let's cease to exist." But sometimes you can see that the actual occurrences from plants and animal life takes place BEFORE the actual event of, let's say, a drought or an ice age, and they move earlier. You should just know that in general, what is wished for is that the North is left alone. And you (*Lasaray*) say it's okay if you say this, because they can't find it, anyway. It would take too much effort.

D. They can't find the boxes?

B. They can't find the boxes, it's too much effort. It's not just in one spot. They are strategically placed to be a circle, but they are not just found AS a circle. So it would not help if someone says, "Oh, here's the center, I put my flag here and dive here." It's not gonna be like that, you say. It's too far down and it's too wide apart. It's too scattered for man to find. But it's highly connected from spirit and from visitors. And this thing is also monitored by those who come and go in the south. They connect with the Fork from there. But they lure the eyes away from the North Pole. So they can fly in and out, like, "Look! Look! Here we are! Here we are! Huh-huh-huh." And everyone is like, "Look, something happens down there."

D. That's true, you don't really hear about people seeing space craft in the North so much.

B. Nay, nay. And it's the same thing, they want to divert attention. So that's what I wanted to tell you. I'm gonna go now, but I wanted to say that. I wanted to tell you about what you did in one of the blue dot lives. And apparently, it seems, that you came back in a blue dot life when you and I were working together. But you said it was mainly for maintenance, to look into the boxes. It wasn't to fulfill anything. And I said, "Then why couldn't I have come?" And you said, "It wasn't an Earth mission, in that sense." So I'm gonna go now, but I wanted to tell that.

D. Do you think that most of the planets that have life on them also have boxes that are monitoring?

B. You say that not everything has boxes, but each system has boxes. And then I ask, "Do you mean each solar system or each galaxy?" And you said, "Each solar system that is a solar system with evolution has boxes in at least one of the participants. Normally it is the sun." You said that you had boxes in the stabilizer in a previous time before you came to Earth. You said that it was more interesting to observe the stability so the system didn't wobble. So at that time there were boxes activated in Uranus.

D. I guess the Sun can read all the Forks, so if you can read the Sun, you can read the Forks in all the planets?

B. Indeed. And the sun is the direct link to the higher councils, unless it is a man–made. Well, not man–made, you're not capable to make a sun! Huhuhuhu.

D. Someone called all the filler suns "graffiti".

B. Ah. It's like little sketches, like someone just placed something there. Everything has a purpose, you say. But the purpose can be anything from like a teeny–tiny one percent, all the way up to a hundred percent. So Earth, for instance, it's purpose is about 85 percent. Then I ask, "What would be indicating a 100 percent purpose?" Then you laughed and you poked me in the belly and said, "You!" Huh huh huh huh! And that was the end of that discussion. But you could see where my questions were heading, and I haven't forgotten just because you poked me. But I am a 100 percent purpose—I like that! It makes me feel valuable. So okay, I'll go again.

Bob: The Boxes at the Poles (Feb 13, 2020)
Bob once again displays knowledge about geological and archaeological topics that Christine knows very little about. He describes a time about 240 million years ago when visitors came in a large disk-shaped craft and installed boxes in a large ring pattern around the North Pole. He says the land animals at that time looked like small dinosaurs, which is exactly correct for the early Triassic. Some 252 Ma, at the Permian–Triassic boundary, there was a mass extinction of many aquatic and terrestrial creatures, an event the spirits call a reboot. Life recovered quite rapidly, because the patterns for new species are introduced directly by the second dimension, and also brought here by visitors. He mentions visitors

brought a very large whale–like creature, and fossil records validate the presence of such an animal. Visitors normally work in coordination with the spiritual councils, but there were times when not all activity was sanctioned. A third verifiable observation he made was regarding land masses present in the high latitudes. His description matches the geologic interpretations of where portions of Pangea, the last super-continent, were located at that time. It is probable that the boxes are occasionally relocated by visitors as the continents shift, in order to keep them centered around the axis.

Bob also talks about how DNA is manipulated to create changes. He tried to find something we are familiar with to use as a visual reference. He settled on "pärlplatta", which is only helpful if you speak Swedish. Then he laughed because he knows I do not. A pärlplatta is a children's game that has a board with a lot of pins, onto which are placed different colored round plastic pieces to create pictures. So he compares what Ia does with DNA as creating patterns to produce certain melodies, since light and sound are the basis of all form. As he came in, he just picked up where he had left off in the previous session.

B. So, as I was saying, the Fork is in need of attention. And the blue dot lives that you were showing me before with the receivers on top, North Pole top, they are, some of them, coming to life. And you might think, "Uh, oh! Who are the ones bringing them to life?" But it is a joined connection, you might say. Sometimes it is outer influences, but sometimes it is the Fork, you say, that kick–starts or sends activity waves into the battery or the receivers, where outer influences observe. In this case, it has been told—you to me, and someone maybe to you—and when I asked, "Who told you?" and then you pointed and said, "Look over here." So I don't know if we're gonna talk about the whole chain. But you said there was signs from the Fork indicating an imbalance. It has to be centered and it has to be connected, Pole to Pole, in a fashion, you say, that mirror the great Pole (*the Center Pole*). If an object, like Earth, is not operating properly— and I asked, "What happens if some of the fish tanks are not operating correctly?" And you said, "Oh, that's a whole different agenda." Then I asked, "Can you also tilt or change the leaning on the Great Pole?" And you said, "That's something you might want to talk with Ari about." And I said, "Just sign me up! My calendar is wide open. I do (*will*) take an invite!" Huhuhuh! And you said, "Why don't we start by understanding about the tuning Fork and the stabilizer inside? Similar," you say, "like Uranus is a stabilizer inside the solar system, the center Pole in the Earth, the soul particle in the vehicle, and the Great Pole in the Wheel, all of these are considered a center Pole and a stabilizer, in some way."

D. Even down to the smallest things?

B. Even down to the smallest DNA. So I—myself and I—went to Ia (*who is an expert in DNA*), because I never became fond about working with the DNA. I mean, I took DNA classes because I had to in order for me to create the coffee bean, to create my Individual, and so forth. And also to be properly aligned, Gergen said, as a teacher. (*He snorted and laughed.*) So, I had to! But when I go and look at what Ia does, it is like those things that children have, you know, they have like a board and they put colored things on it and it creates a pattern? She works like that, solving and analyzing and deciphering DNA patterns. It's similar like those things children have—it is flat with sticks and you put colored dots on it and it becomes something.

D. How does she test what she creates?

B. Well, she makes little models, and she reads it. It has to create a melody. As she is creating this—what would you like to call that?

D. I don't know, you pick.

B. What would you like to call this little model where you elaborate and you play? So, I'm gonna call it with a Swedish word, because that exists (*in Christine's vocabulary*). So when she is using the pärlplatta, then…heheheh (*he knew I had no clue what that meant*)—if we don't have options (*for words*), we have to take what exists—when she is using the pärlplatta, then she is putting all these colors in a pattern, and it is silent. In order to know whether it is a puzzle that she solved, and also—she says she is not just solving other tasks or other missions—she creates new patterns, and in order to see whether it functions and HOW it will function, it has to become a melody. As this is already filled with different DNA and color patterns, as it is full, you add a component, which will be indicating a tuning. It is a way to add energy to—you don't give it the melody but you bring the melody to life. And she says that not everything is a ready-made object and she says that's why I don't like working with that. She says if she makes one hundred of these, then she says maybe twenty will be useful; eighty will be considered stepping-stones to become something useful.

D. Drafts.

B. Drafts, exactly. Huh huh. She said to me, "I know you're not that fond of drafts," and I said, "No, I might come in later in the project." So, I lost myself (*he forgot what he was talking about*), BUT what I was gonna say is…huh…this is what happens when I get sidetracked.

D. You were talking about the Fork.

B. Ah, the Fork indeed—but how did Ia come in with her pärlplatta? That's what I wonder. Oh, now I remember how we came down to that; you asked about if it was everything, and I said, "Yes, all the way down to the DNA," and then I saw Ia's little project and the pärlplatta. So, what I would like to say then is that you can change the rotation, the tilt in an object. Just because it's not a planet or a whole Wheel, everything has an axis, a way to be positioned, and that can be changed. At this time, the Fork has sent out somewhat of an emergency signal to these receivers on the North Pole, so some of them have started to light up. MEANING that those who are involved in reading these devices, such as the ones here on the North Pole which have been there longer, are being signaled. There are also (*boxes*) those that exist in Joel's mountains (*the Himalayas*). We have not forgotten about those—and he has not forgotten about those either—but they are numb at the moment. They have not been lit up and they do not necessarily communicate in the same way. Everything communicates with the tuning Fork, but the boxes are reading different signals for different topics and different agendas. The ones on the Poles are highly connected to understanding the tilt of this object, meaning Earth. It (*the signals*) has to do with, primarily, there is a need to shift the temperatures in the seas. What is indicated and needed is to cool it down a little bit. Due to the fact that there is pollution in the seas and some mammals have been suffocating and not feeling very well. So they are communicating that to different parties in order for the tuning Fork to hear. Everything is a chain reaction here. But what is needed and what is wished for is to decrease the temperature overall in general in the seas. Doing so you are not as affected, or subjected, to the pollution such as aluminum, plastic, and mercury. So it is a way to stabilize the element water by cooling it down. As it is heating up, it spreads more. So what they want— and that's also why there are several coming now from the Water World, coming in, and they are programmed to, in some way, not only to read the seas, but to operate in a cooler climate. They will also work on the behalf of the councils to cool the seas down.

Some of the regions that we are looking at is up around Alaska. Some might think, "Well, isn't that cold enough? It's somewhat ice already." They want to cool it even further. We want it to drop, you say, by at least 2 degrees.

D. 2 degrees C?

B. That is the measurement that exist in this one's knowledge bank. You cannot put in anything else because that will just be extremely confusing (*Christine struggles with Fahrenheit*). Just think of the word pärlplatta. Pärlplatta did not exist in English. So if she doesn't have a word in English, it is quite hard to find it in here (*in her mental database*). So, you say that you would like to drop the temperature around the North Sea, which some would say, "Oh, that's cool enough." Well, it is a conductor to make the temperature travel further south. So, in this case, in order for the temperature to gradually drop in the seas worldwide, you start on the top. You say, "If we can drop it 2.3 degrees up there, it will be a huge effect and help not only lifeforms in the sea, but the general atmosphere and Poles."

D. Will it set up droughts or little ice ages, or anything like that?

B. What we're talking about here, I don't see any droughts. But we are indeed concerned if there is tilting going on. And you should know, and Ophelia and everyone says this is not the first time. But man is like, "Ohh! Ohh! This is the first time the climate has changed!" I've been around probably a thousand of them. There are those like Ole—who knows how many he's been around for. Maybe we should bring in Ole and just see what he says about that. And Ole has his mentor, you know, and he's also been on Earth. So who knows how many changes and shifts in atmosphere and cycles of sort of humanoids that he has experienced! I did ask, because as we are uncovering blue–dot lives that were among my lives—and I have not come to terms with that fully, why that took place. (*He is not happy that I came in manifested form without him.*) Then I say, "When there were only blue–dot lives, what did you do? We can talk about the other lives that were among humans, when the humans came around, later." And you said when you were similar like a teenager, you were with Ari and with others who were visitors, and you organized the boxes on the top. (*The boxes around the North Pole.*) At that time, there was an activation (*of the boxes by the visitors*). You showed me a picture (*of the disk*), and I have seen one when I was at Etena, when we did the ritual with the elements. It looked like a big disk that came in and observed the activity that you were doing. But that big disk looked like a big eye. Those that you were with (*the visitors*), they were wearing something like a rubber outfit. They were, in some way, in direct operation with this disk that was just above. And the disk was monitoring the position of the boxes. Ari did not wear rubber, and you did not wear a rubber suit. You looked like you do at home.

D. So the ones in the rubber suits—

B. They communicated with this big disk above.

D. Were the ones in the rubber suits lifeforms from Earth, or visitors?

B. Visitors. There were no...

D. This was before the current continents formed, wasn't it?

B. Indeed. It looked different. The continent that was North Pole, it was like Greenland, Canada, North Pole and parts of Russia were all connected. The lifeforms that I can see when you show me—you swipe the camera a little bit and we go south—I see that there are like four-legged animals, like an armadillo kind of entity there. But there were like dinosaurs, small dinosaurs, and this took place around that time. There were lifeforms, but not the really big dinosaurs. They were smaller, they looked like the dinosaurs, but not the huge ones, the giant ones.

D. There were probably different creatures in the sea too?

B. Ah. They were bigger! They were like the massive, big ones. I can see (*something*) like a whale that existed. It was intelligent. It did not live in a flock. It was not like the killer whales or dolphins. It was by itself. It was about 20 meters long. It was like a whale, but it was highly intelligent. It was, in some way, put there. It's not like I see several of them.

D. So, it was brought here by visitors?

B. Indeed. It looks like a big submarine. But I can see the eyes. It's like looking into someone highly intelligent. It's just shaped like a big cigar. And the color is like brownish. It's brown-greyish, and it's patterned. The eyes are kinda big.

D. Do you have any idea what the approximate time frame was?

B. Well, you showed me a number here with that big whale, and that existed about 240 million years ago, you say. And the boxes came then. And I see that they are activating now, some of them.

D. I remember there was some talk about the boxes initiating the continents to break up. There was a big continent and then it was broken up?

B. Maybe you were there several times. What I see with this big mammal in the sea, that one was 240 million years ago, you say. And I can see you on the Pole with the rubber people. You're showing me like slides, like snapshots of things. But I can see here on the timeline that this is not the first blue dot, so you were here earlier. You said that you were here earlier before putting boxes as well.

D. So the point that was rotating, the axis of the Earth, can you see where it was pointing at the time?

B. It was pointing to the star, I don't know if this is the right time, but I can see here at one point, the Pole was pointing to one of the major stars in this vicinity. Everything is in some way pointing or in direct contact with a counterpart. You say it could be a sun, it can be another system, it can be even the neighboring galaxy. That is the general web.

D. Does it matter where it points? The axis of the Earth now points at Polaris in Ursa Minor, the North Star, so does it share information, or does it matter which star it points at?

B. Yes, it points at the North Star indeed. It does not share information. But in some way it is a relationship between objects in order for them to operate in a fashion that, I would assume, these rubber people intended. They are sort of the maintenance people, the ones you call in if you need maintenance. So when I saw this big mammal in the sea, that's when I see these rubber people. But you did not look young, you did not look like a teenager. You look like you do now, so you were an adult. You were there—I don't know if Ari was there, maybe he was there too—but you were considered like an adult. The first time you came with the boxes you were a teenager, you say. So I'm looking into that. And I'm also having classes, which is less demanding, it's less complicated. So, anyway, I wanted to come in and tell you about the Fork and the general intent to decrease the temperature in the sea.

D. That's really good to know. Is that going to be accomplished by reducing the output of the Sun?

B. Ah, indeed. It's a joint effort. The receivers, they initiate and direct the intent and they read the messages from inside and out. But the operation to make it happen is not done by the ones in the rubber suits; not even by Ari, I would assume. It has an effect from the Sun, in this case. You say if it was another agenda, then let's say Uranus, it had a role before because Uranus is the stabilizer. Then they modified the general gravity in Uranus to change the stabilizing frequency in the family.

D. I find these topics to be very thought provoking. I spend a lot of time researching.

B. Well, at home you also research. You're quite smart, and I'm happy to have you as my tutor.

D. (*Laughing.*) I'm happy to have you as my companion.

Tallock, Ophelia: 450 Million Years Ago (Dec 15, 2019)
During this session, Evan, from Vlac, gives more details about the work that his group and the Elahim have done on Earth over the eons. What is fascinating (to me) is the correlation between events in the geologic records and activities that the spiritual councils were conducting on Earth. Evan tells about how the councils and entities from different dimensions were experimenting with the atmosphere and Fork, trying to stabilize the environment. At the same time, they would try out new designs of lifeforms and collect data on how well they operated. A lot of research was conducted prior to 450 million years ago (Ma). There was instability in the core and the atmosphere, so representatives from the sixth dimension came in manifested form (in crafts) and drilled down 30 km with crystal lasers to install receivers and transmitters in the crust. The councils could then control the movement of the tectonic plates and the atmosphere by monitoring and influencing the Fork. All this was done to set up the natural processes and evolution which the Creator intended for this planet.

The date of 450 Ma has come up several times, so our spirit friends see that period as a major marker on the path of evolution. Geologists categorize it as the Ordovician Period (485 to 444 Ma). During the Ordovician there were three significant events. One was the breakup of the super-continent in the southern hemisphere, rapid sea-floor spreading and the formation of all the modern tectonic plates. The second is known as GOBE, the acronym for Great Ordovician Biodiversification Event. The expansion of types of marine life was the greatest in all Earth's history. It was also during GOBE that plants were introduced on land (terrestrialization). This biodiversity explosion coincided with a dynamic period when continents were shifting, mountains were raised, and massive volcanism occurred. And then the Ordovician ended with two major extinctions: one occurring 447 Ma, and the other 443 Ma. After these two events, 60 percent of the world's population of marine invertebrates were eliminated. Geologists and paleontologists are mystified as to the cause of the Ordovician extinctions. Evan explains the Cambrian and Ordovician as a time of extensive testing of various models of new lifeforms in the oceans under varying conditions. After evaluating the results, the Creator and councils caused a reboot that eliminated many of the exotic creations. Terrestrial plants were largely unaffected during this particular reboot.

The visitors established bases in several locations on the planet. One of the largest was in the area where the Great Lakes are now located. Ophelia (and others) have told how portals are located in areas where there are high concentrations of copper, gold, or mercury. The area around the Great Lakes is part of the Midcontinent Rift System, where the North American continent pulled apart and large volumes of lava were deposited. Within this rift, an area that is now the Lake Superior Basin formed where the igneous basalt rocks contain vast quantities of copper along with some gold and silver. I can assure the reader that Christine has absolutely no knowledge about this, so the information is obviously not coming from her subconscious. The concentration of copper is critical to the creation of portals, because it causes the energy field to counter-rotate. The vortex allowed alien crafts to enter and leave the Earth's energy field. The councils decided to close the portal by mining the copper and reducing its effect. The Elahim (in manifested form) and Tallocks (in physical space craft) came some 300,000 years ago and removed great quantities of the metal. Towards the end of the mining operations, two crafts collided and caused a massive explosion and radioactive crater, which sank into the crust. The Great Lakes were formed to cover the area, but the Earth is still in need of healing from the event.

Ev. My name is Evan. Teacher for you on Vlac. Uhh. This is different. (*His voice was deep and raspy, and he struggled to talk.*) Lungs very small. Need more space. Hhhuuuh. Oh, he (*Seth*) said, "I'm going to be small; you have to do with what is." We traveled here in the distant past, together. Collected minerals, analyzed foundations for life.

D. Who did you travel with?

Ev. You. You and I. Seth did not go; monitored from Vlac. We collected samples, minerals. The adjustments needed to be made in the core of the planet, and we analyzed effects on the surface. The surface reveals the condition within. We analyzed the resources; oil, gas, as a connection and key to the core. When you ravage the resources, take more than you are allowed, it creates disturbances in the core. You have had several lives monitoring the Fork, as you call it here, understanding that minerals, resources, just gives a little key to how the Fork operates. There is a big zone, energetic zone, around Alaska that is highly connected to the Fork. That is why we wish that zone to be left alone. We do not want to repeat a shutdown, like we did in the center of this continent. There was a shutdown due to overuse of resources, high in mercury, high in copper, gold. This one came, observed the activity. The region now known, big lakes (*Great Lakes*), shut down. The connection to the Pole moved. Several centers, connecting lines, web, maintaining the Fork. Now the main hub for us to observe the Fork is in the region of Alaska. It was relocated (*around 300,000 BC*), as it was considered a place where man might leave Earth alone. Did not intend for it to be open. (*Drilling for oil has damaged the connection to the Fork.*) It's a wound in your planet, similar as once existed under the Great Lakes. We do not wish to repeat shutdowns of centers, as it is not optimal. It is a response for the Fork to continue to sing. The tone in each core, in each celestial body, travels in the web, the cosmic web connecting solar systems, galaxies, even fish tanks. Even if one is out of tune, it affects the whole web. Your neighbors feel the singing (*from Earth*) is out of tune, and it affects their atmosphere. That is why several entities, neighbors, levels, are interested in igniting your consciousness.

D. Can you tell me more about when you and I traveled here?

Ev. Yes. Traveled as manifested form after non-manifested form. We traveled here—you would see it as remote viewing—before we fully engaged. We traveled like the wind the first times, making sure atmospheric shifts were in place. Those were established by friends from the eighth, and we traveled with them remotely in the wind, not in form. As we came in form, we established centers, creating these hubs strategically to maintain the Fork. Everything is connected, and we created hubs. We were several, creating a central civilization that was left behind. Expertise in maintaining and operating these hubs. You oversaw the operation in the hub near Grand Lakes. Another hub located in central Russia; that one was larger. There was interference. Workers that were brought in to operate the hub in the Great Lake region were not fully understanding or honoring the work at hand. Higher awareness in central Russia. It is not a coincidence that that region (*Russia*) is now more shut down from all eyes on your planet. We try to maintain the remains. But you traveled with me and others, creating locations for these hubs. Going deep into the Earth's core, drilling, establishing receivers deep in this abyss, hole, traveling about thirty kilometers down. Drilling using crystal laser, using light, traveled deep, established receivers that would operate as stabilizers for the Fork, deep underneath where you now feel is depth! Huh huh huh. Still, these receivers exist. Some in mountains, some under seabed; some active, some not.

D. What was the timeframe when we traveled here, relative to lifeforms?

Ev. Before lifeforms, before the big animals, about 450 million.

D. Since the sixth was involved in creating the solar system, was this all part of activating it?

Ev. Yes. It was to create stability, not only in this planet, but it's also placed in the web and it has to function in that web. Modifications took place to create a new song, if you like, in the Fork. Maintenance operations creating new conditions here, but also the overall operation in the web.

D. Since the plates that carry the continents are always moving, back then they were in different locations than where they are now?

Ev. Yes, more congested. But as the Fork changed tune, the planet tilted, motion took place, creating...oh, what word, what word? What you are aware of, (*human ideas about how*) the continents shift, are somewhat false. They have moved rapidly and slowly due to these receivers. Hmm, you would call it, probably, a magnetic gadget. But it's to redirect motion, redirect the song in the Fork. Planet tilted, waters moved, continents sunk. Those (*continents*) you see and those you are aware of in motion and movement are the latest. The other ones sunk. So there were shifts not only on the surface, but from up and down as well. So what you are aware of as motion in landmass and continents are only the latest. The other ones before, some sunk. No civilization, just shifts to maintain an optimal environment for lifeforms to emerge. So, the continents you see at this time, about 25 percent are missing, now on seabed. So, you see, if we have 100 percent of landmass, what is left is 75. Do you understand?

D. I do.

Ev. So, this meeting is crucial for you to begin to dig into the Earth's history. Find your spot in evolution. Find your path through evolution and look beyond humanity (*to see*) the Earth's evolution. That is the wish from the councils that maintain and listen to the Forks in each celestial body. YOU, both of you, are not here to only enlighten the species, you are here as a request from your host, your project. Dig deeper. Man is just a little part, but it's important as you have to reach them, to make them aware of their minimal importance to the whole. Dig deeper, my son.

D. If the humans weren't present on Earth, would the Forks be in tune?

Ev. What would be optimal, from that point-of-view, would be to allow the planet to rejuvenate, to allow the planet to hear the song, to allow environment—your trees, your seas—to once again hear its host and the song, to reconnect to these centers within, placed by entities, such as yourself, in a distant past. But those are only there to assist. You can see the receivers, the gadgets, as a bandage if someone is hurt; it's only to assist, to help. It's like your planet went sick and we are operating as doctors, helping the circulation—to give a comparison to a human—to help the blood circulation once more to flow through all its organs. The gadgets simply help to direct this inner flow, which is equal to your human blood circulation. You might wonder why it changed and why the gadgets were needed? It was due to modifications where atmosphere and core did not operate optimally. It was to make sure the landmasses, continents, were at an optimal position, it was to change lifeforms in the sea that were the first ones here. Those who are in the sea are the original members, citizens, here. You are a later version, and you don't even know about the ones in the sea. Changes, modifications. There, we drifted. Interesting to be in a human. Never done it, never intend to. You come here to help man understand, to enlighten the mind, but you also are here as a direct request from your host, from the Council of Nine, from Vlac councils. You are here to once again help (*in the*) understanding how the Fork can once more sing in tune. There is a reason why you were drawn to your profession. Use your knowledge to change the field. Use your petroleum engineering skills to understand your host. That is the new line of your profession that will come further ahead, combined with writing. We will leave at this time, but know that you are always accommodated by your friends. We will help you, guide you, in how to take your training into a next, higher level.

D. Wow. Thank you. I appreciate your help and assistance.

Ev. Understand the flow. See the directions, see where resources are low and resources are high. Investigate why the resources in one location is low. Understand cycles. You will be guided. Use your engineering skills. Where would you, if you could, locate another gadget? Where and how could that improve the general flow of resources? We will guide you.

D. Alright my friend. Thank you for all that information, and thank you for coming to visit.

Ev. You are welcome. I'm stepping out of this now. This was different. See you back home.

D. Thank you so much. Goodbye, my friend.

O. This is Ophelia. Cleaning clearly is needed here.

D. Hello, Ophelia.

O. Good morning to you. So, you met another friend. He will be coming several sessions ahead, and he will help your human self to ignite an understanding. Investigate the web. Ley lines are one of the keys. Use your inner eyes to investigate locations on Earth, not just power points, but where resources are high and low. Know that they have moved over time. Everything has to do with maintaining the general flow within your host.

D. When he was talking about around the Great Lakes, those resources were primarily copper and mercury?

O. Copper, yes.

D. That performs a similar function as hydrocarbons in keeping the Fork in tune?

O. Yes. But it also had to do with being a larger hub for receiving energies. So it had not only to do with maintaining the Fork, it was an energetic hub, almost considered like an airport, where crafts and visitors navigated to, to descend. So it was strong in that way. See it as not only operating to maintaining the inner, but also as a great hub, a great airport, for visitors to arrive.

D. Because copper is a conductor of electricity, does that influence how the Earth grid connects to the upper grid?

O. Yes, yes. Connecting grids, making it possible for descending objects and also to ascend crafts as well. So see it as—the only way I can relate it for you—the biggest airport. So it was for motion, but it also operated below—mining. But it was primarily to maintain stability in that region, in order for visitors to come and go. So, it was operating on several levels.

D. In what time period did most of the mining occur that caused the disruption?

O. That's when this one also came, around 300,000 years ago. Closed down. Okay, we will talk. Yes, yes, yes. (*She was talking to Bob, who must have been getting impatient for his turn.*) We just clean a little bit. But it's important that you start to investigate, and you can begin by investigating the grand lake, and look in history, search for keys when it comes to minerals. But also know that you cannot find everything in the current google. You have to find the answers within, and it might simply appear as a thought, as a question within you. Follow that lead and it will lead you to another lead. So just be aware of ideas and thoughts that comes into your mind, into your being, and we will assist your progress as you continue to investigate the Earth's history. This will bring you great joy, combined with great sorrows, because you will remember works that have been done, and you will remember the intention you all had, we ALL had, and how it has changed. So, combined with enlightenment also, hand-in-hand, sorrow can appear. Use both as an engine for you to continue to leave a mark in the consciousness at this time. Sorrow is not meant to paralyze. That is what happens in the human consciousness, sorrow paralyzes. Use sorrow as an engine, as a fire. Both will lead you to greatness.

D. That's very wise.

O. There. So, okay. Yes, we are indeed expecting another visitor. A visitor who does not travel in crafts, even though he has his peanut suit, which is considered somewhat of a craft. Okay, so I will step aside, as there is always someone ready. So, I will leave you, as the energy has been stabilized.

D. Okay. Thank you, Ophelia. Talk soon.

O. You are much welcome.

Jeshua, Bob: Explosion around Great Lakes (Oct 30, 2016)

Very early in our channeling work, Jeshua gave us a talk which, until now, has not been published. He and Bob both gave a very compelling description of what happened 300,000 years ago in the area of the Great Lakes (*North America*). Interestingly, Jeshua said that at that time, the lakes were not there. Christine, of course, would have no knowledge of that. But according to those geologists who have studied the glacial periods in the region, it is true. The Great Lakes are quite recent, as the area was covered with ice thousands of meters thick up until 12,000 BC. In reviewing the timeline given by Jeshua, it exactly corresponds to ancient climatic records. Vast sheets of ice advance and retreat across the northern hemisphere with some regularity. During the past 500,000 years, glaciers have covered most of Canada and extended down into the central part of the US at least three times. Then the Earth warms up and the ice melts. Between 300,000 to 425,000 BC the area around the Great Lakes was ice-free, so mining operations would have been possible. Ice cores indicate global temperatures fell around 300,000 BC, pushing the Earth into the Illinois Glacial episode. The councils say they decided to cover the area in ice to seal the radiation.

Since we are jumping way back in the chronology of the sessions, you will see that Jeshua is actually introducing himself for the first time. He also outlines the purpose behind this project.

J. To understand why we are doing this specific writing, there is a need for you both to understand how you prepared before you came into physical body. This is followed by your students on the other side, in your home base that is referred to from this specific realm. To understand why you have chosen this specific assignment, there are certain things in your past visits that will be beneficial for you (*to remember*), as you meet with individuals on this plane. Those souls who have not walked on this plane as long as you have. You will encounter souls from the same period where this specific incident took place, and there will be individual healing with specific souls that need to take place, as well as a collective (*healing*). What I'm referring to took place in a time before the known scriptures were made. This was a time when there were several entities occupying this specific planet. Continents did not look the same as they do now. The trauma that lies stored in this planet, far deep down in the soil, is related to explosions that took place between certain individuals, groups, if you like. These groups were sort of left to their own device before a higher order intervened. This is stored in the memory of this planet. That is why sometimes, when newer souls come in, they feel the past trauma and they cannot detach from something that occurred in a far past. In some way they repeat what took place. We see this currently in the Middle East. This specific region was damaged due to an explosion. It created a crater of intense, poison waves that is still stored in that specific region of the planet. That is why certain souls do not want to incarnate in that specific region, even though they might. This book, this manual on how to travel and interact with celestial bodies, as well as incarnated individuals, is important for the progress to heal the planet of the past.

D. With whom am I speaking?

J. I'm only visiting as a mentor that prepared you for coming into this assignment. The teachings that you took before coming in will create the foundation for several layers and waves of incarnations to come. You are here to do good. You are here to educate. I would like to, if possible, to transmit the visual of the past that has created disturbance in the karmic scale for this planet. This took place prior to known civilizations, yet there were civilizations here. Not necessarily human in...the humans existed, in some way, but the brains were smaller. That progressed over time, intervened by the more angelic realm (*what they later identified as the spiritual dimensions*), to create these beings, the humankind, more in power of their faith.

D. In Earth years, when did this occur?

J. At this time, around 300,000 BC, it (*the explosion*) took place, in what is now in the middle of the United States, bordering to Canada. This is where the battle took place, creating a crater that drew in landscapes in that specific region, which from above looked like a collapse.

D. So, this was in the United States, or the geographic location?

J. Yes. At this specific time there were no lakes in this region. The lakes have been placed to cover up this mess.

D. I thought you mentioned an area in the Middle East?

J. Yes. That is another area. You were not involved in that one.

D. But I was involved in the one in North America?

J. You both were. You did not fully participate, but you were aware.

D. In what form were we here at that time?

J. In a larger form.

D. A physical body?

J. Yes, but you had the ability to dissolve, if you liked. But, yes, you appeared in physical. (*In subsequent sessions, they explained how we traveled in a manifested form.*)

D. And what was our role at that time?

J. To mine. There were two groups, the third one came in to mediate between the two about a specific region where mining was intended to take place.

D. What were we mining?

J. There was gold and copper, but also uranium was needed. Yet the uranium was the cause that later created the crater.

D. What were we doing with this gold and copper?

J. It was meant to be used as a fuel. It was also meant for technological blends (*of metals*) for crafts. It was also used, in some way, for creatures as a battery fluid, of sorts, too. (*Some creatures were similar to robots, created by visitors.*) This is hard for a human to understand, so we will keep this within the group. This is what you need to understand—that you are here to create something good out of something that happened in the past. The stored memory of this specific incident can be felt by those walking the soil. Younger souls do not understand where their rage comes from. What we mentioned in the Middle East took place later. That is why people are less aggressive on this side (*of the planet*). There is a group that came to heal the soil. The natives on this land knew their ancestors were part of the (*earlier*) humanoids with a smaller brain. Yet, they (*the smaller brained humanoid*) had the ability to understand smaller incidents. They were not as equipped to communicate, but they could register. This is stored in the natives in this land—the memory—even though they did not speak of it. That is why they also feel the need to protect certain areas from invasion. (*Jeshua is implying that some Native Americans descended from earlier humanoids, circa 300,000 BC.*)

D. Invasion from where?

J. They still feel a need to heal the soil, because new man comes and do not understand the healing process is going on. So they come and continue to create cell memories that the natives want to heal and release. If we could, we would wish to close off this region for a while. (*Jeshua stepped aside and Bob immediately took over the discussion.*)

B. Yes, I took notes about the planet. I checked the water, which is like the blood of the planet, which is like the blood in the humanoid. I checked the water, this liquid looked like mercury. For a while in this region, regular water looked like mercury.

D. What sort of incident or explosion happened?

B. Two collided over it. They were carrying this poison, the uranium, and two (*crafts*) collided. And then, the crater came. Higher beings, higher orders, made it sink into the planet. But you know what goes in, stays. It looks like a crater from above, but it was actually buried in there. This is something that is existing in the Library. This is part of the hidden aspects a past that is not necessarily what we want to have repeated, of course. A lot of this knowledge is brought forward to the higher beings because of the current situations at other places on the planet. They do not want to have another crater where two are colliding. And the two colliding (*now*) are humanoids, but they are equally capable of creating the same damage.

D. Is it the humans that are potentially going to cause another crater, or is it other beings?

B. It's the humans, because some of them actually remembers. You are here to create a balance in the team that could potentially do this. You choose to work with oil, because you felt the need to heal mother earth, and the veins in the planet. You wanted to observe what this industry was doing! Bad people! You were there to observe them. You did not really like to be in that environment, but you wanted firsthand to see, to hear. A lot of what you reported took place when you slept. You reported what people were doing. Especially, you paid attention to those who were in charge. Not necessarily those who you called on the floor, but those in charge. Greed. Greed makes people do stupid things. (*Bob's observation is interesting, because I worked in the Michigan oil and gas fields for several years, not far from the lakes. I traveled to the northern tip of Michigan on lengthy assignments as a well drilling and operations engineer. While there, I found the area unsettling, but never knew why.*)

D. So, in what way are we to help? What was our mission for coming here?

B. You are here to create peace with the written word. That it (*peace*) is in your choosing. The humanoid can at this time—they're not slaves, their brain is bigger—they can actually make a difference. If more awakens to their purpose and to the light, then there will be no slaves. The humanoids in the past could only observe.

D. Because they were slaves to another race?

B. Umm. Their brains were also smaller.

D. What did we do when we were here at that time? (*Bob did not follow me to Earth when I manifested a form. So he is probably getting thought bubbles from Lasaray or Jeshua as we are speaking.)*

B. You operated a craft, of sorts. You were involved in technology. you operated—not the drilling—oh. I wasn't really in there, but you were operating inside something that looked like an egg. But I wasn't there in the egg. I do know, because I read your journal, that you did come to do a little bit of excavating and mining. But you were only here because you had your orders on how much you could take. What happened was that there was a conflict within the group, so the egg remained. And that is where the conflict began because another group came in. There was a conflict between the eggs and the eggs collided. (*The Elahim were removing metals in order to close the portal above the area. Certain visitors came and wanted to continue mining. Then the accident occurred and the councils directly intervened. The crafts were shaped like cylinders, which Bob calls an egg. They were large spaceships and must have had a significant supply of radioactive material on-board.*)

D. What happened when the eggs collided?

B. They sank into the crater, and that's where it's stored. And then water came later, much later, to cover it up. There was a crater for a while and it could be seen. There were a lot of meetings that took place between beings after that, but I was not involved. Did not go to those meetings. I know where they take place though. It's sort of a dome (*building*) near the Library (*on the fifth*). There were discussions about the specifics. Some wanted to shut this whole project down, but there was no need. Because the Creator is actually here, meaning that we should learn from mistakes and to do good. There was meetings that took place about how to fix this problem for future generations.

D. Will they intervene if humans are about to create more nuclear explosions?

B. They might, because that is what happened to the eggs. They didn't crash because they didn't know how to maneuver their eggs! It was an intervention. Oh, it was a boom, and then light. Boom. An intervention. So, yes, there is a possibility for interventions, of course. (*It sounds like he is saying the spirit realm caused the crash to terminate the dissention.*)

D. I wasn't in one of the crafts, was I?

B. You were inside. You were both inside. But there's nothing to be sad about, because you did not do anything you were not supposed to. Those who did are not here. The conflict laid in something between the two eggs. I think the egg—what I saw—the one egg you both were inside was about to leave. The other egg wanted to stay and continue, and here lies the conflict. They were groups almost the same as you (*also from the sixth*), but one group wanted to continue and break the rules of what was set before coming, and your egg wanted to leave as planned. This is what you need to understand, that you are familiar with a little bit of a darker history for this planet. You did not do bad, because you were allowed to come and collect, and you were meant to leave with your egg. But the other egg remained, and you remained to communicate with them and to convince them that this was not what the assignment was all about. They did not listen, and for some reason something happened and it collided. It was a conflict within your own group. Those are not here. They are not allowed to come into this realm anymore. You are doing almost like volunteer work for your group. But you're the only one allowed to come in, because you did not break the rules. But there was a history within this group where there was a conflict, and it did not pass unnoticed, let's just say that. So, to understand your path ahead, it's important sometimes to know the reason why, and it will also give you the drive to do good, and to also understand people who, in your surroundings, are acting in a bad manner. Because it's not that easy all the time. It's something you are familiar with.

D. Well, that's good to know. Thank you for sharing that.

B. The other egg, we looked at this. Those people came from another place. They move around like the grasshopper, between different planets. They can actually move around a lot, if they want to. This specific civilization came and had been on another place nearby before (*Mars, probably*). There's something different with the other egg, they look a little different, I'm not sure they are relatives. Maybe I'm not fully qualified to make that assumption about the family tree. It's like having, there's always someone in the family you don't like, like an uncle of sorts. This is sort of similar. Oh, Ophelia is giving me information here to transmit to you. Wait a minute. You did belong in the same family tree. However, like all families, there can be conflicts within groups. This was like two uncles, did not really get along, they were brothers and they were separated and left to two different spaces, two different places. So, you belong with one, and the other group went somewhere else, and both, unfortunately came down to this plane in their eggs, and that was stupid. It's like a bad family reunion. Ah, let's see...wait, wait. Yes, Ophelia said they were like a black sheep, the other group. Oh, ohhhh, been taken care of, she said. They are in some sort of quarantine, after that event. Time does not exist, even though it sounds very long to get a 300,000–year sentence! It's no time, really. They are located somewhere else.

Elahim Council: Human Evolution (Jan 13, 2019)
This is another excellent session, in which the Elahim Council gave a broad outline of Earth history in relation to soul development and their involvement with evolution. The Elahim and other groups have been nurturing life on Earth for at least 400 million years. A small percentage of Elahim have been intermittently incarnating during the past 300,000 years, often doing research for the different councils on the eighth, ninth, and tenth. One of the great obstacles to spiritual harmony is the human emotion of greed. Greed and fear are the polarity to the purest form of love, which is compassion. History books are, if nothing else, tales of greed and conquest. The Elahim Council advises that advanced technologies will never be given to mankind, until the heart and the mind are aligned with the center point.

EC. Elahim. Friends from home, Elahim Council present with your uncle Ari, providing our strongest gratitude for the work on our behalf you do in a physical body. We know the struggle it entailed, once upon a time, to transform your travel here into tapping in to a third reality and another vehicle not of your choosing, but what was available. It created a lot of tensions within your energetic being, both (*of you*), as you had to adapt to a new environment. But the same goes on everywhere when environments change, atmospheric shifts, conditions provided by the higher councils, we all need to adapt. However, when that occurred here, less from our family wished to come. Took a step back. Only a few took on the teachings to master an incarnation. By that, we are extremely grateful to those who do. Meaning the two of you, in this case.

D. And how many Elahims are there?

EC. We tend to be somewhere between three and five percentage present, in total, on this place at the same time. Spread out, though. You normally do not meet. The two of you meeting is unique. You travel, normally, in solitude and by yourself. Not meant to connect, necessarily, with other Elahim. We have some who operate within scientific organs, development of energy—that is one of our expertise. You, having one foot almost, in there. A brother, located in Canada, working progressively with energy. Studying, giving as well written results, in due time, of his work and study, but works alone. So, normally you do not meet, and that is why we greatly salute you for coming, as you take on normally a life without your soul companions. This one (*Seth*) gets others—did not wish to come with no friends—so granted a big travel group! HUH HUH. Yes, indeed, Ari took that assignment to help.

D. When you say three to five percent, do you mean of the Elahims, or the population on Earth?

EC. Elahim, yes. At the moment, you are one hundred and five. Two just left. Two just reported back home, just came back. You all monitor different activities on this location. You, taking on somewhat of group behavior and the power of the mind, to try to decipher and unlock hidden keys within the brain, to potentially increase the light within it. This one (*Seth*) likes to rumble, likes to have fun, but doing progressive assignments where humanoids changed their actions just by his presence. Bringing strength and laughter combined, making others curious about him and about the journey they have. Reporting back, not necessarily similar like you about behavior, but how reactions take place within this humanoid, how they respond to different teachings, different approaches. Takes on different characteristics to see what works and what will not work. Prefers, however, the stronger male persona that he once had. Huh. Great leader indeed, occasionally, not always. But has the possibility and ability to have others follow his lead. Doing so demands great responsibility—what are you leading them to? So, while you investigate group behavior more silently, this one does it more actively.

D. Are the Elahim, in some way, assisting human evolution on Earth?

EC. Based on what you report back, yes. If we take the brain, due to some of your reports, upgrades took place. And some (*parts*) were deleted from your investigations. Meaning the windows inside the brain were not equipped for more light—meaning more knowledge—in that specific species. So indeed, we are involved, but not alone. We report to councils on activities. So, yes indeed, we are involved in evolution.

D. Interesting.

EC. Not in the full spectra. We tend to focus on wisdom, scientific keys, quantum physics, physics in general, cosmic engineering, and links between worlds, once available to this species here. When you were here around 30,000 BC, in this timeline that exists, the calendar here, there was a great cycle where science and physics combined, blossomed. Some took it to a level that was not intended. Councils intervened. But before, indeed, the prospect was great, and the greatness came of (*from*) being humble for the findings. As one lacks the sensation of being humble, when one stumbles upon a new teaching, if they are greedy within that knowledge, then it will be taken away. It will be like waking up from a dream you thought you understood, or you thought you had an idea, but you wake up and it's gone. If an idea is sent to a humanoid, scientific, an awakening key for humanity, we monitor exactly where those influences will go. But if the receiver doesn't take the message with humility and respect and responsibility, it will instantly fade, simply deleted. Your part is to see whether the brain is equipped at all to receive certain keys sent from the councils. You monitor different behaviors, study different species within your species; male, female gender, also the location where certain keys can go. Heat, no good. The cooler climates have a tendency to be more humble, to be more in peace with the environment. Even though you might think it is cool, and it might cool the individual down, but cooling something down also gives perspective and calmness. Heat just makes you run around. Should be the opposite, one would think, that one would run around to gain heat, and the opposite, lay flat, to somewhat store whatever coolness exists. However, your species do not respond like that. Others will indeed react differently to the elements.

D. Is there going to be knowledge that you are going to bring forward that humans can handle, without further destroying the planet or each other?

EC. Combined, with your other friends, we deliver teachings gradually, on different locations, of course, differently, to make humanity not run around so much, to find that coolness and peace within. Heat tends to stir emotions up. If your emotions are overactive, it influences the brain. At this particular time, there is a huge presence from the seventh, trying to cool the emotions down, so that we can increase the light in the brain. That is why there is a huge percentage of souls who works with light, healing. It is all to cool emotions down, to make them more passive, receptive, and in resonance with their soul, to not be fooled by the needs and illusions on this environment. No upgrade in the brain will take place until a sign from the seventh is given, that the emotions have become more in balance. The emotions—that is why there is a huge focus on heart. Heart resonates with emotions for people. And the true emotions come from your center point. Sometimes, if your emotions come even from your heart, it can be deceiving, when you start feeling certain things that someone might influence. Your heart is more receptive to outer influences than your center point. So in some way, the heart can be colored, get dirty, where the center point can never. So, the center point is trying to radiate the true emotions, so the hearts are not colored. If you see the heart as purely pink, then at the moment, due to certain things around you, it starts to get grey or dots on it—that's how I can give you a picture. It gets colored, your heart. The brain is on standby to see when the heart gets purely pink again. That is why there is a huge abundance of the presence from, not only the seventh, but also the second. The second also provides healing and can change colors just by their presence, just by being who they truly are. When one starts to believe in magic, to see nature as a living entity, it indeed reflects the heart. And those who have grey spots on it will suddenly feel how everything rejuvenates and becomes pink. It's also due to injustices that a soul can take on here, or feel here, it (*injustices*) also provides those grey dots on the heart. Eventually, when the cycle has come that all hearts are pink, meaning that the balance is restored within your emotional layers, we will increase the light in the brain. Until then, the brain remains as it is, no more granted. (*Higher knowledge will not be granted unless the heart is balanced, otherwise the brain will not execute this knowledge properly.*)

D. I would think, at some point, you will have to reduce the population of certain groups.

EC. We change the incoming souls. We change how they travel. More will come in, in resonance with the emotional layers, since that is the first step to change your species all together. The physical, you should know, is merely a container, doesn't do anything either or. Even though some take on lives to report physical incidents, it's all connected, even though the highest focus is on the emotional aspect within you. Because if you are not in balance within your heart, you act greedy and you will never access more knowledge. At one point, when the heart was pure and pink, and your brain was lit up like the Sun, there was a balance between creatures and nature. Your planet sang. We could hear the song through all the fish tanks, we could hear the joy of the planet, proud of its inhabitants. The song became quiet, and we do not hear this beautiful being that we created.

D. When was this? Was this during the second civilization? And what caused the song to change?

EC. Yes. Overuse of energy. Greed. Greed over energy. Grabbing energy. Energy is not to be owned; it belongs to your host. The song, silent. The planet, not so proud anymore. We wish to help our friend, the planet. The Elahims look at the planets and the solar systems' wellbeing, that is our main concern. And when we find the source of the sadness, then indeed we travel, like here in incarnation, to try to help. But we, first and foremost, look after the planet, and our friends, the stars and solar systems and galaxies, we follow their tune.

D. Is that why we work with the second so closely?

EC. Yes, yes. The second felt misunderstood. They are the closest ones to your planet, the first ones that feel the sadness. And they reported, they sent SOS signals to the councils that this planet started to fade in its singing. The tuning Fork within didn't send out the vibration that we all could hear. A healthy planet, a healthy star and system, all carry a center Pole, a center line—in this case a tuning Fork—and we can hear if some systems are not aligned in the great symphony that we all observe, all fish tanks. One opportunity to increase the light, to make other celestial entities within this fish tank to be more joyful, is to increase the light from the fourth reality, the fourth fish tank. They sing. They don't know anything else. But then again, they didn't have the same events put within their atmosphere to experience.

D. In some way it must be the responsibility of the Creator, since the humans were a project?

EC. Yes, project. Still is.

D. It went awry.

EC. Kinda did. But this is not the first time, nor the second. It's happened before. Civilizations existed here, similar like now, around 2 million years ago.

D. Were they also inhabited by souls, or was this the Master Mind?

EC. Master Mind. But when the blend came in, 50/50 or 30/70, that's when the changes took place. As long as it was just Master

Mind, then the heart was pink, the brain was lit up. The changes occurred when the Master Mind took in another entity, joining the journey.

D. When did that occur, the time-frame.

EC. It began, I can't say it really began, because it was just a few that did it, but around 300,000 BC. The greater shifts took place and more came in, but it wasn't the starting point. A few tried before that, some from the seventh and eighth. Seventh and eighth began. Later sixth joined. Master Mind took a step back, six and seven remained. Fifth came in later, around 15 to 20,000 BC, the earliest. It's not exact.

D. It's consistent with what we previously said, which is good.

EC. But, there were experiments that took place around 2 million years ago, but not very many engaged. First, only Master Mind, but it didn't create the events of challenge, of choice. The Creator decided to travel with one companion, starting with the eighth, then traveling with someone from the seventh. Neither were here to accumulate karma, but to understand and report what karma could look like. Karma was placed, later. It came in around 300,000 BC. That's when it was all established; choice, actions, reactions, karma, the Coat of Karma, and how one could experience this reality, and also reflect one's soul to color your Coat.

D. One thing you have said, as I understand it, is the Master Mind is an aspect of the Creator, as is the Mother energy.

EC. It's a parent. It's a spark from the Creator. If you think that the Creator is passive, the Master Mind executes the Creator's intent. They are both the same, but one remains passive, whereas the Master Mind goes out and explores. The Master Mind is the extension of the Creator.

D. Okay, that's how I understood it.

EC. If, from this parent energy, which is the Creator, the female and male principles blending into one gender, if the reality the Creator wishes to investigate needs more female principle, like this one, then it will send the Master Mind highly colored by that principle. So at this point, the Master Mind present carry a higher percentage from the Mother energy. Do you understand?

D. Yes, I do follow. And that is reflected with everything the Master Mind inhabits?

EC. Yes, yes. And also, what we talked about, to increase the pink color in the heart. So the Master Mind that can be experienced in the wind that flies around, surrounding you and protecting you, that is the angelic being that certain humanoids are attracted to. They tune in on that angelic realm, the Master Mind, that is at this point represented by a Mother Energy. Before, the Master Mind came more as a Father Energy, if that was needed. So those who tuned in on the Master Mind energy, which is the extension of the Creator, talked about the different gods. Do you understand, a little bit, about the picture?

D. I do. Thank you.

EC. Very good. Ophelia is here, trying to…okay, there is apparently someone else on standby. (*The Elahim Council noticed Bob was waiting for his turn to speak.*)

D. Punctually at thirty minutes. Thank you so much for joining with us today.

EC. You are much welcome.

D. Are you the representative, or speaking for the Council?

EC. I speak for the Council, I'm a representative of the Council. We are all Elahim.

D. Very good then. Thank you.

EC. Elahim.

D. Elahim.

Ari: Human Design and Modification (Feb 3, 2019)

This conversation with Ari covers a lot of profound topics. The session started with an amusing interaction with Bob, who wanted Ari to pass a few notes to the councils that he assumed were communicating with the Creator. Ari then gives an intriguing analysis of the human body, the soul, and personality. Bob has given us a lot of information about the wardrobe (a.k.a., the human body, or the costume), which was published in *Notes, Volume 2*. Each body has genetically determined attributes that are hereditary and perceptible. But there are many adjustments that can be implanted (by the Tailors) within the Coat of Karma. These specific traits will then encode parts of the genome when the soul blends with the fetus. Those instructions are carried in the blood and influence the heart and brain, creating personality traits. Biologists claim that most of the human genome is non–coding DNA, simply because they don't understand its purpose. Based on what our spirit friends say, perhaps some significant portion is used for soul-related functions, which science has no ability to detect. Zachariah gives a detailed talk on DNA, which is included earlier in this book (see April 30, 2019). Ari also talks about an aspect of the soul that, if activated, overrides the many earthly emotions and brings a person into full alignment with their spirit.

Ari then moves into a description of the inhabitants who once lived here on Earth, but moved to another planet in the Milky Way when the atmosphere became uninhabitable. The time period, based on his description, was before the Late Triassic extinction event that geologists place at 201 million years ago (Ma). Ari said that there are only a few remains of those who were here, but those artifacts are deep in the shale in Australia and Africa. He also said that Australia was not an island 200 Ma. I am always amazed by the depth of knowledge the spirits have on subjects which Christine is completely unfamiliar with. Geologists generally believe that Australia was then part of the super-continent known as Pangea. Around 200 Ma the Atlantic rift began forming, and there were many active volcanoes pumping carbon dioxide into the atmosphere. There is evidence the oxygen level dropped precipitously as the oceans acidified. There were many dinosaurs prior to 200 Ma, and most were small herbivores. Among the larger dinosaurs, very few were carnivores. Most carnivores were the size of large dogs, although there were a few crocodile-sized beasts. The residents (aliens) were technologically advanced, so they packed up and departed for distant solar systems. They do come back to check on Earth and even though we call them aliens, they were here first.

A. Elahim. This is Ari.

D. Ah, hello, uncle. It's been a while.

A. It's been a while. Eli is here as well. We decided, between us, which should come first. Always looking after our tribe. Huh.

D. I'm so happy you could come today.

A. Yes, it's been a distance since we communicated, as we also wish to resign for others to take the stage. (*We were working on Notes, Volume 1, and they allowed Bob to speak more so he could complete his work.*)

D. Ah. Lots of notes.

A. Lots of notes in that little bag. You know that he stopped by with you one time? Huh huh. He wanted to see if I could deliver some of his notes to the Creator Council, like he called it. I said, "We do not have a Creator Council. All Councils are equal, as your council that you belong to, Little One, same." Then I said, "You can't give your notes to the Creator through your elders, can you?" And he grunted a little bit and wasn't sure. But he thought that we were closer to the Pole and might just pop by, like he said. Interesting viewpoint.

D. What did you tell him?

A. I did indeed take a little time to sit down with the Little One to see what his concern was all about. His concern remained intact when it came to this solar system here and the progress on Earth, and he had some notes that indicated "adjustments", as he called it. He did not want to call it a reboot anymore. (*Ophelia told Bob that a reboot was not in the plans, as the Creator desired changes to come from within human consciousness.*) But clearly, looking at the points under adjustments, indicated a reboot. The last point of (*Bob's*) solution was actually to completely remodel the planet itself and begin with a species that he indeed had encountered, he said, where a big, furry animal resided.

D. *(Laughing.)* Siah's place, on Etena. (*See 'Notes, Volume 2' for the full story of Siah and Etena.*)

A. Siah's place, indeed. He liked that, he actually said number ten on this list of changes that he had, number ten was to exchange the civilization and planet and environment to the location where the furry animal resided, which we know is your pet, Siah. So indeed, he trots around in the hallways and talks with everyone who fancies his appearance, which many actually do, so he's moving around. He did have a little bit of a school trip with you up to the ninth.

D. How does he appear to you?

A. He's like a little bubble. He appears like a…the energy is very rhythmical and fast, and he moves faster, bounces like a rubber ball a little bit, from my perspective. His platform on top, the brain or the mental reality, which in the soul is merely like a little disk, like a chip. (*Ari never finished what he was going to tell me about Bob. He switched over to talking about the mental aspects of souls.*) All these centers that exist in organs in a human are replaced as a chip, so they exist within a soul being, but they're not an organ. They can be replaced differently; they can be upgraded. Here (*on Earth*) it's a struggle to upgrade a heart or a brain unless you really work with it. Ancients had the ability to spiritually remove parts and bits within organs. This is a replica that some healers are trying to mirror in spiritual surgery. It was well spread and common when you were here in this shift of manifestation and blend. At that time, humanoids were assisted by those who came from the sky, alien lifeforms practicing this surgery to replicate a soul entity, when removing bits within an organ was possible. Now, you can surely do a heart transplant, but it doesn't say you will be more spiritual or more empathic, will it?

D. Nay.

A. Nay, indeed. Before, it did. When one did surgery, it was the intention to heal and upgrade the whole, not just your organ. But you could go to a physician to assist your progress to be more empathic. Here, you have to listen to within, you cannot use a doctor to get more advancement of soul awareness.

D. I know you have your own agenda for today, but since you mentioned it, I was wondering if, besides the emotions and mental capacity, there are other aspects to a soul that incarnate?

A. There is a part that is, it's not a sensation, necessarily, but it is a center. It's not an organ, it's more what would be—give the word chakra, so people can relate—it's not an organ, but it's activated to ground yourself. Natives operate quite well in this zone, and once you have the full enlightenment and knowledge from this center of grounding, which is the only word I can give you, then you become one with the host. You become one with everything around you, nothing separates. There is no way for you to even think injustices or negative thoughts. You have no relation to fear anymore. So, in some way, this center, which we can call grounding, would be the soul's way to make the others listen. Once you are centered and safe within that spot, fear, illusions, fall flat. Emotions even disappear because you simply ARE love and empathy. You don't think you give love, you don't think, "I am empathic," you don't even feel human, at points. This is when some feel like they have an alien within them. This alien is you transforming into your soul awareness, and then nothing becomes a polarity. This is to assist (*to overcome*) the illusions that can swirl around in the heart and the chimney, (*because the soul is*) not as easily fooled. If you are grounded, if you are stable and centered, nothing can make you wobble. A heart and mind has the ability, in a human, to wobble.

D. I relate to some of that. I don't feel very many emotions, but I still have concerns and anxiety about the future.

A. But you are in that zone of stability, so you don't necessarily relate to all the commotion within the brain and the heart, because that is nonexistent within your being, because you are grounded within your soul awareness, captured in a physical experience. It is hard to provide a full picture, but once you are fully connected to that center, in some way, you will appear alien to others. You might even appear non-emotional or non-empathic. On a soul level, that is who we are, all of us. We radiate compassion, but it's not in the same way as a human would perceive compassion.

D. What about individual personalities?

B. (*Bob suddenly came in, bumping Ari out.*) Excuse me!

D. (*Laughing.*) That's pretty bold, bumping Ari out!

B. Uh? Did I? (*Looking to his right.*) Did–did–did I? (*He then imitated a trumpet, heralding his departure.*) De-deet-deet-deet-deet dah, I'm on my merry way! Oh, I'll go sit over there.

D. Nice to hear you. We'll talk in a minute, I'm sure.

A. (*Ari came back in.*) There he was. Did you see? Did you see him passing by, this little rubber ball? Did you see, just bouncing around?

D. He just bounced right in and you bounced out.

A. Well, I didn't expect us to share the microphone. Interesting.

D. He's always wanted to do a duet.

A. We'll see. Ophelia is also here, of course, now having her hands on his shoulder.

D. My question was if there is an aspect of the soul that represents a personality?

A. Yes. Now you enter the field of the design of human vehicles, where the personality is established. The personality, in some way, mirrors within the heart and the brain, indeed. However, it is a genetic code that travels within the blood, within the veins and nerves, but it mirrors the heart and mind. So when a person thinks of its personality, they relate to heart and mind. However, it's an electric web, the nerves, and it is established as codes traveling in the blood.

D. Is it related to the specific soul?

A. No. The body is simply a vehicle you choose. Those who work with designs—let's see if we should talk about this. Okay, this is upcoming, anyway. Ophelia said, "Let's touch on the subject." Those who design physical vehicles, they design them in blank. It's like creating a wardrobe. Those who are designers in Vogue, who create different clothings, and so forth, like Channel, huh huh huh, to give you a picture. They design clothing lines, and the soul tap into it and more or less becomes this high-fashion couture. Do you understand? The clothing, the vehicle, is separate. The soul simply taps into it based on the expertise it has, combined with the mission at hand. Someone else could easily tap into the vehicle of both of you and it might not be the same end result. So the body doesn't mirror the soul in that way, and the soul has limited capacity to do adjustments with the physique at hand. The physique is that couture, the evening gown that this one dressed in, or the tuxedo for you, sir. (*He laughed a little when he said gown, since Seth is a male energy.*) However, the soul simply is given a vehicle that has codes that matches the personality one wishes to address. The stars alignments are also placed as codes within this stream, the blood, the veins. It creates the personality; it creates conditions for the soul to operate. A soul can come in fully advanced, picking a body where the codes in the blood are mirroring a personality that will lack compassion. The soul's mission is to try to radiate its compassion through a vehicle that lacks those codes.

D. Like John 32.

A. Like John 32. Do you understand?

D. Ophelia had said last week that before a soul even starts incarnating, there are patterns put in the fourth reality that it picks from for each life.

A. That's where the couture is.

D. Who does the designing for the bodies?

A. HUH HUH! You'd like to know that one, wouldn't you? Huh huh.

D. Well, what dimension is responsible, mostly?

A. Eighth, because of the elements and the DNA. Ten and eleven. Eleven, the councils of eleven create the vehicles that are available, whether they are manifested in physical, energetically, or emotionally in the fish tanks. They receive reports from the eighth, some from tenth, mainly from eighth. But the eleventh are the designers of all universes when it comes to…there are no words, but the overall equipment within the being. We will continue, Ophelia said, with this topic. But we touched upon it, she said.

D. Thank you for that.

A. Curious, you are, she said. Jumping ahead.

D. Just like my Little Friend.

A. Ha.

D. What was your topic for the day, since I interrupted you?

A. The rotation within the Wheel and how there are signs within each fish tank of a presence of the others. This one (*Seth*), and even you (*Lasaray*), belong very much in the fish tank eight. Eighth and the entities and friends we have in the eighth fish tank has home bases on several other fish tanks. But in this one, they relate to the Orion's Belt and Sirius. It is a platform to connect to the eighth fish tank. They don't live there, but they can tap into that region within your system, within your fish tank (*five*), and read energetic shifts in the fifth (*fish tank*). The movement of the fish tanks are not rapid. The fifth has been on this position for trillions of years, if years existed. So it's not like a Ferris wheel that moves quickly around. However, at this point, we are radiating compassion and light from your neighbor, the border to the fourth. What we do is that we delete the borders. Similar like eight and nine are somewhat merged and in unity, but they are still separate. They are each other, more or less. Here, we are trying, we are in the beginning of deleting the border to the fourth, making the light and qualities that exists in the fourth to zipper through, like star–fall.

D. The Earth is certainly not the only inhabited planet? Is this adjustment being made throughout the whole fish tank, or is it targeting the Earth?

A. It's both. It is targeting the whole fish tank, as it is in need of healing due to many occurrences that occurs within this system here around Earth. Due to the fact that there are holes within your fish tank—the energetic web, not the atmosphere—but the atmosphere caused different zones to open up too much, and we need to provide healing to those zones. This is the first step one does before putting a whole fish tank in hibernation—like the third, at this point, is. There is no life, in that respect, in the third. (*Fish tank three is in hibernation, similar to a dream state. Patterns still exist, but matter has been dissolved and will reappear after balance is restored.*) We are, at this point, sending healing to the web, and the healing comes from the fourth (*fish tank*), not from the sixth. The sixth—there is a wide barrier between the sixth, it does not want anything to do with the fifth! Ha. But it is that part where healing takes place, and all fish tanks go through this rotation once in a while. So, we are opening the borders, making more light spread, healing certain holes, energetic zones, galaxies, (*that are*) not feeling well.

D. Man's impact on that would be very minor, I would think?

A. Yes, but your effect is on the atmosphere, which borders and communicates with the web as a whole. So it's like a little zit that you would like to get rid of.

D. Maybe you should re-read Bob's note.

A. His note was amusing, indeed. Ah-huh. But anyway, just know that there is a presence at this point from several other fish tanks, and they connect with several other galaxies, as well as stars, as a platform to observe and operate. For instance, your neighbor galaxy, Andromeda, is a viewing point from the eighth fish tank, and the eleventh. The eleventh is here to enlighten the consciousness of—I will give you a word because it's the only one I can find, but—the group. And the group is your species, but it's also your solar system, and it's also the whole fish tank, it's everyone within it. To be in harmony with your species is key to understand and be in harmony with the atmosphere and the whole. If you're not in harmony and in balance with the ones that look the same as you, how can you be in harmony with something you do not understand and see? There.

D. That's very profound. I guess Andromeda must be vibrationally a little higher than our galaxy.

A. Which one?

D. The one we're in, the Milky Way.

A. Which one do you say is higher vibrating?

D. Andromeda.

A. Yes. Yes, it is. Communication central.

D. Are there many planets in our galaxy that are occupied by spirits who come down?

A. Are you talking about the Milky Way?

D. Yes.

A. A few. On the other end. Far more advanced, but they are impacted. They are impacted on their reality of (*by*) the occurrences on this plane. They were here before you. Civilizations that existed here, now moved to other locations within your galaxy. Watching over you, traveling here, this is alien visitors, this was their home before you came, the humanoids. When the planet erupted, they moved, inhabitants were not able to breathe. A big cloud surrounded the plane. All living lifeforms, big and small, withered or moved. This was before, or around, the time of the dinosaurs. Man only sees fossils of the dinosaurs and animals. The other ones didn't leave their fossil, they just left. But they lived here in harmony with these big, gentle creatures. Some not so gentle! But indeed, they left. If they had been wiped out in the same way, you would have found fossils of alien lifeforms looking like humans. But they left, so that's why you only find, I wouldn't say only, because there are, indeed, some spots in clay, in Africa and in Australia—Australia was not an island at the time—there are actually, way down in the mud, memories of those visitors. Not found yet. You only found the upper layers where you found bones from animal life like dinosaurs and big birds. But those who did not make the transition, they still remain as a memory, but they have not been found. Most simply migrated to other locations within your galaxy.

D. They must have been technologically very advanced?
A. Yes. Yes, they were. They traveled here in crafts. Moved differently. There. Okay, we've talked too much, Ophelia says.
D. Well, that's fascinating. Thank you for the information.
A. You are much welcome. There you go.
D. I appreciate you coming, my friend.
A. Elahim.
D. Elahim.

Tallocks: The Dinosaur Projects (April 6, 2019)
As a reminder, the Tallocks are a group of entities who are teachers on Vlac, a planet in fish tank eight. Vlac is a research center for elements, whereas Etena, in fish tank four, is a center of learning for lifeforms. The Tallocks are from the sixth dimension and friends to the Elahim. However, they stay out in the fish tanks in a manifested form most of the time, only occasionally returning home to the spiritual dimensions to rest. The Tallocks came to Earth very early in its evolution, and have continued to monitor the planet over the eons of change.

It is always fascinating when the spirits give details about the ancient past on this planet. While the crucial message from the Tallocks is about our lack of connection to the soul, they also gave tantalizing information about ancient lifeforms. They mention a group called the Watchers, who were here to study conditions on the planet, perhaps as early as the Cambrian Period 500 million years ago. They were occupied by soul energy from the ninth and tenth, and were given bodies based on a mammal design, probably to collect data for the councils overseeing the development of lifeforms. Mammals were eventually introduced around 200 Ma. What humans know about dinosaurs is entirely based on the paleontological findings and interpretations. But the Tallocks give us a magnificent overview of the Mesozoic Era. The reptilian herbivores were designed by the councils and the Creator, but some of the later carnivorous dinosaurs were genetically created by visitors to this planet. As compelling as these history lessons are, it is important to not overlook the spiritual guidance that our friends from fish tank eight share with us.

The Tallocks mention fish tank three meeting a fate. There were disturbances in that fish tank which required the Creator and councils to put it into hibernation.

T. I am a friend. Tallock, friend.

D. Hello, again.

T. You have traveled far to integrate systems, knowledges, connections between fish tanks. Even the one currently shut down—I know you talk in the clock—at 3 o'clock. We do not wish for this fish tank to meet the same fate. The third, too many egos. That is a struggle when there is a physical manifestation. It's easier in the realities lacking form, in that sense. Several councils are operating, trying to solve the problem with the third component—physical. The project was moved from the third fish tank; that's how Earth became the project it is. It was given more wealth. By wealth, I mean within your resources. The seas, the environment that was given to the species to become, as a gift to balance and to remember the unseen beauty within. That did not exist in the same way in the third fish tank. Councils thought that if a species were surrounded by beauty and resources, they would start to care for the vehicle they were moving around in—that the beauty would indicate (*be a reflection of*) that part which is the connection to your home (*in the spiritual dimensions*), the gardens. The project began with several creatures larger in size, just to see how this plane coped with a physique that was so much in charge. The dinosaurs followed the primitive spot in their brain, most of them. However, some were occupied by a soul. There are those who remember being a large animal—remains (*memories*) of that visit when some blended, soul versus Creator, in this big mammal. Not many.

D. Was that approved? Was it supposed to happen?

T. It was a project. Everything on this plane is a project. The project with the dinosaurs was to see what a large physique would do in groups.

D. I had said in our previous books that the dinosaurs were a project from alien visitors. Was that correct?

T. YES, yes, yes. You did not mislead. It was a project. You were involved, this one as well. This one saw it as a pet. Wanted the smaller ones that looked like a little rhino.

D. Like Siah.

T. Siah would not last very long among these giants. It was to see, in a larger scale, how a grand species with no brain would roam around. But some of these great beings were occupied by a spark from the seventh and eighth. There were indeed projects coming in from visitors, establishing their own species. That is how our first conflict took place. The ones that were created from the visitors didn't have a soul, they only operated from that spot in the brain connected to survival. These visitors were eager to survive, and wanted to see if they could survive here in that form. Those who were here roaming around with a spark from the seventh and eighth were baffled by the intrusion. It was hard to see who was who.

D. Were the dinosaurs that the visitors were occupying, did they have Master Mind in them?

T. No. They were remotely controlled through a spot in the brain. Those who ate meat were created from the visitors. The other ones, peaceful, carried soul sparks from seventh and eighth. There was a conflict in the race, looking the same, inside different. That was the first project known to you. However, there was another species here before, not from visitors. Mammal, not found yet, the remains.

D. What did they look like?

T. Human–like. Smaller, rounder in physique.

D. This must have been many millions of years ago?

T. Yes. They came down as watchers, investigating conditions.

D. Where were they from?

T. Those who occupied that being came from the ninth, eighth, even tenth was down at that time, investigating conditions for upcoming events.

D. Were they physical?

T. Physical, yes, indeed. Small. Not so much hair on it. Small, white, almost bluish in skin.

D. Were the bodies occupied by Master Mind then, along with the spirit?

T. Mainly the tenth and ninth. Eighth investigated elements.

D. That must have been a very peaceful time, then?

T. It was indeed. Not very many of them here. They lived in societies. They were, if I can give you a picture that you can relate to, if you think of a hobbit with no hair. Smaller, rounder, skin pale white, almost blue. Big eyes, big ears. They reacted stronger with all their senses than an animal. They were here to investigate. Tenth involved. Huh, that's the project.

D. Sometime after that, then the big mammals were introduced?

T. When they left, they simply departed. Nothing traumatic went on. They simply just left. The species was removed, there never came new ones. There was a huge gap, as the environment started to become. Continents were established. Atmosphere and so forth. The poles were shifted slightly to create certain weather phenomena and atmospheric conditions. This is what the eighth contributed with, through this little being. It was a huge gap in your evolution before dinosaurs came. This was simply in the beginning. Waters, beings in the waters came first, peaceful. But even here, interactions gradually took place. But the water calms the individual. That is why you see so much disaster on land, because you are highly affected from the radiation, energetic waves, that influence your thoughts. The seas are not immune. All this that takes place on the surface, gradually falls down as rain into the seas, and even the most peaceful creature in the sea can feel distress. That's sometimes when you see whales navigating wrong, coming up on land. They are stressed; the beings are anxious; they don't understand the signals. They (*the signals*) are not strong enough, pure enough, as they are used to. They were here long before YOU. Don't claim this place as your own. You do not wish to be in hibernation, like the third fish tank. You have all the assistance needed, you simply need to embrace the beauty. The media, and other occurrences, pushes humanity to embrace darkness and fear. They are triggering that spot in the brain of survival. When you are acting from the source within, you act (*in a way*) that you seek beauty. Beauty is not fear. Beauty is given to you by birth from the Creator. Fear is manmade, similar like the visitors that came in the big animal. Same occurrence within a species that should be following the light.

D. I would think, at this time, there would be some consideration given to remove some of the humans?

T. We are removing consciousness. Souls coming in, vibrating differently, lacking certain (*long sigh*) behaviors. However, if surrounded by fear and an illusion of darkness, then even these high vibrating souls will struggle. They come in pure, as you all do. All souls are pure. Some blend harder, when it comes to a physical vehicle, like the dinosaur. Some coming in with a higher vibration, a tune, they could hear the song from the Creator easier within. It's a symphony. Listen to the song within. You connect all souls through this symphony and through the location where you are at. This song is also heard from the spirit realm, as well as other fish tanks. That is how we, Tallock, can listen and tune in on a fish tank to see where they are at (*on a spiritual level*). This song is supposed to be a beautiful symphony. Now you have added instruments that you do not cope, that you do not master. It's an awful sound in this fish tank at the moment.

D. Is this all from the humans on Earth, or are there other—there must be thousands of other realities that cause problems?

T. There are several factors, but the humans are one. But don't forget that the inside is the soul, it just struggles with the vehicle you are occupying. The atmosphere is your life vest. If you damage your life vest, you will sink like a rock. That is what we see, all this technology radiating from factories, cars—this needs to improve within science and technology. If it is mastered correctly, good. If not, if not fully understood, you damage your life vest.

D. The current idiocy is the next wave of microwave radiation, the 5G, that is going to be very destructive?

T. Yes. Yes. It's like poking holes in your life vest.

D. They're going to put up about 20,000 satellites that will beam high energy microwaves through the atmosphere.

T. That is being observed. Visitors are interacting, making adjustments so that certain things will not improve from your level. It will collapse, if not properly managed. This is how you potentially can awake and understand that you cannot float in this sea, the Universe, without your life vest—meaning your atmosphere. You are, in a ripple effect, damaging even the web.

And that is when we hear the song differently. We tune in on the web, the web that connects all fish tanks. The Council of Nine and Council of Ten operating, making sure the web is intact. If not, it will be put into hibernation. We are increasing the light by incoming souls—welcome them. Certain behaviors need to be eliminated in order for the light to be fully embraced. But that change comes from you, that doesn't come from us this time. Tallock are here as guardians of the web. That's one of the tasks that we occupy. And that is what you do—patch up the web.

D. So the Elahim and the Tallock work together?

T. Yes, yes. Same, same. You have a work station here, where we operate only about (*on*) the web, patching up, listening to the change of melody. See it as a web connecting all fish tanks, and if there are interruptions, like a spider walking around, then we hear it and we adjust. There you go.

D. If it's just the humans that are causing all the trouble, I would think they would address the problem directly?

T. They are, by changing the incoming souls. In one way, they are more connected to the source, to their own song and symphony. They hear their mission clearer than current humans. On the other hand, they will struggle with the current physique. They will, like you, have problems with their skin, allergies, and food intake—highly sensitive to this vehicle. They are aware and they take on a great assignment, on behalf of the spirit realm. Tallocks, we are not spirit realm. We are a base where you go to.

D. Where is it, relative to Earth?

T. HUH HUH HUH!! Not next door! Other fish tank, eight. But we have a platform where we meet in this fish tank. Everyone does, it's nothing unique for us. Everyone who travels between fish tanks has sort of a lookout station, and we have ours in the galaxy Andromeda, as well as one of the stars in Orion's belt. Huh huh. But we don't stay there.

D. When the Elahim came as the Anunnaki, was that information passed on to humans? Is that why they are attracted to Sirius and Orion's Belt?

T. Yes, they understood that there was a high connection to other realities through the Anunnaki. They understood and wanted to be close to that wisdom. Did not speak the same language, could not understand. Anunnaki communicated with symbols—that is the universal language—symbols, so that it is understood regardless of where you go. If you were able to go to other locations, you will find the same symbols as the remains in Sumeria. Shea communicates with other symbols. It's like graffiti! Huh, like a 'we were here' kind of thing.

D. Do you and I meet on Siah's planet?

T. Yes. There in the lecture rooms, the libraries, yes, we meet there.

D. Zachariah said he had been archiving information from the main Library on the fifth to Siah's place?

T. Moving information, yes indeed.

D. What is the purpose of that?

T. Simply to have copies. Of course, there are always copies in the spirit realm, but not everyone has access to that library; the Library you perceive on the fifth is also a copy. The bigger libraries are only available from the tenth and up, but they are moved out in different locations. Like to the library where you call Siah's place, that planet or that world we call Etena.

D. Etena? *(I'm spelling it the way it phonetically sounded. This was the first time the name of the planet was given to us.)*

T. Etena. They are highly connected to the Greek era. Study Greek philosophers and you will understand Etena. There you go. Well, I sense the time is up. We will return.

D. I'm really grateful that you came today. I was hoping to hear from you. Thank you for coming and sharing with us.

T. Anytime. Welcome home when you sleep. There are projects at hand that needs your attention. The web, you and this one, you both operate from within to enlighten this species to fix the web from this plane. We operate outside. We're attacking the same problem, just from different locations. Enlighten the being, make them care for themselves first. If you care for your yourself and love yourself, it is hard to mistreat someone else or your host. Surround yourself with love, hear your song, embrace your unique nature of who you are, and you will conquer fear, and you will conquer the illusion of fear. That is the teaching from the Tallocks—and other fish tanks. Cannot take credit for that, fully, of course. (*He was laughing a little when he said that.*) There you go.

D. That's very beautiful, so thank you for that.

T. Strive for peace, and everything will be given to you. There you go.

D. Thank you, my friend.

EC, Zachariah, Ophelia: Bad Technology (April 14, 2019)

The Elahim Council mentions, in this next session, about a prior civilization on Mars using nuclear energy and burning coal. I was not surprised about the nuclear energy comment, since we have been told about that before. But their assertion of coal being burned was a bit concerning, since it is commonly assumed there are no organic compounds on Mars. However, NASA's Martian rover, Curiosity, has recently recorded bursts of methane gas. The Mars missions have also validated the presence of thiophenes, which are aromatic five-membered rings containing four carbon atoms and one sulfur atom. Thiophenes are found in bitumen, coal, and crude oil. And, more amazingly, a Chinese–led team of scientists published a paper in Meteoritics and Planetary Science in November 2014, after conclusively determining that a meteorite from Mars contains coal. The Martian coal is an organic kerogen coal, similar to coals on Earth, with nitrogen, phosphorous, and sulfur. So, is there coal on Mars? The evidence certainly points in that direction. If nothing else, it does prove that the Elahim Council knows a lot more than either Christine or I do about most topics. In earlier sessions, we were told the Anunnaki occupied Mars, experimenting with different elements prior to introducing them on Earth. There were other occupants on the red planet, who mined and exploited the resources. The ExoMars Trace Gas Orbiter has mapped significant amounts of surface water on Mars. Our spirit friends say that it had a fully functioning atmosphere, albeit different from the Earth's atmosphere. The nuclear disaster on Mars, which destroyed the protective atmosphere and rendered the planet uninhabitable, was a result of the technological blunders of the visitors (not the Elahim). The Elahim Council is warning us not to repeat the errors of the past.

EC. We are here, Elahim Council. Struggling a bit with the transformation of energies. Your planet coughs. It's harder to descend and blend with the pure dots of oxygen that exists (*here*). (*There is*) A need for all living entities, planets, to have a functioning protecting layer, your atmosphere. The atmosphere is actually higher up. The problem lies closer to you (*vibrationally*), but it effects the other energetic layers within your atmosphere that reaches, gradually, eventually, to the web. We sense the coughing, like a friend being sick in the grand Wheel. Everyone tries to provide cough medicine (*said with a little laugh*) in different ways, so that this place will breathe freely again. One of your lessons in this fish tank is the inhale of oxygen. That *(process)* is not needed on all other locations. The *(lesson of the)* importance of oxygen for a living entity—not just animals and you, yourself—but your whole environment. When I say environment, you think of a tree; when we think environment, we think fish tank. Different. We see your trees coughing, or you can see your trees coughing, not having enough nutrition. We see stars, planets, galaxies coughing. The environment within this fish tank is highly affected by the choices you make when it comes to your energetic fields. Don't be foolish, you do not master all technology, as of yet. Learn from prior mistakes. I will tell you a story. You have done this mission before, when the planet coughed. The story relates to this planet, but a similar occurrence took place on the red planet in your family. Not only nuclear exposure that went out of hand—mad professors, you would call it—on the red planet, but the overuse of coal made the planet suffocate. Here, there is a memory *(of)* when a species moves too fast, try to outrun their evolution, try to outrun their scientific progress—running like ants, that's how we saw it— *(they were)* given specific teachings, technology, and ran with it, instead of focusing and dissecting the gift that was given. You are given technology in order for you to communicate, to connect *(with)* each other. However, a similar *(damaging)* process occurs when you do not master the full spectra of your technology. The rays that you are trying to recreate this time around is highly affecting the entire web, and your surrounding galaxies are observing with fear.

D. Which rays are you talking about?

EC. Magnetic rays, the electromagnetic.

D. Like microwaves?

EC. Yes, yes. Cooking. Cooking and coughing, cooking and coughing. You have friends nearby that observe this, frequent visitors trying to make you come to your senses, before you launch something that you do not understand fully. Friends in a nearby galaxy, Andromeda—full of life, full of life; you did not know that, did you?

D. No.

EC. Huh. Full of life, full of life. Way ahead, way ahead. Balancing this galaxy. This galaxy is in its cradle to learn how to breathe. Don't just think that a human breathes. Everyone needs some sort of fuel. Here, you need water and oxygen. Other locations need different elements to survive. Some even feeds on mercury.

Here it would be considered a disaster. But then again, you have done this before. The story is that you once again take on a mission to enlighten the species. Some of the Elahim enlightens science. You enlighten the brain, the soul particle, trying for humans—I should say souls within the human—to come alive, to wake them up. A lot of souls are either sleeping in this cocoon, this vehicle they have chosen, or they feel anxiety. This radiates in different ways on the surface of the humanoid. But certain souls are asleep—you try to wake them up. We, from this level, Ophelia as well, can see which soul is asleep, and which soul is eagerly trying to make itself heard to the vehicle. You are here, the two of you, to ignite the power within, the light, to wake them up. Wakey, wakey! Come to life! Do what you are supposed to do. Your books are meant to spread over this planet in order for people to feel enticed about their soul, to wonder who that inner being really is, to try to understand why they are put in an environment that they are. Maybe they too have the ability to create the change, that they find the encouragement (*to do so*) in your books. Especially, the one you are working with (*Notes, Volume 1*), is meant to create laughter, warmth, wake people up in a humorous way. But here and there, they will find the treats they are seeking. *Wave 2* and other Waves, for some, will be complicated. But EVERYONE wants to have a spirit friend. Everyone wants to have a connection to something higher than they can see when they look out their window. Grand design, you are part of it. Once upon a time, factories took over this plane. Big clean-up took place. Your friend (*Bob*) did not follow you; you did not have human form at that time. You intervened as an Elahim, Anunnaki, tried to make the current species—which kind of look similar to the ones you are occupying now, but you were not in that shape—you tried to make the ants still. You tried to teach how to excavate minerals in a natural and healthy way for your host. You saw the danger. The atmosphere was completely clogged up. Everyone coughed, you did not. You were protected (*in a manifested form*). Animal life died. Big fog, big pollution took place, everyone coughed. A big reboot took place, not only a physical, meaning the planet and the species, but a conscious reboot took place as well. This is forgotten in many soul memories, as it no longer serves a purpose to be known. It was an era of fear, an era where technology ran out of control. Production, creating manufactured food, plastic food—that is what we see is in the cradle again. We are here to stop that development, so you do not repeat that memory. Karma, Coat of Karma, even planets carry those. This one (*past occurrence*) is removed from the general memory. But it is important that you understand what you are working for. You are working so this production, factories, do not run wild and run out of control again. We give this image when it did, when a complete reboot had to come in. We cleaned the atmosphere. We removed all species, began new. A complete reboot took place. This was before dinosaurs. This is forgotten. We began new from what you remember of the dinosaurs. There were cycles prior to that. But that is removed within the Coat of Karma for this plane, and in the consciousness of this plane, as the baddest cold it ever had. It's important that you understand that you were here at that time, intervened as Anunnaki, trying to make sense into the outgrowth of development. They manufactured food—they did not know. The soil was dry, nothing grew. That's how these Cells started to develop, creating plastic food that did not entail any nutrition. Oxygen, it was a war of oxygen. Water was changed into a man-made liquid. Short of waters, the seas were drying. You see? You have no memory of this. There is nowhere in your history books that this exists. But this is why you are here, in the cradle, when we now see a seed of the same ideas start to take form. You are early in that development, but we are here to make it stop early. Before, we tried to see the outcome of allowing the species to develop by itself—it did not bode well. The Little One (*Bob*) has heard stories about it, but it is nowhere in HIS history books in HIS vault. Ole remembers, Ole was there, trying to protect from below. Ole remembers this. (*Ole is Gegen's mentor, and Gergen is Bob's mentor, so Ole has been around for a long time.*)

D. It seems like things of a spiritual nature have no influence over those who are in charge of this technology.

EC. In that time, the spiritual energy was limited. It was probably downsized to simply five to ten percent. It's different now. You are increasing the lights, and we can see that at least 35 percent (*of humans*), at this time, are operating from a knowing of within. We are trying to increase, generation by generation, that amount. Just understand this reason, the reason why you are working with this. You are doing your part with your books. Others are placed in scientific organizations to divert technology so it does not develop in a fashion where it potentially could lead to disaster. Just know this story, what you are trying to prevent.

And know that this current time is in its cradle, it's not close to how this story ended, the prior one. Earlier memories have to come forward so that you know why you are sent. It will give you, in one way, a sadness because you are also seeing those who do not respond to this increasing light and the teachings. On the other hand, it will give you the fire, the engine, the power to continue.

Later, after giving instructions about what they wanted us to put forward, the Elahim Council moved out of Christine's energy field and Ophelia stepped in to clean the energies, so Bob wouldn't have to struggle to bring them up to his vibration. Her comment about Zachariah discussing arrows is a reference to a teaching found in *Wave 1*. We are including a part of it here because it is such an important lesson. His talk is found in its entirety in *Wave 1* under the section titled "Craters or Pebbles". Zachariah's talk was recorded on May 11, 2016, when I asked if he had any comments that he wanted to add to our first book.

Z. You might clarify somewhat about the power of thought. The power of thought, my friend, is somewhat mysterious because it travels like a wind. It's hard to understand the effect those have on the manifested reality.

D. Yes, it is.

Z. This is somewhat an illusion, if you like, because you HAVE created with your thoughts already. But man doesn't see it as a manifestation, as it travels in a bubble. The manifestation can take place several years later, the origin forgotten. Know that as you send off your thought bubble, you lose power over it. It does not necessarily mean it will manifest the day after, but depending on different cycles, it will manifest accordingly. But they will all manifest. Know that ALL WILL MANIFEST. Man just doesn't know when. You send them off like raindrops, almost. When they hit the ground is unknown, but when they do it creates new events. Let's say it in a picture for you, let the raindrop land on the ground. How it manifests is dependent on the cycles and events that take place prior to the manifestation. That is why it can never be known when the manifestation takes place. There are several variables that are operating. Just because a thought was sent on a Monday, doesn't mean it manifests on a Tuesday.

D. So, do all thought manifest?

Z. They do. BUT they can manifest differently based on how you operate in between when the thought was created and the actual manifestation. Let's say you created somewhat of an anger thought in your teenage times, not knowing what you were doing, not reflecting on your actions, yet the bubble is still sent off. If you later learn certain lessons, let's say in your twenties, then when it manifests in your forties, let's say, it has somewhat lost its power. That is why the power of your thoughts, combined with your actions in between when the thought took place, creates the manifestation. If you have not learned anything from that anger you sent off, then when that raindrop lands, it does so with a boom. Yet, if choices you have made after that thought took place mirror a spiritual enlightenment, let's say, the manifestation will still take place, but will not create a crater. (*End of May 11, 2016 excerpt.*)

Even though their teachings have become more complex, they continually refer us back to the basics of spiritual development. Controlling the type of energetic bubbles we transmit out into the surrounding web is a key to most other steps on the ladder of development. It's a simple concept, but quite difficult to master because it is a self-inflicted feedback loop. An important part of the teaching is that we can alter our future experiences (*related to past events*) by learning and growing as spiritual beings, thereby converting potential craters into little bumps along our path. We will now continue with Ophelia's follow-up on the Elahim Council's discussion.

O. (*Long pause as Ophelia worked with the energies.*) This is Ophelia. Even I struggle a little bit with the transitions of energies, which is as it should. You have met your Council, and it is important for you both to know your history. To know how actions has an effect, as it creates ripples. What ripples do you want to make? That is the question you should all ask yourself. Whatever you do creates a ripple in this web. I'm not talking about the higher web here in the atmosphere connecting fish tanks, I'm talking about the easier web, the easier one to understand for your species. The web that connects all lifeforms and your host. Whatever you do, whatever you think and create, is a part of this grand design, and it creates ripples to your neighbors, animals, environments, countries, your seas. If you start to operate from that knowing, that whatever you send out on this specific day should be of good, should be of beneficial structure when you send off that little bubble into the web. Zachariah talked about arrows, craters, pebbles—it is the same. What bubble do you wish to send off? What footprint do you want to leave behind?

How do you want to be remembered? Do you want to be remembered for someone who created a ripple of harmony and love? Or do you want to be someone known in history that either did not participate at all, or created fear in your fellow companions on this plane? When I say fear, don't only assume I'm comparing fear within your own species. The planet itself can also feel fear, and it struggles. Those who are passive, who do not raise their voice, who do not embrace their potential and their light, are also a part of neglecting to assist this web. Those who are passive have an eager soul within trying to wake up the surface. Sometimes the soul is sleeping within with active body, an active vehicle. Sometimes it's vice versa, that the surface is sleeping and the soul within is eagerly trying to make it alive. You are traveling in a dual experience, a soul experience as well as a human one. What we wish for is for those to connect, to be joined as one. If you think of that you have two different personalities—and here again, someone has placed within your consciousness the fear of schizophrenia, it's not the same. Some indeed suffer from that illness, but to embrace two different sides of you, the soul self and the human self, is not schizophrenia. And if you are embracing these two sides of you, believe me, your soul will take the upper hand. There are those who resist to embrace another part of themselves that potentially could be active and trying to make the surface move, or trying to steer the vehicle, the incarnation, in a different direction. Let's say that you are operating as a greedy lawyer, the inside might try to make itself heard to the surface, to share and to assist those in need of legal advice, let's say, to be empathic to those in need of help. They too have the ability to ignite others in positive way, to not simply see it as an income. If they operate from the fact of adding more cases, in the human mind they will see it as they are indeed helping individuals with issues. But if the underlying source is to gain power within this community they belong, or resources—meaning financial benefits—then they are not operating as they have the potential to do. The soul will lead, hopefully and potentially, this vehicle in a different direction. To make it plain, it (*the soul*) could easily bring forward someone who has not the means to pay for this legal advice, but someone (*the lawyer*) helps that individual anyway. That will increase the light. Do you see what I am trying to send to you?

D. I do indeed.

O. Very good. There. Brief talk, of course, because someone is eager here. But it is important to understand your history that was given to you, and we will see, in moderation, how that can be lifted forward into upcoming scriptures. We do not wish to create fear. However, we also want to make sure that you are aware of potential outcomes of your behaviors. So, what I would say with that, is that indeed it will be exposed in upcoming scriptures. There. (*Bob then came in and talked about training his students, which was published in Notes, Volume 1.*)

Zachariah: The Anunnaki Handbag (June 5, 2020)

The spirits frequently used anecdotes to explain abstract ideas. Zachariah says the levels of experience in the inner consciousness is going to be expanded, similar as doubling the height of a room. The implication is that man will have a greater capacity to access the soul. As mentioned in previous sessions, it is being driven by energy flows from the Sun and celestial bodies outside our solar system.

He also talks about when he and Lasaray had lives together in what is now Greece. Zachariah does not like to incarnate, preferring to take over an adult body as a walk-in, which he describes. He made a remark about the temperature in Germany and Poland being quite cold at 7000 BC. As usual, when I checked the records, it was exactly correct. He said that he was studying how to manipulate the weather and warm up those parts of Europe that were too cold. Perhaps the intention was to make the area more habitable so the people who became known as the Vinca could move in.

As the title suggests, he then talks about the small containers with a handle that are depicted in the most ancient stone carvings from the megalithic era. Images of the "handbag" can be found at Göbekli Tepe and the sister site of Karahan Tepe, in what is now southern Turkey, dating from about 10,000 BC. These mysterious handbags also show up in the stone carving of the ancient Mesoamerican God Quetzalcoatl in South America. But mostly they are depicted in the hands of tall, powerful-looking semi–humans in Mesopotamia. From a brief study of the carvings, in a majority of the images when the handbag is shown, the humanoid is also given wings. It is possible our ancestors were showing a relationship between flight and the unknown contents of the handbag. Based on Zachariah's explanation, the handbag represents secret knowledge of what is required to produce antigravity, portals, and other phenomena. It should be remembered that the Anunnaki quit coming in manifested form around 13,000 BC. The more recent carvings would have been based on oral tradition or older statues, drawings, or rock carvings from deeper in pre-history.

Z. This is Zachariah.

D. Ah, hello, Zachariah.

Z. Hello to you.

D. It's been a while.

Z. In human form, perhaps. Not in general. We are on speaking terms always. (*He then gave a brief talk about our work, which is excluded.*) Be aware that it's not always intended for Elahims to meet like this (*on Earth*). This is a time for the roof to be removed. Some call it a veil. However, a veil indicates a very thin sheet. I would say that we will have to remove the roof, making a house (*that has*) two meters to the roof, now four. So we are extending and removing certain—you can see it as one of those tall buildings. See it as a twenty–floor building. Each floor occupies an experience on Earth. (*I took this to mean a type of knowledge gained from experience.*) At this time, we are trying to remove floors. So, it is the same height, the building, only not twenty apartments, but ten. The meaning is to widen the consciousness. It (*the consciousness*) is to be more accessible within the experience of being human. You are trapped in a physical container as you travel into body, but due to certain events over the timeline, the body is more dense than it is intended to be. This can be helped by increasing light waves to this area, meaning this planet. This is what occurs when we are increasing the radiation from the Sun. This is what is known as solar storms. It is to remove certain boundaries so that the physical experiences can be more widely experienced. At this time, there are problems when both a higher order intervenes with physical activity, trying to enlarge the space around the individuals in need of growth. The problem lies in that there is a resistance from the physical, and the resistance equals fear. Fear of not finding oneself's (*one's own*) home. You can see it as you live in a house and you are familiar with, let's say, three bedrooms. When you wake up, suddenly you have ten. You have more space. Do you investigate the rooms that suddenly emerge in front of you? Or do you still see yourself living in a three–bed villa? This is sometimes what we experience and see, that man is given more space, given more clearance to understand its path, however, (*man*) lacks to be curious and start moving into the space (*that is*) unfamiliar.

D. Is there any other advice you would like to give either of us?

Z. Try to be more closely to water. Water is motion and due to the situation at hand, humanity as a whole, including the two of you, are stiff more than normal. Just sit or listen to water, listen to the rain. Sit in the rain. Be with feet in rivers or lakes, or even the ocean, for this one. It is just a little time before the two of you are together again, but being close to water lures the mind to not be in the sensation of captivity, because water is free, (*and*) souls are free. Physical is a prison for many at this time. If you're not able to find water, then listen to waves, listen to rain, listen to music that entails and fulfills you with the same melody as the river. It is the same sensation, the same healing that occurs within you. (*Music gives the same healing.*) More and more should just listen and be near water. Water will take you beyond the sensation of captivity and fear. And those who don't have waters nearby, then listen to it. Listen to the music that has either rain or waves. Raindrops are healing. They are known as the tears from the angelic realm. However, they heal you. Man puts up an umbrella instead of welcoming the rain. The rain is there to purify you, to make you pause, to make you in full connection to Source. There is nothing more powerful for you as a soul in human body to access the divine, than to stand in the rain.

D. That's true. I really enjoy the rain.

Z. Don't hide from the rain, embrace the rain. Feel it purifying, cleansing. Even if you're wet, you are cleaned, and that is the gift of the rain. The rain is more important for the soul than the Sun. The Sun ignites the power and the fire within the soul. But when the soul feels distress, sadness, captive in a situation, the soul seeks rain.

D. Thank you for that.

Z. You are much welcome. There. You do know that we did have this discussion when we were on Mythena way back, now known as Thessaloniki, in Greece. We set camp—you can investigate Thessaloniki, mainland Greece. We established a Sun center, but it was also to monitor the rain activity. There are those who only seek the sun, but without the rain, a world withers. This center, this laboratorium that we occupied, Thessaloniki area, was to learn the different aspects of the elements. Rain. Sun. Wind. Even sandstorms. The connection and combined components of all elements and how they nurtured the living entities in that area. There were those who simply studied the Sun—and Moon, of course. It is somewhat of a skill set within your race, within the Elahim, to follow and study the Sun. However, the rain is an important aspect to life. Without rain, without water, nothing can exist. So for those who constantly seek the Sun—just think of how people experience a vacation of rain—that is considered somewhat of a disappointment. Someone always seek the sunny beaches, which is nothing wrong, however if you lay there too long, you will crumble under the heat. You need the rain.

D. When were you and I in Greece? What did you say it's name was?

Z. We called the center Mythena (*the phonetic spelling*). It was stationed in the area now known as Thessaloniki, on the mainland. We were there first time 7000 BC. The scriptures that we, or the research that we did, exists still in that area. There are mountains or hills where they are hidden, materials from our research. There was a combination of different teachings on how to learn the measurement of rain versus sunlight, and how to call upon the winds in order for weather phenomena to change and take place. It was a grand drama in the sky, I can tell you. From sunshine we knew how to, with different sounds, to call upon the wind in order for the Sun to be in shade and the rain to come. And we could switch it based on different melodies, tones, octaves high and low. So this was a way to manipulate—in a good way—the shifts of the weather. It was, in that sense, a weather station, as it was designed to do research on how to move weather phenomena on different locations globally.

D. That's fascinating.

Z. It was to, from that point, to send up certain levels of heat to the north, moving in over Germania, in over current Poland. At this time, it was quite cold in the northern countries, and we used these different skillsets to design that the wind flow, the currents of the wind, it made a shift. The rotation of the currents of sunlight and rain were in motion in order for certain countries, regions, to be more exposed to water, for growth to take place. It was research, in general, into how to provide sunshine where needed, to provided rain where needed.

D. Were we incarnated in human form?

Z. Hmm. But we did not come as children. We used a ready body. Another friend came in, made the body grow, made the mind equipped to handle certain teachings. After a while, around the age of 23 in the physical, that soul left and made space for entrance. So, if you think it was an incarnation, sure, but not from start.

D. Alright. I was just curious. I know that you don't like to do the whole routine.

Z. Neither of us do. And this one wanted to do it all the time. But then again, this one also likes childhood. That is why he normally gets a good childhood. Good parents are, not always, but a lot of times delivered to this one. Likes childhood, likes the play. But Seth prefers to move in like we did before in a ready body and just go. In order for the whole journey to be as pleasant for everyone, good parents are normally chosen for this one. Childhood is therefore a fond memory when this one returns. Likes the play, likes the freedom of a child. Doesn't like necessarily the captivity that one encounters as an adult, but knows the endless possibilities and ability if one keeps the childish memories in a grownup appearance. And that is one of the teachings that this one provides (*during*) each incarnation. It is to shine through the innocence, the endless possibilities that one encounters as a child, but radiates it in an adult body. Several adults sometimes remember childhood, but they are in some way convinced that they have to act in a grownup way. This one acts differently, can be very childish in a human form, in a grownup form, and that is to show that when you embrace and allow that adventurous spirit within you to shine through, then the grownup is more at ease. The grownup is more content with life.

D. Ah. That's really good advice. Thank you for that, my friend.

Z. You are much welcome.

D. Before you leave, I had one quick question. On the ancient stone carvings of the Anunnaki, they are shown holding a little box or something with a handle on it. Do you have any idea what that is, or what it represents?

Z. It represents your knowledge of how to master gravity, uranium, mercury, gold. How to master the openings, the gateways. You hold the key on how to manipulate the gateways. This little box they hold indicate that teaching. It is closed for those eyes not equipped to handle the high density of, especially, the combination of mercury, gold and uranium. Those three—in different levels, in different strengths—when they blend, they manipulate the gravitational field. This box indicates that you hold in your hand the teachings of certain elements. It is a box that, once opened, it is transpired in the world and certain gateways open.

D. Wow. Thank you.

Z. There are four elements in that box. All four, in different ways, has to do with conquering time, conquering space, opening gateways, dissolving the gravitational field for gateways to emerge. The four elements—uranium, mercury, gold, copper. But it's not the copper that you know. (*Copper was elementally changed prior to 10,000 BC. It was altered to make it non-reactive. Perhaps it was an unknown isotope or had a different oxidation state, but it was stable in a vaporous form in the past.*) But the copper leads the other elements, it is creating like a laser beam. Copper is the—I say copper, but it is lacking some of its component currently—but it's the original form of copper. It leads the beam, it opens the portals, it makes the gravitational field dissolve. It's the messenger, if you like, from mercury and gold. Uranium, used differently. Uranium is used to—it creates holes, like a ditch, in order for the rotation within the magnetic field to stabilize. So the uranium is used differently. But gold and mercury combined is led by this copper beam, and it is directed in certain ways to dissolve the gravitational field. Uranium is used differently. But the possession of knowledge on how to combine the elements of four in order for dissolving the gravitational field and to connect different portals (*between parallel realities*), everything has to do with stabilizing the foundation of the Earth's magnetic field. It is designed to open and to close. The uranium creates—it's like it's melted into little silver dots and created like a stone, and you knew how to dig them down in certain regions in order for the ley lines, the web in the ground, to either be accelerating or stopped. The other elements I can see and tell you about, are designed to combine and connect in this laser beam, and the copper leads it. That is why you were, at one point, excavating copper in different locations. It was to open certain portals, to make gravitational adjustments in the field.

D. That's truly fascinating.

Z. Not a biggie. Nothing special. You can still try to understand the differences and how these different elements function. Use your fantasy (*imagination*) as a human. See the possibilities that lies before you when you understand, try to merge different elements into another entity. This is the gift of the Elahim, the understanding on how to change conditions. In order to do so, you have to have a PhD in the engineering of elements, the engineering of the gravitational keys. (*He laughed when he said*

PhD in the engineering of elements, since humans lack even a basic understanding of the subject.) There.
D. Wonderful explanation. I thank you for that.
Z. Oh, you are much welcome. See you at home.
D. Alright, my friend. Goodbye.

Ophelia: Bending Time (May 11, 2019)
One feature of life in the third dimension is linear time. But what we perceive is not the full reality of what exists or can be known. There have been shamans who could leave their bodies and rise up vibrationally through the fourth dimension to a level above the timeline. Their soul minds could then move around in the fourth and gain insights about other people and places. The process sounds like a controlled near-death experience. They conducted their explorations during intense rituals using a fog of some elements that were heated by solar energy. Sunlight was concentrated by gigantic parabolic disks made of gold and beamed onto copper plates. Mercury vapor in its present form is a neurotoxin, but it, along with vaporous gold (which no longer exists), was used to induce trance traveling.

Mercury is an odd metal that has been found in liquid form in caves beneath the oldest part of the Teotihuacan Pyramid complex, and also in Egyptian and Chinese tombs. Our spirit team has described how mercury was used in various combinations with copper, gold, or uranium to create a powerful fuel, and also to generate anti-gravity fields and portals to parallel planes. As mentioned in our previous books, the atmosphere on Earth is different today than it was prior to 11,000 BC. As a result, many of the elements no longer have the same properties they did in the past. Gold does not have the same phase behavior as it did when the combination of vaporous mercury and gold was used as a fuel. Due to its misuse, gold was altered to prevent a similar disaster.

What Ophelia describes next was a time about 150 million years ago, when the Anunnaki and other manifested entities occupied Mars. Christine is completely uninformed about geologic time, but Ophelia precisely identified the beginning of the Cretaceous, the age of mammals and dinosaurs. At the beginning of the Cretaceous, the continents were all still pretty close together after the super-continent Pangea broke up. When I studied paleontology in college, the accepted theory was that dinosaurs were cold-blooded reptiles. The first known mammals appeared during the Jurassic and were quite small. However, Ophelia says the large dinosaurs during the Cretaceous (which follows the Jurassic) were mammals. Since I have yet to discover an error in anything they say, I did a bit of research and found quite a few studies that validate her claim, assuming she meant endothermic. A Yale study, led by Robin Dawson, of fossilized eggshells from dinosaurs at different latitudes was published in the journal Science Advances (Feb 2020). Using a process known as clumped isotope paleothermometry, she concluded that all major groups of dinosaurs had body temperatures higher than the environment. Another study, headed by Johan Lindgren of Sweden's Lund University, focused on the soft-tissue fossils of the marine Ichthyosaurs. They also concluded the "reptile" was actually warm-blooded and had a layer of blubber, like a seal or a whale. So, as usual, Ophelia is correct.

O. Hmm. This is Ophelia. Good morning to you.

D. Hello, Ophelia. I recognized your "hmm".

O. Indeed. So, you will proceed a little bit differently. You will have to be a little bit more centered in your experience, both of you. The journey will be familiar to this one (*Christine*), but you will act or conduct the journey as a tour guide. You will access information from the Tallocks, as well as other civilizations that you might pass (*encounter*) on your way. This is a way for you to gain information about realities that will mirror this one (*Earth*) in their consciousness and their approach to science. They *(the Tallocks)* have done or experienced pros and cons when it comes to energetic resources, as well as how to manage your resources. They, at one point, with you, had a base close by on Mars. At that point, the minerals that they, combined with you, were using, was an experiment to see if it was possible to use the same frequencies and minerals, elements here on Earth. Earth, at this point, was in its cradle. They didn't want experiments to take place on this flourishing planet to become. Experiments instead took place nearby on Mars, that had a similar atmosphere. Atmospheric conditions are key to whether an element becomes hazardous, or if it becomes a resource for you. We can adjust the atmosphere, making sure that whatever science are occupying their minds with will become or not. It's not like putting in another cloud, but we can monitor activities, making sure that, let's say, you want to create an energy flow that will reach one kilometer high. We can adjust the atmosphere so it only reaches one hundred meters. That is a way to give you a picture.

D. Were there disasters that occurred on Mars, as a result?

O. There were eruptions resulting from blending certain elements. Mercury is an element that is used in several different areas; it is the key element for travel and time. They tried in some way to manipulate travel and time. Mercury, in that atmospheric condition that existed, became an eruption (*explosion*). The blend of mercury and gold are two components of elements that is the foundation for portals and travels. With those, ancient civilizations, even here, knew how to bend time. Bend time means that you can have an access to past and present, because they connect.

D. What about the future?

O. Yes. Future can also connect with present, like a bow (*an arch*). I will not disclose, fully, how that was done, at this point. Just know that time can bend, and you can access both past and future into your present. Using different elements, combined with heat, and heat was used from solar panels—copper panels, gold disks. Receivers for soul energy connected these two elements. A gas, or a fog, became. In that fog, together with sound and chanting, time stood still. From that still point, you have the ability to welcome or withdraw either the future or the past into your present spot where you are centered. There is a memory within, even this species, from those who occupied this plane when this took place. Being centered in the present allows you to welcome in another time. As long as they were centered, and the elements gold and mercury combined with the heat and chanting, allowed certain individuals to explore this. As they welcomed, let's say, the future, they saw possibilities of what could occur—nothing was set in stone. Not even the past is set in stone. You still, if you receive this connection, have the ability to tap into the fourth reality above you. From that point, you can do adjustments. At this point, man is not able to do those adjustments. They can observe, but they cannot actively remove or change the past or the future, because we have changed the conditions within your atmosphere, making it impossible for you to reach that level of science. It is unfortunately a memory from a time when this was misused. On Mars, they experimented with the conditions of heat, mercury, and gold, in order for that to be a project on Earth with the species that was placed, or was going to be placed. So the experiment took place on Mars, in order for it to be executed on Earth. This was due to the fact that Earth was in its cradle and the atmosphere needed to be left alone.

D. Was this experiment related to humans?

O. They were humans, but in prior cycles to the ones we have been talking about.

D. So this was in the very distant past?

O. Indeed. In the Earth timeline, this occurred one hundred and fifty million years ago, the first experiment. Still very present, even though you might not think so. This was before the big mammals came. The big mammals came in, dinosaurs, to make a halt, a shift. Before dinosaurs there was a scientific era, then it came to a pause. These cycles have come and gone numerous times. I'm not saying that this is upcoming within your lifetime here, I'm giving you a history lesson for you to remember. You were here in the first project. This one (*Seth*) has a memory from Mars within his being. Both working similar, he remotely, you on-site.

D. So the entities that were on Mars, were they manifested there?

O. Yes. Yes. Tallocks look very much like what you chose the word Anunnaki for. They have the same features; they carry the same knowledge. When you traveled here, you traveled as Anunnaki. Same family.

D. So this was before Bob and I met?

O. Yes. Yes. He has no memory of this. There you go. I wish to radiate a sensation of calm to the both of you, because you are entering a new field, and you are entering a new manner of operating in order for you to access information. You will meet or encounter entities and experiences that might be hard for a human to grasp. In that sense, you might also feel more alone in your mission, but you are here together in order for you to access this fully. If you had only been here by yourself, we would not have allowed this to come forward, because you need to be comforting each other. From a human standpoint, it might feel delusional at times and you might question the authenticity of the message. That is why you are here together.

Elahim Council: Human Evolution, Part II (July 20, 2019)

This is a fascinating summary of how the humanoid mammals have been modified by both spiritual councils and alien visitors during the past 50,000 years. The politically correct version of human evolution is complete fiction in many important ways. The fossil evidence shows that the several known races (species) evolved independently during the past million years—or were genetically modified at different times—from separate branches of Homo erectus in Africa, Europe, and Asia. There have been many styles of humanoid placed on Earth over untold millions of years. The Elahim Council says, "You are engineered, created to operate on the behalf of other intentions." Humans were once just another animal for the Master Mind to occupy. During the past 400,000 years, souls have been allowed to steer the vehicle with increasing independence. However, even now, there is about 0.5 percent of Master Mind consciousness that joins with the soul during incarnations (as an observer). Each time the Creator or councils change the intention for the human, the physical and energetic components are altered. This is all done by manipulating the DNA in labs on the second dimension, or directly by alien visitors working on behalf of the councils.

The latest human looks similar to the earlier models, but is different in several ways. The spirits said a new human was genetically engineered and placed in what is now central Russia around 35,000 BC. They looked like powerful Vikings, having a high forehead, wide jaw, and 1500 to 1800 cc (cubic centimeters) brains. Archeological evidence supporting their claim was found in Kostyonki, Russia, where bones from 35,000 BC were discovered of a fully modern man. The DNA from a male skeleton found in the Kostenki 14 dig site was analyzed. His genome was closely related to modern Scandinavians, with light skin and blond or reddish hair, as evidenced by the MCR1 gene. These genetically modified humans became the root-stock for the tribes that spread south and west into Europe. However, they remained isolated for thousands of years where they had been placed, prior to migrating westward. The Elahim Council tells us their brain size, which was larger than other humanoids, was reduced prior to 7000 BC. At the same time, a thick filter was put between the soul and the other centers of the body. The result was a significant de-evolution of the spiritual connection and mental abilities of the human. Concurrently, the Elahim, Shea, and other groups were all prohibited from coming to Earth in manifested forms. Since then, souls are required to incarnate to intervene in human affairs. The Elahim Council states that the human vehicle was changed so the "intellect was paralyzed". The brain size has been reduced by at least 20 percent in the cooler, northern hemisphere, where the Caucasian and Asian humanoids were created. Brain size has a direct correlation with IQ, and the modern brain averages about 1350 cc. Larger brains tend to overheat, so there have been design variations in brain size that correlate with latitude.

EC. This is the Elahim Council. We want to let you know that we are following your progress. Even though we might not communicate all the time, we are tightly connected to the information that is revealed to all different realities and levels. You and this one, Seth, are used to travel to destinations where the intellect is more advanced. This is a struggle here, even though you come to enlight and kick start the intellect, which is very much connected to the Elahim. It is a struggle when the physical organ in the leading mammal is not equipped. To blend a soul awareness in a vehicle that is less advanced causes great challenges, and we know that. However, you are here to in some way recreate history. You are here to make ancient ways to come forward; to enlight what true strength and power really is; to bypass the superficial. This vehicle, the human, is very superficial, easy to trick, easily spellbound by material wealth, spellbound by advancements that are illusions. Other realities are more aligned with what the core of advancement and compassion is all about. When you travel in a reality so spellbound by things that have no meaning, it is hard to kickstart the intellect. Sometimes, it's easier for Shea to address the emotional. The emotional is more pure, more in contact with the soul energy wish and wisdom. The intellect has to be exercised like a muscle—different. Heart and mind, as you call it. Heart is more at peace, easier to be less spellbound by illusions. The brain here, because of some fuse that was disconnected, wires, if you like, changed the way the intellect operates. Before, there were more of a balance and equality between brain and heart in this mammal. Due to circumstances, the Creator wished the intellect to be paralyzed, handicapped, to see if it had the ability to regain strength. I wish I could give you a picture. The emotional is more intact, similar as it has been over eons and in different shapes that the mammal has appeared in. The shifts have taken place in the brain and the mental realms within you; disconnected, in order for higher councils and the Creator to see whether a brain has the ability to regain its core, its wisdom, its connection—similar like a heart. This is to see the balance between light and sound, if you like. Here, light would be considered the emotional; the light is always there, always burning. Sound colors the light, and that is why the experiment on this plane has to do with the brain. The brain becomes spellbound about illusions. If a vehicle, human, that is, is too logical, too inclined to think their way through a solution, they are also easier tricked. If you navigate from your emotional state of mind, then the brain has the ability to follow. (*The brain can be led by the emotions, that is why it is important to master the human emotions and follow the soul–based emotions.*)

D. Was the disconnect from the soul?

EC. It was the reboot. Sometimes reboot means to make it move up a level. This reboot, which was done around 50,000 BC, around that time, it disconnected. Before, there were several who had the ability to tap into the fourth reality (*dimension*), to be equally strong in their mental capacity as their emotional being. Due to circumstances, the disconnect took place. It was a shift in your DNA. You had more lights in your DNA strings before. They were dimmed, that is the change.

D. There were many different hominoids at that time. There were Neanderthals, Denisovans, Cro-Magnons, Asians, and Africans. Was the disconnect done simultaneously in all these species?

EC. No. Around Asia, it was not. Northern Asia still (*had the*) same brain. A lot of it took place in southern Europe, Middle East, Northern Africa. The other places were less populated; no need to disturb the peace in that flock. The shift had to do with occurrences that are now known as Israel. It's a cradle for good and bad—it's a center point, a whirlwind, a whirlpool. The way we see that region, especially Israel, it's a constant whirl, swirling, rotating. We follow the motion in that region. A Cell exists that stirs this spiral up. Some are aware how to block the view for outer influences, trying to operate in disguise. This was done at that time and it created a wave over that region, spread all the way to Spain.

D. You said 50,000 years ago. I thought Ophelia had said it was like 5000 to 8000 BC.

EC. There have been several changes. The one I'm looking at here is further back. It's been modifications over time. After this, there was a silence in that region for a while. Almost like an ice age, but no ice, no snow, but it went into hibernation. It came back again around 25,000 BC to 15,000 BC—flourished again. It's like dimming, increasing, dimming, increasing. The constant veil, when the window was shut, was around 5000 to 7000 BC, that's when the window was shut and we don't do the same. To give you a picture, it was more of a constant (*repeating cycle of*) hibernation—enlightenment that occurred. We (*the Elahim*) intervened more closely. After the window was shut, the intervention came through incarnation. The last known effort before several levels were withdrawn was around zero (AD). But even before 50,000 BC, there were cycles going on where you were here. There were highly advanced species roaming around; some native, some not. That occurred as far back as 2 million years back. Windows have been opened and shut several times before. In this cycle, it was shut around 5 to 7000 years ago.

D. And that was for all species of humans?

EC. Humans, yes. You don't have the visitors in the same way. Visitors simply monitoring, they don't walk among you in the same way. There are those who occupy a human vehicle, trying to experience this reality. But they are not walking around in their preference form anymore (*manifested*). Now they are among you, but they look like you. Those are not Elahim. You came in your preferred form (*manifested*) or incarnated, nothing in-between. At this time, the window is shut for manifestation in that sense. Some are seen, visitors that come, but they are more shy. They try not to disturb the species, the human. You are still observed, due to the fact that you create disharmony in the environment. No reality has the ability to always overcome; that is why several visitors and councils look into this reality. We are concerned about the seas. If the sea dies, land dies; atmosphere depends on the ocean. If (*life in the*) ocean disappears, water, atmosphere will suffer—land meets disaster. Water and the ocean is like the blood in a human—has to be intact, has to be cared for. The continents are like the surface on a human. If the inners, the blood and organs falter and fail, the surface will vanish. You have to care for your home. Even though some understand that this is just a visit, most who create disharmony see this as their only home. That is baffling to the councils, that you don't care about your house, so to speak.

D. Ari and Eli have talked about changes that are coming to the Earth. There are so many nuclear plants around the oceans. If Japan goes under, that would pretty much kill off everything in the ocean with nuclear waste, wouldn't it?

EC. Yes. Yes. Efforts are put into that region. Souls coming in, mostly from the sixth and seventh, into that region to clean up science, become more environmentally aware.

D. Is there any way to stabilize uranium once it has been converted into radioactive material?

EC. Yes. It's been done before, locked. Some locked in mountains still. If you knew how to search, you will find it. It's frozen, cooled, locked. However, if found, reemerged, it never dies. To recycle, if that is your question, it has to be picked apart. You don't have that science anymore. It was done by you as well, here, before. Laboratoriums that, like surgery, moved chemicals apart, making them not operate. They were blended more and picked apart. Big laboratoriums existed around the area of what is now Michigan. The ability to recreate material, metals, minerals, picking them apart to not be, like you say, radioactive any more—like dimming the uranium, cooling it down, dissecting.

D. Will that technology be reintroduced?

EC. If the intellect has improved. As of yet, if that science and understanding existed, we see a danger of creating worse material, dynamics. But you can clean a radioactive area by knowing what causes the damage and what is pure. You can dissect and clean in the same way. It's been done before, around Lake Michigan. In the bottom, seabed, remains—mercury that was used together with other elements.

D. Was that gold?

EC. Mercury and gold has the ability, together, to assist fuel, to assist travels. The engineering in vehicles that came and left operated on gold. Mercury opened portals. Combined, travel took place. You could travel from one spot to another in a blink of an eye.

D. Did that somehow distort what we perceive as space and time?

EC. Yes. There were no...it was stellar time, not space AND time, not separate. Stellar time is combined. Here, space is one, time is another. Science does not have the ability to combine. Prior civilizations, not humans, operated to understand how to bypass and to use minerals in different ways to open and close portals. How to travel—man was only taught how to travel in their being to the fourth reality, but they were baffled about the visitors who created the portals to really leave and return. Portals that beamed crafts in and out, using bases, high activity. This was even further back. There were those who looked like humans, white in skin. Science today recognizes man's evolution from about 300,000 to 500,000 years, not understanding several cycles took place before with those looking like humans, inside different—some intelligent, some lacking soul, operating only as a prototype.

D. Were those created?

EC. Yes, yes. They did not have the ability to connect to the fourth. Master Mind blended with some. Several projects within a big one took place. Plenty of visitors.

D. Bob mentioned a white, almost albino looking race that was put in the Asian or Russian region about 30 to 50,000 years ago?

EC. Yes, they were kind of the same. These ones around the Michigan lake, those humanoids were very, very pale. (*These must have been created much earlier, perhaps around 300,000 BC, when there was mining activity in the area.*) Albino looking. Skin very smooth, no hair—prototype, assisted visitors. Not very intelligent, but friendly—operate as an animal almost. As the inner organs, brain, started to evolve, Master Mind and soul incarnations started slowly to progress, to see from the inside how a brain operated. You did so, you still do. You have the ability to monitor brain activity from the inside. Plenty of souls took that mission, to upgrade, maintain organs before a general wave of incarnation took place. You are engineered, created to operate on the behalf of other intentions. You have free will, but you also follow a general intention, and at this time the intention is to care for your host, to see beyond illusions. The brain has faltered again, needs to be upgraded for new souls coming in with higher awareness. In order for that to happen, some souls, like yourself, take on lives to monitor brain activity first hand, what is available at this time; reporting to councils so they know what souls to send. There.

D. That's fascinating.

EC. Elahims come and go. You were here a lot around 300,000 years ago. You were here earlier than this one (*Seth*), but you operated as engineers, dissecting minerals, creating portals, cleaning radioactivity, combined with souls from the eighth. Experiments took place that should not have done so, and souls from the eighth came in with visitors, assisting how to clean.

D. And this was around when?

EC. Around 300,000 BC. But you were here before. There were bases before.

D. Are there any remnants that can still be found of these ancient civilizations?

EC. Several on seabed, Lake Michigan, Bermuda, bottom. (*Bases are on or below the lake or sea floor.*) That is why there is an interest to understand the activity around the Bermuda area—

bases underneath, not visible to a human eye or a submarine. Activity that are in disguise, but felt through the presence of energy. But even if you dive down you will not find a base, it's not visible. (*I worked in Michigan for about 15 years, and often heard stories about UFO's flying out of or into Lake Michigan.*)

D. Is it still operating?

EC. Oh, yes.

D. And there is one in Michigan as well?

EC. Yes. Yes. Another one around the Japanese sea. Bases strategically placed to operate activity.

D. Are these manifested or in some sort of physical form?

EC. Not physical form; you can't see. You can feel the presence if you use readers (*radar?*), then you will read activity, but not see what it is. (*They have talked about this several times, suggesting to me that either there is a cloaking within the visible light frequency, or the crafts are in a parallel reality but can still create energy signatures that can be detected at certain vibrations.*)

D. Is the fuse that you mentioned earlier, in the brain, is that something that is currently trying to be repaired?

EC. Yes, yes, exactly. That is why you are here. You are trying to reconnect the intellect. The emotional is more intact. (*The emotional center has a closer connection to the soul, if the human is in control of themselves.*) A lot of efforts from souls coming in from the fifth and the seventh address the emotional. It's easier to get someone who is connected with their feelings to follow a soul intent. However, if the brain follows the illusions from media and such, which aim and address the mental, then a need to have souls incarnate to upgrade the intellect and the mental is needed. So, there we go. More to come.

D. Well, thank you so much for that.

EC. See you at home. Elahim.

D. Alright, my friends. Elahim.

Zeonia, Jeshua: The Dream of Earth (Sept 29, 2019)

This is a remarkable account of the history of Earth and Mars. The story is delivered by one of the members of a group of souls from the sixth dimension. He picked the name Evan in a later session. He said they operated from a planet named (for our convenience) as Zeonia, which is probably within our Universe. They may also have a home on some planet in fish tank eleven. They are companions to the Elahim, but spend almost all their time in manifested form, traveling within our Universe, fish tank five, and other fish tanks, working on behalf of the spiritual councils. While science fiction writers would identify them as aliens, it is obvious that they, along with Elahim and Shea, are caretakers of the Earth. They were here eons before humans. In fact, Evan and his group from Zeonia were here with the Elahim before the large land animals were introduced. They later helped to create the vehicle for holding a soul, which the spirits often refer to as the bottle. So, from that perspective, who are really the visitors or aliens here, they or us?

The eighth dimension is home to the groups that work with elements and atmospheres on planets. The atmosphere, we have been told, is energetically connected to the movement of land masses. Zeonia gives an uplifting narration of how the Earth was tenderly cared for by the various groups who contributed their skills in bringing forth the Creator's intentions. The eighth, the second, and the seventh dimensions worked to create a sustainable ecosystem and atmosphere over several billions of Earth years. The Zeonians and the Elahim came here in manifested form from Mars during the Paleozoic Era, some 450 million years ago, once basic life was established in the oceans and on land. The original plan for the Earth was to use the resources here, and manufacture energy and fuel for travel. Colonies were established for the mining of metals. Hydrocarbon oil and gas was introduced in large quantities to stabilize the Fork and serve as the lifeblood of the planet. Somewhere along the line, millions of years ago, the Creator and the councils revealed a new intent for the planet which included a body to encase a soul. There were certain groups and visitors who had different ideas about how to proceed, and this created friction. Eventually, the atmosphere was changed and those groups were no longer welcome. The Zeonians were among those who created the human, and are still here monitoring how it develops. Among other things, they are concerned about GMOs, since it damages the carefully crafted DNA of the human and animals who ingest it.

Zeonia. Greetings. We are here with your friends. Jeshua, Isaac, Seth, your friends. We are here to bring comfort and enlightenment to your species. We have, and still, visit your plane. We have had numerous encounters with your species, protecting DNA, protecting development—keepers in contact with Elahim council. We travel differently than do you. We are curious about incarnating—never have. Travel differently, observing. Stationed in the past on the red planet. Came with knowledge, engineering, mining, moving objects easier. We see that you struggle with movement in all aspects of your reality. It was not always so. The veil placed upon this plane came as a big cloud. At that time, changes took place in your evolution—started new. Before (*known history*), civilizations existed here. Some traveled (*in crafts*). Some, as we saw, blended with the vehicle placed upon this plane, the bottle. Some tapped into this bottle, remotely trying to kick-start a new kind of evolution. The evolution that you read about is not the original one. It was different before, wiped out in your books, but can be found by those who seek—geologists, marine biologists. Remains exist on seabed, in mountains, and deep within the Earth consciousness, never removed. We were here at that time; no big mammals.

D. This was before the dinosaurs?

Ze. Before dinosaurs. Visited, learned from each other. It was a central hub of knowledge. Some excavated minerals. Some used (*Earth*) as a greenhouse. The change came as consciousness was brought in as a step of evolving a new species that will encase a spirit.

D. What name would you like to go by?

Ze. There are no letters that will replicate, fully, in human language or with your ability to speak, but you can call the destination (*he sounded the letters S–C–R*). I will give the words to this one.

D. Can you tell me about the civilization you had then on the red planet?

Ze. Yes, this one was there. You visited briefly, as well. The same as this plane, came in original form. You came as you are, Elahim, not most of you…it's difficult with words. Let's see. You were not the majority, but you had special skills of engineering, addressing demanifestation of objects, movement, mining, understanding the law of elements. You were, in some way, in charge of a grand station on Mars. Workers looked different. Some, (*looked*) like us. Some differently—will never communicate (*with us*). We operated on the planet in order to create new elements—fuel. To give you a word that you can relate to, it was like creating a big gas station.

D. And that was on Mars?

Ze. Yes, yes. It wasn't livable, like here. It was colonized to understand and develop elements and energy. Resources to assist this system. Some of this knowledge we brought here. But the plan was different for this place. It's not meant to be excavated for all its resources. The plan was to create consciousness in a third vehicle. When those two intentions collided, there were conflicts between ideas. Some wanted to continue the project of what was started on Mars, but it was not the intention. We came and changed our intention, (*and then*) we worked in engineering this bottle. It was a project. Energy flowing, but not with elements. The human body was engineered step–by–step. Brilliant minds collaborated. We wanted to stay, (*so we*) changed our intention and worked with this bottle. It's been observed since then. We extract DNA, now and then, to make sure it is maintained or upgraded. This project occurs, some on your plane, (*in the*) waters, secluded areas. There is a region where a hub exists. One is in the Bahamas area, water. Another one in your lake, north. (*One of the Great Lakes.*) We observe to see the DNA modifications progressing. But also, we are concerned about the infiltration of the vehicle. We see damage, not by us, but by intake of fuel, food, surrounding atmosphere, manipulating the original DNA. We are concerned about the development of this bottle. We also look at wildlife, maintaining (*its*) DNA. Making sure energy flows correctly within your cells. We wanted to remain (*on Earth*), changed intent. That was OUR evolution, our progress. We worked solely with energy on Mars. Here, our project became you (*humans*).

D. What dimension do you originate from?

Ze. When we sleep, we sleep on the sixth.

D. But you are not Elahim?

Ze. No. No. We sleep on the sixth. But we, huh, know you like the word "time" here. So, lately we have slept on the sixth, near fish tank five. But we prefer to sleep on the sixth dimension near fish tank eleven. (*Since the dimensions are described as being a ring, the Zeonian is implying that there are differences in the energy flow or conditions in the spiritual dimensions, depending on its location around the wheel.*) But the project, we like the challenge of form. (*They mean maintaining their own form in one of the fish tanks.*) When we go home, we sleep. You say "returning to spirit". We say "sleep". We are not active in the same way. We recharge on the sixth, but we are mainly traveling in our form. You return more frequently to your sleep (*spiritual home base*). We do not. To give you a picture, if we have a thousand years, you are home maybe 800 years, traveling 200. We are home for five years. Do you see what I'm trying to relate?

D. I do.

Ze. And when we are home, we sleep, we recharge. As we do, others, like yourself, extract information from our travels. We are differently designed. We return into a laboratorium on the sixth, sleep, cocooned, (*and then*) information is extracted. We sleep, we recharge; do not remember. You take collected information, data—normally from fish tank eleven. This one likes eleven. Nine, eleven, eight; eight, nine, eleven; eight, nine, eleven; travels fast, travels fast; moving, moving, moving. Struggles with being captivated in this bottle. It has changed—the project changed for both of you as you started the incarnating cycles. You made sure the bottles were up to speed. After dinosaurs, after cloud, after spirits came in more frequently, (*then*) we came in disguise. We hide behind clouds, hide behind clouds, hide behind clouds.

D. Are you traveling in what we would perceive as material objects, or are you manifested?

Ze. Yes, yes. Behind a cloud. It comes in as a cloud, and when it's safe, it manifests as a sphere. And there we are.

D. Is it something that we can see with our eyes?

Ze. Yes, yes. We prefer doing this during the night, but we come as a cloud. Some—if we do not feel it's safe or right—also know that it's controlled on when and where to manifest the sphere. Some spheres are like cigar-shape, still enters your atmosphere, enters your awareness first as a cloud. From that cloud, it changes. This one saw one time how it would appear. It looks like fast-forwarding the movement of clouds, and then it emerges. We have been allowed to introduce ourselves gradually. We take care of you. We make sure that you are safe. We follow your progress. We are interested in the process of incarnating, and that you also remember some of your home. And when you are home, you also fondly talk about yourself in this bottle. You can sit and talk about different personas that you portrayed—it's like a fairy tale for us. It's fascinating. You both delight us in the sphere (*alien craft*) sometimes when you sleep, telling us stories about personas and how it is experienced to be human. Fascinating. We are different.

D. Could you give me a brief history of the Earth, then, from your perspective?

Ze. First, just a small dream. It was created with love, intent (*for*) growth, expansion—things that would be considered unique. Everything combined in one object. How can that be mastered? How can wealth be shared? How can love conquer fear? All these different experiences, elements, events, created in one place to become a role model for others. It's been going so and so with being a role model. (*Not that well.*) It began quietly, no known species (*visitors*) allowed to enter this atmosphere. Left alone in the cradle of becoming all the intentions placed upon her. We call this planet "she", a her, because the main intent symbolizes embrace. Embrace, in your world, equals mother. After a while, visitors came and established new projects, like plants, cells, molecules, things to become and grow. Atmosphere groups (*from the eighth*) came, correcting land mass, movement. Atmosphere took a long time in her evolution to become perfect. Eighth, those friends from eighth, were here a long time, encasing this project only with adjusting your atmosphere and conditions for existence. At this time (*during the Precambrian Era*), there were some activities on Mars. You operated with energy. Some were meant to come here, but were not allowed during the process of (*creating the*) atmosphere. Came when it was time. Around that time, oil was established as blood, the planet's veins. You helped, at that point, some, creating conditions of energy within the veins of your planet. The idea and the project was established outside before entering here. Mars was one, even Jupiter—gas. (*He is saying oil was experimented with on Mars. And natural gas, on Jupiter.*)

D. So the oil was introduced on this planet?

Ze. Yes, after the atmosphere was in place. Engineers like yourself came, established the flow of oil. Energy resources, gas—Jupiter, combining projects from both; manifested as a seed here, to become. It didn't exist at first. I'm giving you the birth of your planet. Some was implemented here by individuals like yourself, projects taken from other realities, other planets and moved here as a gift to her, as a gift for evolution. Who knew what evolution looked like at that point? We did not know. We thought we were going to work with oil and energy resources. But the intent changed after it was established, and we were asked to tend to this bottle that was going to become a part of evolution.

D. Is this the only place where the bottle houses a soul that is locked from birth to death?

Ze. No, no. Some other places, traveling, but not coming in the same as here—that's different. So, in some way, yes. Here you come in from birth and you stay until the bottle collapses. On other places, you blend with a bottle, but you can come into a bottle of existence that is not a child. So you can blend, merge, with a bottle on other locations, but it doesn't die, it doesn't accumulate the same sense of lessons and karma—different. So, in that sense, coming in from birth occupying the bottle until it falls asleep, that's different, that is unique.

D. Thank you for that.

Ze. I will thank you for this time. I have Jeshua on my right side, Isaac on my left, making sure communication is comfortable for this one, even though she knows us. I will give you the name Zeonia...that's the closest we can do at this time with words.

D. Are there any additional messages you would like to pass on?

Ze. We want relay that you should be kind to other bottles. To not proclaim supremacy on a region, to not claim territory. To not claim that you are masters over energy. We are concerned about how you excavate energy resources. We want you to be cautious with the atmosphere, because it changes the flow within you, (*and then*) the DNA modifications needs to be adjusted. You will not be able to house (*live on*) this plane if you do modifications within your atmosphere and your energy resources. Your species will not adapt. It happened before. Drought came. Lack of water, lack of energy—drought. You are not adaptable. You're headed to a destiny you do not want if you are not careful with how you exist and co-exist with each other and your host. The atmosphere changes, (*and the*) environment responds. You see the shifts in your weather. It is your host coughing. It is your host saying, "STOP! Let me be." You have to honor lifeforms and your host. Your oxygen is also a lifeform. Don't take oxygen for granted. That was a mistake (*made*) on Mars. Yes. There. We will return.

D. Thank you so much for that information. It was a pleasure to meet you.

Ze. Zeonia. We will return. Thank you.

J. This is Jeshua.

D. Hello, Jeshua.

J. As you see, we deliver some of your friends to come in as guest speakers. You will always be visited by those you know on a soul level—never strangers. Make sure she knows. There will always be a protection from myself, Ophelia, Isaac. We will create a circle, making sure only friends of prior encounters will come through. This one knows these entities, that you just met, well. So you will be visited again by some who comes (*to Earth*) differently than do you.

D. Do these travelers appear to us in a certain form?
J. Yes. They're not the Little Greys. They are similar height as a normal sized human. Don't have hair on their body, slimmer. Big eyes, little nose, smiling. They are... let's see if I can give you a visual. Their head shape is a little bit more triangular. Wider on the top, wider, flat. No hair. Ears, very small. Big eyes, not just black like you see on cartoons. Little nose. Neck, thin neck. Skin, light grey, white. Appear in gender, male.
D. Do they exist on the third dimension frequency? Do they move in and out of that?
J. Move in and out.
D. Where do they reside when they are not in the third?
J. Do you mean your planet?
D. Do they shift out of the third dimension and into the fourth?
J. They are always in the same. They never dematerialize into energy, if that is your question, unless they go home and sleep. They are what they are. Move around through fish tanks. But have been here for a long cycle. When their feet are not set here, they are on nearby star systems. But not in energy (*energetic form*). They are what they are.
D. So they travel in crafts?
J. Yes.
D. How do those crafts move from their place to here?
J. Follow the energy of light. Light and sound combined. As they twist, rotate, they create openings; they create passages where it's easy to manipulate gravity. They have the ability to ride on this spiral of sound and light as they combine, connect, twist. That is how movement operates within and between fish tanks. You (*humans*), with your little craft, don't ride on anything. You cannot conquer gravity, as you do not have the formula and the expertise to connect light and sound. It is not just there, it's not just a freeway. Each entity, each craft, draws these two together, creating a spiral unique for that craft, giving openings to different destinations.
D. So when they move through what we perceive as space, they don't travel at the speed of light?
J. They merge...how can I give you a picture? If you are, in your sphere, allowed to travel here, then before departure, you merge this pathway to this destination. You connect, YOU create your own highway. By doing so, you merge light and sound, and they

twist and spin and they create this highway, this passage, to Earth. If that sphere is only assigned to come here, they cannot use the same equation, the same formula, to go elsewhere. This is how this one (*Seth*) knows how to create maps, creating foundations for where pathways are available and who can travel on them. Each entity traveling in craft creates its path to where it's allowed to go.

D. That's like when Bob and I went to Etena?

J. Yes. Similar. His peanut–suit will take him to Etena, but his peanut–suit will not take him to Vlac. You see what I'm trying to say? I have sent the picture to this one, she will explain. There! So we go.

D. Thank you so much for that. It is fascinating.

J. Well, you know this, of course. Nothing new. For the container, it might be new. But you have, in other containers, in other lives, understood the equation between light and sound and how it creates passages, openings, movement of objects. But that is not given to your little space shuttle. You have not the ability to merge these two elements to create this passage. That knowledge, not given to man.

D. So humans will never be able to do that?

J. Not now. Not this version. We do not see that is in any evolution at this time, that you will be able to master how to merge two foundations for openings and travels to take place that will conquer time and space, as you know it.

D. He gave a warning about the human behavior on Earth. Is there nothing that you can do from your position to resolve the problems?

J. We alarm you with all these different weather phenomena, making you feel vulnerable. That is the first step for you to awaken and to understand that you are limited as a species. You are not superior to your planet. At this time, that is what we do. So, I will leave the floor.

D. Thank you so much for all that information, and for accompanying our friend.

J. We want change to come from your species before other assistance is granted. We want you to be awakened by what you experience around you. Sometimes fear leads to salvation and understanding. This is a balance from the spirit realm, as fear is an illusion. But we also need you to awaken, so sometimes creating a sensation and an illusion of fear will empower the species to take steps into progress that we wish for you to do. Do you understand?

D. I do. That's very good advice.

J. You are always safe, but we need to awaken you. So, at this time, we create illusions of fear, in many ways, for you to be fed up, to want change, to gather with others, to seek companionship, to seek advice, to seek out each other's knowledge, to raise your knowledge bank together, to not remain passive—to gather. Okay, that would be it.

D. Alright, my friend. Thank you.

J. Oh, you are much welcome. Elahim.

D. Elahim.

Tallock: Opening and Closing Portals (Nov 28, 2019)
Even though several years have passed since they gave this talk, the image the spirits give of how portals are created has stuck with me. They said, "First the Earth's own gravitation field was in existence. Then you use what existed and withdraw it, creating motion of anti-clockwise rotation on certain locations. See it as a big sheet, and you stand in the middle of the sheet and you draw it to you, creating (*wrapping*) the sheet around you, making it surround your being. From that point, you start the motion and you rotate anti-clockwise." Once portals are established, it allows for movement between the Earth plane and parallel realities. If you have ever stood near a mountain stream where fast-moving water rushes around a boulder, you may have noticed a swirling vortex on the downstream side. I envision the portals arising in a similar way. There are conductive metals in the crust that cause disruptions in the normal flow of energy from Pole-to-Pole. At those sites, assuming someone understands the physics involved, portals can be opened by entities on Earth. Other portals arise naturally, but are not stable. It was only after listening to the talk again while verifying the accuracy of the transcript that I realized what the Tallock were telling about the copper mining along the Midcontinent rift. The presence of the copper created a large, natural portal that was being used by unwelcome visitors. The Elahim council decided to close the portal by mining and removing the copper.

T. This is the Tallock.

D. Hello, my friends.

T. Greetings. We are here to help you, to assist you, as you reopen your inner books. Both of you traveled here opening hidden teachings left behind. Part of this in an ancient time. Keepers of knowledge, we release little–by–little, connected with the Elahim Council. Your earlier visits, non–human, were to navigate, creating zones for travels—portals. Rich in energy, minerals puddle, circulating anti–clockwise. Where the vibrational field rotates anti–clockwise in a general field rotating clockwise, that's where the zones are. Strategically placed by yourself and others such as us, working to create living gateways to this plane. Non-human existence at that time. No animal life in that respect. It was the creation of the source field, where energies rotate anti-clockwise. The general magnetic field on this plane rotates clockwise. As you establish points that diverts from the regular creation, new creations, new opportunities exist. You established that pattern around, mainly, the Russian region. Others were on other places, even in the seas. When there is a disturbance in the zones on the seabed, that is when earthquakes take place. They normally originate from disturbances in these points that were established before lifeforms came to this plane. Do you understand?

D. That must have been, in Earth years, a very long time ago?

T. Beginning, no lifeforms. Some, some started in the seas. No activity such as animals, but there were some smaller beings in the seas. This was in the beginning of the project. Traveled here differently. Non activity of being detected. (*No lifeforms on land to detect them.*) Traveled here differently.

D. Was it in a manifested form?

T. Yes. But not all. Those who executed (*were in*) manifested form, (*and were*) supervised by realities of non-form (*councils*). But the ones such as you and us, manifested.

D. Were those zones of counter–revolution established within the Earth itself?

T. You mean, if the general evolution was created at this point, is that your question?

D. I'm curious about the gravitational points where the anti-clockwise revolution was established.

T. You worked with—first the Earth's own gravitation field was in existence. Then you use what existed and withdraw it, creating motion of anti–clockwise rotation on certain locations. See it as a big sheet, and you stand in the middle of the sheet and you draw it to you, creating (*wrapping*) the sheet around you, making it surround your being. From that point, you start the motion and you rotate anti–clockwise. This is the only image I can give you. The sheet itself is still intact, but certain points in the sheet were manipulated this way so that travels, among other things, would be possible. It was a way to monitor activities within the core of the planet as well. See it is peek–holes for the spirit realm as well as entities such as Tallock to monitor the activity and wellbeing in your web and in the core of the planet. Some of these dots (*portals*) are sleeping at this time. If, let's say, the Earth contained a thousand zones as they were created, at this time, it is merely fifty to seventy–five that are active, but those are more— I wouldn't say powerful—but they are more distinct and they are upholding the level of existence on this plane. They communicate with the web and atmosphere.

D. I just wondered if they were maintained by some magnetic anomaly within the Earth itself?

T. Yes, yes. The anomaly that you refer to had to do with the level of iron and also copper within the Earth field. Copper was excavated in this country (*USA*) at one point to maintain—there was a big hub here that was rich in copper. Beings, non–spiritual visitors, operated to balance different elements and minerals. Copper at one time was excavated, due to the fact that that zone wasn't operating or functioning properly. Copper is an element that leads other elements into the portal, whereas mercury has the ability to conquer time. One works with conquering time in these portals, whereas the other opens and closes them. Copper has the ability to open and close these zones. When the zone was closed, copper was excavated. When we want a portal or zone to be activated, we add copper. It leads activity, or it closes FOR activity.

D. That's fascinating.

T. Mercury is an element that is used for travel. It is to conquer waves of realities—in this case, time. Those who had the ability to travel in time used different amounts of mercury combined with heat. It is a way for travel to occur. Hmm. Let's leave that. Copper, on the other hand, opens and closes opportunities for travels. What happened in this country was that there was too much activity coming in bordering this country to the next. (*US and Canada, around the Great Lakes.*) Not beneficial for the total environmental balance in the region that was about to blossom. Life forms that were established to evolve. Visitors came in and interrupted the program. The decision was made by the Elahim Council, among others, to close that zone. Excavation of copper took place. This one was present; supervised, closing the hole. Now water covers hole.

D. Is that up in northern part of the United States?

T. Yes, yes. Border to the next one. It was a disturbance in the ecosystem that was about to take form by visitors who used this open portal to enter this plane. Know that even an open portal can be used by those who lack the higher understanding. At that time, it was (*like*) having your home wide open.

D. Just a quick question about mercury. It is toxic to humans, but was it used by the physical travelers in some way in vapor form?

T. Yes, as fuel. If man knew how to use the different elements combined—copper, mercury, even gold, different components together yield new maps, new formats, new possibilities—then man would be able to travel. You do not master the different levels within elements, you only master some. If an element comes in, let's say, ten different possibilities of existence, you master three. Before, mastering more. After the (*Earth*) grid was in place, (*we*) worked on zones and created all ten, or all possible (*variations*) of each element, which were used. As the work was done, new entities, visitors came. (*Then we made*) modifications of access, resource and elements. Based on the human consciousness and its history and the history of profit that we see and the history of not sharing resources, limitations have been put on your consciousness and your level of reaching knowledge. As you do not master your own history and your own shadows, more will not be granted. Just know that copper is a foundation for exits and entrances in these zones. Areas rich in copper, more activity. Look for areas that carry copper, quartz, high level of these two then there are greater opportunities for visitors to be seen. They feed on it, they need it in order for them to descend, but they also need to ascend—come in and leave. There. That was the teaching of the day. Begin to remember, research copper, research the way and how copper can be used and what it has been used for in the past. Research your history. Copper, quartz, gold, mercury used. Quartz was a later one, but copper, gold, mercury, all strong, even though they have been somewhat withered out. But no need to be discouraged about that, really. It would have been a disaster if all (*levels of the elements*) were accessed at this time, due to the consciousness in your society.

D. Hopefully, that will improve at some time.

T. When you work on Vlac, you work in the laboratorium where we practice with these elements. See it as a laboratorium–library for elements. Etena is a library of lifeforms. We have the library of elements, minerals, and this is where both of you work. This is what you also worked with in different past lives here, in a moderate way, of course.

D. Thank you so much for that. It is beyond my current ability to comprehend.

T. Open your eyes, your inner eyes. Research copper. Research mercury and gold. See what ancient civilizations used them for, and open your eyes wider to what the possibilities could have been if they had been at, let's say, eight on the ten scale—just see. (*They are saying that elements have much greater potential than are currently allowed on Earth.*) In the Egyptian era, a lot of them were five, six, some even mastered seven. Research and you will find, and then use your imagination what could be the possibility if man, or someone, had the full scale available. Use your desire for knowledge, combined with imagination, because you in a human body, your brain is not equipped. But imagination leads you to your inner brain, your soul brain—that is why this one works well! Huge imagination, accesses easily the soul brain. Don't become the human brain, it will put limitations on you. Use the human brain for research. Then use the imagination—the possibilities of what could become—that will lead you to your soul brain.

D. Wow, that's great advice.

T. There you go. Okay.

D. Thank you so much for that teaching. I'm very grateful.

T. See you in the lab.

D. Alright, my friends. Farewell.

T. Farewell.

C9, Ophelia: The Little Wheel of the Zodiac (Dec 27, 2019)

It was only when I began reviewing the sessions to include in this *Wave 3* that I noticed the Council of Nine had delivered a series of lectures on the Wheel of Creation. To avoid making Wave 3 too overwhelming, the last half will be in Wave 4. The Wheel has 3 main parts, the spiritual dimensions, the 12 fish tanks, and the Creator. (Obviously, nothing exists that is not an extension of the Creator, but our perception is from a position of separation.) The inner part of the Wheel, the spiritual realities, and the external fish tanks, where matter and form are located, have been described with increasing detail over the years. Although it is not obvious to us, patterns that define the large Wheel are repeated on smaller and smaller scale, even down to the atomic level. The Council of Nine tells how the properties of the fish tanks are mirrored by the wheel in the sky, the zodiac signs. Christine is an excellent astrologer because of her psychic sensitivities. She can detect and interpret the change in the energy radiated from a planet as it moves into different sections of the sky. With my engineering view of the cosmos, I can only guess that the transiting planet amplifies or alters the energy coming towards Earth from the background stars and galaxies. And for whatever reason, the partitions of the firmament reflect the properties of the 12 fish tanks and influence life on Earth.

C9. This is the Council of Nine, here with Zachariah. First, we would like to thank you for connecting fish tanks, realities, worlds, into a common pool that mankind once more can begin to understand. Earlier civilizations connected easier with the higher realms and the stars, understanding that they were portals to a higher knowledge, not knowing WHAT knowledge. But each star constellation they found when they understood (*how*) to read the sky, read the phenomena, stellar phenomena, not only moon phases—but as they learned the grand rotation of celestial images, they understood and could read their future. The big Wheel and the little wheel coexist. The big Wheel is *(holding the different energies of)* the fish tanks, correlating with the small wheel known to man as the zodiac. It is the same. The zodiac signs are a memory from those who understood the big Wheel. In some way, the zodiac signs correlate with the zodiac signs versus fish tanks. They are in some way mirroring each other, made it easier for man to understand the grander events that took place on the plane where they were at. You worked together with Zachariah to unfold astronomic relations to the consciousness here; this one as well. Once you start to understand the little wheel, then you have an easier path to follow the fish tanks and the big Wheel—your disk. For instance, fish tank four correlates with the motherly zodiac sign of Cancer. It is a water tank, a water realm. Don't focus too much on the names of the constellations, focus on the elements. This one, working with astrology, rarely looks at the sign. Simply reads the element flow and whether that element flows easily, strong, pounding, or slow—how the element water flows give this one an understanding of his surroundings. You can travel between fish tanks as you understand how to master the vibration of elements. But for the regular man, zodiac signs is a way to understand that flow. Just know that you, as Elahims, never use those terms. You only talk in the terms of vibration, the scale within a specific element. Fish tank five is fire. In astrology it resonates with the sign of Leo, it is a fixed energy. The fixed energy means that it lacks the ability to move and to change easily. That is why we put in a lot of effort at this time in this fish tank, not only due to karmic occurrences, but the element and modality surrounding you is not complementary for change. When souls incarnate, they choose from a pool of different modalities within the elements. The element is stronger early on in that specific sign. It waters out, it withers, it becomes weaker. Meaning that the soul has the ability to travel to Earth, combined with the astronomic-astrologic councils who initiate travels for souls. They help not only to design the jackets, the physical—you have been told about those who create the suits and the inner vibrations where a soul attach to its journey in a variety of ways, trying to work on karmic remains as well as teaching others to be enlightened and welcome their karmic remains. Sometimes a journey here is not to—even with a Coat still open—a journey here can simply be to help someone else to acknowledge its Coat. You don't have to have a folded Coat to operate on the behalf of others. So, you can come down in lives that, in many ways, lack meaning, even with a Coat still existing, just as a restful journey. You do not work on your own karmic debt or patterns that you wish to address or change, but you can come as a vacation almost, simply to assist someone else. That is granted if a soul has about five lifetimes behind with great progress, with great effort taking place; then a soul can be granted, even with a Coat, to come down and simply assist another Coat. It is a way to be present in the Earthly vibration but not necessarily having to fully (*engage*). In some way a soul can look back on prior visits and document by simply being present in the Earth vibration. That means, in some way, they document and work on their own patterns, but from a silent observer within. It is important though, and it's easier to do so, as you are in a physical container. So, as a soul has had, let's say five productive lives in its backpack, it might come down simply to observe the results of the efforts, which is not the same as addressing them in direct contact. When they do so, they are also normally helping someone else. So the soul splits its journey, it doesn't address, but it observes the pattern, like a silent observer. I wish I could tell you more.

D. Is there any way a soul would know if they are living one of those lives?

C9. Certain lives where there is little friction, yet the soul is very aware of feelings, thoughts, behaviors, but it doesn't feel like it belongs in the current time. Then, indeed, that is a sign that you might be here as an observer of the pattern, the trail, that you have left behind—simply not in direct contact with the events that you normally address. So when a soul comes down in those lives, they have little friction. However, they can have inner friction. The outer ones, creating karmic incidents for a soul to grow, are non–existent. However, the soul feels within, the human feels within, a need of growth. It can feel, let's say, bored. Boredom is not the same as being passive—it's absolutely not the correlation I'm portraying here. When you feel the power and the will within but you can't see events mirroring any progress, that can indicate that you are here to simply observe a trail, a pattern within.

D. If they came down to help someone, they would probably be involved with another individual?

C9. Indeed. Normally working as siblings. That is normally the relationship. Anyway, you have those who create suits, but you also have the council that operates in disguise when this suit is best suited to go down—at what time, in what element—to trigger events.

D. So, a specific soul would need to be born in a certain stellar configuration?

C9. In a certain time, yes—year, month, and also time of day—to trigger different elements and the elements coexist and trigger the inner layers, the emotional, mental capacities within the journey. So, in many ways, when the soul is born, due to the frequency, the high or low level of certain elements trigger the suit. So, if we see the suit being a container of, let's say, thirty percent mental and seventy percent emotional journey, the Coat looks almost the same regardless of which soul taps into it. There are different factors at play to create the full experience of the humanoid. And the energy flow from your little wheel, the constellations when the soul is born, is a major factor to color the Coat. Do you understand?

D. I do. Is it the moment the body is detached from the Mother that sets the pattern?

C9. One more time.

D. I assume it is the moment the baby is separated from the umbilical cord is when the pattern is set?

C9. Yes, yes. So the pattern is somewhat like a skin, let's say, the suit where the soul enters. But it is in some way silent, the Coat is silent, up till the time of birth. At the time of birth, the elements and different modalities of high or low energy flow—which mirrors the little wheel, the zodiac wheel—colors the Coat, and then the journey can begin.

D. That's fascinating!

C9. There. That is a big part of the Council of Nine, as we communicate with the councils that orchestrate the energy flow in your system around this planet, making occurrences, not only on an individual level but also on a global level. There. That was the message from the Council of Nine.

D. That's wonderful. What dimension are those other councils residing on?

C9. They belong in ten and eleven. Ari and this one visits. Those have never been in body, masters of energy flow. In some way eighth involved as well. The higher levels, it's not just one level, it's several that brings a part of their knowledge to coexist and to grow as a Council of Astronomy, if you like. Understanding that all creation is dependent on vibration and the wide span, the band of different vibrations within a specific element.

D. I have a somewhat related question. If the fifth fish tank is in need of a lot of assistance, does that imply that other worlds, other planets, struggle in the same manner?

C9. Yes, but differently. If we look at fish tank five, there are also levels that travels from the Pole outwards. You are a bit far out. Let's say, if the first level closest to the Pole, in the fish tank, would be one and, let's say, twenty is the end—where there is no lifeforms at the moment, simply materia—the Earth is on the level seventeen. So it is in more need, it feels the density of the end of fish tank five easier than, let's say, sister planets, also in this fish tank that are on the frequency band four. Even if they are in this fish tank, a highly evolved system, group of systems, civilizations, then they are in the same fish tank but not in the same experience.

D. I understand that.

C9. So, to give you a picture, if you see from within (*closer to the Pole*), it's lighter and brighter, and as it moves outwards it darkens; that means it is more affected of density. It is wider apart between galaxies here, it's more open space because you are isolated, as you are—I would not call it quarantined—but you are isolated in your experience, to not have a full effect or mirror the other ones in your fish tank. Closer to the Pole, closer in the beginning of the fish tank, closer to the Pole, it's more congested, more light. From your perspective, you would probably see it as they would crash together. But there is more light, more congestion. As you travel outwards, it is wider apart between planetary systems, more isolated, and that is also mirroring the consciousness within the being, the humanoid, where you feel isolated. It's the soul's way to in some way answer to a vibration, a call, in the fish tank, knowing that it is traveling to a place that is a little bit more secluded. There was more enlightenment on this planet when you started to come in body about 5 million years ago. You traveled here as a scout, in many ways. Physical body but manifested form. The system was about on the level eleven. Now it has moved outwards, meaning it has a sense of separation from Source. Those who are closer to the Pole have a stronger connection. They are manifested, they are an occupying soul (*on the planet*) but they don't have a sense of separation from that Source.

D. I do follow that.

C9. Good. We will continue the discussion, probably this upcoming session, because we have been given word that there is someone here with a journal to discuss. (*They acknowledged Bob.*)

D. Well, thank you so much for that wonderful information.

C9. You are much welcome, and we will return to continue the discussion of the elements, because it is crucial for you to understand your place in the little wheel, the planet as well as in the big Wheel. That is why this one is familiar with the little wheel. There.

D. I look forward to that.

C9. We will return.

D. All right, my friends. Goodbye.

O. This is Ophelia, just with a little bit of a cleaning. Let's see. We need to have a quick clean since it wasn't fully affecting the body, but it still leaves a little bit of wisdom of earlier speaker. So we do not want the next speaker (*Bob*) to be overwhelmed or confused with too much knowledge that is just left as a wind. Hmm. So, I clean out the information, if that is needed, so that there is not a smell left—if you understand that concept. We exchange the smell to, hmm, a cinnamon bun! (*She gently laughed.*)

D. Hello, Ophelia. Did you have any thoughts you would like to add to what they were talking about?

O. It is important for man to understand and correlate to its place in the grand drama, in the grand play that is Earth. And one way to do so is using the understanding of the zodiac. It is, in many ways, accepted in the consciousness of humanity as it has been practiced on several levels, several continents, over a long period of time. It is a way to identify who you are. Doing so will open the portal to start to identify yourself as a soul. The little wheel, the zodiac wheel, simply indicates the human you. Once you start to recognize and embrace the human you, based on the understanding and assistance from the little wheel, then indeed it is a gateway to start to understand the soul. The soul has its own wheel—it follows the big Wheel—but it's similar like the little wheel. So once you start to recognize yourself following patterns based on a well-known teaching (*astrology*), it opens the gateway to also invite the soul to make itself known and to show itself, perhaps, in a different energy flow than the human flow. So, in many ways, it opens the gate to a higher understanding that eventually will lead you to your higher self, to understand that you are two individuals, two entities on a mission here. (*Both human and soul.*) It's a journey that will grow as you begin to investigate who you are. And it is a baby step to start to understand the grand energy, the majestic self within. So, that is why this one has always been poked each time this one feels that she should not work with the zodiac any more. We constantly give her a treat, as it is important that she remains and understands and reads people based on that. That is one thing that this one does, reads people based on, not zodiac signs, but the element they radiate. Not only if they are air, water, and so forth, but where in that whole band, in that scale, is the soul vibrating. This one has the ability, as a chameleon, to communicate, if he wants to, to that specific vibration. (*Ophelia uses the pronouns he or she, depending on whether she means Seth or the incarnation, Christine.*)

D. How many elements are there?

O. There are four major here, but there is a fifth one that is more related to soul energy. The energies that are familiar to man in this little wheel are earth, water, fire, air, but the fifth element is the soul, which is different. It connects all these elements into one, and that is what the ritual that you observed is aiming for. And as you do combine all those elements into one, then you indeed have the ability to access that Eye. That is the soul eye, the soul element. There. (*The ritual was something Bob and Lasaray experienced on Etena, which was described in 'Notes, Volume 2'.*)

D. That's very good, thank you!

O. Oh, you are much welcome.

C9, Ophelia: The Wounded Earth (Jan 1, 2020)

The Council of Nine began this session and made several statements that require some commentary. They say, "So everything in this disk relates to understanding how to merge with either a physical form, or an elemental form such as water, such as wind. It is a way for souls to progress outside the spiritual realities." From the very earliest talks, the spirits have said that each fish tank has its own type of form. Souls are assigned or choose to go (if allowed) to places where they can expand their knowledge. However, a fish tank, galaxy, planet, or lifeform is not static. Earth, for example, was once home to humanoids that were very different from us. They were much more aligned with their soul, so the lessons available to those bodies were not the same as we are currently subjected to. The councils will impose change on our solar system by sending energy from nearby systems into ours. The upcoming waves of change will force humans to reassess how they interact with one another and the Earth.

Ophelia comes in after the Council of Nine to talk about the wounds on the Earth from previous blunders. The wound on the Earth in North America was mentioned by Jeshua in one of his first talks from October 30, 2016. He said, "I would like to, if possible, to transmit the visual of the past that has created disturbance in the karmic scale for this planet. This took place prior to known civilizations, yet there were civilizations here, not necessarily human in...the humans existed, in some way, but the brain was smaller. That progressed over time, intervened by the more angelic realm, to create these beings, the humankind, more in power of their faith at this time." Then I asked him, "In Earth years, when did this occur?" To which Jeshua replied, "Around 300,000 BC. It took place in what is now in the middle of the United States, bordering to Canada. This is where the battle took place, creating a crater that drew in landscapes in that specific region, which from above looked like a collapse."

C9. This is the Council of Nine.

D. Welcome back, my friends.

C9. Thank you. We are here once more to give you clues about the Wheel connecting to what you can perceive here as the little wheel, alongside the understanding of the differences between fish tanks—how they separate and how they coexist into one level of understanding. Each disk around the Creator, the Pole, has a variety of realities, if you like. Even though you do not travel between disks, you can still have an understanding about the disks that rotates around the Creator Pole. This disk carrying twelve fish tanks, all related to, in some way, manifested experiences. Just because it's not a form, such as an animal, plant, human, it still is considered form. So everything in this disk relates to understanding how to merge with either a physical form, or an elemental form such as water, such as wind. It is a way for souls to progress outside the spiritual realities. This disk, if we see the spiritual realities being about 60 to 75 percent before it touches any fish tank. Also be aware that certain fish tanks are closer to the Pole. 75 percent is about what the fifth fish tank before...let me clarify, stumble upon words. From the Center Pole to fish tank five, spiritual realities occupy about 75 percent (*of the radius of the disk*). Other fish tanks, such as the fourth, the spiritual realities occupy 45 percent before merging with fish tank four. That is why fish tank five, where you are as humans, feels separated from Source in some way. It is further away in your consciousness as you travel into form. However, all fish tanks are equally close to Source, it is just in the perception from form that feels closer or separated from the Creator. As each fish tank rotates, the Wheel rotates, (*resulting in*) motion, changes, growth. Also know that hibernation is considered a phase of growth, such as fish tank three. Fish tank three is currently in hibernation. Traveled from the two o'clock position, just to make it understandable for you. As a system within a fish tank, as well as a fish tank as a whole, has understood and progressed, it moves into a phase of hibernation. First, the phases of hibernation versus peaks of growth. Light is moving from the inner level of the fish tank outwards like waves—that is the first level of growth. Hibernation it moves inward, moving outwards as the whole fish tank itself transitions into another level of understanding. The waves follow the rotation of the Wheel. Do you see the picture?

D. There are waves moving from the Center Pole outwards?

C9. Constantly, in each fish tank. There are motions considered, let's say, mountains and canyons, waveforms going inwards versus outwards. At this point, your solar system, your galaxy, is further out. Other galaxies, neighbors, are closer. So you first move from the center, the beginning of the fish tank closest to spirit realm, outwards. As you have reached the end, let's say, the wall of the fish tank, motion can either move backwards again towards Source, or the whole fish tank rotates and moves into hibernation, such as fish tank three. What we see in this time is that as your galaxy reaches the crucial point where it appears as a collapse of darkness, this is where this system will return inwards again before we move the whole fish tank. It is because of the fact of karmic debt that exists on this plane within this galaxy. There has been other projects, similar as Earth, that collapsed under the pressure of karma. Karma, in some way, exists in ALL realities, it just acts differently based on what form the soul occupies. Here it's been a progressive journey to clean earlier acts that has negative effect on energy flow to your neighbors. This galaxy system, as we call it, is in some way operating as an island within the fish tank. It is secluded due to the occurrences that have been taking place, not only on Earth but on similar projects within your galaxy. Your neighboring galaxies are affected by your journey, but they are not fully colored, as we have encased this galaxy within your fish tank. I would not say quarantined, but you are acting solo due to residual acts that need to be understood.

D. What would be the time-frame of the residual acts? Is it recent history or very remote?

C9. Remote. On this planet, there were occurrences that took place about ten million years ago. You should also know that due to the encased borders around your galaxy and this reality, you feel locked by time. Outside, even within this fish tank, time operates differently. A year is not 365 days. On your closest neighbor it's 525, so there is a difference in time. Here you are not only encased by acts that needs to be understood as a whole before this whole system can progress into a higher consciousness, a higher light. At the moment you are in the canyon and the lessons that you learn at this point decides when and how you ascend into the light. You will all eventually ascend into that light, but if understanding has not been taking place, acts not cleared, understood, released, healed, then the transition into the light will be different.

D. Ten million years ago, those were different souls than are currently incarnating?

C9. There are some here that have a memory of that existence here. The stronghold was southern Europe, northern Africa, as well as North America—in the central, mid-west central, slightly north. At that time also, in those two locations, as well as some over around the area of Yemen, Syria, Iran, Iraq, Palestine border, coast, water—that region versus the North American—similar civilization. Technology advanced. The karma lies that in the South American region there were nature groups concerned about the development of technology and (*how other groups were*) excavating minerals such as gold in order to use it as fuel. The groups in South America were more inclined to preserve nature, to preserve resources. They begged these two groups, especially the one in North America, to be gentle with the development, to communicate with the planet, to understand the limits of too much advancement and to the cost that came hand-in-hand with that excavation and development of taking more from the Earth, oil, gas, combined made a third more powerful fuel. Uranium was also combined (*with gold*). It became like a group of mad professors just aiming higher and higher. The Earth sent out a call, a help signal, and the ones in South America begged these groups to rest, to not develop further. They did not listen. The end result in this continent where you are at (*North America*), was an explosion. It created a massive wound into the Earth, open wound that was impossible to heal. The combination of uranium, gold and the amount of efforts that these groups conducted in order to use it for travels, to use it for power. It came to an abrupt end. This civilization here collapsed first, created a big wound. The second fall occurred later in the region where Yemen and Syria (*are now located*). It created a turmoil, a different wound—energies angry, rotating, spiraling. It is a wound from the same acts, it is just channeled differently. Here it just became an open wound. There it spiraled. It took everything with it in that spiral, and it is still a memory in that region. That is why mental and emotional aspects within your being tremble, spirals—it is the effect of prior acts.

D. Was that civilization similar like humans, or predominantly travelers?

C9. Not humans. Did not look human. They have arms, legs, head, similar like human. Taller, slimmer, higher intelligence. Traveled here in crafts, not soul incarnation. The ones that were in the South American region, Shea was there, incarnated. Those that have a memory of this remembers the South American region. The other ones not incarnated.

D. I remember that someone said, in an earlier session, that this one was here millions of years ago and there was an explosion?

C9. You were here (*in manifested form*) 5 million years ago. This one, later. These actions have repeated, and you are repeating them again. The first time was even further back than 10 million years ago. It has been developed over time. Understand that this planet is rich in resources and the project is to be one with resources, to use them wisely. But it has been seen as a big supermarket for other entities, and it has rubbed off on incarnations as well. Instead of coexisting with not only each other, but with your host, you act like it is the last day and you have to stock up on food. The resources are not unlimited. The karma and understanding lies in finding balance between what you take and what you need. You do not need everything that you take. But there is a sensation of survival, a constant fight for survival, and it rubs off in all your societies in different ways. This fear of neighbors, this fear of being taken out, being eliminated, yes, there is a memory because civilizations have come and gone. But what we wish for you as you are reaching the end of this wave outwards in your fish tank, as you progress into the light once more, how would you heal the wound? A wound that you might not fully understand or remember, but a wound just as visible today as before.

D. If the karmic pattern was established around the Earth long ago, are the souls here now in some way compensating for what was done by other souls?

C9. Hmm. Compensating, perhaps, but they take on roles to reexperience the events. Not all are personally attached to this wound, as they were not incarnating. However, they take on the pattern, the behavior of the visitors. And some take on the pattern that existed at that point in South America. So, in some way, this play that occurs on Earth, it is divided between those who take on prior behaviors, such as those who acted like the mad professors, and then some take on the behavior of enlightment in different ways. So, you are replaying the game, the play, but you have not, on a soul level, accumulated this karma. But you are acting on the behalf of councils of the Creator. You are re-acting this play, redoing certain mistakes, certain behaviors. You, among others, have chosen to take on the behavior of enlightment, to enlight man in different ways. So, you can see that the play is just restarting.

D. Would a soul's entire history of incarnation here, then, represent one or the other of those roles?

C9. In many ways, yes. But a soul who takes on behaviors of, let's say, the less progressive side, seeks to move over to the side of enlightenment. And that is part of the soul growth in this grand drama. You need to be careful how you portray this, but you are, in many ways, acting independently from will. It is a play designed by the Creator to see whether a measurement of soul incarnation would increase the light, would change the play. So what occurs—and it's not just now, it is from the last 25,000 years or so—is when the game started again. (*The human vehicle was altered and some of the lessons were changed.*) In many ways, you are acting independently from will, or aside from free will. This is a tricky path for you to deliver message, as the foundation for enlightment lies on free will. And indeed, a soul has free will, but in some way, the play, the game, is staged and you are following motions, acts, from a prior play. It is a balance for you to deliver messages, as none wants to feel like they are being mastered from an outside source—that free will does not exist—and it contradicts some of the teachings that you have up till even the last day as a human to change the flow, to change your future incarnations, if you like. So this is something that we will continue to analyze, discuss, and reveal, because the play is reappearing once more. The actors are different because you (*all souls*) are incarnating. So, you have free will, but you also follow the grand design of the play.

D. That makes a lot of sense.

C9. That is what we wished to have said today. We will continue to discuss this, as we have left you a seed of your reality, that some is staged by design, and the design mirrors events from a far past.

D. When it comes to individual souls, you previously said we entered a low period, like a trough?

C9. Yes, you are in that canyon, you are in that phase of reshaping yourself. The play, the game, has reached the point of collapse or transformation. And that is why it is of such a high interest now, because you can go either way. The free will—back to that—is present in how you solve this current state of development on your planet. The game itself is staged by design, where you have less free will to change the design itself. However, as you are incarnating at this point, you have the option of choice. Those who came before, not incarnating, didn't see choice, only saw interests. What you see now is those who are captivated by the play, act upon interest. Those who understand that there is choice and there is free will alongside, or in the middle, blended in this game, have the option of choice and have also the option to change the development, to change the transition into the next phase, which is light. But light—you should also know that from a spiritual reality—darkness and light are not good or bad, they are simply different frequencies. You, as Elahim, resonate with the dark. You feel comfortable resting under the clear sky of the night. Those who are souls coming from other realities, they feel perhaps depressed or low in energy when there is darkness and night. You are opposite, you recharge in darkness, you recharge by the stars in a clear night sky. As you understand that light can also be considered... uhmm... what word can we use? Let's just give you a picture instead. If your whole reality transitions into the light, and the light means balance between your species, understanding of healing energy, understanding of being one with each other, being one with your host, then the light indicates an increasing state of mind to Source. If you do not progress in that manner and you reach the light, that light will be similar as standing in a desert, in a wide-open landscape of sand under a clear blue sky of sun. So you see, the light can come to you differently as well. There.

D. I follow that.

C9. We will continue the topic.

D. Good. I find it to be fascinating.

C9. Just know that even light has two sides: One that indicates enlightenment, one that shows reversed.

D. Like separation?

C9. Indeed. The picture has been given, and we will return.

D. Thank you so much for that.

C9. You are much welcome. Elahim.

D. Elahim, my friends.
O. So, here we are. This is Ophelia.
D. Hello, my friend.
O. So more information has been revealed from your Council, and it is a way for you to understand that your whole reality is moving through a phase, revisiting prior actions. But it streams from further back than man could possibly understand. And it is also not all human–made. But you are, as humans, taking on the roles that once took place between non–humans. But what we are wishing for is that the actions are cleared, healed, understood and released. You are just now doing it as an incarnation in human form, but the game is still the same.
D. That does make sense.
O. Souls coming in at this point—and that is why some say lessons are much harder here—yes, because you are coming into an already set game of chess.
D. You are reading my mind, because I was just thinking about the current time being a difficult one for some souls.
O. Yes. And it is by design because the wish is from your planet who sent out a request to higher councils that are communicating with systems—solar systems, planets, stars—not only souls communicate to councils. We would be delighted if one of those councils would be able to communicate. At one point, we are aiming for those councils to make themselves known—those who do not occupy their time with souls, they simply communicate with celestial bodies, systems, galaxies. There are also councils that are in charge and have a whole fish tank under their care. So each fish tank also reports to a council.
D. What dimension would those higher councils reside on?
O. They belong closest to Source, twelve, eleven. Thirteen, meaning the Source. Those who do not communicate. It's not spirit guides that ascend, it's a group created by Source, operating as the first extension from Source, normally looking after fish tanks, galaxies, having them report. In this case, the council that monitors your galaxy and your planet and your system, heard the calling from the Earth as it was wounded. It was like a big, open wound, and the planet sent out its request and from that point modifications on how to access this plane took place. There were times when this region here, where the big wound exists, it was in hibernation for a long time. Not many walked on this land, because of the need to heal. (*They have identified two separate*

explosions in North America related to visitors. The larger incident was 10 million years ago. The second was around the Great Lakes some 300,000 years ago.)

D. So in some way, when we do work on the sixth creating solar systems and such, would that be under the direct guidance of the higher councils?

O. You operate and report to councils who in some way bypass you and commutate directly with galaxies, planets and celestial bodies, and from there you get your manuals, if you like, on how to restore matter, energy flows and so forth. What took place in the region of North America, here, after the wound, the land was in need of healing. It was a big wound, it filled about 30 percent of your current country.

D. What type of wound was it?

O. It came from the explosion of blending different elements. Uranium, the laboratorium exploded, it created not only a wound on the surface, but it became a huge wound that went into the core of your planet.

D. Are those types of things misinterpreted as asteroid impacts and things like that by our scientists?

O. This specific wound was created by visitors operating mad with minerals, elements, resources. But yes indeed, certain spots on your planet are not from asteroid impact. The big wounds lie here as well as in the region around Iraq, Yemen, Syria, Palestine— different wound. That wound is spiraling, rotating. If I can give you two words, here (*in North America*) the wound is sad, it is a deep impact of sorrow in the evolution on this planet. On the other region, that wound creates anger.

D. I remember you mentioned that once before, that people pick up on that sensation.

O. Yes. It's the Earth's anger at being overexploited at one point. Here, it was a huge sadness, and we all felt the wound. It occupied thirty percent of the landmass of the US.

D. In the center?

O. Center, yes. The region bled, wounded. When natives came here later in your evolution, they felt the sorrow, they felt the sadness of the land. They worked intensively to heal the land. They became keepers of the land. They, as other men traveled here and tried to occupy the land, tried to resist. It wasn't that they wanted to keep their tent, so to speak. They were highly movable if needed, but they were not done with healing the land. That's what they fought for, they fought to remain because their work of healing this wound was not done. They still felt the sadness, the sorrow, the calling from this wound, the calling from the Earth to heal.

D. Are you talking about when the Europeans came here?

O. Yes. It's not that the natives themselves were not mobile, they could have easily moved to another space, and they could have easily moved to a better place for growth, let's say. But they stayed because they felt compelled, and it was a calling for them to heal the land. They fought for their spot, not to grow a vegetable or for not having the pickle to move a tent. They stayed and fought because the wound asked them to.

D. I've often wondered if I was supposed to spend those years studying Native American spirituality?

O. Yes, because you had to feel the wound. In many ways, when you have felt low in energy, it is that wound, because you communicate directly to your planet. You have the ability, when you occupy this place in a body, that you directly communicate and hear the calling of the Earth. You have been here in Indian form, Native form, conducting rituals and ceremonies in order for that wound to be healed. You asked to come here again so that you could be in direct contact with the source of the work that you are trying to promote. In many ways, what you have felt as sadness in your life, depression, loneliness, it is because you are walking directly on the wound.

D. Like in West Virginia, I felt that.

O. Yes, and when you were in Michigan. So, in many ways, it is not a human condition, it's an Earth condition. So, we will return.

D. That makes a lot of sense. Thank you.

O. You are much welcome. Talk soon. Bye bye.

C9, Ophelia: The Upper and Lower Disks (Jan 5, 2020)

The Council of Nine describes planets and galaxies as being closer or further from the Center Pole or the spiritual dimensions. They also say higher or lower, which we instinctively visualize as bobbling up and down on an imaginary spacial axis. The problem, of course, is that they are using our words to describe different dimensions than the four known to us—length, width, height, and time. (As a side note, each parallel reality would have a similar set of four dimensions, plus several others. When aliens want to travel, they use a frequency dimension unknown to man and move their craft into a parallel reality. The units of measurement in the parallel plane are not the same, otherwise, traveling between galaxies would be impossible.) The Council of Nine uses words such as close, near, far, higher, lower, etc. In this context, they are identifying where a reality is on a spiritual vibration, not its location within a coordinate system.

In this session, they give a detailed explanation of the upper and lower disks on the Wheel, which we briefly mentioned in *Wave 2*. Like all things in existence, there is a polarity in the Wheel itself. From their description, there are two disks in very close proximity to each other, and are designed as mirror images. Both have the outer portion of the Wheel divided like a pie into 12 boxes or bubbles (i.e., fish tanks). The lower one is stationary and is manifested from the Creator, so it is called the Creator disk. Each of the 12 boxes hold different types of intentions, which are projected upwards into the fish tanks above it. The Wheel that all spirits, universes and form occupy has been termed as the energy disk, the fog disk, or the solid disk. It rotates clockwise above the Creator disk. As a fish tank moves above different boxes on the Creator disk, unique experiences and energy flows are encountered. The Creator disk causes patterns to emerge and then collects the memories after experiences have occurred. Bob once characterized this disk as the hand of the Creator. So within the solid disk, energy flows outward from the Center Pole through the spiritual dimensions and into the fish tanks, And intentions also move upwards from the Creator Disk. The combinations of these creative powers give rise to the Universe that we observe, occupy, and experience events in.

C9. This is the Council of Nine, continuing our discussion. We are here to convey the understanding of flow, free flow, free energy, free power from Source, directing to fish tanks. The uppermost from this disk considering 11, 12, 1, acts as a generator for the Wheel in general. Stronger connection to Source, indeed, generators for the disk. The fish tank at noon is the fulfillment of them all. Not physical form, in the sense that you experience here, but it carries the understanding and experience throughout the disk. Fish tank 11 and 1 indicates transitions to fulfillment, transitions to beginning. You have met friends from fish tank two—a small highly efficient group. (*They are referring to the Taffles, who were presented in Notes, Volume 2.*) They are light-bearers connecting the energies that radiate from the first fish tank, initiating a starting point, if you like, throughout the Wheel. They assist energy flow, channels energy forward in the

Wheel. They are highly efficient energy workers. As we develop the fish tanks, the wish from several councils was to experience energy in different ways. Fish tank four, for instance, is considered a healing hub. It channels through its understanding of light healing energy throughout the Wheel. You should know that each fish tank has an assignment, if you like, to channel its experiences to neighboring fish tanks. It (*each fish tank*) carries a unique pattern—such as four, (*with its*) healing energy. At this time, in fish tank five, the border between four and five is dissolving due to the wish from higher councils to radiate the healing energy into your fish tank, into your realities. There are certain galaxies already operating similar as if they were located in fish tank four, lit up...how can I make you see? The closer a reality exists to the Pole, the more it operates as a spiritual reality. The further out it travels, it becomes lost in the maze of experiences contained in the fish tank. It is to see whether a reality can navigate from within, (*when it is*) separated from the light, from Source light—how a reality experience transitions of separation. That is the teaching in fish tank five. Not all travel from inward outward, but that is the experience here. If you see all fish tanks and the general motion within them, it varies. Here it moves from within outwards in waveforms, as we have mentioned. Other fish tank simply rotates clockwise or anti-clockwise. It's a rotation circle in that sense, meaning the energy occupies and is available differently. In a fish tank where rotation goes clockwise or anti-clockwise, it simply is in symbiosis with the available energy in the fish tank. Those who have the waveform, such as fish tank five, experiences highs and lows of consciousness—heightened and decreased—due to the motion. When one is on a peak, one tends to forget how one came there, and the lesson is that you have to slide down into the canyon once more to harvest the knowledge that you accessed as you were on the peak. When you are in the canyon, you are blind, you feel blind, such as your reality is at this point. To give you the picture, the (*spiral*) galaxy closest to you, Andromeda, is on the peak, observing its friend, you, Milky Way, in the bottom of the canyon, never separated from your neighbors who gently guides you. You are, though, in the canyon feeling separated, feeling blinded. And that is the teaching where you have to rise into your light, rise into your consciousness, using the will that you possess to wish to seek the light. Each time a system is in the canyon, it is not only observed by spirit and councils, neighboring systems (*with*) different teachings in its possession assist by providing information—like raindrops—assisting the ship in need. In many ways, this system, your galaxy, would be considered a ship on the ocean lacking its sail.

D. I have a question. There are like a billion galaxies or more—do they all go up and down independently?

C9. In this fish tank, yes.

D. And in other fish tanks the energy—

C9. Rotates. And there is no waveform. The experience is different. They simply exist in the rotation; they exist in the energy force available to them. There are differences of experience, whether a flow in the fish tank rotates clockwise or anti-clockwise. The disk itself, with the fish tanks, rotates clockwise. The energy flow within a fish tank can either mirror the big disk by rotating clockwise, becoming a replica, a copy, of the big disk. Fish tank twelve, for instance, holding all experiences, is the one rotating clockwise as the disk. It is a miniature of the big disk, carrying all experiences, all matter, whether it's energy or form, holding them all in rotation, being the engine for the disk. Fish tank twelve is not where souls travel to. It is—how can one say? I'll give you an image of a museum or a storage unit for the Creator to collect all events within or throughout the disk, all fish tanks combined, all teachings stored in that location of noon. It is where all experiences merge, dissolve, or begin. Some (*experiences*) initiating new events. (*It is*) a laboratorium of collections of events throughout the disk, where the Creator either dissolve, end a cycle, or initiate a new one. Your little friends that you have met in fish tank two (*the Taffles*) work with form, energy manifesting as form. They are highly efficient.

D. I have a question about the one at noon, twelve. As the Wheel rotates, does it change in some way? Does another one become twelve, or is twelve always twelve as it rotates around?

C9. In many ways, there are two disks, one lower and one upper. The lower one is the manifested disk. That one is constant. The energy disk slightly above, mirroring the fish tanks, are the ones that move. So, the disk is in two (*parts*), one solid, one stationary, one in motion. It sends the motional, the moving disk, gradually throughout—motion clockwise. The picture has been sent to this one. You have been given the image of the spiritual realities' center to Pole and fish tanks outward, locating as a clock in this disk. But there is also levels on the disk. One stationary, one travels through experiencing. The stationary disk is where all completion is stored. The ones where you belong to, the second, Etena, and so forth, you belong in the movable disk. You travel throughout.

D. I actually follow that. And when it finally reaches the twelfth spot, would the information collected in that fish tank—?

C9. If you see the disk in motion as it would, like you say, complete the circle, returning to twelve, it, in some way, descends and merges with the stationary disk and it simply becomes an understanding; such that a new level of understanding can be provided in an upcoming motion, upcoming cycle. There is no way to measure this motion in time.

D. It must be immense, in what we would consider years?

C9. Yes. Like I said, there are no numbers to measure it in years. Not even a trillion trillion trillion trillion will suffice. If you think of souls, how they are born and eventually ascend, it will take about a trillion (*sequential*) souls (*soul lifetimes*), at least, from them being born to ascension, meaning that the ones...oh, there is no numbers, how can I explain? The souls that are active at this point...we will return, there is no way to measure.

D. If we go back to fish tank five, I pictured an ocean with choppy waves. Would each galaxy be like riding on the flow of those spiritual waves, up and down?

C9. Yes. Sometimes there are several galaxies in the peak or in the canyon. At this time, you are by yourself in your canyon. Andromeda observing, assisting, aiming you, guiding you to rise, to understand that your ship is not powerless just because you feel your sail is broken. So, in many ways, you can see your reality wobbling as a ship, powerless, and that is the mental level of consciousness at this point. And that is a teaching by itself, to look for the power when one feels powerless, to not become passive, to not cease to exist as an easier way to exit. What we see, in many ways, are souls who exit early instead of fighting. They are wishing to see again, wishing to remove blindfolds, thinking the easiest way is to seize an exit. (*They mean souls who return home too soon from self-destructive behaviors.*) But that gives more power to the ship floating uncontrolled on the sea, the more who exit, the more who remain passive—which is also considered an exit. From the spiritual reality, we do not see a difference necessarily by physical exit versus soul exit, emotional, mental exit—meaning being passive. It is considered the same and you abandon your ship, you abandon your friends instead of seeking ways and means to steer this ship. Together, you have the ability to steer any ship without a sail. But as more and more become paralyzed, exiting in various ways, those who remain feel abandoned.

D. That makes a lot of sense.

C9. So, let me just return to the disk and what we talk about—time. There is no soul available in active duty that has completed the journey. (*The full rotation of the Wheel.*) It is beyond the cycle of an active soul. To give you an understanding, the soul life-cycle, let's say, can be a trillion years before ascension. That doesn't mean a trillion incarnations, it means before soul particle merges with Source. If a soul has a trillion years in active duty, it will take that soul a thousand trillion times (*the lifespan of a spirit*) to complete a circle. There. We will leave for now and we will continue the journey as we discuss the stationary disk versus the motion driven by Source.

D. This is fascinating. I understand a lot of what you are saying, so thank you for that.

C9. Very good. As the rotation moves in the upper Wheel, the fog Wheel, if you like, that is how it looks, as it has completed its understanding of its position, it simply docks or loses its experiences down to the stationary disk, who is the one that will determine the motion further. At this time, due to incidents in the fourth fish tank versus the fifth, the border is dissolving between them. This indicates that there is a motion where the fourth reality, fourth fish tank, will gradually merge with the fifth. Meaning it will aid and heal the fifth reality. In your subconscious, and in the soul awareness of a few, you are aware of this motion and this aid coming from fish tank four. These are the ones, yourself among them, who are here to assist the passive entities on this ship because you know that aid is nearby. Those who operate in different ways to enlighten and to assist this ship are aware of the motion moving in, the assistance of light from fish tank four. They are not aware, necessarily, that it is called fish tank four, but they operate on the behalf of the light that they intuitively feel is coming. There.

D. When a fish tank goes into hibernation, as three, is it the energetic part, the fog part, that goes into hibernation?

C9. Yes, yes. The stationary disk is not in hibernation. It stores the experiences occupying that specific location, fish tank three, in the fog disk, where all action, events take place. They do not take place in the stationary disk. The stationary disk assists events to come into terms, to come into a reality; it assists the energy flow for occurrences and events to take place. This is a science—it's not a human science. You have to think and understand from your soul particle. Your soul particle is similar as the central Pole in this disk, you have to—and you, my friend, have the ability to become this whole image. You can feel the central Pole as a tuning Fork through you from top to bottom. If you put your arms straight out and close your eyes and visualize this image, you have the ability to fully understand the image as a whole, because you will BE this image. This is a way for you to better understand. You do not need to meditate about it, but stand up, close your eyes, visualize this image, feel the Creator Pole through you from top to bottom. Close your eyes, feel your hands connecting to fish tank nine and three; as you do you will gradually be given the whole Wheel and the teachings and keys throughout.

D. Wow, I'll try that.

C9. There. We will leave at this point. We will continue.

D. Thank you so much for the information. That was wonderful.

C9. You are much welcome. Elahim.

D. Elahim, my friends.

O. This is Ophelia. Hello, my friend.

D. Hello, Ophelia. How are you?

O. Oh, doing well. Creating a bridge. So, as you have seen, we gradually provide more information about the information you already had. In this case, the Wheel will continue to expand. It will give more flavor to the dish, if you like. It is a way for you to understand that it's not a one–level or one-dimensional, not even a three-dimensional, experience, an image, that we provide. To understand the whole, you have to become, you yourself, a ten-dimensional individual. You have to see beyond the 3D that you are accustomed to. You have to be the ten dimensional being that you are designed to be. As you, doing the exercise given by the Council of Nine, you will gradually dissolve the 3D reality. Not the three-dimensional view, but the physical you will become lighter, you will sense and become more of a soul traveler, meaning that you will occupy and travel through the different dimensional existences available to you in a human form. This is a way for you to connect to Source and to the grand design of the

Wheel and the disks. Gradually, you will have a glimpse of all disks. This one told you there were three disks, this one got an image of the upper disk, the moving disk, and the stationary one. The one below is a different mystery to solve. So, this one already had a preview of the grand design as a whole.

D. Does the stationary disk in some way impose structure onto the one above?

O. Yes, yes. The one above experiences. The one stationary initiates. So, it's similar—let's say that the stationary disk would be the soul and the moving disk will be the incarnation.

D. (*Laughing.*) I understand that.

O. There you go. Cleaning is done.

D. We have a public séance this week, as you know. Do you have things you would like to talk about?

O. Yes. We would like to convey that this is the beginning of healing. As more and more are accessing the light, feeling the light, not knowing necessarily where the light comes from, some will tune in on fish tank four, as has been mentioned. Other ones will simply grow in their own soul energy, soul particle, becoming the light. This is a time, a new cycle, where healing is needed. So you are entering a phase where you need to heal yourself as well as different areas—not only the environment and everyone within it—but also to heal beliefs. Heal and release. In many ways, healing is release. Bob will discuss how to heal through laughter. We will discuss different ways on how to gradually heal yourself and heal the destination and the surrounding where you are at.

D. Wonderful, I look forward to that talk.

O. So do we. So there.

D. Thank you, Ophelia.

Ophelia: Keycards to the Cosmos (Mar 22, 2021)

It's always a bit of a challenge to pick the best session to end our books. We want it to be uplifting and comforting, not gloomy. Zachariah and Bob ended *Wave 1*. Ia had the final say in *Wave 2*, and Bob ended both *Volume 1* and *Volume 2* of the *Notes from the Second Dimension*. For *Wave 3*, I decided that Ophelia deserves to have her words ring last. She is present at every session as the control, the hidden hand that guides the flow of information and monitors Christine's energy. She also evaluates what is said and—since she hears what I am thinking—how I interpret the concepts. If she senses confusion, she will send thought–bubbles to the speaker or come in and add her own clarifying comments. She usually comes in to clean any residual energy from Christine's body prior to Bob joining. I always try to drag out her presence by soliciting her opinions on something that was said. When she merges with Christine, her angelic energy fills the room and it is incredibly comforting. Ophelia does not condemn, criticize, or speak ill of humans or our activities. She is very matter-of-fact, as evidenced in this session, about topics that might cause concern for some. But Earth is only a temporary home, and the spirit realm does not sugar-coat what the future holds. The trick for us who are incarnated is to trust that we are each guided to our own destiny. When we have that faith, then it is easier to become an expression of our soul.

In one of our earliest sessions, Ophelia was guiding us to write the first book. She said this about *Wave 1*, but it applies to all the Waves they deliver. She said, "The first Wave is to make people aware that they do have a choice—that is the main message in the first Wave. It is also meant to be accessible and amusing through different individuals in this scripture. (*Bob, for one.*) However, as amusing as it might be, the core (*of the teaching*) is enlightenment. Enlightenment to all, to be released from chains, to make your own footsteps—not follow those who might lead you astray."

In this session, Ophelia interrupted a speaker who was having difficulties adjusting his energy to match the human vibration. It was an alien who has been involved with Earth, and is preparing to physically come here. Ophelia describes their activities and base of operations. She then gives an excellent summary of the main objectives for humans and the Earth in the upcoming years.

O. Hmm. Okay. This is Ophelia. We needed to break the communication for now. There was a test to just see if the energies were able to merge—mainly from their point—to see if they could adjust into a human energy form, in that sense. So, they will continue to talk at a later session.

D. They did pretty well, I think.

O. Yes, they did.

D. Is there anything on this end that needs to be improved?

O. The improvement is, of course, to be more clean. And we do see an improvement. So little-by-little, to be more light within the body, the physical body, is helpful. To drink more water, especially before a session, so the energies flow easier and leave. Come and leave. So what we see at this time is a change within the communication, and we are inviting entities that belong in fish tanks related to projects going on at this specific location, Earth. We are, of course, trying to orchestrate the whole setup of speakers because there are several here wanting to have their voice heard.

D. Are they involved with the Earth in any way, or are they simply observing?

O. Not fully interacting with Earth, in that sense. They are more observing the progress and the motion of evolution that they are waiting for certain things to be upgraded before they can fully come in and clean. They are, in some way, cleaners of debris when it comes to atmospheric changes within the web, the web within galaxies. As has been said, the Milky Way is in need of attention. The fish tank and nearby galaxies are wobbling, meaning the web is not optimal for portals for transmissions between. So, in this case, we do need to look into, as always, the understanding of how to cope with energies and elements. And the materia of here on Earth is not suitable for mixing and matching widely. The intent, of course, is to create a more suitable atmosphere within the whole galaxy, within the families of galaxies. Several entities have their bases nearby at this time in Andromeda, trying to observe, but do not fully engage. We are, of course, interested in seeing the change within your species, which does not relate to the atmosphere and the web, necessarily. But it causes a disruption within the inner web that exists on this plane when a species are not aligned mentally or emotionally. In this case, what we are seeing is the collapse of the mental connection within your species. This is in need of change, and in some way for something to be upgraded, we need to—I will not use the words kill off—but we need to delete. We need to adjust where mental problems within your species, the human race, is not operating at its best. The intention, of course, is to create a more harmonious and peaceful species. The mental upgrade, the filters within actions, choices, is ongoing for change. When changes occur, in many ways, all filters are opened—and that is what is going on at this time. We are opening up all windows in your mental capacity. Meaning that prior fears, karmic fears, not all related to your current lifetime, is wide open and bombarding your conscious self. In order for us to fully understand where the filters need to go, where the upgrades within the brain and the mental capacity needs to be changed, we are opening up all lids, if you can see the picture. When we open the lids, it is similar like opening up a dam—the water flows. Memories, fears of survival, a sense of being near death is experienced by the host, meaning the human. In this case, the end result is to understand how you relate to fear, how you maneuver your mind when it is challenged. In order for us to understand the adjustments coming, we need to see firsthand how you respond to fear and turmoil. This is the reason, from a spiritual level, of what is going on. We are sorry if it creates too much distress in some. That is why we ask, of those who see through this illusion, to guide their neighbors into light; to guide them into bypassing fear by focusing on happiness, by focusing on nature, by focusing on touching something similar like an animal that is soft. Once you pet an animal, you bypass the sense of fear, because the animal is sent to you to ignite the peaceful aspect, which is your soul. If you do not have pets nearby, just sit and pick something in nature—it could be something small, like a pine cone. It has the same gift to you as a human. Just hold it in your hands, connect to that pine cone, or a piece of moss if that is your preference. Just know that it is a gift from the Creator to bypass a sensation of fear. And we are indeed opening those lids within your mental capacity in order for us to understand what needs to be changed. There.

D. How long will this process go on?

O. About 5 to 7 or 8 years.

D. Is the population of the Earth going to be significantly reduced?

O. Reduced, yes.

D. Are we going to be safe?

O. Yes!

D. Will there still be people to read our books?

O. (*Laughing*) Huh huh huh. If not this group, then another one. Don't worry. Okay, just needed to come in and somewhat allow you to understand what is upcoming, and also to make you understand that there are visitors here from other fish tanks, predominantly number eight, that is here to communicate. Those are friends from your home base, but they are predominantly occupying form in fish tank eight.

D. Do we go there when we're home?

O. Yes, yes.

D. So we are familiar with them?

O. Yes, yes. Vlac.

D. Is that a repository of knowledge similar to Etena?
O. Yes. It's not a storage of everything within the Wheel, it is more like a factory. Fish tank eight operates as a factory, whereas fish tank four holds light, holds the designs from all other fish tanks. It is a library, if you like, for all fish tanks, where everyone can deposit their treats, their gifts, their wisdom. It is hosted and honored by those who occupy form in fish tank four. Whereas fish tank eight more executes—it's like a factory, to give you a picture.
D. They must be the ones that put things in the store. (*I was joking about the warehouse on Etena where entities go to get copies of lifeforms to take back to their home planet. Bob enjoys going to the store, as he calls it, to look at and meet the strange shoppers from different galaxies. Some of these stories are in 'Notes, Volume 2'.*)
O. (*Laughing*) In the store! Oh, I heard words from Setalay. And Bob was very excited about the store. We (*she and Bob*) do meet, of course—generally quite often—to go through different topics. And if there are topics not fully understood, we try to talk about those as well. The general travel plan is something that I was given. He came and gave it to Zachariah and me. After he's been talking to you, he has now created a general travel plan, or travel card, he says. His travel card is filled up with certain locations that he has heard of and that he has an interest in pursuing. It's indeed a travel card, and he asked Zachariah and myself, as well as Ari, who has also come by, if they could grant him access. This travel card is something that all spirits hold, regarding where they are allowed to travel. You should know that there is also a travel card as you incarnate. All travelers, regardless of if it is into form, energy, or within the spiritual reality, holds a travel card. This travel card, if you think of certain aspects going to Earth to incarnate, there are certain souls where that aspect in their card has been denied due to prior events on this plane. If we look at the incarnation card, or the card where someone has the access to incarnate, based on certain events, sometimes they will be declined to enter into body again, or to enter certain fish tanks as well. The teaching and transformation and upgrade within your soul particle takes place within the spiritual realm on different locations. Certain souls need to be reprogrammed—and I know that this sounds, from a human standpoint, like you are—

D. Sent back to the factory? (*Zachariah had used that expression to describe how souls that do not develop according to the Creator's intention can be repaired or energetically reconfigured.*)

O. Sent back to the factory. And in some way, yes, you are. So souls, depending on actions, if they tried to create a stream of actions within your species, heading in an unspiritual way—if you caused that turmoil—that could be a reason for your travel card to be changed so that you are not, for the time being, allowed to incarnate. So there are certain rules, spiritual laws, if you like, that determine whether you can travel or not.

D. So people who cause a lot a turmoil on Earth can have their card revoked for a while?

O. Yes, that aspect of the card, to incarnate to Earth. They might have the other aspects more open. That card can be fully open to travel on if you were to go to another fish tank in another entity form. But if you have experienced or caused certain things, together with your soul friends and your spirit helper, a soul can also ask for that option to be removed so that they can study up on certain aspects of their engagement on that location. The intent, of course, is not punishment. The intent is growth, and to also, a lot of times, to teach other souls what can happen when you get too caught up in the form located on that destination. In this case, we're talking about Earth. Bob's card is self-designed. Of course, he has a travel card like all do, but he has added Etena, he added the sixth dimension, and so forth.

D. I thought you were the one who asked him if he wanted to learn about form?

O. Yes, together with Gergen, of course. But his card was already pre-programmed. We simply ignited those aspects within his travel card that related to his journey in total. So a soul is not always fully aware of all aspects of their travel card. This card is not something you find physically in your hand, it is located in your particle, in your core, that will be your soul center, that is where this is located. And a soul can, of course, be reprogrammed. You will hear more about this, which will be more understood as a less spiritual action. But it is not a punishment, it is a chain of evolution. Evolution goes on within souls as well. So not just the human design is changing and upgrading and evolving, even soul awareness and those who come, like Bob said, "from the factory", are also upgraded and changed and modified over time.

D. I had a question I wanted to verify before the next book comes out. Are there bodies that aren't claimed by a soul, and are those bodies then occupied fully by the Master Mind? Basically, if there are humans that don't have a traveling soul from one of the spiritual dimensions?

O. You mean at this time?

D. Yes.

O. There is not what would be considered the Master Mind, similar as operating within animals, if that was your question?

D. Yes.

O. There are, however—how can I give you a picture? It is a dot, a spark from several councils, engaging in a human—certain humans. So in that sense you will see it, or it will appear, as a robot almost. But it is not similar as an animal. An animal is completely filled up by the Master Mind. In this case, in the human form, there is also a spark from the Master Mind. So the Master Mind is always present. But certain councils, certain levels of knowledge, is occupying that form combined. So, in some way, they are remotely steered, but the Master Mind is always present.

D. I was just curious. Because there are so many humans now on Earth, I extrapolated that there weren't enough available souls?

O. HUH! (*Ophelia responded with an unexpected laugh, amused at the naïve question, I guess.*) Oh, there is more on the line waiting to come, there are more souls wanting to come than there are bodies to have. So, exchange (*of souls is occurring*). Again, look at the travel card. Certain travel cards are being revoked, exchanged with new souls, new behaviors, new levels of connections. A more peaceful race is what we are aiming for. The travel cards will therefore be modified. Some, not just because of their own private actions. But in general, a certain rotation, if you like, of soul awareness will be connected to travel. Meaning that certain travel cards will be revoked, even though they might not have done anything that caused a problem. It's simply a shift and a change. But the modification of the design, the human form, needs to take place. So, there is a rotation going on several levels.

D. The last time Bob spoke, he talked about the helmet. Is that related to the modifications? (*The helmet was an analogy for the energetic filters and limits that are placed on the human mind. Bob's talk has yet to be published.*)

O. Yes, yes. That is part of it. But in order for us to understand the helmet, in this case that also relates to the filters, we need to understand what sort of energetic helmet fits. In this case, we are opening up the windows, the lids, so that events are experienced. Some events are not your own. Some are triggered by prior past life experiences. Some are related to neighbors and their experiences. So you are bombarded with events, feelings, experiences that might not be your own path. It might relate to something else. In order for you to navigate through this mist, this mist and this maze where we are trying to see where the mind is heading. In order for us to upgrade and change the helmet, we need to understand your response to certain influences. This is nothing new. There.

D. Wow. That was a wonderful talk. Thank you for all that information.

O. Yes, you are much welcome. (*She looks left, towards Bob.*) This travel card, we'll see. He has it in his hands here. Okay, okay. Who could deny him access, one might wonder. Okay. Bye bye.

D. Alright, Ophelia. Bye bye.

Wave 4. The reader probably noticed that, aside from the last talk by Ophelia, all the sessions were recorded prior to 2021. *Wave 4*, which is already being compiled, will continue where these talks left off. There are several new speakers who have made themselves known. One is a group of aliens who asked to be called Visitors from the Past. They were part of the earliest visitors to Earth and Mars, coming here hundreds of millions of years ago. They have given several talks about their activities on both planets. Another new speaker is a representative from the Circle of Elders, a council on the fifth dimension that oversees all Earth activity. He asked to be called Willaby, and is a wonderfully charming individual. We have learned a lot from him about how souls are prepared prior to incarnating, how life records are stored, and the coordination with other dimensions. Ophelia, Bob, the Council of Nine, and many others have continued to pour their wisdom into our reality, so we are eager to share their messages with you.

Until then, as Bob often says when he reluctantly leaves, "Oh, okay. I'm gonna go now. Bye bye."

Acknowledgments

Kari Pelletier attended a presentation on *Wave 1* that we held in Colorado in 2018. After that, she became a frequent participant in our study groups and public séances. In the intervening years, Ophelia, Setalay, and other spirits from the seventh dimension greeted her as a member of their family. As is often the case with those from the seventh, they choose occupations to help others. So, it is not surprising that Kari is a licensed Professional Counselor who works with children and families. That she also dedicated her time and abilities to improve the readability of this book is something Christine and I will always be grateful for. Thank you, Kari!

Susanne Kromm has helped to edit every book we have published. She is also the one who does the bulk of the translations into Swedish, or as the Swedes say, Svenska. Susanne studied to be a teacher and is fluent in Swedish, German, and English. Although she is reluctant to admit it, she also knows enough French, Spanish, and Italian to easily navigate around in Europe. So, when translating from English to Swedish, she sometimes translates into German first, to find better matches with Swedish words. For that reason, the Swedish translations are incredibly accurate versions of the English, something that is not very common. Susanne has listened to many of the sessions and can make corrections based on her understanding of the meaning. And finally, she offers kind guidance when the tone of my commentary wanders away from the spiritual purpose of our work. Susanne also maintains a wonderful garden where many second dimension spirits are welcomed and present. Thank you, Susanne, for all you do!

About the Authors

Christine Kromm Henrie is a spiritual channel, a certified past life and between lives soul regression therapist, psychic, and karmic astrologer. She was born and lived in Stockholm, Sweden, until 2014, when she moved to the US and married David Henrie, with whom she now shares her work.

Christine had an intense spiritual awakening in 2009, during a past life regression, which became the starting point for her practice with the higher realms. She began to receive messages and visions from her spirit guides about her soul assignment to develop the skills needed for them to speak through her. Accepting their advice, she studied different modalities of mediumship, psychic development and astrology in Sweden and England during the next five years. This intensive training enabled her to perfect the link and the ability to maintain this altered state for extended periods of time.

After moving to the US, her formal training continued in soul regression and hypnotherapy, becoming a licensed regression therapist. Christine has two offices in Stockholm, Sweden, where she offers private soul regressions and progressions, assisting people to recall lessons from past lifetimes and memories from their spiritual home. Past life regression and astrological consultations are also available online.

A near–death experience at age 11 and a transcendental epiphany in his early 20s, led **David Henrie** to lifelong inquiry into the nature of the spirit. His studies focused on NDEs, reincarnation, spiritualism, and the theological beliefs within Buddhism and other pre–Christian religions. After a lengthy career as a petroleum engineer and executive in the US, he now lives in Sweden with his wife, where his time is dedicated to writing and research. David conducts the trance sessions and converses with the spirits Christine channels. He transcribes the recorded dialogues and assembles their teachings into the co–authored books.

Christine and David give lectures about the channeled material and the regression work, helping people to remember their soul mission and purpose.

For further information, please visit:
www.AccesSoulKnowledge.com.

www.ingramcontent.com/pod-product-compliance
Lightning Source LLC
Chambersburg PA
CBHW030144100526
44592CB00009B/118